THE NEW MIDDLE AGES

BONNIE WHEELER, *Series Editor*

The New Middle Ages is a series dedicated to pluridisciplinary studies of medieval cultures, with particular emphasis on recuperating women's history and on feminist and gender analyses. This peer-reviewed series includes both scholarly monographs and essay collections.

PUBLISHED BY PALGRAVE:

Women in the Medieval Islamic World: Power, Patronage, and Piety
edited by Gavin R. G. Hambly

The Ethics of Nature in the Middle Ages: On Boccaccio's Poetaphysics
by Gregory B. Stone

Presence and Presentation: Women in the Chinese Literati Tradition
edited by Sherry J. Mou

The Lost Love Letters of Heloise and Abelard: Perceptions of Dialogue in Twelfth-Century France
by Constant J. Mews

Understanding Scholastic Thought with Foucault
by Philipp W. Rosemann

For Her Good Estate: The Life of Elizabeth de Burgh
by Frances A. Underhill

Constructions of Widowhood and Virginity in the Middle Ages
edited by Cindy L. Carlson and Angela Jane Weisl

Motherhood and Mothering in Anglo-Saxon England
by Mary Dockray-Miller

Listening to Heloise: The Voice of a Twelfth-Century Woman
edited by Bonnie Wheeler

The Postcolonial Middle Ages
edited by Jeffrey Jerome Cohen

Chaucer's Pardoner and Gender Theory: Bodies of Discourse
by Robert S. Sturges

Crossing the Bridge: Comparative Essays on Medieval European and Heian Japanese Women Writers
edited by Barbara Stevenson and Cynthia Ho

Engaging Words: The Culture of Reading in the Later Middle Ages
by Laurel Amtower

Robes and Honor: The Medieval World of Investiture
edited by Stewart Gordon

Representing Rape in Medieval and Early Modern Literature
edited by Elizabeth Robertson and Christine M. Rose

Same Sex Love and Desire Among Women in the Middle Ages
edited by Francesca Canadé Sautman and Pamela Sheingorn

Sight and Embodiment in the Middle Ages: Ocular Desires
by Suzannah Biernoff

Listen, Daughter: The Speculum Virginum and the Formation of Religious Women in the Middle Ages
edited by Constant J. Mews

Science, the Singular, and the Question of Theology
by Richard A. Lee, Jr.

Gender in Debate from the Early Middle Ages to the Renaissance
edited by Thelma S. Fenster and Clare A. Lees

Malory's Morte D'Arthur: Remaking Arthurian Tradition
by Catherine Batt

The Vernacular Spirit: Essays on Medieval Religious Literature
edited by Renate Blumenfeld-Kosinski, Duncan Robertson, and Nancy Warren

Popular Piety and Art in the Late Middle Ages: Image Worship and Idolatry in England 1350–1500
by Kathleen Kamerick

JEWS AND CHRISTIANS IN THIRTEENTH-CENTURY FRANCE

Edited by

Elisheva Baumgarten and Judah D. Galinsky

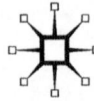

First published in 2015 by
PALGRAVE MACMILLAN®
in the United States—a division of St. Martin's Press LLC,
175 Fifth Avenue, New York, NY 10010.

Where this book is distributed in the UK, Europe and the rest of the world,
this is by Palgrave Macmillan, a division of Macmillan Publishers Limited,
registered in England, company number 785998, of Houndmills,
Basingstoke, Hampshire RG21 6XS.

Palgrave Macmillan is the global academic imprint of the above companies
and has companies and representatives throughout the world.

Palgrave® and Macmillan® are registered trademarks in the United States,
the United Kingdom, Europe and other countries.

ISBN: 978–1–137–28719–9

Library of Congress Cataloging-in-Publication Data

Jews and Christians in thirteenth-century France / edited by Elisheva
Baumgarten and Judah D. Galinsky.
pages cm. — (The new Middle Ages)
"This book centers on changing paradigms in research and history
of Jews and Christians in medieval Europe and specifically in northern
France. It seeks to outline both the animosity and the intimacy that
existed between these communities during the thirteenth century, a
period of great changes"—Provided by publisher.
Includes bibliographical references and index.
ISBN 978–1–137–28719–9 (hardback : alk. paper)
1. Jews—France, Northern—History—13th century.
2. Christians—France, Northern—History—13th century.
3. Christianity and other religions—Judaism—History—13th century.
4. Judaism—Relations—Christianity—History—13th century.
5. France, Northern—Ethnic relations—History—13th century.
6. France, Northern—History—13th century.
I. Baumgarten, Elisheva, editor. II. Galinsky, Karl, 1942– editor.

DS135.F81.J49 2015
305.892′404409022—dc23   2014043565

A catalogue record of the book is available from the British Library.

Design by Newgen Knowledge Works (P) Ltd., Chennai, India.

First edition: May 2015

10 9 8 7 6 5 4 3 2 1

CONTENTS

Part 1   Learning, Law, and Society

Part 2 Polemics, Persecutions, and Mutual Perceptions

Part 3 Cultural Expressions and Appropriations: Art, Poetry, and Literature

FIGURES AND TABLES

Figures

Tables

ACKNOWLEDGMENTS

This book is the product of two grants supported by the Israel Science Foundation—Elisheva's grant (#328/06) on Gender and Piety and Judah's grant (#1342/07) on The French Tosafot. Our conversations and joint interests led to the organization of an intensive seminar sponsored by the Israel Science Foundation and the Israel Institute for Advanced Studies.

We thank the Israel Science Foundation and Robert Arnold of Bar-Ilan University who coordinate these grants and the Israel Institute for Advanced Studies and Smadar Bergman, Ronit Forer, and Lea Prawer as well as their entire staff. This volume contains articles that went through an extensive process of review. We are most appreciative of all the scholars who consented to serve as anonymous reviewers. The reader for the press made suggestions and comments that were very helpful and gave this volume its final form, and we are grateful for them.

We thank Brigitte Shull, Bonnie Wheeler, and Ryan Jenkins at Palgrave Macmillan for patiently and expertly shepherding this book into print and for constantly urging us on as we worked, and are grateful to Rena Bannett, Fray Hochstein, and Gabriel Wasserman for their editorial help.

ELISHEVA BAUMGARTEN
(Hebrew University of Jerusalem)

JUDAH D. GALINSKY
(Bar Ilan University)

ABBREVIATIONS

AJS Review	*Association for Jewish Studies Review*
BT	Babylonian Talmud (Standard editions)
IMHM	Institute of Microfilmed Hebrew Manuscripts
JQR	*Jewish Quarterly Review*
JSIJ	*Jewish Studies, an Internet Journal*
PL	*Patrologia, series latina,* ed. J.-P. Migne
PT	Palestinian Talmud (Standard editions)

CONTRIBUTORS

★Cyril Aslanov is a professor in the Department of Romance and Latin American Studies at The Hebrew University of Jerusalem. His research interests are in the study of languages in contact, especially Romance and Semitic languages. His recent publications include *Le français levantin, jadis et naguère: à la recherche d'une langue perdue* (Paris, 2006); *Parlons grec moderne* (Paris, 2008); and *Sociolingüística histórica de las lenguas judías* (Buenos Aires, 2011).

★Elisheva Baumgarten holds the Prof. Yitzchak Becker Chair for Jewish Studies and is an associate professor of medieval Jewish history in the Departments of Jewish History and of History at The Hebrew University of Jerusalem. She studies the social history of medieval Jews in northern Europe with an emphasis on gender and Jewish-Christian relations. She is the author of *Mothers and Children: Jewish Family Life in Medieval Europe* (Princeton, 2004); *Practicing Piety in Medieval Ashkenaz: Men, Women and Everyday Religious Observance* (Philadelphia, 2014); and numerous articles.

★David Berger is Ruth and I. Lewis Gordon Professor of Jewish History and Dean at the Bernard Revel Graduate School of Jewish Studies at Yeshiva University. His teaching and research interests are medieval Jewish history, Jewish-Christian relations, anti-Semitism, contemporary Judaism, and the intellectual history of the Jews. In addition to his *The Jewish-Christian Debate in the High Middle Ages* (Philadelphia, 1979), he has published numerous studies that have recently been collected in two volumes—*Persecution, Polemic, and Dialogue: Essays in Jewish-Christian Relations* (Boston, 2010) and *Cultures in Collision and Conversation: Essays in the Intellectual History of the Jews* (Boston, 2011).

★Susan L. Einbinder is a professor of Hebrew and Judaic Studies and Comparative Literature at the University of Connecticut. Her teaching and research deal with the relationship between history and literature and have focused mainly on poetry and literature from both northern and southern France. Her first book, *Beautiful Death: Jewish Poetry and Martyrdom in Medieval France* (Princeton, 2002), examined northern French Hebrew poems of martyrology and her second book, *No Place of Rest: Jewish Literature, Expulsion,* *and the Memory of Medieval France* (Philadelphia, 2009), reconstructs French-Jewish memories of expulsion in a variety of literary texts.

★Jessica M. Elliott is a visiting assistant professor in the Department of History at Grand Valley State University. Her teaching and research interests are in religious conversion and Jewish-Christian relations in medieval Europe, urban culture in high and late medieval Paris, and cross-cultural encounters in the premodern world. Her dissertation, "The Changing Status of Converted Jews in Thirteenth- and Fourteenth-Century Northern France" (University of California, Santa Barbara, 2014), reconstructed attitudes of Christian intellectuals in France toward the possibility of Jewish conversion and examined the socioeconomic integration of converts into the working world of medieval Paris. The research for the dissertation was funded by a Bourse Chateaubriand from the French Ministry of Foreign Affairs. She is currently working on a monograph that contextualizes the heightening of Christian concerns about the status of French converts in the fourteenth century within the larger world of Jewish-Christian relations in medieval England and northern France.

★Judah D. Galinsky is a senior lecturer in the Department of Talmud and Rabbinic Literature at Bar-Ilan University. His teaching and research interests are in the fields of medieval Jewish rabbinic literature, Jewish-Christian relations, book culture, and the practice of charity in the Middle Ages. He is the author of a number of studies, most recently: "The Significance of Form: R. Moses of Coucy's reading audience and his *Sefer ha-Mitzvot*," AJS Review *35* (2011), 293–321; "The Evolution of the Monetary-Tithe in Ashkenaz," *Journal of Jewish Studies 62*, 2 (2011), 203–232; and "The Different Hebrew Versions of the 'Talmud Trial' of 1240 in Paris," in *New Perspectives on Jewish-Christian Relations: In Honor of David Berger*, (Leiden, 2012), 109–140. He is currently working on a book project which focuses upon late thirteenth-century rabbinic culture in northern France.

★Ari Geiger teaches medieval history in the Department of General History at Bar Ilan-University. His teaching and research interests are intellectual and religious history of medieval Europe, Christian Hebraism, and Jewish-Christian polemic in the Middle Ages. He recently published "Historia Judaica: Petrus Comestor and His Jewish Sources," in Gilbert Dahan (ed.), *Pierre le Mangeur ou Pierre de Troyes, maître du XIIe Siécle* (Turnhout, 2013), 125–145 and "A Student and an Opponent: Nicholas of Lyra and his Jewish Sources," in Gilbert Dahan (ed.), *Nicolas de Lyre, franciscain du XIVe siècle, exégète et théologien* (Paris, 2011), 167–203. His book on Nicholas of Lyra and Fourteenth-Century Christian Hebraism is forthcoming in 2015.

★Ephraim Kanarfogel is E. Billi Ivry University Professor of Jewish History, Literature and Law at Yeshiva University's Bernard Revel Graduate School of Jewish Studies. Among his recent books are *"Peering through the*

Lattices": *Mystical, Magical, and Pietistic Dimensions in the Tosafist Period* (Detroit, 2000), and *The Intellectual History and Rabbinic Culture of Medieval Ashkenaz* (Detroit, 2012), which has won the Goldstein-Goren Prize from the International Center of Jewish Thought at Ben-Gurion University and the Schnitzer Prize for Best Book in Biblical and Rabbinic Studies from the Association of Jewish Studies. His current book project, *Brothers from Afar: Rabbinic Approaches toward Apostates and Apostasy in Medieval Europe,* focuses on the attitudes of medieval rabbinic authorities toward conversion and reversion in their historical contexts.

★Rella Kushelevsky is an associate professor in the Department of Literature of the Jewish People at Bar-Ilan University. Her teaching and research focuses on Hebrew stories written in medieval Germany and northern France. She recently published *Penalty and Temptation, Hebrew Tales in Ashkenaz* (Jerusalem, 2010) and is currently preparing a diplomatic edition of *Sefer ha-ma'asim,* a Hebrew story collection from thirteenth-century northern France.

★Daniel J. Lasker is Norbert Blechner Professor of Jewish Values in the Goldstein-Goren Department of Jewish Thought at Ben-Gurion University of the Negev, in Beer Sheva. His areas of interest are medieval Jewish philosophy (including the thought of Judah Halevi, Maimonides, and Hasdai Crescas), the Jewish-Christian debate, Karaism, and selected issues in Jewish theology and law. His first book, *Jewish Philosophical Polemics Against Christianity in the Middle Ages.* (New York, 1977; 2nd ed Oxford/Portand, OR, 2007), details the use of philosophy in the medieval Jewish critique of Christianity, and subsequent works have included editions and translations of a number of polemical treatises. *From Judah Hadassi to Elijah Bashyatchi: Studies in Late Medieval Karaite Philosophy* (Leiden, 2008), describes developments in Byzantine Karaite philosophy from the twelfth to fifteenth centuries, and his latest book, *The Sage Simhah Isaac Lutski. An Eighteenth-Century Karaite Rabbi. Selected Writings* (2015), presents annotated editions of Lutski's treatises.

★Anne E. Lester is an associate professor of History at the University of Colorado at Boulder. Her teaching and research interests cover medieval religious women, the Cistercian order, Capetian France, hospitals and charity, and the crusades. She is the author of *Creating Cistercian Nuns: The Women's Religious Movement and Its Reform in Thirteenth-Century Champagne* (Ithaca, 2011); and co-editor of *Cities, Texts, and Social Networks: Experiences and Perceptions of Medieval Urban Space, 400–1500* (Farnham and Burlington, VT, 2010); and *Center and Periphery: Studies on Power in the Medieval World in Honor of William Chester Jordan* (Leiden, 2013). She is completing a monograph on the movement of relics from Constantinople and the Latin East into France and Flanders during the thirteenth century provisionally entitled *Fragments of Devotion: Relics and Remembrance in the Aftermath of the Fourth Crusade.*

★Sara Offenberg is a lecturer in the Department of Jewish Art at Bar-Ilan University. Her teaching and research interests are Jewish-Christian relations in medieval art and literature; the image of the Jew in art and literature; German Pietists; *piyyut* commentary; and Hebrew illuminated prayer books. She is the author of two books: *Illuminated Piety: Pietistic Texts and Images in the North French Hebrew Miscellany* (Los Angeles, 2013); and *Antisemitism and the Jewish Response in the Art and Literature of Thirteenth Century France* (Jerusalem, forthcoming). She is a coeditor of the journal *Ars Judaica*.

★Samuel N. Rosenberg is Professor Emeritus of French and Italian at Indiana University, where he taught language and linguistics—including translation—and literature of the Middle Ages. He has translated numerous medieval works into English, including trouvère poetry and Arthurian narrative. His translations, like his philological scholarship, have appeared in a wide variety of publications, both American and French.

★Yossef Schwartz is a professor of Medieval Intellectual History at the Cohn Institute for the History and Philosophy of Science and Ideas at Tel Aviv University. His research focuses on late medieval and early modern science and philosophy, with emphasis on theory and praxis of translation, Latin Hebraism, and Jewish European receptions of Latin Christian thought. Among his publications: *"To Thee is silence praise": Meister Eckhart's reading in Maimonides' Guide of the Perplexed* (Tel Aviv 2002) [Hebrew]; Yossef Schwartz and Volkhard Krech eds., *Religious Apologetics – Philosophical Argumentation* (Tübingen, 2004); and Yossef Schwartz, Alexander Fidora, Harvey J. Hames (eds.), *Latin-Into-Hebrew: Studies and Texts*, volume 2: *Texts in Contexts* (Leiden 2013).

★Karl Shoemaker is an associate professor of History and Law at the University of Wisconsin, Madison. His teaching and research interests are in the history of criminal law and the historical development of legal and political institutions concerned with punishment, dispute settlement, and social control in the high and late Middle Ages. He recently published *Sanctuary and Crime in the Middle Ages, 400–1500.* (New York, 2011) and is currently working on a monograph that examines the legal career of the devil in the late Middle Ages.

★Lesley Smith is Professor of Medieval Intellectual History, Fellow and Tutor in Politics, and Senior Tutor at Harris Manchester College, University of Oxford. Her research interests are history of exegesis, manuscript studies, history of the book, and history of medieval schools and universities. Recent books include *Masters of the Sacred Page: Theology in the Latin West to 1274* (Notre Dame, 2001); *The* Glossa Ordinaria: *The Making of a Medieval Bible Commentary* (Leiden, 2009); and *The Ten Commandments: Interpreting the Bible in the Medieval World* (Leiden, 2014).

*Margo Stroumsa-Uzan is a lecturer in the Department of Arts at Ben-Gurion University of the Negev and teaches at Shenkar College. Her teaching and research interests focus on the social history of art in the Middle Ages with a special emphasis on the history of illuminated manuscripts, women's studies, and death. She is working on publishing her first book analyzing the impact early books of hours had on the lives of secular women, based on her dissertation entitled "Women's Prayer: Devotion and Gender in Books of Hours from Northern France ca. 1300" (Ben-Gurion University of the Negev, 2009). She is also the author of "Jonah of Aquileia: A Gesture to Constantine the Great," published in *Between Judaism and Christianity. Art History Essays in Honor of Elisheva Revel-Neher*, eds. Katrin Kogman-Appel and Mati Meir (Leiden, 2009).

*John Tolan is Professor of Medieval History at the University of Nantes (France). His teaching and research interests are in the history of religious and cultural relations between the Arab and Latin worlds in the Middle Ages. He is the author of numerous articles and books in medieval history and cultural studies, including *Petrus Alfonsi and his Medieval Readers* (Gainesville, 1993); *Saracens: Islam in the Medieval European Imagination* (New York, 2002); *Sons of Ishmael: Muslims through European Eyes in the Middle Ages* (Gainesville, 2008); *Saint Francis and the Sultan: The Curious History of a Christian-Muslim Encounter* (Oxford, 2009); and (with Gilles Veinstein and Henry Laurens) *Europe and the Islamic World* (Princeton, 2013). He currently is director of a major project funded by the European Research Council, "RELMIN: The legal status of religious minorities in the Euro-Mediterranean world (fifth-fifteenth centuries)" (www.relmin.eu).

INTRODUCTION: JEWS AND CHRISTIANS IN THIRTEENTH-CENTURY FRANCE

Elisheva Baumgarten and Judah D. Galinsky

This collection of essays explores a variety of perspectives on Jewish and Christian life in northern France during the thirteenth century. The incentive for this volume was the changing paradigms within the field of medieval studies connected with Jewish-Christian relations and the growing understanding that has characterized the past decade and a half of scholarship, underlining not only the animosity but also the intimacy and similarities between the two faith communities.[1] In light of the growing tendency to view both religious communities as more closely linked than in the past, this work aims to examine these relationships on multiple levels and in a variety of disciplines. It sets as its goal an examination of the thirteenth century specifically as it is somewhat overlooked, sandwiched between the "twelfth-century renaissance" and the late thirteenth- and fourteenth-century famine and disease that changed the face of Europe and, in the case of the Jews, the persecution and expulsions.[2] This book seeks to examine the thirteenth century in particular—although a long thirteenth century, broadly defined—specifically through the prism of the changes that took place within the Jewish and Christian urban communities. Our objective has been to outline the continuity alongside the changes and the similarities as well as the differences in a coherent way.

Over the years, attempts have been made to describe and characterize the uniqueness of the thirteenth century. Some have focused on the formation of classic scholasticism and the contribution of the translation movement. Others have chosen to emphasize the various political and administrative developments as well as the growth of the legal profession and that of bureaucratic institutions. Yet others devoted attention to the "machinery of persecution" against heretical movements, Jews, and others as a defining feature.[3] The thirteenth century has also been portrayed as the period when educational institutions such as the university developed, urban centers expanded alongside the concomitant growth of religious piety, especially lay piety, and the innovation in the arts. William Jordan nicely captured this lack of clarity in defining the thirteenth century when he wrote in his prefatory remarks to the century:[4] "It has been called the 'Age of the Cathedrals', the 'Age of St Louis', the 'Age of Thomas Aquinas', even the 'Age of Synthesis'." What does emerge from all of the above is that, even after limiting our exploration to northern France, there is no simple way to describe the major developments of this century.

Concerning the study of the Jews of France, it is worth noting that there has been a marked tendency among scholars to group together the Jews of northern France and those of Germany under the broad category of "Ashkenaz," arguing they share a common cultural heritage.[5] Others, however, have seen the need to make clear distinctions between these geographic settings.[6] In this volume, the authors have made an effort to question in what way French attitudes and culture differ from that of Germany (see chapters 5 and 10). In addition, by studying the Jews of France in conjunction with scholars looking at their Christian counterparts, one can better draw the lines between geographies, and not only those between religions. At the same time, we have not ignored the fact that much of what occurred in France can be viewed as a reflection of broader European trends, whether in culture, religion, law, or education. With this in mind, at times, some developments mentioned below are described as "European."

The primary rationale behind the geographic limitation is that it allows us to explore, with a certain degree of confidence and control, the Jewish and Christian communities and the relations between them. A widening of the scope would have made such an effort far more complex as each geographic region has its own institutions, political structures, and mindsets. For example, if we consider the two major modern northern European countries—Germany and France—in the medieval period, these two areas (which were distinct in ways uncommon with their modern counterparts) were of significantly different character. During the thirteenth century, northern France had a strong monarchy and dynamic educational institutions that attracted students from all over Europe; Germany had neither. Despite these differences, scholars have more often treated both geographic regions as one rather than as separate entities, discussing the Jews of northern France and Germany together. This is true both of Jewish Studies scholars and of those studying Christian attitudes to Jews.[7]

A good example that has served as a model is the book edited by the late Michael Signer and John Van Engen, *Jews and Christians in Twelfth-Century Europe*. This collection has served us as a point of departure in its emphasis on the intimacy and distance that existed simultaneously between Jews and Christians in northern Europe as well as the importance of singling out a century that is so often discussed as part of a larger process.[8] At the same time, we sought to limit our scope even more in order to address the unique characteristics of the communities in France alongside the features they shared with their northern European neighbors at large.

This book seeks to probe the limits of these similarities and differences on a number of levels. One level of difference pertains to language. French and German Jews communicated, both among themselves and with their Christian neighbors, in the vernacular, adopted from their immediate surroundings.[9] Along with these, some of our authors question whether they also adopted certain traits and inclinations (see chapters 5 and 13–16). Urban life also had distinct features—most notably in Paris as opposed to other locations. The rise of the universities in Paris (and Orléans) as centers of law and learning and the development of the book trade had great impact on Christian life in the city.[10] Many students flocked to Paris, and the city grew in unprecedented ways. As part of this same development, the Jewish community expanded as well. It is not surprising that Paris became a meeting place of sorts for a number of French Tosafists during the first half of the century.[11]

Conversations that were taking place outside of Paris, with the involvement of Parisian masters and theologians, also had great import for Christians and Jews in France. The Fourth Lateran Council (1215)—one of paramount events of the century in that it codified changes that had been brewing and created new realities—was an occurrence that has been central in discussions of Jewish and Christian life. For Jews, this council contained not only the repetition of traditional guidelines related to the employment of Christians by Jews and shared commerce, but also the requirement that Jews (like Muslims) wear a distinctive sign.[12] Although this canon was not quickly implemented, it has been seen by many scholars as representative of ominous changes. Scholars of Christian society have studied the canons of the Fourth Lateran Council from multiple perspectives, focusing on the definitions of heresy and the guidelines for the sacraments and for the laity that it contains.[13] Yet, few studies have studied these perspectives together. The Fourth Lateran Council is central in many of the chapters in this volume, allowing a joint assessment of some of its implications.

As is evident from these words of introduction, by situating French Jews and Christians side by side, we hope to start a more inclusive conversation. Jews were a distinct minority among medieval Christians in France and there is merit in looking at Jews among their neighbors specifically within this century as their position changed quite radically from the beginning to the end of the century. This attempt to discuss Jews and Christians together does not undermine the distinction between the two faith communities. Rather, it serves to emphasize the importance of understanding how the two societies were intertwined—for better or for worse—throughout the period and how this connection developed and unraveled during the thirteenth century.

At the beginning of the century, we see Jews living among their neighbors in relative peace, despite royal demands and insecurity. A major turning point in relations between the King and his Jewish subjects and for their sense of security and self-confidence was the Talmud Trial of 1240 that took place in Paris.[14] This was the first time that Christian authorities, led by Pope Gregory IX and King Louis IX of France, felt that they had the legitimate right to intervene and to judge the Jews' most important post-biblical religious work.[15] The sub-sequent burning of the Talmud seared this breach of trust into the consciousness of French Jews and beyond. From the perspective of Christian-Jewish rela-tions, this event was most significant. The trial highlighted Talmudic passages that seemed to blaspheme Jesus, Mary, and others and that seemed to condone anti-Christian behavior on the part of Jews. All of this contributed to the cre-ation of an atmosphere of suspicion and hatred between Jews and Christians in France. [16] Yet, as some of the studies in this volume show, some changes came sooner than others. Imperial edicts against Jews or revised halakhic understand-ings of Christianity preceded suspicion on the ground, as part of daily life (see chapters 9 and 10). Many of these comparisons remain to be further fleshed out, beyond the studies in this book. The chapters presented here are meant to high-light the intellectual, social, and cultural changes that took place in medieval French society during the thirteenth century among both Jews and Christians and the ways these changes related (or did not relate) to each other. The areas explored, in both Jewish and Christian societies, are by no means exhaustive. Rather, we view our efforts as a modest beginning. Our hope is that this book will spark the curiosity of our fellow medievalists to continue exploring this century and its unique features.

A secondary but no less important goal of this collection is to break down the artificial boundaries that divide the various academic disciplines and those that separate "medieval studies" from "Jewish studies." The inclusion of a wide variety of literary genres and methodologies allows for a broad perspective on cultural and social changes during the thirteenth century as well as shifts in mutual perceptions of Jews and Christians. The overarching goal of this work is to focus attention upon the unique trends that characterized European society and culture during the thirteenth century.

In order to fulfill our goal of illustrating some of the unique features of the thirteenth century as observed in the two faith communities of northern France, we have chosen to focus upon three broad areas of investigation: learn-ing and law and their relationship to society; developments in religious polem-ics and aspects of persecutory policy; and cultural developments in the areas of literature and art. These include the study of the Bible, legal developments, religious polemic, gender, social history, perceptions of the "other," language, literature, and art.

Part 1: Learning, Law, and Society

The first section of the book discusses continuity and change relating to law and learning and their impact on society—a focus of many of the major developments during the thirteenth century. Two well-educated canon lawyers, who studied theology as well, became Popes—Innocent III and Gregory IX—initiated some of the events that are seen as crucial to many of the changes that took place during this period, such as the convening of the Fourth Lateran Council under Innocent and its role in formulating religious beliefs, both concerning the Christian communities and the Jewish ones. Definitions of heresy and of the rights and obligations of minorities as well as the emphasis on educating the clergy, and through them the laity, were part of the declared goals of this council. These same Popes were also central in the growing suspicion toward Jewish customs and texts. During the thirteenth century, and specifically in northern France (as well as in Italy) the university developed as an educational institution. Franciscan and Dominican masters of theology played a central role within the confines of the faculty of theology in Paris and their attitudes—both toward the laity and toward the Jews—had an impact on daily life and beliefs. The chapters in this section all relate in different ways to these broad themes and, to some extent, it is our hope that positioning them side by side allows additional insight as well.

Lesley Smith—in her study of thirteenth-century theological commentaries to the Bible and particularly the Ten Commandments—notes that, to a large extent, the commentaries follow the lead of those produced in the twelfth century. The standardization of the university curriculum did not leave much room for innovation. However, once one turns away from the official commentaries to other genres, such as works devised for pastoral care, one finds novel interpretations. Smith points to change outside of the faculty of theology at the university and explains the innovative genres that become typical of post-thirteenth-century scholarship. Smith also demonstrates how one object, the pocket Bible, was central in developments within university studies.

Another central object in this context is the prayer book and, specifically, the Book of Hours, which evolved into an independent book during the late thirteenth century, and this development can be seen prominently in northern France. **Margo Stroumsa-Uzan** outlines some of these changes during the thirteenth century and looks specifically at the Books of Hours as an object used by women for their personal devotion. She suggests a contrast between the Books of Hours used by women and Psalters used by men. By examining the contents of these books and especially the illuminations chosen for them, she shows how they led to an expansion of secular women's religious life as part of burgeoning urban culture and lay piety. As she notes, these new trends were of import for Jewish prayer and piety as well as for prayer books created for, and used by, Jews. This theme is further explored from a Jewish perspective in chapter 13 by Sara Offenberg.

Also following Smith and looking at a different aspect of biblical commentary, **Ari Geiger** writes about the dramatic change between the twelfth and thirteenth centuries concerning Christian Hebraism. He asks why Christian interest in Jewish commentarial traditions to the Bible decreased drastically in the thirteenth century. After offering a number of suggestions such as the turn to an interest in moral–ethical issues and the dominance of the mendicants in the faculties of theology, Geiger goes on to demonstrate that Christian interest in Jewish learning did not disappear, but rather, became focused in other areas of learning, such as Aquinas' and other theologians' interest in the Maimonidian synthesis between Aristotelian philosophy and the Bible and those active in religious polemics took new interest in the Talmud.

Moving to the legal realm, **Karl Shoemaker** writes about change in the application of the "ius commune" in France. His study addresses the law as influenced by legal developments within the universities. He argues that, although content remained much the same due to local and political necessity, with regard to procedure, things did change. According to Shoemaker, from the beginning of the century, French lawyers stood ready to implement modes of trial that they had appropriated from the classical jurists and repurposed for French courts. In these new modes of trial, judges exercised considerable control over the initiation of legal processes, the leveling of charges against suspects, the acquisition of evidence, and the examination of witnesses. These procedures also required literate judges and legions of scribes to record the copious testimonies extracted by the inquests. In short, one could argue that, in France as in much of south-western Europe, a growing body of professional lawyers worked within a common, learned world of law that was very different from what existed in the previous century.

Whereas the first four chapters focus on broad developments in thirteenth-century Christian society, the fifth chapter in this section by **Judah D. Galinsky** looks at internal Jewish changes and addresses the new genres of writing among northern French Jews during the thirteenth century. His chapter suggests that northern French Jews, like their Christian counterparts, were more interested in providing accessible knowledge to the laity than their German Jewish colleagues. By comparing between halakhic literature written in northern France with that from Germany, he notes a clear tendency among French scholars to make their work accessible in an attempt to educate the laity—a trend that cannot be found in Germany until the last quarter of the century.

The final chapter in this section by **Yossef Schwartz** brings together the developments of learning and law to examine the Talmud Trial that took place in Paris in 1240. He points to the unique level of cooperation between the King of France, the Pope, and the university masters during the course of this event, and suggests that such early collaboration should lead to reconsideration of the changing roles the masters of theology played in external matters. According to Schwartz, the evidence from the trial demonstrates that, even before the reign of Philip the Fair, the masters of theology were called upon to assist the monarchy in the process of judgment outside of the university community. By positioning the trial against the Talmud within political developments not related solely to the Jews, Schwartz provides a more integrated understanding of the Talmud Trial within the northern French Christian context.

Part 2: Polemics, Persecutions, and Mutual Perceptions

The second part of the book leads from the more general trends related to knowledge that typified the thirteenth century to the polemic and animosity between Christians and Jews that has been central in previous research. The desire to convert the Jews of northern France has frequently been underlined as well as the general lack of success in this effort.[17] So too, the expulsions of the Jews from parts of the French Monarchy—in 1182 (return in 1198), then in 1306 (returned in 1315), and, finally, in 1394—have been central in the history of the relations between northern French Jews and Christians.[18] Discussions of these complex relations in our collection include both the outright polemic between Jews and Christians recorded in treatises devoted to polemics as well as comments on converts and on interreligious antagonism and competition.

The chapters in this section of the volume are devoted to providing both assessments of research to date and new perspectives. The chapters by Daniel Lasker and David Berger both look at the treatises that describe the Jewish-Christian polemic. **Daniel Lasker** focuses on one polemicist—Joseph Official—as a symbol of thirteenth-century French polemic. He studies his rhetoric and structure to demonstrate what typified northern European Jewish polemics. Joseph was from a family originating in Provence and the author argues he was a polemicist by profession. He contends that, unlike the debate in Iberia and southern France with which Joseph was familiar, when writing for a northern European audience, Joseph deliberately avoided philosophical ideas or rational formulations. Rather, he penned a collection of exegetical remarks and biblical interpretations through which he critiqued Christianity. Moreover, his writing is replete with vulgarities and harsh descriptions that were not part of the polemics south of the Alps. In fact, he omits the rationalistic arguments that one could have expected to find in southern polemics. The author explains Official's writings as the result of the Talmud Trial in the mid-thirteenth century when northern European Jews felt a need to put to paper a fuller polemic with the Christians, yet Joseph provides a decisively northern French flavor to this polemic.

David Berger, in his wide-ranging essay on both Christian and Jewish polemicists, addresses the question of change and continuity in the Jewish-Christian debate from the twelfth to the thirteenth century. In the first part of this study, he takes issue with a number of the conclusions found in Amos Funkenstein's classic article on this topic. According to Berger one cannot find true evidence for the use of *ratio* as a polemical tool to prove Christian truth before the fourteenth century. The language of *ratio* as distinct from *auctoritas* appears and even becomes standard in some Christian works, but it is lacking in polemical force. In the continuation of his study, in agreement with Lasker, he notes the difference in tone between thirteenth-century polemical works written in northern Europe in contrast to those composed in the South. However, according to Berger, it was not the thirteenth century that gave birth to the use of profoundly insulting rhetoric. Rather, this development was the product of Franco-German Jewish culture, as can be found in non-polemical writing from previous centuries. In the last part of his study Berger, reexamines the two major polemical events that took place in Paris during the thirteenth—century—the famous Talmud Trial of 1240 and the much less known religious debate of 1270 conducted by Pablo Christiani of Barcelona fame. He concludes his study by noting that, in contrast to the twelfth century, there is no evidence that Christians were committed to a serious missionary effort aimed at Jews. Pablo's missionary activities in both Spain and France reflect a very different reality.

Polemics were not just an expression of antagonism between the religions; they were also an ongoing conversation between them. Another vehicle for expressing sentiments against the other religion—as is evident already in the first part of this book—is legal writings. Admittedly, the existence of a law does not mean that it was in fact observed, but the legal discourse allows for a better understanding of the intent of the legal hierarchy if not of those following their instructions. Writings accompanying laws clarified the intents of their authors. Two chapters in this section look at specific laws and the ideas behind them that were related expressly to Jews and Christians. **John Tolan** discusses Innocent III's attitude toward the Jews at the beginning of the thirteenth century and, specifically, his concern about the polluting effect Jews could have on Christians through their contacts with them. Innocent III, in accord with earlier church authorities, ruled against Christian presence in Jewish homes as servants and wet nurses and against Christians buying Jewish meat and wine. His reissue of these restrictions is evidence of the extent that they were not strictly observed. However, as Tolan argues, in contrast to previous authorities, Innocent's numerous letters on the matter reveal a fear of pollution that was unprecedented. Focusing on milk and blood—a matter crucial when discussing wet nurses—Tolan outlines how the concerns raised in the early thirteenth century became more central in conversation about Jews over the next decades.

Moving from Christians to Jews, **Ephraim Kanarfogel** addresses aspects of the other side of the same coin, Jewish legal discussions of daily contacts with Christians. He collects and analyzes the various legal approaches taken by rabbinic authorities in France and Germany on permissible and forbidden business relations between Jews and Christians. He begins by asking: how exactly were Christians perceived? Were they classic idolaters who were to be avoided in all ways? He demonstrates that, over the course of the late twelfth and early thirteenth centuries, northern European Jews more and more readily did business with Christians and reconsidered classic prohibitions on them that assumed they were idolaters. The main body of his chapter reviews various opinions on buying Christian clerical and ritual objects or taking them as pawns. He demonstrates the complexity of opinions on the matters and a growing hesitancy of some rabbis, alongside lenience on the part of others. He connects these changing opinions with Jewish awareness of Christianity and especially with Jewish perceptions of the growing authority of clergy and their influence on the laity.

Both Tolan and Kanarfogel demonstrate the extent to which Jewish and Christian legal writings—while no longer read, as in the past, as positivistic representations of reality—are a key genre because of their relative richness and the insight they provide on the changing attitudes of members of one religion toward the other. Above all, both chapters show the nuances in the formulations used to address the other religion, alongside a growing reticence, during the thirteenth century.

The final two chapters in this section allow for reflection on the association between theory and social realities and between the prime case study in this book—the Jewish minority and other groups under the church's scrutiny. **Jessica Elliott** examines what can be seen as the effects of both the polemic rhetoric and the legal restrictions. She asks how Jewish converts to Christianity were perceived by authors of Christian chronicles. Elliott compares the rhetoric of those who wrote before the Expulsion of 1306 to later authors. As part of the polemic and legal restrictions of the thirteenth century, many Jews did, in fact, convert to Christianity. She studies how these conversions were understood and argues that, while the pre-1306 writers tended to present a positive picture of the Jewish converts, those from the fourteenth century had a decidedly different rhetoric. The later stories contain tales in which Jewish children were forcibly baptized and adult Jews sought baptism, feigning devotion, so that they could desecrate the sacred objects of Christians. These anxieties and doubts provide valuable clues about the Christian understanding of Jewishness and the degree to which Judaism was believed to be inextricably linked to identity after the turn of the fourteenth century in France.

The last chapter in this section provides a unique comparison to the focus on the Jews. **Anne E. Lester** studies a different group that was being categorized and persecuted by the church—that of religious lay women. She explores how these women, who did not belong to formal orders and who lived in their homes, were redefined in legal documents as *mulierculae* or little women. Their form of religious life was typical, as she indicates, of the northern French landscape. Lester, in her study, explains how their label— that of little women or even ridiculous or silly women—served multiple purposes and was part of an attempt to marginalize them and their spirituality. She points to the connection between these women and their Jewish neighbors and even to a joint execution of one such woman—Marguerite Porete. She suggests the need to further investigate and recognize the commonalities of lay religious women and Jewish communities. In this way, her chapter provides a path to incorporate medieval Jewish history in France— not just within the narrative of other Jewish communities, but also within the dynamics of classification and categorization of various Christian groups among whom the Jews lived.

Part 3: Cultural Expressions and Appropriations: Art, Poetry, and Literature

As part of our focus not only on persecution or on the world of learned men, but also on the communities that lived side by side, Part 3 looks at art, poetry, and literature. These developed independently from more ancient traditions and also as part of the growing interest in the laity. Within the medieval urban setting, new practices and objects became central during the thirteenth century.

Sara Offenberg looks at a Hebrew prayer book created at the same time as the expanded manufacture of the Books of Hours described above. She examines the Miscellany (which was an expanded prayer book) created by a scribe named Benjamin who may have been from Metz but who used this book and completed it in Paris. This beautiful and elaborate manuscript includes both unique prayers and illustrations. Among them is a poem commemorating a martyr—Samson of Metz, who was burned at the stake in 1276 and an illustration of the biblical Samson. Offenberg seeks to connect between the poem, the biblical illustration, and the scribe of the Miscellany and points to the way Samson was portrayed in picture and prose in light of Jewish-Christian tensions. Her chapter underlines the close connections between Jewish and Christian artists and scribes.

The next two chapters in this section also focus on prayer and poems as the site of creating cultural identities among late-thirteenth-century Jews. In these cases, language—and not art—are at the center of the inquiry, focusing on Jewish prayers written in old French (in Hebrew letters, known as Judeo-French). **Cyril Aslanov** examines the 1288 lament from Troyes—written after Jews from this location were burnt at the stake. He uses this lament that has been studied a number of times over the past years as an opportunity to discuss the language spoken by the Jews in northern France and its cultural implications. Aslanov argues for the dependence of the lament on other Hebrew texts but in a less restrictive manner than one would have expected had the poem been in Hebrew. He is especially interested in the factors that led to the development of Judeo-French (a parallel of sorts to Yiddish and Ladino). He argues that, by the late-thirteenth century, French Jews were isolated and distinctive to the extent that they developed their own language, which could have developed further if they had not been expelled. The decision to write in Judeo-French was crucial from his perspective as Jews may have spoken like their neighbors, but writing a prayer required a unique combination between spoken language and particular cultural models.

Addressing a different poem, **Susan L. Einbinder** provides an analysis of the way an anonymous Old French poet translated a classic Hebrew poem—*Ansikha Malki*—during the late thirteenth century. In the appendix to the chapter, translations by Einbinder and **Samuel N. Rosenberg** into English of both the original Hebrew and its medieval French translation are provided. Einbinder's analysis underlines a question that has not received due attention as a result of the paucity of Judeo-French sources. Seeing that the Jews in medieval France did not speak Hebrew, in what way did the French vernacular impact upon their thinking, beliefs, and practices? How would a Judeo-French repertoire (that seems to have existed) alter the way we understand medieval Jewish culture? Much like Stroumsa-Uzan, Einbinder situates the translation of classic Hebrew poetry within the thirteenth-century culture of affective piety and sees it as a symbol of a community that sought to understand Jewish symbols and holiness within the vernacular. Her chapter raises the opportunity to reflect on these aspects of daily life and practice that are only minimally evidenced in the sources that have survived.

Rella Kushelevsky continues the theme of the embeddedness of the Jewish communities in Christian culture by looking at one story from a central northern French Hebrew collection of tales—the *Sefer ha-ma'asim*. Her chapter demonstrates the dependence of the Hebrew tales on medieval French tales that were current. In this case, her examination of the story "A Slave for Seven Years"—a story not known in previous Hebrew versions—is compared to a story with similar contours—the Life of St. Alexis. At the center of the story is the abstinence of a man from his bride. Since abstinence is emblematic of a central difference between Jewish and Christian attitudes toward marriage and sexuality, it allows for an examination of the way medieval Jews adapted themes from their Christian cultural environment. The similarities between the tales, alongside their differences, allow for a better understanding of the way medieval French Jews saw themselves amid their surroundings. This chapter opens an additional cultural frontier for comparative research—that of belles lettres—that has hardly been studied to date.

All in all, we see this section of the book as an invitation for future investigations of independent developments within each culture, but especially of cross-cultural comparisons between Jewish and Christian cultural products such as poems, stories, and art. These contributions also allow expression of aspects of daily ritual and culture that are often overlooked when situating Jews within their surroundings and focusing on relations with the rulers, governing bodies, or anti-Jewish sentiments. The cultural developments point to the ways medieval Jews adapted ideas from their surroundings and expressed them.

The chapters in this volume shift in focus, at times emphasizing cohesion among Jewish communities, inside and outside of northern France, and, at times, preferring geography to religion. These shifting loyalties are not contradictory in our eyes, nor must one chose between one and the other. As the thirteenth century came to a close, but also throughout the entire medieval period, one can assume that Jewish communities would have felt a close affinity to each other, despite cultural differences. Nevertheless, this would not have invalidated a sense of belonging to specific places.[19]

We end this brief introduction with one of the most manifest texts from medieval northern France in which a Jew expresses his "frenchness." This text was written by an unknown Isaac sometime during the fourteenth or fifteenth century. In his poem, our poet describes his travels from France to Germany.[20] Playing with the verse in Jeremiah 51:5 ("For Israel and Judah were not forsaken *ki lo alman yisrael*"), the author uses the Hebrew word *alman* and the French word *Alleman* (Germany) to suggest, tongue in cheek, that German Jews are not part of the Jewish people. This poem is both sarcastic and humorous and the impetus for its composition is unknown.[21]

When I left France
And went down to Germany
I found a folk cruel
As ostriches in the desert heat.
    But Israel is not forsaken! Straw's not to be compared to wheat!

I hoped for salvation
For tranquility and rest
But what they offer is worthless.
My heart is broken.
    Oh Israel is not forsaken! Straw's not to be compared to wheat!

I sought throughout Alsace
And there's nothing worth knowing
Except that unnaturally
The women rule, the men effete.
    Oh Israel is not forsaken! Straw's not to be compared to wheat!

I'm sick and tired of the Germans.
All of them are vulgar
With beards like goats.
Don't trust them for they always cheat.
    Oh Israel is not forsaken! Straw's not to be compared to wheat!

Notes

1. See these recent historiographical surveys: Ivan G. Marcus, "Israeli Medieval Jewish Historiography: From Nationalist Positivism to New Cultural and Social Histories," *Jewish Studies Quarterly* 17 (2010): 244–285 and David Malkiel, *Reconstructing Ashkenaz: The Human Face of Franco-German Jewry, 1000–1250* (Stanford, 2009), 1–61.
2. For a recent account of the twelfth century, see R. N. Swanson, *The Twelfth-Century Renaissance* (Manchester, 1999). For a concise survey of the fourteenth-century developments see William Chester Jordan, *Europe in the High Middle Ages* (London, 2001), 289–325.

3. R. I. Moore, *The Formation of a Persecuting Society: Authority and Deviance in Western Europe 950–1250* 2nd ed. (Oxford, 2007) and *The War on Heresy: Faith and Power in Medieval Europe* (London, 2012).

4. See Jordan, *Europe in the High Middle Ages*, 179.

5. This was the standard approach in all writings on the Middle Ages throughout most of the twentieth century, as can be seen from the works of Jacob Katz, Hayim Hillel Ben-Sasson, Ephraim Urbach, and others. Even today, there are some scholars who retain this usage of the word. See Malkiel, *Reconstructing Ashkenaz*, in his preface, ix.

6. The first to clarify this in writing was Avraham Grossman in a number of early studies that were then summarized in his *Ḥakhmé tsarfat ha-rishonim* (Jerusalem, 1995), 539–586.

7. With regard to Jewish studies, see above n. 5 and, with regard to the study of Christian attitude toward the Jews, see, for example, Moore, *The Formation of a Persecuting Society*.

8. *Jews and Christians in Twelfth-Century Europe*, ed. Michael A. Signer and John Van Engen (Notre Dame, 2001), especially 355–359.

9. See Kirsten A. Fudeman, *Vernacular Voices: Language and Identity in Medieval French Jewish Communities* (Philadelphia, 2010).

10. For an accessible survey of the educational developments from the twelfth to the thirteenth century, see Lesley Smith, *Masters of the Sacred Page: Theology in the Latin West to 1274* (Notre Dame, 2001), 3–34.

11. See, meanwhile, Ephraim Kanarfogel, *Jewish Education and Society in the High Middle Ages* (Detroit, 1992), 58.

12. Kenneth Stow, *Alienated Minority: The Jews of Medieval Latin Europe* (Cambridge, MA, 1992), 245–251.

13. Regarding issues of belief, heresy, and sacrament, see R. N. Swanson, *Religion and Devotion in Europe c. 1215–1515* (Cambridge, 1995), 10–38, with regard to the laity, see 25–30.

14. See the extensive treatment of this event by Robert Chazan in *The Trial of the Talmud: Paris, 1240* (Toronto, 2012), 1–92.

15. On Gregory's role in the trial, see Joel E. Rembaum, "The Talmud and the Popes: Reflections on the Talmud Trials of the 1240s," *Viator* 13 (1982): 203–223. Also see Jeremy Cohen, *Living Letters of the Law: Ideas of the Jew in Medieval Christianity* (Berkeley and Los Angeles, 1999), 317–363.

16. On these thirteenth-century developments, see William Chester Jordan, *The French Monarchy and the Jews: From Philip Augustus to the Last Capetians* (Philadelphia, 1989), Susan L. Einbinder, *Beautiful Death: Jewish Poetry and Martyrdom in Medieval France* (Princeton and Oxford, 2002), and Sara Lipton, *Images of Intolerance: the Representation of Jews and Judaism in the Bible Moralisée* (Berkeley, 1999).

17. See Einbinder, *Beautiful Death*, 72–73, 114–116, 180–181.

18. See Jordan, *French Monarchy and the Jews*.

19. See Susan L. Einbinder, *No Place of Rest: Jewish Literature, Expulsion, and the Memory of Medieval France* (Philadelphia, 2008), 137–157.

20. See Elisheva Carlebach, "Early Modern Ashkenaz in the Writings of Jacob Katz", in *The Pride of Jacob. Essays on Jacob Katz and his Work*, ed. Jay M. Harris (Cambridge MA and London, 2002), 65–83, where she discusses this poem in a different connection.

21. This original Hebrew poem was first published by Avraham Meir Haberman, "*Shirat ha-ḥol shel yehudé ashkenaz ve-tsarfat*", *Moznayim*, 5 (1958), 403–408 and recently reprinted in Avraham Meir Haberman, *Talmud Me'ir. Collected Articles*, ed. Avigdor Shinan (Jerusalem, 2010), 132. The translation presented below is that of Susan Einbinder. The poem was originally translated by T. Carmi, *The Penguin Book of Hebrew Verse* (New York, 1981), 453.

PART 1

LEARNING, LAW, AND SOCIETY

CHAPTER 1

CONTINUITY AND CHANGE IN THE STUDY OF
THE BIBLE: THE TEN COMMANDMENTS IN
CHRISTIAN EXEGESIS

Lesley Smith

Given that the Latin text of the Bible remained, broadly speaking, constant in the period covered by this volume, it must be reasonable to ask
why we might expect there to be anything *other* than continuity in the Bible
and its interpretation in the thirteenth century, why there should be change.
In order to address this question, we need also to step back and consider the
antecedence of "the thirteenth century" of this volume; that is, a period of
development and consolidation that sets thirteenth-century France as the
stage on which a new and important play will be enacted. For each of the different topics dealt with in this book, the key points at which change happens,
or the spread of time over which we can see a sustained change occurring,
will be different; for each, there is a different point—beyond the literal—
where this conceptual thirteenth century begins. For scholars of the Bible
and exegesis, it is impossible to consider the situation at the beginning of the
thirteenth century without keeping in mind the innovations of what is generally described as the twelfth-century renaissance.[1] Indeed, it is tempting to
begin the "biblical" thirteenth century around 1110 and to run it forward till
around 1340; and, although we will resist that temptation, nevertheless, we
cannot ignore the twelfth-century changes altogether.

Why Expect Change?

The first part of an answer as to why we might expect change in the study
of something as comparatively static as the Bible is that there was a *contextual*

change in *who* was making exegesis, *where* they were doing it, and *who* they were working for, that is to say, what audience they were expecting. During the twelfth century, the cutting edge of biblical exegesis (though, obviously, not all exegetical activity) moved from a monastic setting to a world of secular schools (that is, non-monastic, but necessarily clerical classrooms). Initially, these were schools attached to cathedrals and mostly presided over by a single scholar, but, as the century drew on, the constellation of schools in Paris coalesced into something appreciably more solid than the classes offered by individual teachers; they became the proto-university of Paris. Paris, indeed, became the European center of academic work on the Bible and theology, drawing in scholars from across the continent, and the place where popes came for academic advice.[2]

Moving the center of biblical scholarship from monasteries to cathedral schools to a fledgling university meant more than a change of place: it signaled also a change in who was doing exegesis and for whom they were working. Crudely put, this was a movement from monks working for themselves (contemplatively?) and for fellow monastics; to clerics working for fellow clerks in (often the lowest of) holy orders, who may or may not have been intending to continue pursuing a scholarly life; and finally to university teachers who (increasingly during the thirteenth century) were mendicant friars working for fellow friars whose vocation was centered on work among the laity. Whereas monastic study could be unstructured, schools and universities required (again, increasingly over the thirteenth century) a syllabus, examinations, and qualifications that recognized achievement of a certain standard. Students had to produce work that followed set models in order to be considered qualified.

The second major reason we might expect to see change in biblical interpretation is more solidly rooted in the thirteenth century—the influence of the Fourth Lateran Council of 1215, one of the aims of which was to provide for the education of both clergy and (indirectly) the laity.[3] Lateran IV and the new mendicant Orders had a symbiotic relationship because the mendicants provided the personnel for the Lateran reforms; and there was symbiosis, too, in the relationship between the Paris schools and the Lateran Council. Without the need for a more educated clergy and the encouragement of the mendicants, the proto-university at Paris might well not have thrived as it did; without the financial underpinning that the mendicants (ironically) provided, the theology faculty might not have attracted enough students to survive, since in 1219 the university had been forbidden by Honorius III from teaching the money-spinning subject of civil law.[4] For the mendicants who increasingly made up the body of teachers and students at Paris, the schools were a preparation for work outside academia and, in response to this, the sorts of material that mendicant scholars produced broadened and diversified the traditional mode of biblical commentary.

Manifest Changes

Against this background—even drawn as sketchily as we have had to here—it should be clearer why, even in a subject such as the interpretation of the Bible, which might appear to be a conservative activity, reliant upon authority and tradition, we might indeed expect to encounter change. But how do we see such change manifest in the thirteenth century? We can highlight three areas in which change in the study of the Bible can be seen to have given rise to a practical effect.

The first is a change in the Bible as a physical object. Throughout its Jewish and Christian history, the Bible had seldom been copied as a single text (a "pandect"), but rather as a series of volumes (whether in codex or scroll format), each containing a group of biblical books.[5] From about the middle of the twelfth century, the comprehensive biblical commentary, known as the *Gloss* (Latin *Glossa* or *Glossa ordinaria*), became the Bible of choice for scholars, who were much more likely to want a copy of a glossed biblical book than of a plain, uncommented text.[6] Because the *Gloss* combined the complete scriptural text with a relatively substantial exposition, the Bible as a physical object grew and grew, so that a typical set of Glossed biblical books could run to 20 volumes. With even an unglossed text running into half a dozen or so volumes, for the peripatetic mendicants of the thirteenth century the Bible was impossibly unwieldy. They commissioned pandect, hand-sized "pocket" Bibles in large numbers. The Dominican community at St Jacques in Paris was at the forefront of thinking about the types of materials the Order needed to go about its work.[7] Their need to use the Bible on the hoof, outside the classroom, the monastery, or the parish church, further impelled these mendicant scholars to create or utilize a series of aids for finding and interpreting the text, such as indexes, concordances, and a version of Jerome's interpretation of Hebrew names that became a standard addition to most pocket Bibles. Concern with the accuracy of the text produced lists of corrections to the standard circulating version.[8] Instead of—or rather, as well as—a text to be pored over slowly in preparation for contemplative meditation, this mendicant Bible became a ready-reference edition, made for quick consultation and use in the world outside the convent.[9]

There was also change in the form in which biblical exegesis was presented. The thirteenth century has been characterized as the century of the *summa*, that is to say, a work which gives comprehensive coverage of a thematically arranged subject, where explanation proceeds by questions, rather than being ordered around a single text such as a biblical book. There is much to be said for this observation, but the *summa* by itself is not the whole story of thirteenth-century scholarship. The base material for the compilation of theological *summae* is generally biblical exegesis, so the commentary form did not disappear from the scene. In addition, the twelfth century had its own *summae*, in the form of ordered collections of *sententiae*—"sentences" or opinions on debated issues. The most famous of these was Peter Lombard's *Four Books of Sentences*, but there were a number of others.[10] Lastly, exposition of single biblical books continued throughout the thirteenth century. The relative obscurity of thirteenth-century biblical commentary as it appears today is, at least in part, a result of the priorities of modern scholarship. Most of the material that has been edited and studied is taken from *summae* or individual treatises, rather than from more rambling, less immediately involving commentaries. But the commentaries are there, and commentary work done in the thirteenth-century classroom was the foundation of the new forms of treatise.

Finally, there is change in the form of an expansion of the focus of biblical exegesis. A common narrative of the arc of medieval commentary portrays interest as moving from the spiritual senses of scripture to a literal and historical interpretation of the text. To an extent, such a shift is observable, but it is not exclusive: interpretation that includes the spiritual senses never disappears. Moreover, the change takes place over a much longer period than the thirteenth century alone. It also involves an expansion of the definition of the literal sense to include some of what were once thought of as spiritual meanings. The possible reasons for such a change are multifarious, and too complex to go into here; but I would note their link to the interests of a few individual medieval scholars, rather than to a more general abandonment of the spiritual senses. The great scholars of the thirteenth century are recognizably individual in their work and, for me, the narrative of spiritual to literal exegesis is driven by modern knowledge of the work of some very particular commentators, rather than necessarily by a more common overall thread.

The Decalogue

So much for the theoretical possibilities for continuity and change. Now let us test them in medieval practice. To do this, I have chosen to look at the exegesis of the Ten Commandments as a sample text. Why the Decalogue? First, and most obviously, because the Commandments are in themselves a central text for both Christians and Jews: the precepts appear twice in the Hebrew Bible [Exod. 20: 2–17; Deut. 5: 6–21], and are revisited in the Gospels, both as a context for the Sermon on the Mount [Matt. 5–7], and as a refrain for some of Jesus's pronouncements, especially the assurance that he has come not to destroy the Law but to fulfill it [Matt. 5: 17]. Secondly, because the Decalogue is not just a set of random biblical verses, but a self-contained portion of scripture, it is perceived as a self-contained unit both in other parts of the Bible and in subsequent biblical interpretation. Thirdly, it is a useful example because it was included in Peter Lombard's key text, the *Four Books of Sentences*. This meant that, from the early thirteenth century onwards, everyone studying to be a master of theology at Paris had to expound the Commandments text, because writing a *Sentences* commentary was a prerequisite for graduation. Hence there is no shortage of material on the Decalogue, and the material is comparable. Finally, the Decalogue is useful because, in the years after the Fourth Lateran Council, when the ideas of the Council passed into local diocesan legislation, the Commandments was one of the texts commonly cited as being among those the laity should be taught, along with the Pater Noster and the Creed. If there is a move toward an increasingly pastoral focus for biblical interpretation in this period, the interpretation of the Commandments should chart it.

The Decalogue before the Fourth Lateran Council

What were the important components of interpretation of the Ten Commandments up to the thirteenth century? To set the scene, I have distilled some general points from the discussions in the *Gloss* and in Peter Lombard's *Sentences*, the two key mid-twelfth-century texts that had both contemporary and subsequent thirteenth-century influence.[11] The outlines of the exposition were set by Augustine, who treated the Decalogue in two sermons.[12] Origen and Isidore were also employed, especially in the *Gloss*, but Augustine was the major influence.[13] In particular, Augustine was a main source for the Lombard in his *Sentences*, so all commentaries on the *Sentences* are also influenced by Augustine's priorities and discussion, noticeable for what the commentators do *not* consider, as much as for what they do.

Exposition begins by laying out how the Exodus text was to be divided into *ten* commandments. This is a more complicated question than may at first appear, since the biblical text does not itself number the precepts, and the relevant passage is slightly different in each of the Exodus and Deuteronomy versions. What, for instance, was the extent of the first commandment? Did it encompass the text only as far as having no other gods, or did it include the prohibition of graven images? This decision necessarily had a knock-on effect on the phrases at the end of the Decalogue about coveting goods and wives, if there were to be at least ten, but only ten, commandments in total.

Once the texts of the individual ten precepts had been decided on, the question of the division of the Decalogue was continued, so that it now considered how the Ten were to be distributed across the two tablets of stone handed down to Moses: one tablet, it was argued, contained the commandments pertaining to God; the second, those pertaining to one's neighbor. The Jews (generally quoted by Christian exegetes in the person of Josephus, whom they knew through Jerome or Philo) divided the Ten equally, five and five.[14] Christian tradition posed a more difficult problem since Origen and Augustine disagreed, dividing the precepts four–six and three–seven respectively. Augustine's system prevailed: his pattern incorporated two perfect numbers (three and seven) and managed to work in the Trinity, although it left him (and every commentator who followed him) the awful task of having to explain why the prohibition of concupiscence was divided over two separate commandments.

In both the *Gloss* and the *Sentences*, these questions of number and counting, disagreements between traditions, division of the commandments between God and neighbor, and their distribution on the tablets of stone, take up a surprising amount of the discussion, at least a quarter of the exposition, before the individual commandments are reached. Even when these divisions of the text are out of the way, we are a long way short of getting down to the practicalities of the precepts pertaining to one's neighbor. Before reaching them, the texts cover, for example, the differences between an image, a likeness, and a similitude; a taxonomy of types of worship; and whether (and how) it is just for God to punish the children of sinners down through four generations.

By the time both texts finally reach the commandments referring to one's neighbor, they have almost run out of steam. Both rely on Augustine to provide definitions (for example, of the difference between fornication and adultery), and the general principle is that the commandments are to be interpreted broadly: the whole is to be inferred from the part, making the precepts a shorthand way of ordering people to avoid evil and do good to their neighbor. The *Gloss* runs through these interpretations swiftly, but the *Sentences* has a further very long excursus that skews its treatment of the Decalogue even more. At least another quarter of the Lombard's discussion is given over to the single commandment against bearing false witness, which he interprets as meaning a prohibition of lying and swearing false oaths. He takes his material from Augustine's two short treatises on lying (*De mendacio*; *Contra mendacium*[15]) that detail eight types of lies and their potential for sin, along with a consideration of oaths (a particular form of truth-telling) and perjury (a particular form of lying). Judged by length of discussion, in comparison to this commandment, none of the others seems to be very important.

The Decalogue after Lateran IV

The expositions of the *Gloss* and the *Sentences* were the springboard for the work of the thirteenth century, to which we now turn. The commentators from whose work I will draw were, unless noted, all mainstream Paris masters. What we cannot fail to notice for all these commentators is the importance of tradition in their work, especially in regard to the overall shaping of the material. Whether it be in a biblical commentary, like Hugh of St Cher's *Postilla*, or a *Sentences* commentary like that of Alexander of Hales, the similarities to previous exegesis are much more striking than the differences.[16]

The concentration on the numbering and division of the commandments remains important; the focus on the commandments of the first tablet—the precepts about God—is sharper than the more general expositions of the precepts about neighbor, always with the exception of the commandment against false witness, and the exposition of lying and oaths; and the discussion as a whole employs the ideas, structure, and preoccupations of authoritative Christian writers, especially those of Augustine. Continuity, here, outplays change.

I would argue that this continuity is attributable to a great extent to the context of the Paris schools and their rapidly solidifying edifice of syllabus, set texts, and qualifying exams. The type of education the masters had experienced and the type of work they were expected to produce fixed their approach. We can see this when we consider Decalogue commentaries by two scholars working not in Paris but in thirteenth-century Oxford, Simon of Hinton and Robert Grosseteste. Simon was a Dominican who had studied in Oxford and taught there as a master of theology. His questions on the Ten Commandments follow an academic order, but with additional authorities from outside the Paris mainstream and a number of digressions by Simon himself.[17] Robert Grosseteste seems not to have studied formally in Paris, and much of his knowledge of the Bible and theology was self-taught.[18] His interpretation of the commandments is quite unlike those of his contemporaries, ignoring division and numbering, interested in commandments (such as honoring parents) that others neglect, yet hardly considering lying or oaths at all. There can be no other explanation for something so odd than that he was not a product of the schools. Change outplays continuity here, but it is because Grosseteste was not part of the Paris system.

Continuity or Change?

Does this consciousness of tradition mean there is no change in Decalogue interpretation among Paris masters? Not at all. The most obvious movement is in the expansion of the discussions, which is so marked as to be in need of explanation. It is more than just a case of greater material survival.[19] Thirteenth-century biblical and theological material becomes more and more prolix: there is never a sense that the writers might impose upon themselves a word limit, nor consider that short and structured might be better than long and expansive. What reasons might we adduce for why these discussions of the commandments expand?

First of all, there is an expansion in the way the commentators contextualize the Commandments and the Old Law. They want to fit the Law (capital L) of the *Torah* into the edifice of law in general, often with elaborate organizing schemes. In doing this, they ask how law creates obligation; how the Old Law relates to the New Law; which parts of the Old Law survive into the New, and why; what exactly a commandment is; and how, if "the letter kills but the spirit gives life" (2 Cor. 3: 6), any of the Old Law is still important. Most of these questions are touched on in Peter Lombard's *Sentences*, but they acquire a much greater prominence in the thirteenth-century commentaries.[20]

Secondly, along with the taxonomy of law, commentators show a greater interest in the psychology of the commandments: they ask how the precepts command thought, word, and deed, and how (whether?) commandments should attempt to restrain motivation, such as anger or envy.

Thirdly, the expansion of Decalogue exposition is fuelled in part by the addition of greater detail, more examples, or more authorities, to spell out what is basically the same meaning. The so-called scholastic method was (among other things) *additive*: once a question or topic entered the debate, it was almost impossible to dislodge it. Peter Lombard's discussion of the Decalogue, for example, includes two topics found in Augustine's treatment of the commandments—a comparison of the commandments with the ten plagues of Egypt (Exod. 7–12), and a question about whether or not Jacob lied in pretending to be Esau (Gen. 27). Both are absolutely thankless issues for any scholar to expound: as the plagues grew more serious (ending with the death of the firstborn), the commandments grew less so (concupiscence of neighbor's goods); and Jacob clearly declared himself to be "Esau, your firstborn son." Readers gained little by following the twisted logic involved in justifying either example. But the additive nature of the scholastic method precluded them from being dropped from the discussion.

Despite the interest in questions of law, of motivation, and the increase in detail, there is continuity, in that discussions of the commandments do not shift their focus to the individual precepts. What it actually means to kill or steal or not keep the Sabbath, for instance, never becomes the place where the debate is centered. From this, the reader may think that continuity wins out after all, that interpretative ideas about the commandments remain static, and that the questions raised by the individual precepts are not really of interest to post-Lateran IV commentators, despite their obvious practical application to everyday life. Must we then conclude that Lateran IV has no effect on interpretation?

A New Context

There is another aspect to the argument; but to discover what medieval theologians thought about issues of adultery, killing, theft, and so on, in greater practical detail, we must turn away from the commentaries of the schools and look to different types of work—to material produced outside the Paris university syllabus. A good example of this is the treatment of the Commandments in Thomas of Chobham's popular and influential *Summa confessorum*.[21] Chobham's handbook for confessors is an early [c. 1220] and very good example of what became a thriving thirteenth-century type. After a brief treatment of the sacrament of penance as an idea, Chobham begins by looking at vices (and the virtues they oppose). He looks at such general topics as the seven deadly sins, the difference between venial and mortal sins, and pride as the root of all vice. This section includes his discussion of the Decalogue, alongside a consideration of which vices and virtues are associated with it, and—the old chestnut—a comparison of the commandments with the ten plagues of Egypt.

Chobham has little specific to say about the individual commandments: his treatment here is much more like the university commentaries than anything we might have expected from a confessor's handbook. For example, he links the first three precepts with the persons of the Trinity, he discusses similitudes and likenesses, and he gives broad definitions of the commandments about one's neighbor: all rather disappointing.

Luckily, this is not the only place in the *Summa* we can look for the issues contained within each of the commandments. Chobham has detailed sections that cover matrimony (encompassing questions of adultery and fornication, for example), the sin of *luxuria* (again including adultery), homicide, superstition (which theologians generally discussed under the first commandment), theft (and its companions, robbery, sacrilege, usury, simony, and restitution), lying, oath-taking, perjury, and vows. In fact, it might almost be said that Chobham's text is itself meant as a detailed exposition of the commandments of the second tablet.[22]

The precept against killing is a good example of his two approaches. For the academic commentators, killing is—surprisingly—one of the least important of the commandments. They note, at most, that killing means homicide, not judicial killing; that it includes suicide but excludes the killing of animals; and that circumstances are to be taken into account when judging whether or not the precept has been broken. Chobham's treatment of killing *within* his Decalogue questions is among the shortest.[23] He notes that the will to kill as well as the act is forbidden, citing 1 John 3: 15: "whoever hates his brother commits homicide." But fortunately for us, this section is far from being his main discussion of killing. Thomas returns to the subject under his treatment of the broader topic of anger (*ira*), since anger provides the motivation to kill.[24] Here, Thomas raises 36 separate issues about killing, dealt with under four headings, including not merely lawful killing, but "meritorious" homicide, which covers war, judicial killing, defense of others, and the killing of heretics and Jews.

What Thomas Chobham shows us is that the same biblical material can be dealt with in the thirteenth century in different ways, even by the same people, or those trained under the same system. The importance of tradition in the schools, with their system of learning by commenting on authoritative texts by means of authoritative texts, makes it easy to see continuity in the training of academics and of their work. This is not to say that there were no fashions in the choice of which books were taught, but that the Bible and patristic authority remained at the heart of the syllabus. Even when new sorts of material entered the syllabus to be commented on (as the *Sentences* had done, for instance, in the 1220s), the texts used to interpret them were mostly well-established themselves, as was the *method* of reading and commenting. All of this may make it seem as though continuity stifled any urge to change. But there is change; and it comes about through the expansion of biblical and theological *genres*. By dealing with the same issues found in the Ten Commandments, but in a different written genre—not in an academic commentary, say, but in a handbook utilizing biblical material—scholars could shift the terms in which they considered the same subjects. Some questions were immoveable—Chobham's discussion of lying, for instance, still includes a discussion of whether Jacob lied[25]—but the confessional genre allows him to move into areas of practicality and to a variety of responses that would be inappropriate for the more theoretical genre of commentary, where the exegesis of the text, perhaps surprisingly, is much less nuanced.

Genre and Change

While we are used to talking about genre and the importance of form in medieval literature, the notion of genre in theological writing has been largely ignored. Although we know that there was a wide variety of types of theological material produced in the thirteenth century (some of which, if not new, were nevertheless newly minted), we are not used to thinking that their response to the Bible might be different, depending on the genre in which they are found. A Ten Commandments commentary from the schools must forbid killing, in all but the most restricted circumstances, just as it repudiates adultery. But in the more immediate world of the confessor, the same material can be dealt with at once more strictly and more leniently. More strictly, in that the questions are delineated in more detail, with comprehensive coverage of practical situations. More leniently, in that the blanket bans of the academic are nuanced to fit pastoral necessity. These are authors responding not just to students and theories, but to the everyday imperatives of the parish. They know that what is suitable in one situation will not work in the other. Here then we have continuity *and* change—but side-by-side, rather than one after the other. Rather than force new developments into old forms, commentators and theologians invent new genres, giving themselves the freedom to produce new forms of interpretation—forms in which they can speak to a wider world.

Notes

1. The term became common after Charles Homer Haskins published *The Renaissance of the Twelfth Century* in 1927 (Cambridge, MA), and is echoed in the excellent volume of essays published to celebrate Haskins's contribution,

Renaissance and Renewal in the Twelfth Century, ed. Robert L. Benson and Giles Constable (Oxford, 1982). A more recent account of the subject and bibliography is given by Robert N. Swanson, *The Twelfth-Century Renaissance* (Manchester, NY, 1999).

2. For accounts of the schools and the early university systems, see Hastings Rashdall, *The Universities of Europe in the Middle Ages*, rev. and ed. F. M. Powicke and A. B. Emden (Oxford, 1936); Gordon Leff, *Paris and Oxford Universities in the Thirteenth and Fourteenth Centuries: An Institutional and Intellectual History* (New York, 1968); the essays by Jean Leclercq, Richard W. Southern, John W. Baldwin, Nikolaus M. Häring, and Richard H. Rouse and Mary A. Rouse in Benson and Constable, *Renaissance and Renewal*; Beryl Smalley, *The Study of the Bible in the Middle Ages*, 3rd ed. (Oxford, 1983); Hilde de Ridder-Symoens, ed., *A History of the University in Europe, vol. 1: Universities in the Middle Ages* (Cambridge, 1992); John van Engen, ed., *Learning Institutionalized: Teaching in the Medieval University* (Notre Dame, 2000).

3. For the text (Latin and English) of the Fourth Lateran decrees, see Norman P. Tanner, ed., *Decrees of the Ecumenical Councils*, vol. 1 (London and Washington, 1990), 227–271.

4. For Honorius's prohibition see Henrich Denifle and Aemilio Chatelain, *Chartularium Universitatis Parisiensis* (Paris, 1889–1897), 1:32. For the mendicants in the schools, see Smalley, *The Study of the Bible*; M. Michèle Mulchahey, "The Dominican Studium System and the Universities of Europe in the Thirteenth Century," in *Manuels, programmes de cours et techniques d'enseignement dans les universités médiévales*, ed. Jacqueline Hamesse (Louvain-la-Neuve, 1994), 277–324; and Mulchahey, *"First the Bow Is Bent in Study..."*. *Dominican Education before 1350* (Toronto, 1998); Bert Roest, *A History of Franciscan Education (c. 1210–1517)* (Leiden and Boston, 2000).

5. For a short readable account of this history, see Christopher. F. R. de Hamel, *The Book. A History of the Bible* (London and New York, 2001), and his bibliography for the Introduction and ch. 1. Cassiodorus describes a copy of the Bible divided into nine volumes (Genesis to Ruth; Kings and Chronicles; Prophets; Psalms; Wisdom; the "biographies," Job, Tobit, Esther, Judith, Maccabees, Ezra–Nehemiah; Gospels; Epistles; Acts and Revelation), but there was no single agreed division; indeed, Carolingian library catalogues can use the Latin *bibliotheca* (library) for a complete copy of the Bible.

6. See Lesley Smith, *The Glossa Ordinaria: The Making of a Medieval Bible Commentary* (Leiden and Boston, 2009).

7. Richard H. Rouse and Mary A. Rouse, *Manuscripts and Their Makers: Commercial Book Producers in Medieval Paris, 1200–1500*, 2 vols (Turnhout, 2000), and see their essay in Benson and Constable, *Renaissance and Renewal*; see also Mulchahey, "Dominican Studium System."

8. Smalley, *Study of the Bible*, 331–337; Laura Light, "Versions et révisions du texte biblique," in, *Le Moyen Âge et la Bible*, ed. Pierre Riché and Guy Lobrichon, Bible de tous les temps 4 (Paris, 1984), 5–93; Lesley Smith, "What Was the Bible in the Twelfth and Thirteenth Centuries?" in *Neue Richtungen in der hoch- und spätmittelalterlichen Bibelexegese*, ed. Robert E. Lerner (Munich, 1996), 1–15; Gilbert Dahan, "La critique textuelle dans les correctoires de la

Bible du XIIIe siècle," in *Langages et philosophie: Hommage à Jean Jolivet*, ed. A. de Libera et al. (Paris, 1997), 365–392; Dahan, *Les intellectuels chrétiens et les juifs au moyen âge* (Paris, 1999), 272–285; Lesley Smith, "Hugh of St. Cher and Medieval Collaboration," in *Transforming Relations: Essays on Jews and Christians throughout History in Honor of Michael A. Signer*, ed. Franklin T. Harkins (Notre Dame, 2010), 241–264.

9. I should add an excursus here, to say that this period sees an expansion in non-Latinate—or non-literate—versions of the Bible, such as vernacular translations and paraphrases, copies which incorporate commentary, such as the *Bible moralisée* or *Bible historiale*, and texts that rely on pictures. Such "Bibles" are a topic in themselves and I shall not address them here, partly because of the limitations of space, but also because the link between those texts and biblical commentary is not yet well understood, certainly not as far as the influence of the vernacular on the Latin versions is concerned.

10. Peter Lombard, *Magistri Petri Lombardi . . . Sententiae in IV Libris Distinctae*, ed. I. C. Brady, 3 vols (Grottaferrata, 1971); see also, for example, Cédric Giraud, *"Per verba magistri": Anselme de Laon et son école au XIIe siècle* (Turnhout, 2010) and Peter of Poitiers, *Sententiae Petri Pictaviensis*, ed. Philip S. Moore and Marthe Dulong (Notre Dame, reprinted 1961).

11. Peter Lombard, *Sententiae*: the section on the Decalogue is book III, dist. 37–40. No modern critical edition of the entire Gloss exists, although there are editions of the Song of Songs and parts of Lamentations by Mary Dove and Alexander Andrée, respectively. The version of the Gloss given in Migne's *Patrologia Latina* is very partial and not a true reflection of the medieval text. The most convenient way to read and cite the twelfth-century text is in the facsimile of Rusch's *editio princeps*: *Biblia latina cum glossa ordinaria: facsimile reprint of the editio princeps Adolph Rusch of Strassburg 1480/81*, ed. with introduction, Karlfried Froehlich and Margaret T. Gibson, 4 vols. (Turnhout, 1992).

12. Augustine: Sermon 8 on the Ten Plagues of Egypt (*De decem plagis aegyptorum et decem praeceptis legis*); Sermon 9 on the Ten Strings of the Harp (*De decem chordis*), in *Sancti Aurelii Augustini. Sermones de vetere testamento*, ed. C. Lambot, Corpus Christianorum Series Latina, 41 (Turnhout, 1961). For further discussion, see Lesley Smith, *The Ten Commandments: Interpreting the Bible in the Medieval World*, Studies in the History of Christian Traditions 175 (Leiden and Boston, 2014).

13. Origen, *In Exodum homilia*, ed. Marcel Borret, Sources chrétiennes 321 (Paris, 1985); Isidore of Seville, *Mysticorum expositiones sacramentorum, seu quaestiones in Vetus Testamentum*, ed. J.-P. Migne, *Patrologia Latina*, 83: 207–434.

14. In fact, there were also debates among the Jews; but Christians recognized a single Jewish position as reported by Philo Judaeus, *On the Decalogue*, ed. F. H. Colson, The Works of Philo Judaeus, 7 (London and Cambridge, MA, 1937).

15. Augustine, *S. Aureli Augustini. De fide et symbolo, etc.*, ed. Josephus Zycha, Corpus Scriptorum Ecclesiasticorum Latinorum 41 (Vienna, 1900); trans. R. J. Deferrari, in *Augustine. Treatises on Various Subjects*, Fathers of the Church 16 (Washington, DC, 1952).

16. Hugh of St. Cher (ca. 1190–1263) joined the Dominican Order in 1225 or 1226 and was one of its greatest early scholars and administrators, becoming the first Dominican cardinal in 1244. His writings are prodigious. There is no modern edition of his great biblical commentary, the *Postilla in totam bibliam*, but there are several early printed copies (see B. Carra de Vaux, "La constitution du corpus exégétique," Annexe 1, in *Hugues de Saint-Cher († 1263): Bibliste et théologien*, ed. L. -J. Bataillon, G. Dahan, and P. -M. Gy (Turnhout, 2004), 43–63, at 56–57). I have used the Paris, 1533 edition. Alexander of Hales (ca. 1185–1245) was an English theology master, teaching in Paris; he joined the Franciscans in 1236. He is credited with introducing Lombard's *Sentences* as a compulsory element of the Paris theology syllabus. Alexander of Hales, *Glossa in quatuor libros sententiarum*, Bibliotheca Franciscana Scholastica Medii Aevi, 14 (Quaracchi, 1954), 3: lib. 3, dd. 37–40.

17. Simon of Hinton (fl. mid-thirteenth century) was an English Dominican teaching at the Oxford convent. He discusses the Decalogue in his most popular work, the *Summa ad instructionem iuniorum*, which also circulated in an abridged form, the *Exceptiones*. The *Summa* is printed among the works of Jean Gerson: "Tractatus de decem praeceptis," in *Joannis Gersonii. Opera omnia*, vol. 1, pt. 3 (Antwerp, 1706); the *Exceptiones* are edited in P. A. Walz, "The 'Exceptiones' from the 'Summa' of Simon of Hinton," *Angelicum*: 13 (1936), 283–368.

18. Robert Grosseteste (ca. 1170–1253) came to theology only after studying science. He taught theology to the Franciscans in Oxford (although a secular cleric himself), but we know nothing of his own theological education: he may have been self-taught. *Robert Grosseteste, De decem mandatis*, ed. Richard C. Dales and E. B. King, *Auctores Britannici medii aevi* 10 (Oxford, 1987).

19. Much more material exists by thirteenth-century biblical and theological scholars than by those of the twelfth century. Apart from chance, and the increasing amount of material from each century closer to the present, this may also be because twelfth-century scholars worked in a predominantly oral teaching culture and did not expect to "publish" their works. See Michael Clanchy and Lesley Smith, "Abelard's Description of the School of Laon: What Might It Tell Us about Early Scholastic Teaching?" *Nottingham Medieval Studies* 54 (2010): 1–34.

20. John of La Rochelle (d. 1245), for example, was a Paris Franciscan master especially interested in questions of law, and his commentary begins with a consideration of the wider questions of how to place the Law among law in general. His Decalogue commentary is part of a treatise known as the *Summa fratris Alexandri*, so-called because of its association with Alexander of Hales, with whom John worked closely. The editors of the Quaracchi edition have shown that John was the most likely author of at least books 1 and 3: *Doctoris Irrefragibilis Alexandri de Hales Summa Theologica seu sic ab origine dicta "Summa fratris Alexandri,"* ed. V. Doucet, vol. 4 (Quaracchi, 1948).

21. Thomas of Chobham (d. before 1236) was a secular cleric known for his pastoral writings. *Thomae de Chobham Summa confessorum*, ed. F. Broomfield, Analecta Mediaevalia Namurcensia 25 (Louvain and Paris, 1968); on the Decalogue, art. III, dist. 1, qu. VIIIa.

22. Chobham, *Summa confessorum*: matrimony (art. 4, dist. 2, qu. VIIa; art. 7, dist. 2, qu.XIIIIa); *luxuria* (art. 7, dist. 2); homicide (see note 23); superstition (art. 7, dist. 5); theft (art. 7, dist. 6, qu. IIa-XIIa); lying, etc. (art. 7, dist. 11–12).

23. Chobham, *Summa confessorum*, art. 7, dist. 4, qu. VIa, VIIa, VIIIa.

24. Chobham, *Summa confessorum*, art. 7, dist. 4.

25. Chobham, *Summa confessorum*, art. 7, dist. 10, qu. Va.

CHAPTER 2

PSALTERS FOR MEN, BOOKS OF HOURS FOR
WOMEN: ARRAS AS A CASE STUDY

Margo Stroumsa-Uzan

Following the grant of a commercial charter by the French crown in 1180 AD, Arras became an important production and trading center for wool and cotton as well as a moneylending center. Commerce generated new wealth, and this, in turn, enabled the town to become a cultural center of the region. The growth of a commercial bourgeois, which adopted aristocratic habits, contributed significantly to the dissemination of education for both religious and secular purposes. Arras also became a center for performers—a consequence of the role assigned to jongleurs in the legend of the holy candle, which had long been associated with Arras, and that, since the early twelfth century, had cured many pilgrims suffering from the fatal disease of *ignis sacer* (holy fire) or St. Anthony's fire.[1] Furthermore, the town was already the site of the oldest organized annual poetry competition, the *Puy*, dedicated to the Virgin Mary, in which knights and clerics, aristocrats and peasants, and women as well as men would all participate. Finally, secular plays were written and performed in Arras long before medieval drama spread all over Europe.[2]

It is within this vital and prolific milieu that the production and use of books in Arras should be viewed. In this paper, I will examine devotional books—psalters-hours and books of hours—in an attempt to show that the proliferation of books of hours during the second half of the thirteenth century was connected to gendered expectations of the shifting roles of women in the growing urbanized milieu. The working assumption behind this investigation is that illustration cycles found in illuminated manuscripts reflect gendered attitudes within their cultural values. As this collection of papers deals with Christian and Jews in France during the thirteenth century, I will refer briefly, at the end of this article, to Jewish society as well.

As much as Arras was a center of commerce and culture, with an esti-
mated population of 25,000–30,000,[3] its situation was not unique and may
be compared with other towns of the time in East Anglia, Flanders, and especially northern France. More specifically, similar conditions can be identified in—to name only a few places—Oxford, Ghent, Bruges, St. Omer,
Amiens, and Metz, all of which had both commercial and cultural connections with one another.[4] So, as much as Arras has its special place within the
urban agglomerations of the late Middle Ages, it can also stand as a faithful
representative of the new urban centers within the whole period.[5]

Books of hours, as independent books, are the creation of the second half
of the thirteenth century. Their appearance can be related to the profound
social changes of the period described above.[6] Already by the beginning
of the century, book patronage had ceased to be dominated by monastic
and other religious communities, and the lay (aristocratic and bourgeois)
population was no longer under the domination of religious authorities that
asserted exclusive control of all roads to salvation. From the mid-thirteenth
century, books of hours were commissioned from urban centers. Following
the appearance of the first books of hours, such as the *de Brailes Hours* from
ca. 1240, their proliferation was rapid.[7] More than 60 books of hours from
the second half of the thirteenth century, composed in England, France, and
Flanders, have been preserved, suggesting that the actual number of books
produced was much larger. While books of hours were, in part, the result of
religious changes, they also promoted these changes. Such changes led not
only to a religious revolution, but also to a cultural-gender transformation.
As yet, however, these phenomena are not well understood.

As books of hours were the medieval version of a bestseller, they contain
within them, according to Leon Delaissé, a record of the changing religious
sentiments of the secular population.[8] In a similar spirit, I would like to show
that early books of hours were mostly produced for the use of secular women,
and, as such, record not the changing attitudes of the secular population as a
whole, but rather gendered changes in religious sentiments. This sharpening
of focus directs light upon the hitherto obscure life and beliefs of medieval
secular townswomen. These urban women left no written records of their
spirituality. Therefore, books of hours that can be proven to have been in
use by laywomen are particularly valuable, for they can provide a mirror to
these women's religious feelings.[9] Yet, while this mirror can show us valuable
insights, it is also apparent that the image contained within it is not static.
Prior to the thirteenth century, it is possible to detect—but impossible to
read any general historical lesson from—an occasional, isolated demand by
lay patrons for private prayer books. By contrast, the proliferation of books
of hours in the second half of the thirteenth century demonstrates a steadily
growing demand that is testimony to a development of private feminine
devotion in this period. Although my task in this paper is to focus upon the
particularities that can be discerned in books of hours attributed to Arras

during the second half of the thirteenth century, the findings may tentatively be applied to other similar towns in northern France.[10] In general, the modern attribution of books of hours to a particular place in which the manuscript was supposedly used is based upon *incipit* versions customary to particular places, and upon the names of local saints inscribed within.[11] Upon these grounds, at least eight psalter-hours and books of hours made between 1250 and 1300 can be attributed to Arras.[12] The earliest example seems to be the *Ghuiluys de Boisleux Psalter-Hours*, which was owned by a lay couple from Arras.[13] Its relation to Arras is attested in the Calendar, the Litany, the Office of the Dead, and in the Hours of the Virgin. Two coats of arms featured in fols. 17v and 129 identify its first owners—Ghuiluys of Boisleux and her husband John of Neuville-Vitasse, two prominent Artois families allied in marriage c. 1246.[14] By the end of the thirteenth century, the book passed into the hands of the (titular) Empress of Constantinople, Catherine of Courtenay (1274–1307/8), and her husband Charles of Valois (1270–1325), whose armorial appears on the fore-edges of the manuscript. Catherine of Courtenay and Charles of Valois are depicted on fol. 17v below the Boisleux and Neuville-Vitasse coats of arms. This full-page illumination, repainted by an Italian painter, shows Catherine of Courtenay and Charles of Valois with their four children—one boy and three girls—praying before the Virgin and Child, who appear within a mandorla. Catherine and Charles' youngest daughter, Isabella of Valois, was born during the year 1305, thus forming a *terminus post quem* for this illustration. A second portrait of Catherine of Courtenay, featured alone, is depicted in the historiated initial D at the beginning of Matins of the Hours of the Virgin (fol. 214).[15] Catherine is shown kneeling before the Virgin and Child while the Virgin crowns her. Underneath this illustration is an earlier picture that depicted another woman kneeling before the Virgin and Child, probably Ghuiluys of Boisleux, identified by her armorial and the armorial of Burgundy at her feet. These are the only changes Catherine of Courtenay had made to the manuscript, and as both illuminations seem to have been executed by the same hand, we can conclude that the manuscript was modified by Catherine of Courtenay between the birth of her daughter and her own death (1305–1308).

This sumptuous manuscript with its 11 historiated initials and 31 full-page miniatures, many of them quadripartite, depicts the life of King David in 62 scenes throughout the psalter.[16] By contrast, the hours are illustrated by three historiated initials—introducing the Office of the Dead (fol. 173), the Hours of the Holy Spirit (fol. 203), and the Hours of the Virgin (fol. 214). As shown by Adelaide Bennett, the David cycle centers on David's adversaries in order to emphasize the legitimacy of his kingship. As both the Boisleux and Neuville-Vitasse families were involved in Louis IX's Seventh and Eighth Crusades to the Holy Land (1248 and 1270), they may have looked upon David as "a viable role model for their morals, leadership, and chivalric ideology," interested as they were themselves in "chivalrous rather than devotional piety."[17] As Anne E. Lester observed, the crusader ideal was a manly alternative to female devotional piety in thirteenth-century northern France. She argued that the expansion and development of the Cistercian nunneries in Champagne in the thirteenth century was the result of gendered perceptions of spirituality that inspired female relatives of men who had taken the Cross to express their own crusader ideals within Cistercian convent walls.[18] Following Lester's argument, it is possible to assume that men who could not travel to the East might find some comfort through identification with David's deeds in the Holy Land. In addition, Richard Leson has pointed to the importance of the relations between the sexes and the roles of women in the domestic, religious, and social spheres in the manuscript's miniatures. In particular, he illustrates the active and positive roles portrayed in the pictorial narrative of Michal, Abigail, and Bathsheba—three of David's wives.[19] Thus, for Leson, while the elaborated cycle depicting King David's victories in the Holy Land may have fired John's imagination, the primary use made of this particular book in the hands of Ghuiluys of Boisleux was as a moral lesson concerning her own marriage.

The family portrait of Courtenay and Valois on fol. 17v is located between the tree of Jesse, following full-page miniatures from the creation to the coronation of the Virgin, and the cycle of David's life accompanying the Psalms. This family portrait, with the Virgin and Child in the *mandorla* looking down toward Charles of Valois, anticipates the psalter and, as such, is related to the models of manhood emphasized by chivalric ideology regarding Neuville-Vitasse. As such, this family portrait has a completely different function than does the portrait of Catherine in the Hours' part.

Owners' portraits are not found in all books of hours; but, in almost all of the cases from this period where they do exist, it is women who are depicted, testifying to feminine ownership.[20] Traditionally, these portraits appear in two locations: at Matins of the Hours of the Virgin and at the beginning of the prayer *"O intemerata"* ("O unspotted"), a prayer addressing Mary and John.[21] In the case of the Ghuiluys of Boisleux's book, both portraits' owners—Ghuiluys of Boisleux and Catherine of Courtenay—are depicted at the beginning of Matins of the Hours of the Virgin. In both cases, depiction and placing seem to be a gendered expression of a convention illustrating woman's place both within devotional books and toward the Virgin and Child.

That both Ghuiluys of Boisleux and Catherine of Courtenay were depicted in their book attests to the importance of the owner's portrait— both as an imprint of ownership and as a way to perpetuate supplication toward the heavenly personage depicted nearby. The fact that the portrait of Ghuiluys of Boisleux was erased in order to depict Catherine of Courtenay testifies to the accepted convention that the depiction described a specific individual. The women's portraits seem to act as mirror images to their devotional intentions, and as expressions of their feelings of kinship toward the Virgin and Child. Indeed, the relationship depicted between the Virgin and Child and Catherine of Courtenay is very different from the relationship represented through her family portrait: here, the Virgin and Child are turned toward her, totally unaware of the viewer, while the family portrait has a frontal-iconic dimension that acts as a representative picture, rather than an intimate representation of Catherine's relationship with the Virgin, intended primarily for her eyes alone. I contend that Catherine of Courtenay re-emphasized the hours' part of the manuscript as a female-orientated product, while the psalter's part remained available to both spouses. Whether the Psalter-Hours were used more by its female than by its male owners is a question that cannot be answered. But undoubtedly, while the psalter's part has a public and formal character, the hours' part reveals a private and intimate realm. Thus, while the Neuville-Vitasse Psalter-Hours is typical of the early stage of a psalter-hours produced for, and eventually used by, a couple—changed and reused by its subsequent owner—it came to reflect the gendered use of both psalters and books of hours that was to become more frequent over the course of the next 50 years.

If we switch our attention to the next examples, which date from the end of the thirteenth or the early fourteenth century, a different conception can be seen affecting the illustration cycle. To begin with, a growing emphasis on the hours gradually leads to their receiving more illustrations, thereby creating a balanced compendium. Indeed, the hours increasingly come to overshadow the psalter, eventually becoming an autonomous prayer book. As both religious communities and laity had used psalters as prayer books, especially since the twelfth century, questions arise concerning the need for the book of hours as a new type of prayer book.[22] What was offered by the new type of book that was lacking in psalters? What was the nature of the social climate that propelled this expansion of (independent) books of hours?

To address these questions, let us turn to a later psalter-hours from Arras. In contrast to the Ghuiluys of Boisleux book, the *Psalter-Hours* from Paris (BnF, lat. 1328) has a modest cycle of illustrations—beginning with three full-page miniatures between the Calendar and the Psalms, representing the Flagellation of Christ, the Resurrection of Christ, and His encounter with Mary Magdalene (*Noli me tangere*).[23] Unusually, these scenes appear in a non-chronological arrangement, with the Flagellation of Christ placed between the Resurrection and Christ's encounter with the Magdalene. A second incongruity of this cycle is that, although prefatory cycles could vary immensely in length, no other example contains only three illuminations so detached in their subject matter from one another. Another psalter-hours from Arras, dated to c. 1300 and kept at the British Library in London (Yates Thompson 15), contains three full-page miniatures (fols. 17v, 18v, 19v) between the Calendar and the Psalms, but each of them is divided into four, thus presenting 12 scenes from the Passion of Christ.[24] The probable implication of these irregularities is that, when the book was rebound, some of its full-page illustrations were left-out and the remainder was not bound in the original order. It is reasonable to conclude, therefore, that the original cycle of Paris, BnF, lat. 1328 once contained a fuller cycle of illustrations arranged in a chronological order probably illustrating the Passion of Christ. Thus, the focal point of the prefatory cycle has changed—from Old Testament to New Testament narratives, from King David to Christ.

Apart from the prefatory illustrations, the Paris *Psalter-Hours* contains eight historiated initials as the traditional French division of the text, dealing with King David in a literal exegesis of one of the first verses.[25] The book's decoration continues with seven historiated initials at the beginning of the seven canonical hours of the Hours of the Virgin, depicting the infancy of Christ,[26] and a portrait of the owner praying before the Virgin and Child inside the letter "O," beginning the prayer *"O intemerata"* at fol. 222. From this short description, it is clear that the same number of historiated initials is found in the psalter part of the manuscript illustrating King David as in the illustrations of scenes from Christ's infancy in its Hours' part. The same division of historiated initials is attested also in London, BL, Yates Thompson 15, mentioned above. Both manuscripts demonstrate a sharp contrast with the mid-thirteenth-century specimen considered above. Although, undoubtedly, the Ghuiluys de Boisleux's *Psalter-Hours* is a much more sumptuous manuscript—incomparable in the richness of its illuminations to either Paris 1328 or Yates Thompson 15—the difference between these manuscripts is not only a corollary of the diverse contexts from which they derive, but is also reflective of key changes that occurred during the half century that stands between them. For, the mid-thirteenth century saw the apogee of the illustrated French psalters,[27] which were owned largely by aristocratic laymen; whereas, by the end of the century, bourgeois-owned books of hours were flourishing, making the illustration cycles of Paris 1328 and Yates Thompson 15 typical products of aristocratic and upper-bourgeois secular ladies.[28] I have already suggested that elaborated cycles of illustration in psalters—in prefatory cycles as well as in historiated initials—depicting scenes from the Old Testament, especially from the life of King David, suited courtly laymen as they contained direct and indirect messages linked to kingship and leadership ideals, and male models of behavior. But as significant as these ideals may have been for men, the shift to the book of hours centered on prayers to the Virgin Mary, and gave rise in light of gendered expectations, to a more suitable model for lay women who were to be preoccupied more by domestic than by public issues, and might have found more resonance in identifying with Mary as a mother.[29]

Although only the hours part remains, New York, PML, MS G. 59 is an example of a psalter-hours very similar to Paris 1328 and Yates Thompson

15, discussed above. It contains a historiated initial D illustrating the owner with the Virgin and Child at the beginning of the Fifteen Joys of the Virgin in French (fol. 68).[30] Although these prayers are well known in books of hours from the fifteenth century, this is one of the earliest examples (dated 1300–1320), and no textual or pictorial tradition existed as yet.[31] This manuscript, together with Paris 1328 and Yates Thompson 15, is of the same genre and shares some resemblance in pictorial schemes, iconographic details, and stylistic resemblance, unifying them as a group perhaps conceived and produced by the same Artesian workshop.[32]

A fifth manuscript—Baltimore, WAM, MS W. 86—is a book of hours with six prefatory miniatures, all depicting scenes from the Passion. The prefatory miniatures, decorated with six scenes from the infancy of Jesus, separate the Calendar from the Hours of the Virgin. Two additional historiated initials are illustrated: King David playing the harp at the beginning of the Penitential Psalms and the Trinity at the beginning of the Hours of the Holy Spirit.[33] There is no indication whatsoever as to the identity of the original owner. Therefore, while it does contain qualities similar to the previous manuscripts, it is impossible to know whether it belonged to a couple, a woman, or a man.

The last manuscript to be considered here is Baltimore, WAM, MS W. 104, a book of hours without a calendar, containing the Hours of the Virgin, Seven Penitential Psalms, Fifteen Gradual Psalms, Litany, the Office of the Dead, and closing with a later addition of eight short imprecations.[34] As for its decoration, three historiated initials are lacking at the Hours of the Virgin: in Matins, Sext, and None. As Lauds, the second Hours, depicts the Annunciation—the first illustration of the infancy cycle—it is reasonable to assume that the historiated initial for Matins of the Hours of the Virgin might have depicted the book owner kneeling before the Virgin and Child.[35] At the beginning of Terce of the Hours of the Virgin however, a historiated initial depicts the Nativity of Christ. On the right-bottom margins of this page (fol. 32v), a woman in the gesture of prayer is kneeling, her knees resting on the foliated page frame (Figure 2.1).

This kneeling woman, with her monochrome dress and a wimple covering her head and neck, seems to be dressed very modestly. Her eyes are looking directly in front of her, meeting the last word written on the end-line—virgo (virgin)—a word forming part of a popular hymn of uncertain origin, known since the ninth century, containing seven stanzas. The hymn's first stanza is as follows:

Ave maris stella
dei mater alma
*atque semper **virgo***
felix caeli porta.[36]

Figure 2.1   Walters Art Museum, Ms. W. 104, Book of Hours, fol. 32v.

The place selected for the depiction of the woman—quite an unusual location—seems to have been chosen in order to establish a relation with the historiated initial above it, which depicts the nativity of Christ. The juxtaposition of images emphasizes the purity of Christ's mother and, at the same time, also the purity of the woman depicted below.

The very idea of virginity must have been challenging for married medieval women. A respectable woman had three possible statuses: she was a virgin, a married woman, or a widow. According to the medieval perception of the great preacher, Jacques de Vitry (1160/70–1240), marriage was good, widowhood was better, but virginity was best. Enjoying a state of virginity was understood not only as a physical but also a moral condition. A "moral" virgin was a woman with integrity and modesty—necessary qualities for communicating with God. In one of Vitry's sermons, he uses the verses from Proverbs, 31:10–13 ("Who can find a virtuous woman? For her price is far above rubies. The heart of her husband doth safely trust in her, so that he shall have no need of spoil...") in order to define the virtuous woman as a married one, living in the material world, performing all her duties both at home and in her community, and who, although she is not physically a virgin, nevertheless deserves all the rights merited by virgin status. His opinion might have been shaped through his relationship with the Beguine sister, Mary of Oignies, during his stay at the Church of Saint Nicolas in Oignies between 1210 and 1216. During the thirteenth century, women who had been married and had children, like Marie of Oignies and Elizabeth of Hungary, and were eventually sanctified, enhanced the moral importance of the virtue of virginity.[37]

Alison Stones has proposed that Beatrix of Dampierre and Hugh II of Châtillon, married in 1287, were the owners of this manuscript.[38] The coats of arms painted in the manuscript have been identified as those of Châtillon of Blois, and of Guy of Dampierre, Count of Flanders (1225–1304). Guy, Count of Flanders, and his second wife, Isabelle of Luxemburg, had seven children. In 1287, their eldest daughter, Beatrix, married Hugh II of Châtillon, son of Guy II of Châtillon, Count of Saint Pol, and Matilda of Brabant. Hugh II of Châtillon was himself count of St. Pol (1289–1292) and count of Blois (1292–1307), whose coat of arms was of Châtillon of Blois—*De gueules a troi pals de devair, au chef d'or, charger d'un lanbeld'azur.* So, the coats of arms of both families are represented by two knights fighting a duel, a depiction of the long and bitter hostility between Hainaut and Flanders. The enmity originated between Marguerite II's children from her first marriage to Bouchard of Avesnes and her children from her second marriage to Guillaume of Dampierre.

The manuscript now has only two prefatory full-page illuminations. The first shows the Crucifixion (Figure 2.2), the second the Virgin and Theophilus. In the Crucifixion, a double-sided sword is simultaneously piercing the hearts of both Christ and the Virgin

This motif is developed out of Simeon's words to Mary during the presentation in the Temple, Luke, 2:34–35:

> And Simeon blessed them, and said to Mary his mother: Behold this child is set for the fall and for the resurrection of many in Israel and for a sign which shall be contradicted. And thy own soul a sword shall pierce, that, out of many hearts thoughts may be revealed.

The appearance of the motif in artistic depictions of the Crucifixion is attested in Cistercian and mendicant Marian devotional circles of German origin from the mid-thirteenth century.[39] It not only served to amplify the

Figure 2.2   Walters Art Museum, Ms. W. 104, Book of Hours, fol. 1r.

contemplative human quality of the Crucifixion, but also to bring into focus the suffering of Mary. Its currency is well-attested by different thinkers of the thirteenth century such as Bonaventure (1221–1274) and the Franciscan friar and Archbishop of Canterbury, John Pecham (1230–1292).[40]

The second full-page miniature depicts the kneeling repentant Theophilus receiving absolution from the Virgin, who stands to his right, handing him a scroll bearing his name—the scroll that he is supposed to have signed previously before the Devil and with his own blood. As observed above, it is plausible to assume that the prefatory cycle of W. 104 also once contained additional miniatures, thus originally forming a cycle of illustration depicting probably Christ's Passion. Nevertheless, it is possible to trace the connection between the two full-page miniatures through the Virgin herself. When we extend the investigation, we encounter many depictions of monks and nuns in historiated initials and marginalia throughout the manuscript. The Litany, which is hardly ever illustrated, receives a historiated initial showing three clerics singing before a lectern, while figures of John the Baptist and Saints Peter, Andrew, and Bartholomew stand in the margins. While it is common to find two or three monks in the historiated initial opening the Office of the Dead, no less than ten monks are gathered behind the coffin. In addition, six monks holding books are depicted in the margins; on the upper frame, two hybrid Franciscan and Dominican nuns sit and hold books, with books also held by another two nuns on the lower frame.

When compared with other books of hours, W104 contains many discrepancies. The prefatory miniatures, the woman's pious dress and head-cover, as well as the unusual placement in the margin in front of the word *virgo*, and the remaining illustrations, reveal the manuscript's religious connection. They suggest that the book might have been copied and illustrated under the close supervision of a religious authority. If Alison Stones is correct that the manuscript belonged to Beatrix of Dampierre and her husband Hugh II of Châtillon, this might reflect the Dampierre's tight connections with the Cistercian nunnery of Flines-lez-Râches, founded in 1234 by the Marguerite II mentioned above. In 1270, Guy of Dampierre, son of Marguerite II and father of Beatrix, departed from the gates of the nunnery to join Louis IX's crusade—a final part of a ritual of departure toward the East.[41] It was also at Flines that Beatrix's younger sister, Jeanne, took her vows.

In light of the limitations of space inherent in a single paper, I will confine myself to pointing out only one general issue concerning the relation of the owners' portraits to the Virgin Mary and Child. Within the manuscripts that have been presented here, there are three owner's portraits with the Virgin and Child, and the family portrait of Courtenay and Valois covering the previous portrait of Ghuiluys of Boisleux described above. The portrait of Catherine of Courtenay with the Virgin and Child, although very sumptuous, can be compared to the two portraits from New York, PML G. 59 and Paris, BnF lat. 1328. In these manuscripts, the owners are depicted in small historiated initials at the beginning of lesser prayers in their books (D, for "Douce dame," beginning the Fifteen Joys of the Virgin, O for "O intemerata," respectively).[42] Inside the letter D, the owner is kneeling with her hands joined in front of the enthroned Virgin and Child, while the Child is turning toward the woman and blessing her. At the beginning of the prayer "O intemerata," the owner is depicted in a similar way—kneeling with hands joined in prayer—in front of a standing Virgin supporting the Child. Both forms—the sitting and the standing Virgin—have precedents in painting as also in the sculpture of the period. These three portraits depict the owners in a private moment of devotion to the Virgin, totally immersed in their prayers. Their meditative state is intensified by the fact that the owners and the Virgin and Child share the same time, space, and reality.

This kind of confidential relationship displayed in books of hours between laywomen and the Virgin and Child is seen in many other examples from the same period. It is safe to say that it represents one of the ways in which the ever-growing Marian cult manifested itself. It is also true that it was an outcome of the religious awakening that flooded the Low Countries and northern France from the beginning of the thirteenth century, affecting the lay urban population with a rapid well-documented expansion of urban mendicant houses.[43] More specifically, however, I suggest that we should also see it as one example of the role laywomen were beginning to play in medieval society: they were becoming the most important link between their families and the Church, responsible for the spiritual behavior and salvation of their clan. In an article published in 1986, Sharon Farmer showed that, in 1215, Thomas of Chobham—an Englishman who had studied in Paris under Peter Cantor—wrote a *Manual for Confessors,* wherein he argues that women should be the focal point of priests' sermons because they have persuasive capacities with regard to their (sinning) husbands.[44] The same idea can be found in the sermons for the *Noble Ladies* of Humbert of Romans (1200–1277).[45] Such ladies, who had received a good education, should care more for their husbands' improper behavior. As they are free from financial problems, he insisted, they must take example from the saintly women who escorted Christ and invest their time for the benefit of the Church.[46]

New literary genres developed during the thirteenth century in Jewish society as well: just as the book of hours detached itself from the *Psalter* and became an autonomous book, so the Passover Haggadah detached from the *Siddur.* Both of these new books were used at home and, despite their differences (the book of hours was a prayer book used daily in privacy while the Passover Haggadah is used once a year by the whole family), both contained illuminations, some of them depicting women reading.[47] Indeed, the first depiction of a Jewish woman reading from an open book appears in the Darmstadt Haggadah; but this is dated to the beginning of the fifteenth century.[48]

The gap between the Christian artistic evidence of reading women from the thirteenth century and its absence at this time in Jewish art might be explained by three gender variables, each dependent on the other: the Virgin's function in the Christian liturgy, women's involvement in religious rituals, and women's role in the family.

The image of the Virgin and her growing importance in the Christian liturgy in the thirteenth century as mediator between Heaven and Earth presented a challenge for Jewish thought—a challenge that had some bearing upon the growing importance of the *Shekhinah*, the feminine expression of God, in Jewish mysticism, as Peter Schäfer and others demonstrated.[49] Recently, Ephraim Shoham-Steiner proposed that the elevation in Miriam's status among Ashkenazic women of the late twelfth century and the thirteenth century was a response to the growing importance of the Virgin among Christian women.[50] This possibility highlights the absence of a Jewish literary genre resembling the book of hours through which, as we have seen, Christian women could unite with a Heavenly female figure. At the same time, it attests to the importance of the gender of role models for the affinity of believers in religious rituals in both societies.

Books of hours as a new literary genre were a primary vehicle through which the Church attempted to include Christian lay women in religious ritual, while also imposing on them responsibility for their children's education and their husbands' salvation. In contrast to this tendency, in the thirteenth century, the Ashkenazic community expanded the exclusion of women from religious rituals.[51] Furthermore, such Jewish women were required to look after the physical demands of young children while the responsibility for their own education was in their husbands' hands.[52] Nevertheless, we should not conclude from this that Christian society was the more equal in terms of gender than that of the Jews, but rather that each society channeled women's activities in different ways.

In sum, I have proposed an investigation of devotional books' cycles of illustrations as reflecting gendered conventions. While psalters' illuminations were centered upon King David, the Virgin Mary took priority in books of hours;[53] the image of King David and its meaning for a high-ranking male dignitary was not one with which women could identify or follow. Although there had been some successful women rulers in thirteenth-century France, they were the exceptions.[54] Books of hours were more suited to women than psalters because women were able to identify with the Virgin in ways that they could not with King David. With his masculine personality, sexual misconduct, hot temper, and warrior image, King David provided neither a maternal image, nor could he offer any domestic comfort or salvation for women. The Virgin Mary as the protagonist of books of hours was the ultimate image and role model for woman to imitate: chaste, devoted, and pure, whereas King David was quite the opposite—an earthly, tormented, craving man.

The second half of the thirteenth century in northern France witnessed the rise of secular women. Although the last decades of gender studies have generated a huge interest in medieval women, historical evidence on the subject is so meager that most studies tend to focus on nuns, beguines, and anchoresses. I do not wish to exaggerate the importance of books of hours, and certainly do not seek to present them as the sole sources of light that might illuminate this obscure subject. They were, after all, only within the reach of the wealthy. Nevertheless, it does seem clear that the study of these books can provide a deeper understanding of the secular aristocratic and high-bourgeois secular women of the (early) late Middle Ages. The rise of the book of hours, with the Virgin Mary as its main protagonist, became an important vehicle for the expansion of lay women's devotional behavior in the growing urbanized society in Arras, and—we may presume—also in other towns with similar characteristics during the late Middle Ages.

Notes

1. Saint Anthony's fire is a disease caused by a fungus (ergot). During the Middle Ages, it often contaminated rye and other cereals. If not treated—as it often was not in the Middle Ages—it produces an intense feeling of burning (medieval victims described it as akin to being burned at the stake) before loss of the extremities.

2. Carol Symes, *A Common Stage* (Ithaca, 2007).

3. Pierre Bougard, Yves-Marie Hilaire, and Alain Nobilos, *Histoire d'Arras* (Dunkerque, 1988), 56–57.

4. For northern France: Alain Derville, "Le nombre d'habitants des villes de l'Artois et de la Flandre Wallone (1300–1450)," *Revue du Nord* 65 (1983), 277–299; Idem., *Villes de Flandre et d'Artois: 900–1500* (Villeneuve d'Ascq, 2002).

5. For a survey, see Adriaan Verhulst, *The Rise of Cities in North-West Europe* (Cambridge, 1999).

6. The broadest survey on the formation of books of hours is Victor Leroquais, *Les livres d'heures manuscrits de la Bibliothèque nationale*, 3 vols. and supplement (Paris, 1927–1943, repr. Paris, 1991). See also Roger S. Wieck, *Time Sanctified: the Book of Hours in Medieval Art and Life* (New York, 1988).

7. London, BL MS, Add. 49999. For a full examination of this manuscript, see Claire Donovan, *The de Brailes Hours: Shaping the Book of Hours in Thirteenth-Century Oxford* (London, 1991).

8. Leon M. J. Delaissé, "The Importance of Books of Hours for the History of the Medieval Book," in *Gathering in Honor of Dorothy E. Miner*, ed. Ursula E. McCracker, Lilian M.C. Randall, and Richard H. Randall, Jr. (Baltimore, 1974), 203–225.

9. An example of a study focusing on England is Kathryn A. Smith, *Art, Identity and Devotion in Fourteenth-Century England: Three Women and their Books of Hours* (London, 2003).

10. A condensed summary on the religious book culture of the region is: Adelaide Bennett, "Continuity and Change in the Religious Book Culture of the Lowlands in the Thirteenth and Fourteenth Centuries," in *Medieval Mastery. Book Illumination from Charlemagne to Charles the Bold, 800–1475*, ed. Adelaide Bennett et al. (Turnhout, 2002), 167–179.

11. Falconer Madan, "Hours of the Virgin Mary (tests for localization)," *The Bodleian Quarterly Record*, 1920/7, 40–44, reprinted in "The Localization of Manuscripts," *Essays in History Presented to Reginald Lane Poole,* ed. Henry W. Davis (Oxford, 1927), 5–27; Leroquais, *Livres d'heures*, n. 2; John Plummer, "'Use' and 'Beyond Use'," in *Time Sanctified,* ed. Roger S. Wieck (New York and Baltimore, 2001), 149–152.

12. Baltimore, Walters Art Museum, W. 86 and W. 104; London, BL, Yates Thompson 15; New York, Pierpont Morgan Library, Ms. M. 730 and G. 59; Paris, BnFF lat. 1328; and Stockholm, National Museum, B 1655–1656. Unfortunately, I have not yet been able to study this last manuscript.

13. For general information on the manuscript, see Bennett et al., *Medieval Mastery*, 182–183 (cat. No. 28); a monograph on the manuscript was written by Veronika Sattler, *Zwischen Andachtsbuch und Aventiure, Der Neufville-Vitasse-Psalter: New York,*

PML, MS M.730 (Hamburg, 2006); Richard A. Leson, "The Psalter-Hours of Ghuiluys de Boisleux," *Arte Medievale* 1 (2006): 115–130.

14. Pictures of the manuscripts can be found at: http://utu.morganlibrary.org/ medren/Manuscript_Images.cfm?ACC_NO=M.730&StartRow=21 (last visited September 1, 2014).

15. D for *Domine labia mea aperies*—the beginning of Matins from Ps. 50: 17.

16. For a detailed discussion of the David cycle, see: Adelaide Bennett, "David's Written and Pictorial Biography in a Thirteenth-Century French Psalter-Hours," in *Between the Picture and the Word: Manuscript Studies from the Index of Christian Art,* ed. Colum Hourihane (Princeton, 2005), 122–140.

17. Ibid., 124–125, 130.

18. Anne E. Lester, *Creating Cistercian Nuns. The Women's Religious Movement and its Reform in Thirteenth-Century Champagne* (Ithaca and London, 2001), 160–162.

19. Leson, "Psalter-Hours."

20. The few examples where men are depicted as owners of Books of Hours before the fifteenth century feature two kinds of men: religious men, as in the Burdett Psalter-Hours where a Hospitaller patron is seen kneeling before St. John the Baptist (Private Collection); or married men depicted with their wives, as in the case of Charles of Valois and Catherine of Courtenay or Joffroy of Aspermont and Isabella Kievraing (Melbourne NGV MS, Felton 1254–3 and Oxford, Bodleian Library MS, Douce, 118). One example of a layman depicted alone is mentioned by Alison Stones in "Some Portraits of Women in Their Books, Late 13th – Early 14th Century," in *Livres et lectures de femmes en Europe entre Moyen-âge et Renaissance,* ed. Anne-Marie Legaré (Turnhout, 2007), 24, where the man is in the right margin before Christ's blessing.

21. Hours of the Virgin—*Officium parvum Beatae Mariae Virginis*—are prayers to the Virgin, divided according to the eight canonical hours beginning with Matins. These prayers, of uncertain origin, were first included in the daily prayers in the tenth century in the Benedictine monasteries of France and Germany. Edmund Bishop, *The Prayer Book of the Lay People,* reprinted in E. Bishop, *Liturgica Historica* (Oxford, 1918), 225–226. The prayer "O intemerata" might originate in one of the Citeaux monasteries. It appears by the end of the twelfth century in four manuscripts, one English and three French. André Wilmart, *Auteurs spirituels et textes dévots du Moyen-âge latin: études d'histoire littéraires* (Paris, 1971), 474–504.

22. Adelaide Bennett, "The Transformation of the Gothic Psalter in Thirteenth-Century France," in *The Illuminated Psalter: Studies in the Content, Purpose and Placement of Its Images* (Turnhout, 2004), 211–222.

23. Paris, BnF, lat. 1328, fols. 14v, 15, 16v. Illustrations from the manuscript can be viewed at the BnF site: http://images.bnf.fr/jsp/index.jsp?contexte=rech ercheCombinee&origine=menuGauche&destination=rechercheCombinee. jsp (last visited September 1, 2014).

24. Illustrations from the manuscripts can be viewed at: http://www.bl.uk/catalogues/illuminatedmanuscripts/record.asp?MSID=8147&CollID=58&NStart=15 (last visited September 1, 2014). One full-page illumination is probably missing after fol. 17.

25. Ps. 1 (fol. 17), 26 (fol. 39v), 38 (54v), 52 (69), 69 (83v), 80 (101v), 97 (118v), 109 (136v). On French Psalters of the thirteenth century, see Bennett, "Transformation," 211–222.

26. The seven historiated initials are: fol. 194—Annunciation; fol. 206—Visitation; fol. 209—Nativity; fol. 211v—Annunciation to the Shepherds; fol. 213v—Adoration of the Magi; fol. 215v—Presentation at the Temple; and 219v—Flight into Egypt. Although there are eight canonical hours, *Lauds*, the second hour was often joined with Matins. For variations of illustrations in the Hours of the Virgin, see Wieck, *Time Sanctified*, 60–72.

27. Bennett, "Transformation," 211.

28. Research on Books of Hours usually centers on the fifteenth to sixteenth centuries, when their production was enormous. As I have shown, there was a first wave of books of hours' production, less considerable in numbers, but no less important, around 1300. Margo Stroumsa-Uzan, *Women's Prayer: Devotion and Gender in Books of Hours in Northern France ca. 1300,* (PhD dissertation, Ben-Gurion University of the Negev, 2010), 1–15.

29. Madeline Caviness argues that not only is it unlikely that secular women could have influenced illuminations in prayer books made for them, but that "even male patrons' control over their books was seldom absolute," "Anchoress, Abbess, and Queen: Donors and Patrons or Intercessors and Matrons?," in *The Cultural Patronage of Medieval Women*, ed. June H. McCash (Athens, Georgia, 1996) 105–115.

30. Beginning "Douce dame de misericordemere de pitierfountain de tous bien..." The owner portrait's inspiration derives from a line in the prayer "etie me agenouilleray .xv. fois devant votre benoit ymage" (and I kneel fifteen times in front of your blessed image). The Fifteen Joys of the Virgin are testimony to a more meditative conception of prayers disseminated by the mendicant orders during the thirteenth century. A simplified form of recitation of the Fifteen Joys spread from the early fourteenth century in books of hours as in New York, PML MS, G. 59. Illustrations can be viewed at: http://utu.morganlibrary.org/medren/Manuscript_images.cfm?ACC_NO=G.59&StartRow=1 (last visited on September 1, 2014).

31. Lucy F. Sandler, "An Early Fourteenth-Century English Psalter in the Escorial," *Journal of the Warburg and Courtauld Institutes*, 42 (1979): 65–80, no. 39.

32. Stylistic analysis of the manuscripts in order to define a workshop is beyond the scope of this chapter.

33. The manuscript is described by Lillian M. C. Randall, *Medieval and Renaissance Manuscripts* (Baltimore, 1992), 113–115.

34. Detailed description of the manuscript can be found in Randall, *Medieval and Renaissance Manuscripts*, 142–145.

35. Two cycles of illustrations accompanied the Hours of the Virgin. The standard cycle depicted events in the life of the Virgin from the Annunciation to the Flight into Egypt or the Massacre of the Innocents. The less common cycle depicted the Passion of Christ from the Betrayal to the Entombment.

36. "Hail, star of the sea, Nurturing Mother of God, And ever Virgin, Happy gate of Heaven". Mary's appellation as 'star of the sea' appears in one of

Bernard of Clairvaux's homilies, *De laudibus Beatae Mariae* – Homily 2, in *Magnificat: Homilies in Praise of the Blessed Virgin Mary*, trans. Marie-Bernard Said and Grace Perigo (Kalamazoo, 1979), 30–31.

37. Clarissa W. Atkinson, "Precious Balsam in a Fragile Glass: The Ideology of Virginity in the Later Middle Ages," *Journal of Family History* 8, 2 (1983): 131–143.

38. Stones, "Some Portraits of Women."

39. This iconography is known also in wall-paintings, ivories, and other artistic media. See Charles R. Morey, "A Group of Gothic Ivories in the Walters Art Gallery," *The Art Bulletin*, 18 (1936): 199–213.

40. "Salve, grandi cum dolore/Iesumma didum cruore/ Cernens in patibulo; Sed hoc minus doluisti/ Quod hunc pati credidisti/ Pro salvando saeculo." The same iconography is attested to in two other psalters-hours from northern France, one from Amiens (ca. 1280, The Hours of Yolande de Soissons, New York, PML, M. 729, fol. 345v), the other from Metz, (ca. 1300, Metz, BM, M. 1588, fol. 204r). A variation appears in the Rothschild Canticles, (ca. 1300, Yale University, Beinecke Library, Ms. 404, fols. 18v–19r).

41. Lester, *Creating Cistercian*, 162–163.

42. Abbé Victor Leroquais defined three categories of prayers in Books of Hours, see n. 2.

43. Richard Emery, *The Friars in Medieval France* (New York, 1962), 90–97, 101–102, 113.

44. Sharon Farmer, "Persuasive Voices: Clerical Images of Medieval Wives," *Speculum*, 61 (1986): 517–543.

45. Humbert de Romans, *De Eruditione Praedicatorum*, XCVI, Ad mulieres burgenses divites, C. Cassagrande, *Predichealle donne delsecolo XIII* (Milano, 1978), 5–42; 43–60.

46. Ibid., 50.

47. Katrin Kogman-Appel, "Portrayals of Women with Books: Female (Il) Literacy in Medieval Jewish Culture", in *Reassessing the Roles of Women as 'Makers' of Medieval Art and Architecture*, ed. Therese Martin (Leiden, 2012), 2:525–564.

48. Darmstadt, Landesund Universitätsbibliothek, Cod. Or. 8, fol. 37v.

49. Peter Schäfer, *Mirror of His Beauty* (Princeton and Oxford, 2002), esp. 128–134.

50. Ephraim Shoham-Steiner, "The Virgin Mary, Miriam, and Jewish Reactions to Marian Devotion in the High Middle Ages" *AJS Review*, 37 (2013): 75–91.

51. Elisheva Baumgarten, *Mothers and Children, Jewish Family Life in Medieval Europe* (Princeton and Oxford, 2004), 85–89.

52. Ibid., 158–165.

53. King David is sometimes represented in the opening of the Penitential Psalms.

54. Karen S. Nicholas, "Countesses as Rulers in Flanders," in *Aristocratic Women in Medieval France* ed. Theodore Evergates (Philadelphia, 1999), 111–137, esp. 136–137.

CHAPTER 3

WHAT HAPPENED TO CHRISTIAN HEBRAISM IN THE THIRTEENTH CENTURY?

Ari Geiger

The twelfth century was an outstanding period for medieval Hebraism and is subsequently the subject of far more research than is the thirteenth. The Christian Hebraists are known for their use of Jewish exegesis as a major source for their own literal commentaries, and are seen as belonging to a general trend of Christian interest in Jewish texts that marked the twelfth-century renaissance, as part of the flowering of Christian literal exegesis.[1] In contrast, in this chapter I will take a closer look at developments in Christian Hebraism during the thirteenth century in Europe, highlight its main characteristics, and describe how it differed from the previous century. In addition, I will demonstrate the connection between these thirteenth-century developments and Jewish-Christian relations during that time. When I refer to the Hebraist movement, I have in mind the broad sense of "Hebraism," meaning not just Christians who could read Hebrew but all those who were interested in Jewish texts and wanted to become acquainted with them—whether to learn or to find material that would be useful for the purpose of disputations.

Christian scholarly interest in Jewish texts was not new in the twelfth century. It was closely linked to early Christian literal exegesis, through two aspects: textual criticism and literal interpretation. This school—always overshadowed by spiritual commentary—had its first flowering in the fourth and fifth centuries, when Jerome proudly raised the flag of "Hebrew truth" (*Hebraica veritas*)—a term he coined to connote recognition of the fact that one must go back to the Jewish sources in order to uncover the literal sense of the Bible.[2] This concept paved the way for Christians of later generations who wanted to enjoy the fruits of Jewish scholarship and could point to Jerome as a patristic authority who encouraged them to do so.[3]

Initially, Christian Hebraism had only a marginal presence until its revival in the twelfth century.[4] Among the many Hebraists in this period, the most important were Herbert of Bosham (d. ca. 1190) and the Victorines (Hugh of St.Victor (d. 1141) and his student Andrew of St.Victor (ca. 1110–1175)).[5] At least some of the Jewish interpretations they incorporated in their work were the result of direct contacts with Jews.[6] It is no accident that Andrew—a radical exponent of the method of literal exegesis who excluded spiritual interpretations from his commentary—also went the furthest in his use of Jewish interpretations and the Hebrew text of the Bible. Similarly, Herbert of Bosham, who was influenced by the school of Saint Victor, chose to write his commentary on the *Psalterium iuxta Hebraeos*, Jerome's Latin version of Psalms according to the Hebrew text that had not been incorporated into the Vulgate. Needless to say, this commentary includes many Jewish interpretations as well.[7]

Scholarly Hebraism in the Thirteenth Century

The Study of the Bible

Deanna Copeland Klepper commences her study *The Insight of Unbelievers* with a comprehensive survey of the scholarly tradition that links twelfth-century Hebraists with their successors in the fourteenth century (mainly Nicholas of Lyra). She offers a chronologically unbroken list of scholars who focused on the historical stratum of the Bible, some of whom studied Hebrew and relied on Jewish texts.[8] Stephen Langton (ca. 1155–1228) passed on the torch from the twelfth to the thirteenth century.[9] Alexander Neckam was another of his generation (1157–1217), who employed Jewish sources and whose biblical commentaries displayed knowledge of Hebrew.[10] They were followed by Robert Grosseteste (ca. 1175–1253), who taught Franciscans at Oxford and was deeply involved with the order before he was named Bishop of Lincoln.[11] One of the Friars Minor who studied with him was Adam Marsh (d. 1258) who later taught the Franciscans at Oxford. Marsh held to his mentor's ideas and passed them on to his pupils, including the importance of studying ancient languages, among them Hebrew.[12] He was also the link between Grosseteste and one of the most important figures of medieval Hebraism—Roger Bacon (ca. 1214–1292).

Although Bacon did not add newly discovered Jewish interpretations, he fought against the entire Church and university establishment, for the need to return to the original texts of the *auctores* and revise and improve translations on the basis of these texts. This could only be done, accord-ing to Bacon, with a good command of Greek and Arabic for the writings of Aristotle and the New Testament, and of Hebrew and Aramaic for the Old.[13] In the field of Bible studies, Bacon stressed the importance of copying Hebrew manuscripts of the Bible and reported that he had made practical efforts in this direction.[14] Moreover, he invested energy in learning Hebrew and even claimed to have written a book on Hebrew grammar.[15]

Klepper is correct when she argues that Hebraism, as a current of scholarship, did not vanish in the thirteenth century. Nevertheless, it is important to distinguish between the Hebraist approach to Bible study in the twelfth century and its counterpart in the thirteenth. As described previously, twelfth-century Hebraism drew on Hebrew sources for biblical commentaries and quoted Jewish interpretations. By contrast, in the thirteenth century, we find relatively little Jewish material in exegetical works.[16] More importantly, even those commentaries that do cite Jewish interpretations do not use Jewish material extensively.[17]

The decrease in the use of Jewish sources during the thirteenth century may be linked to one of the strongest influences on Christian exegesis of that time—the prominence of preaching. Sermons were an important tool in the battle that the Church waged against heresy, which was viewed as a significant threat to its integrity.[18] The conduct of the war against heresy was entrusted to the mendicant orders founded at the beginning of the century that had since grown rapidly, most particularly the Dominicans, whose original *raison d'être* was combating heresy.[19] Because of the emphasis that these orders placed on learning, the Franciscan and Dominican *studia* became key centers of theological and biblical scholarship. The most prominent schoolmen of this period, who also lectured on theology at the universities, were members of the mendicant orders,[20] which explains their significant role in the study of the Bible in the thirteenth century.[21]

These teachers were also preachers, and knowing that their students would one day serve as priests or preachers, they oriented their instruction toward the needs of preaching.[22] Consequently, they emphasized moral exegesis, which employs Scripture to derive religious lessons relevant to the period. This focus on moral exegesis included familiarizing the students with examples of such interpretations in order to incorporate them into their sermons, and having them study the method so that they could devise new and original moral interpretations of their own. Because moral exegesis rests strongly on allegory, the latter gained importance in the thirteenth century at the expense of literal exegesis, which faded, but did not disappear completely. It was only natural that the decreased importance of the literal sense reduced the dependence of Christian exegesis on Jewish texts. In any case, Jewish readings could not be employed in moral interpretation because they were less compatible with Christian morality. The commentaries that grew out of the lectures were oriented toward similar goals and the same audience, and were, therefore, influenced by these processes, as well.

However, Jewish materials relating to Biblical study can be found in other types of works during the thirteenth century, such as tools for Bible study and translations or reworking of Jewish exegetical material for a Christian readership. In the history of Bible study, the thirteenth century may be called "the age of tools"[23] because of the increasing number of works (most of them developed by members of the mendicant orders) intended to serve as aids to the study of the Bible. These were part of the trend that began in the cathedral schools of the twelfth century and continued in the universities of the thirteenth century to turn the study of the Bible into a scientific or academic field. Among these works, some made use of Jewish sources, for example, the *correctoria* texts that drew on accurate manuscripts to present variant readings to the standard text of the Vulgate in some of which the Hebrew text is used as a source.[24] The same is true of the biblical dictionaries (*glossae*) of the age that cite the Hebrew form of entry words.[25]

As has been shown by scholars, the libraries of Oxford and Cambridge and the Bibliothèque Nationale in Paris possess thirteenth-century manuscripts of the Hebrew text of the Bible, most of them of the Psalms.[26] The majority of these texts were produced with the aim of transmitting Jewish knowledge about the Hebrew text of the Bible to the Christian world, along with the meanings of this text. They usually include the Hebrew text of the Psalms alongside a Latin version and, often, a commentary in Latin, based in part on Jewish sources.[27]

An example of a text written in order to convey Jewish exegesis to the Christian world is a commentary edited by Avrom Saltman and Sara Kamin, entitled, "A Historical Commentary on the Song of Songs according to Solomon [=Rashi] (*Expositio hystorica Cantici Canticorum secundum Salomonem*)."[28] Saltman and Kamin concluded that the commentary was written in the second half of the thirteenth century.[29] They demonstrated that it was based on Rashi, adapted for a Christian audience, and employed the Vulgate as its underlying text.[30]

In contrast to twelfth-century Hebraists who quoted Jewish interpretations unfamiliar in the Christian world[31] that they had acquired directly from Jews with whom they had intellectual contacts,[32] in the thirteenth century, the amount of such new Jewish interpretations decreased and most were taken from earlier Christian works.[33] In other words, the sources for Jewish exegesis studied in the theology faculties of Paris and Oxford in the thirteenth century came from commentaries they employed—the *Glossa ordinaria* and Peter Comestor's *Historia scholastica*[34]—rather than from direct intellectual contacts between Jews and Christians.

The leaves of the Hebrew-Latin manuscripts mentioned above do, however, provide some evidence of contact between Jews and Christians during the thirteenth century. Modern scholars who studied these manuscripts have described a picture of cooperation between Jews and Christians—one that also recalls the scholarly ties that existed between adherents of the two faiths in France during the previous century.[35] Nevertheless, these are only conclusions that can be drawn on the basis of an analysis of the manuscripts that, unfortunately, does not give us conclusive information regarding whether the "Jewish" partners in their compositions were converts to Christianity or Jews who remained loyal to their faith.

Klepper has emphasized that most of the scholars identified with the Hebraism of the thirteenth century were English Franciscans (or related to that order in some fashion),[36] in contrast to the more geographically and religiously diverse Hebraists among Bible instructors in the previous century.[37] This thirteenth-century trend according to Klepper, includes France, given the ongoing close relations between English and continental scholars, as many English scholars and students found their way to Paris and stayed there for a number of years, teaching and studying.[38] She conjectures that this contact may have influenced Parisian scholars to employ Jewish sources when they studied the Bible. This, however, may not have been the case as there were differences in the theology curricula in Paris and Oxford despite the personal ties between their scholars.[39] It is possible that this difference resulted in a distinction between the use of Jewish sources in England and in the Continent. One may also wish to consider the senior status of Paris as a center of theology that would make French influence on England much more likely than the opposite. In addition, even if France might have shared in the Hebraist approach when Langton was still alive in the early thirteenth century, by the 1240s this would have become much more difficult (although not impossible), due to the fierce campaign against rabbinic literature being waged there then (on this topic, see chapters 6 and 8). Examination of the materials available to us reveals a larger number of testimonies of the use of Jewish sources in England than on the Continent, during the thirteenth century.[40]

Theology

One of the innovations of Christian Hebraism in the thirteenth century was its expansion into the field of theology. Before then, Christian interest in Jewish texts was primarily for the use of Jewish exegesis in the study of the Bible.

A major development in the study of theology during the High Middle Ages was the emergence of Scholasticism, beginning in the second half of the eleventh century, that sought to combine Aristotelian philosophy with Christian doctrine. The great challenges that confronted scholastic thinkers were melding faith and philosophy and employing philosophy to provide an underpinning for faith. The Jewish scholar Maimonides (1138–1204) is a prominent example of those who followed this path and constructed an entire worldview resting on the twin pillars of Aristotle and the Bible. Consequently, he was taken as a model by Christian thinkers throughout the thirteenth century such as William of Auvergne (ca. 1190–1249), Albert the Great (ca. 1200–1280), Thomas Aquinas (ca. 1163–1243), and Meister

Eckhart (ca. 1260–1327).[41] These scholars learned from Maimonides' methods in *Guide of the Perplexed* to harmonize these two seemingly incompatible domains, and also drew on the content of that work and quoted it with regard to theological problems common to Judaism and Christianity, such as Natural Law and the divine names.[42] Christian biblical exegesis of the thirteenth century was also influenced by Maimonides, particularly on the book of Job. Whereas commentaries were previously influenced by the *Moralia* of Gregory the Great that had emphasized the moral aspect, now the rationalist stream, following Maimonides, began considering the philosophical aspects of the book.[43]

Polemical Hebraism

As noted above, unlike the twelfth century, when intellectual contacts between Jews and Christians were more widespread than at any other time in the Middle Ages, in the thirteenth century the use of Jewish commentaries was generally transmitted via quotations from earlier Christian writings. Nevertheless, one can detect a different and even antithetical goal for Christian interest in Jewish texts developed at this time—what I would term "polemical Hebraism." This was a clear consequence of the uneasy relations between Jews and Christians during that century. A significant portion of Christian interest in Hebrew books in the thirteenth century was motivated by the wish to exploit these works for the purpose of missionary activities and to further the "persecution" of rabbinic literature. As Deanna Klepper notes, whereas the Franciscans of the thirteenth century promoted the study of Hebrew and Jewish texts in order to apply them to their biblical studies, the Dominicans' interest in Jewish texts in this period stemmed from polemic motives.[44] Most of the Hebrew texts translated into Latin in the thirteenth century are related to polemic Hebraism rather than the classic scholarly Hebraism.

This was not a completely new phenomenon.[45] What was new in the thirteenth century was the unprecedented scale of the postbiblical rabbinic material that came into Christian hands. Much material was translated into Latin, and anthologies of rabbinic literature were produced. These compilations became the textual corpus employed by Christian polemicists in subsequent centuries.[46]

Whereas England was in the vanguard of scholarly Hebraism in the thirteenth century, France and Catalonia were the main centers of the polemical Hebraism of that era, beginning in 1239, when the Church declared war on rabbinic literature. In his indictment of the Talmud written by the convert Nicholas Donin that Pope Gregory IX attached to his decree ordering the confiscation of copies of that work, the author incorporated passages that he asserted proved his charges against it.[47] If we ignore his selective quotation and relatively minor but tendentious changes, the passages themselves are faithful representatives of their sources.[48] The war against the Talmud did not end with the trial conducted in 1240 and the great book burning of 1242. A second order to confiscate Jewish books was issued in 1244. The efforts by French Jewry to avert the decree caused its execution to be delayed, pending a thorough clarification of the charges against the Talmud. To make this possible, Odo of Châteauroux (ca. 1208–1273), the papal legate in Paris, together with a staff of converts, collected the passages from the confiscated Jewish books that were considered problematic and translated them into Latin.[49] This collection became known as the *Extractiones de Talmut* (Ms. BN lat. 16558). It contains roughly 2,000 tendentiously selected passages from rabbinic writings, the liturgy and Rashi's commentaries on the Bible and Talmud, rendered faithfully and with identification of their Jewish sources.[50] This anthology provided Christians with their first exposure to a large body of halakhic texts, taken from the rabbinic literature and Rashi's commentaries on the Talmud.

In Catalonia we encounter a different sort of polemical Hebraism, centered mainly in the Dominican mission founded by Raymond of Peñaforte. Whereas the condemnation of the Talmud was part of the Church's war on rabbinic literature, the Dominican missionaries employed it for polemical ends. The leading polemic tactic employed by this school was the use of talmudic texts to demonstrate the truth of Christianity.[51] This was the main axis of the Barcelona disputation between Naḥmanides and the convert Pablo Christiani in 1263,[52] and it was also the underlying idea behind Ramon Marti's *Pugio fidei*, written in 1278, that incorporates an unprecedented number of passages from rabbinic literature. Some of the Jewish quotations are presented as ostensibly christological interpretations by talmudic sages, while others are meant to present rabbinic literature in an unfavorable light.[53] As time passed, the treatise became a resource for Christian scholars to learn about Jewish texts; nevertheless, its primary use was for polemical purposes.

Christian Knowledge of Hebrew in the Thirteenth Century

Despite the fact that the twelfth century was the zenith of medieval Christian Hebraism, very few Hebraists actually had a solid command of the Hebrew language.[54] In this realm, the thirteenth century saw a marked improvement, with more scholars displaying fluency in Hebrew.[55] This trend is apparent in both branches of Hebraism—the scholarly and the polemical. In the former, it involves chiefly the authors of the *correctoria*.[56] This change is not surprising as diminished intellectual contact between Jews and Christians forced the Christians to develop an independent capacity to read Jewish texts. In the polemical sphere, this was also linked to the increased missionary pressure on the Jews. It was during this time that the Hebrew language became a subject of instruction in some Christian schools.[57] The most conspicuous example of this is the Dominican school in Catalonia (founded by Raymond of Peñaforte)—essentially, a training institution for missionaries. One of its graduates was the aforementioned Ramon Marti, who excelled in this area of knowledge.[58]

Conclusions

The thirteenth century follows the golden age of Hebraism of the twelfth-century renaissance, in which prominent Christian Hebraists such as the Victorines and Herbert of Bosham flourished. The dominant cultural trends of the thirteenth century and the worsening of relations between Jews and Christians caused a downturn in this activity. We noted that the weakening in the Hebraist current manifested chiefly in the significant decline in the overall number of Jewish interpretations quoted in Christian commentaries, and in the decreasing number of such new interpretations utilized. The rise of moral exegesis, as a result of the emphasis on preaching, limited those interested in literal exegesis primarily to the Franciscans, whose works were much less "Jewish" than those of the prominent Hebraists of the twelfth century.

The contraction of the circle of Christian Hebraist biblical scholars is also conspicuous from a geographic perspective. Most of the evidence for Hebrew-language study during the thirteenth century comes from England. The definite and substantial decline in intellectual interaction between Jews and Christians in northern France may have been due to the growing hostility between the two religions there.[59] Equally important, the assault against rabbinic literature, which gained momentum in the mid-thirteenth century, made it difficult for Christians to use books that were banned and denounced by the Church as heretical.

Those aspects of Hebraism that were weakened or disappeared in the thirteenth century were supplanted by three new avenues of study: the study of Maimonidean philosophic works that helped shape Christian scholastic theology, acquisition of knowledge from post-biblical texts in the effort to condemn rabbinic literature, and the study of texts to facilitate missionary work among the Jews.

The one facet of Hebraism that did grow stronger in the thirteenth century was Christian fluency in the Hebrew language, as reflected in the areas of knowledge discussed above. Within the scholarly track of Hebraism, we note the creators of lexicons and bilingual Hebrew–Latin manuscripts as well as Roger Bacon and some of the authors of *correctoria*. Further, in the polemicist track, we noted the first attempts to teach Hebrew to other Christians in order to facilitate their missionary efforts. These attempts did not appear to

bear significant fruit, although at least one such scholar—Ramon Marti—
seems to have known Hebrew better than any of his predecessors in the
Middle Ages. The departure from using Hebrew texts continued into the fourteenth
century. The list of Hebraists of that age is quite short. Nevertheless, it was
in this century that Nicholas of Lyra wrote his literal commentary, which is
one of the high points of medieval Christian Hebraism and one of the most
important collections of Jewish sources (chiefly for the study of the Bible)
from that age.[60] In Nicholas of Lyra, the last important Hebraist of the Middle
Ages, we can identify both trends of Christian Hebraism of the preceding
two centuries: the scholarly Hebraism of the twelfth century combined with
the dominant trend in the thirteenth century—the polemical Hebraism. In
addition to his interest in the literal interpretation found in the Jewish texts,
he made use of his knowledge of these texts to deprecate rabbinic literature
and to ground ostensibly Christological interpretations within them.[61] In
this sense, the thirteenth century served Nicholas as both a link between him
and the Victorines' scholarly Hebraism, as well as a generator of the polemical Hebraism of the mendicant orders, which he subsequently adopted.

Notes

1. On the Victorines and Jewish sources, see: Beryl Smalley, *The Study of the
   Bible in the Middle Ages* (Oxford, 1983), 102–106, 149–172; Reiner Berndt,
   André de Saint Victor (d. 1175), exégète et théologien, Bibliotheca Victorina 2
   (Paris, 1991), 221–226; Frans Van Liere, Introduction to Andrew of St Victor,
   Commentary on Samuel and Kings, Corpus Christianorum in Translation 3
   (Turnhout, 2009), 13–16; On Herbert of Bosham: Deborah L. Goodwin,
   "Take Hold of the Robe of a Jew," Herbert of Bosham's Christian Hebraism (Leiden,
   2006); Raphael Loewe, "Herbert of Bosham's Commentary on Jerome's
   Hebrew Psalter," *Biblica* 34 (1953): 48–58; Beryl Smalley, "A Commentary on
   the *Hebraica* by Herbert of Bosham," *Recherches de théologie ancienne et médiéval*
   18 (1951): 29–65.
2. See, for example: Hieronymus, *Hebraicae Quaestiones in Libro Geneseos*,
   Corpus Christianorum Series Latina 72, eds. Marc Adriaen, Germain Morin,
   and Paul de Lagarde (Turnhout, 1959), 1–2; Hieronymus, *Epistulae*, Corpus
   Scriptorum Ecclesiasticorum Latinorum 54, ed. Isidore Hilberg (Vienna,
   1996), Ep. 20.2, p. 105 and Ep. 34, p. 259–264. On this issue see: C. T. R.
   Hayward, trans., *Saint Jerome's Hebrew Questions on Genesis* (Oxford, 1995),
   92–99; Adam Kamesar, *Jerome, Greek Scholarship and the Hebrew Bible* (Oxford,
   1993), 41–81.
3. For example, in the introduction to his literal commentary on the Bible, when
   he declared his intention to quote Jewish sources, Nicholas of Lyra relied on
   Jerome and his guidance with regard to the need to employ Jewish sources
   for the criticism of the biblical text and for literal exegesis. See *Biblia sacra
   cum glossis interlineari et ordinaria, Nicolai Lyrani postilla et moralitatibus, Burgensis*

additationibus et Thoringi replicis (Lugdunum, 1545), 1 :3G. For English translation see Alastair J. Minnis and A. Brian Scott, eds., *Medieval Literary Criticism
and Theory* (Oxford, 1988), 270.

4. With regard to familiarity with Jewish sources until the middle of the eleventh century—the start of the twelfth-century renaissance—we can mention
   figures such as Rabanus Maurus (ca. 776–856), who quoted Jewish commentaries (see Avrom Saltman, "Rabanus Maurus and the Pseudo-Hieronymian
   Quaestiones Hebraicae in Libros Regum et Paralipomenon," *Harvard Theological
   Review* 66 (1973): 43–76) and Theodulf of Orléans (d. 821), who made use of
   the Hebrew text in the edition of the Bible he compiled for Charlemagne,
   see Pseudo-Jerome, *Quaestiones on the Book of Samuel,* ed. Avrom Saltman
   (Leiden, 1975), 4–11. In addition, there are pseudo-Jerome commentaries
   from the Carolingian Age, in which the strong influence of Jewish sources
   is evident. In most cases, however, there was no direct contact with Jews or
   study of Jewish texts, but only citation of Jewish texts from previous Christian
   writings (ibid).

5. To this list we can add Peter Comestor, who included a significant number
   of Jewish interpretations in his *Historia Scholastica.* Unlike the other names
   in the list, the overwhelming majority of the Jewish materials he cites come
   from early Christian works. See Louis H. Feldman, "The Jewish Sources
   of Peter Comestor's Commentary on Genesis in His *Historia Scholastica,*"
   in *Begegnungen Zwischen Christentum und Judentum in Antike und Mittelalter,
   Festschrift für Heinz Schreckenberg,* ed. Dietrich A. Koch and Hermann
   Lichtenberger (Göttingen, 1993), 93–121; Chen Merchavia, *Ha-talmud bi-re'i
   ha-natsrut* (Jerusalem, 1970), 167–193; Ari Geiger, "*Historia Judaica*: Petrus
   Comestor and His Jewish Sources," in *Pierre le Mangeur ou Pierre de Troyes,
   maître du XIIe siècle,* Bibliothèque d'histoire culturelle du moyen âge 12, ed.
   Gilbert Dahan (Turnhout, 2012), 125–145.

6. See nn. 1, 32.

7. See end of n. 1.

8. Deanna Copeland Klepper, *The Insight of Unbelievers: Nicholas of Lyra and
   Christian Reading of Jewish Text in the later Middle Ages* (Philadelphia, 2007),
   14–30.

9. Ibid., 14–15. Langton's commentary includes Jewish material. He also composed Hebrew-Latin glossaries. See Avrom Saltman, Introduction to Stephen
   Langton, *Commentary on the Book of Chronicles* (Ramat Gan, 1978), 29–39. See
   there some examples from Langton's text; Gilbert Dahan, "Les interpréta-
   tions juives dans les commentaires bibliques des maîtres parisiens du dernier
   tiers du XIIe siècle," *Michael, On the History of the Jews in the Diaspora* 12
   (1991): 85–110.

10. Klepper, *Insight of Unbelievers,* 15. See Raphael Loewe, "Alexander Neckam's
    Knowledge of Hebrew," in *Hebrew Study from Ezra to Ben-Yehuda,* ed. William
    Horbury (Edinburgh, 1999), 207–223.

11. Klepper, *Insight of Unbelievers,* 18–20. Robert Grosseteste exerted a major
    influence on Bible study by the Franciscans. He advocated that theology be
    learned directly from the Bible and not from Peter Lombard's *Sentences* (as
    was the custom of the time in Paris and for some teachers in Oxford as well).
    He spoke of the need to master Hebrew and Greek and to apply knowledge

gained from textual criticism. On Grosseteste and Bible study, see: Beryl Smalley, "The Biblical Scholar," in *Robert Grosseteste: Scholar and Bishop*, ed. Daniel A. Callus (Oxford, 1955), 70–97. On his knowledge of Hebrew and the Hebrew texts he owned, see also Raphael Loewe, "The Medieval Christian Hebraists of England, the *Superscriptio Lincoleniensis*," *Hebrew Union College Annual* 28 (1957), 205–252, esp. 211–213.

12. Klepper, *Insight of Unbelievers*, 20–21.

13. Klepper, *Insight of Unbelievers*, 18–23; Smalley, *Study*, 329–332. On Roger Bacon's attitude toward Jewish texts and Hebrew language, see: Smalley, *Study*, 329–333; Samuel A. Hirsch, "Early English Hebraists: Roger Bacon and His Predecessors," in Samuel A. Hirsch, *A Book of Essays* (London, 1905), 1–72; Horst Weinstock, "Roger Bacon's Polyglot Alphabets," *Florilegium* 11 (1992): 160–178.

14. Hirsch, "Early English Hebraists," 44–46.

15. Ibid., 47–57. See also Weinstock, "Roger Bacon's Polyglot Alphabets," 174 nn. 13–14; Edmond Nolan and Samuel A. Hirsch, *The Greek Grammar of Roger Bacon and a Fragment of His Hebrew Grammar* (Cambridge, 1902), 197 ff.

16. For example, in the commentaries of Stephen Langton. See n. 9.

17. As noted above, Andrew of St. Victor and Herbert of Bosham quote Jewish interpretations frequently, something not found in thirteenth-century texts.

18. Karlfried Froehlich, "Christian Interpretation of the Old Testament in the High Middle Ages," in *Hebrew Bible / Old Testament, The History of Its Interpretation*, ed. Magne Sæbø (Göttingen, 1996), 1:509–510.

19. See M. Michèle Mulchahey, *"First The Bow Is Bent in Study," Dominican Education before 1350* (Toronto, 1998), 3–54.

20. For example, Alexander of Hales (ca. 1185–1245), Roger Bacon and Bonaventure (1217–1274) [Franciscans]; Thomas Aquinas, Albert the Great (ca. 1200–1280) [Dominicans].

21. See Froehlich, "Christian Interpretation," 512–517; Smalley, *Study*, 264–265; Bert Roest, *A History of Franciscan Education (circa 1210–1517)* (Leiden, 2000), 130–133; Mulchahey, *"First The Bow,"* 480–526.

22. Smalley, *Study*, 253–263; Froehlich, "Christian Interpretation," 510; Phyllis Barzillay-Roberts, *Stephanus de Lingua-Tonante, Studies in the Sermons of Stephen Langton* (Toronto, 1968), 95–108.

23. Froehlich, "Christian Interpretation," 518 and see as well Smith, chapter 1 in this volume.

24. For example, the *correctoria* of William de la Mare and Gerard de Huy. See: Klepper, *Insight of Unbelievers*, 22–23; Gilbert Dahan, "La connaissance de l'hébreu dans les correctoires de la Bible du XIIIᵉ siècle. Notes préliminaires," *Revue théologique de Louvain* 23 (1992): 178–190. For a list of the correctoria manuscripts we know of (most of which made use of the Hebrew text), see "Correctoires de la Bible," in *Dictionnaire de la Bible* 2 (Paris, 1899), 1022–1026.

25. See Gilbert Dahan, *Les intellectuels chrétiens et les juifs au Moyen Âge* (Paris, 1990), 256, 267. An example of such a trilingual dictionary is Ramsey: *Dictionnaire hébreu-latin-français de la Bible hébraïque de l'Abbaye de Ramsey (XIIIe s.)*, Corpus Christianorum Continuatio Mediaevalis in-4° 4, eds.

Judith Olszowy-Schlanger et al. (Turnhout, 2008) and see as well Smith, chapter 1 in this volume.

26. For lists and short descriptions of these manuscripts, see Judith Olszowy-Schlanger, *Les manuscrits hébreux dans l'Angleterre médiévale: Étude historique et paleographique* (Paris, 2003), 147–302; Raphael Loewe, "Hebrew Books and 'Judaica' in Medieval Oxford and Cambridge," in *Remember the Day, Essays on Anglo-Jewish History Presented to Cecil Roth*, ed. John M. Shaftesley (London, 1966), 36–48; Raphael Loewe, "Latin *Superscriptio* MSS on Portions of the Hebrew Bible other than the Psalter," *Journal of Jewish Studies* 9 (1958): 63–71.

27. See Olszowy-Schlanger, *Les manuscrits hébreux*; Idem., "Rachi en Latin: les gloses latines dans un manuscrit du commentaire de Rachi et les études hébraïques parmi des chrétiens dans l'Angleterre médiévale," in *Héritages de Rachi*, ed. René S. Sirat (Paris, 2006), 137–150; Gilbert Dahan, "Deux psautiers hébraïques glosés en latin," *Revue des études juives* 158 (1999): 61–87; Gilbert Dahan, "Un dossier latin de textes de Rashi autour de la controverse de 1240," *Revue des études juives* 151 (1992): 321–336; Loewe, "The Medieval Christian Hebraists"; Loewe, "Latin *Superscriptio* MSS."

28. Sarah Kamin and Avrom Saltman, eds., *Secundum Salomonem: A Thirteenth Century Latin Commentary on the Song of Solomon* (Ramat Gan, 1989).

29. Ibid., 45–47.

30. Ibid., 7–9, 16–45.

31. Van Liere, Introduction to Andrew of St. Victor, 13–14; Goodwin, *"Take Hold..."*, 67–71, 138ff., 236–243.

32. Here are several examples: For Andrew of St. Victor, see Michael Signer, Introduction to Andreas de Sancto Victore, *Expositio in Ezechielem*, Corpus Christianorum Continuatio Mediaevalis 53E (Turnhout, 1991), 25–26; Van Liere, Introduction to Andrew of St. Victor, 14–15; for Stephen Harding, see Michael Signer, "Polemic and Exegesis: The Varieties of Twelfth-Century Hebraism," in *Hebraica Veritas? Christian Hebraists and the Study of Judaism in Early Modern Europe*, eds. Allison P. Coudert and Jeffrey S. Shoulson (Philadelphia, 2004), 23–24; For Herbert of Bosham, see Goodwin, *"Take Hold..."*, 137–141, 164–167.

33. Gilbert Dahan, "La connaissance de l'exégèse juive par les chrétiens du XXIIe au XIV siècle," in *Rashi et la culture juive en France du Nord au moyen âge*, eds. Glbert Dahan, Gérard Nahon, and Elie Nicolas (Paris-Louvain, 1997), 358.

34. At least until the middle of the thirteenth century, the *Glossa ordinaria* was the standard commentary studied at the University of Paris. It was also an important source for commentators in subsequent centuries. See Froehlich, "Christian Interpretation," 518–559; Lesley Smith, *The Glossa Ordinaria: The Making of a Medieval Bible Commentary* (Leiden, 2009), 193–239; On the circulation of the *Historia scholastica* in the thirteenth century, and its place in the exegesis of that time, see: Mark J. Clark, "The Commentaries on Peter Comestor's *Historia scholastica*," *Sacris erudiri* 44 (2005): 301–309; Mark J. Clark, "Le cours d'Etienne Langton sur l'*Histoire scolastique* de Pierre le Mangeur: le fruit d'une tradition unifiée," in Dahan, *Pierre le Mangeur*, 243–266. In both of these works (the *Glossa ordinaria* and the *Historia scholastica*) we can find Jewish interpretations, especially in Comestor's work, where it appears rather frequently (see n. 5).

35. See Olszowy-Schlanger, *Les manuscrits Hébreux*, 58–66, 144. For a discussion of the identity of the authors of these manuscripts, see Loewe, "The Medieval Christian Hebraists," 216–224.
36. Klepper, *Insight of Unbelievers*, 17–24. See also Goodwin, *"Take Hold..."*, 9–10, 147.
37. By geographical breakdown, Hugh of St. Victor, Peter Comestor, and Peter the Chanter were French. Andrew of St. Victor, Herbert of Bosham, and Stephen Langton were English (though they spent part of their careers in France). Nicholas of Manjacoria (d. 1145) was Italian (see Eva de Visscher, "Cross-religious Learning and Teaching: Hebraism in the Works of Herbert of Bosham and Contemporaries," in *Crossing Borders, Hebrew Manuscripts as a Meeting-Place of Cultures*, ed. Piet Van Boxel and Sabine Arndt (Oxford, 2009), 123. See there for more references); By monastic affiliation: Hugh of St. Victor and his student Andrew were Victorines, Nicholas of Manjacoria a Cistercian, Peter Comestor and Peter the Chanter were secular clerics.
38. Klepper, *Insight of Unbelievers*, 26.
39. For example, the dispute as to whether the Bible should be studied directly or through the *Sentences*. See ibid., 26–28, and the references there; On the differences between theology studies in Paris and Oxford, see also Monika Asztalos, "The Faculty of Theology," in *A History of the University in Europe: Universities in the Middle Ages*, ed. Hilde de Ridder-Symeons (Cambridge, 1992), 1: 420–433.
40. From England we have the *Superscriptio Lincoleniensis* (see Loewe, "The Medieval Christian Hebraists"), the Psalters studies by Gilbert Dahan (See Dahan, "Deux psautiers hébraïques"), the texts of Roger Bacon (see n. 13), the Hebrew-Latin-French Dictionary from Ramsey Abbey (see *Dictionnaire hébreu-latin-français*) and other manuscripts described by Raphael Loewe and Judith Olszowy-Schlanger (see n. 27); Textual evidence of "biblical" Hebraism on the Continent can be found mainly in the *correctoria*. See n. 24.
41. See Dahan, *Les intellectuels chrétiens*, 314–322; Görge K. Hasselhoff, *Dicit Rabbi Moyses: Studien zum Bild von Moses Maimonides im lateinischen Westen vom 13 bis zum 15 Jahrhundert* (Würzburg, 2004); Wolfgang Kluxen, *Maïmonide et l'orientation métaphysique des scolastiques latins au XIIIe siècle*, in *Maïmonide, philosophe et savant (1138–1204)*, ed. Tony Levy and Rāshid Rushdī (Leuven, 2004), 395–409. Aquinas refers to Maimonides in the *Summa Theologia*. For a list of these references, see Dahan, *Les intellectuals chrétiens*, 317 n. 47. Evidence that William of Auvergne was acquainted with the *Guide of the Perplexed* can be found in his *De Universo* and *De Legibus*. For examples, see: Joseph Guttmann, "Gillaume d'Auvergne et la literature Juive," *Revue des études juives* 18 (1889): 243–255 (notes).
42. See, for example: *Mercedes Rubio, Aquinas and Maimonides, on the Possibility of the Knowledge of God: An Examination of the Quaestio de attributis* (Dordrecht, 2006); David B. Burrel, "Aquinas' Debt to Maimonides," in *A Straight Path: Studies in Medieval Philosophy and Culture: Essays in Honor of Arthur Hyman*, ed. Ruth Link-Salinger (Washington, DC, 1988), 37–48.
43. Dahan, "Connaissance de l'exégèse juive," 355.
44. Klepper, *Insight of Unbelievers*, 15–17.

45. Earlier examples of Christian polemic based on knowledge of Jewish material are that of Agobard of Lyons (769–840) and his successor Amolo (d. 852), see Bernard Blumenkranz, *Les auteurs chrétiens latins du moyen age sur les juifs et le judaïsme* (Paris-Louvain, 2007), 152–168, 195–200; Jeremy Cohen, *Living Letters of the Law: Ideas of the Jew in Medieval Christianity* (Berkeley, 1999), 123–145; A. Lukyn Williams, *Adversus Judaeos: A Bird's Eye View of Christian Apologiae until the Renaissance* (London, 1935), 348–365; Merchavia, *Ha-talmud*, 71–92. They were followed by the eleventh to twelfth centuries scholars Peter Alfonsi and Peter of Cluny. See Yvonne Friedman, ed., *Petri Venerabilis Adversus Iudeorum inveteratam duritiem*, Corpus Christianorum Continuatio Mediaevalis 58 (Turnhout, 1985); Petrus Alfonsi, *Dialogue against the Jews*, trans. Irven M. Resnick (Washington, DC, 2006); Cohen, *Living Letters*, 201–18, 245–270; Williams, *Adversus Judaeos*, 384–394; John Tolan, *Petrus Alfonsi and His Medieval Readers* (Gainseville, 1993), 12–41; Both scholars used Talmudic material—Alfonsi due to his Jewish record and Peter of Cluny as a result of the Christian world's discovery of the existence of this literature and the central role it played for the Jews (of which it had previously been unaware).

46. This refers principally to the anthology *Extractiones de Talmud* and to the *Pugio fidei*. On both these compositions, see below.

47. Various arguments were raised against the rabbinic literature. Some of them related to its use by the Jews—namely, that it was the Talmud that kept them from accepting the Christian faith, or its encouragement of anti-Christian behavior. Other arguments, however, such as that which ascribed heretical view about God or defamation of Jesus and the saints to these works, related to the texts themselves, whoever read them; There is extensive literature about the "Talmud Trial." See, for example, Isidore Loeb, "La Controverse de 1240 sur le Talmud," *Revue des études juives* 1 (1880): 247–261; 2 (1881): 248–270; 3 (1881): 39–57; Gilbert Dahan and Elie Nicolas, eds., *Le brûlement du Talmud à Paris, 1242–1244* (Paris, 1999); Jeremy Cohen, *The Friars and the Jews: The Evolution of Medieval Anti-Judaism* (Ithaca, 1982), 60–72; Merchavia, *Ha-talmud,* 227–290.

48. Merchavia, *Ha-talmud*, 238, 250, 288–290 (in detail: 252–283).

49. Ibid., 349–360.

50. On this anthology see: Gilbert Dahan, "Les traductions latines de Thibaud de Sézanne," in Dahan and Nicholas, *Le brûlement du Talmud*, 95–120; Merchavia, *Ha-talmud*, 291–348.

51. On the Dominican mission in Catalonia and its unique approach, see: Cohen, *Friars*, 103–169; Robert Chazan, *Daggers of Faith: Thirteenth Century Christian Missionizing and Jewish Response* (Berkeley, 1989), 67–85.

52. On the Barcelona disputation, see, for example (among many works): Robert Chazan, *Barcelona and Beyond, The Disputation of 1263 and Its Aftermath* (Berkeley, 1992); Cohen, *Friars*, 108–128.

53. Raymundus Martini, *Pugio fidei adversus Mauros et Judaeos* (Leipzig, 1687). On Marti's polemic against Judaism see: Cohen, *Friars*, 129–169; Cohen, *Living Letters*, 342–358; Chazan, *Daggers of Faith*, 115–132.

54. Olszowy-Schlanger, "The Knowledge and Practice," 108 and n. 5; Smalley, *Study*, 155; Michael Signer, Introduction to Andreas de Sancto Victore,

21–22; Frans van Liere, Introduction to Andreas de Sancto Victore, *Expositio Hystorica in Librum Regum*, Corpus Christianorum Continuatio Mediaevalis 53A (Turnhout, 1996), 29–37; For example, Andrew of St. Victor, the acme of Christian Hebraism in the twelfth century, could not read Hebrew texts in the original. On this, see: Signer, Introduction to Andreas de Sancto Victore, 221–227; Berndt, *André de Saint Victor*, 201–213, esp. 212–213; The exception to the rule was Herbert of Bosham, to whom scholars ascribe good knowledge of Hebrew and the ability to read Hebrew texts. See: Loewe, "Herbert of Bosham's Commentary": 48–58, esp. 54; Goodwin, *"Take Hold,"* 152, 164–167, and also Appendix. Goodwin takes a more cautious approach toward Herbert's knowledge of Hebrew, but does not dispute Loewe's statement.

55. Smalley, *Study*, 338–341.

56. See above, n. 24. To this we can add, of course, Roger Bacon, mentioned previously as someone who attained the highest knowledge of Hebrew.

57. See Dahan, *Les intellectuels chrétiens*, 258–259.

58. On the study of Oriental languages by the Dominicans, see André Berthier, "Les écoles de langues orientales fondées au XIIIe siècle par les Dominicaines en Espagne et en Afrique," *Revue Africaine* 73 (1932): 84–102.

59. For example, Stephen Langton quoted Jewish sources but was opposed to all forms of contacts with Jews. See Saltman, Introduction, 30; It is true that the Jews' situation in Latin Europe had begun to deteriorate earlier—in the late eleventh century; but until the Second Crusade and the emergence of blood libels in the 1140s, the massacres associated with the First Crusade could be viewed as a passing and unfortunate episode. In the first half of the twelfth century there still seem to have been open-minded Jews in France who were so heavily influenced by the spirit of the twelfth-century renaissance that their desire for contact with Christian scholars overcame religious and social opposition and resistance to such interchanges. As the century advanced, however, Christian persecution of Jews intensified and the motivation for intellectual contact with Christians was weakened.

60. On Nicholas' use of Jewish sources, see: Herman Hailperin, *Rashi and the Christian Scholars* (Pittsburgh, 1963), 137–246; Klepper, *Insight of Unbelievers*; Ari Geiger, "A Student and an Opponent: Nicholas of Lyra and his Jewish Sources," *Nicolas de Lyre, franciscain du XIVe siècle, exégète et théologien*, ed. G. Dahan (Turnhout, 2011), 167–203.

61. Nicholas' anti-Jewish polemics are found mainly in the polemical works written by him as well as in his *Postilla*. See: Deanna Copeland Klepper, "Nicholas of Lyra's *Questio de adventu Christi* and the Franciscan Encounter with Jewish Tradition in the Late Middle Ages," (PhD dissertation, Northwestern University, 2005); Cohen, *Friars*, 185–191; Hailperin, *Rashi*, 157–184; Klepper, *Insight of Unbelievers*, 82–108.

CHAPTER 4

"I HAVE ASKED FOR NOTHING EXCEPT THE *IUS COMMUNE*": LEGAL CHANGE IN THIRTEENTH-CENTURY FRANCE

Karl Shoemaker

The thirteenth century witnessed remarkable and lasting transformations in law and legal culture in France. The main contours of these transformations are fairly well known to specialists in medieval legal history, although they are not always brought into direct conversation with the other cultural, social, theological, and intellectual changes that marked the French thirteenth century. This essay provides one perspective on these changes—seeking to trace the manner in which thirteenth-century procedural reforms led to the growth of royal bureaucracy and brought France more firmly within the legal framework of the emergent Roman-canon law.

At the beginning of the thirteenth century, legal practices in the regions of Europe now called France were localized and varied—characterized more by multiplicity, insularity, and contestation than by unity or coordination. Powerful landed lords exercised hereditary jurisdictional powers that French kings were only gradually able to bring within royal control. The thirteenth century saw the power and reach of the French monarchy grow significantly. Provinces that had enjoyed significant, even total, independence from the French crown in the twelfth century were largely within the ambit of royal control by 1300. For example, whereas Louis VI (r. 1108–1137) had controlled only, and sometimes just barely, the Île-de-France, his great-great grandson, Louis IX (r. 1226–1270), aggressively extended his rule so that only parts of Brittany, Guyenne, Burgundy, and Flanders remained outside French royal control. Louis VI had been styled "King of the Franks," but his grandson, Philip II (r. 1180–1223), was styled the "King of France," as were his successors. By 1285, beginning with Philip IV, French kings even took the style "King of France and Navarre." The expanded authority of French kings came at the expense of the French barons, who found themselves increasingly answerable to royal law. In the twelfth century, French kings struggled mightily against recalcitrant nobles ensconced in strong castles. The most powerful and troublesome baron in twelfth-century France, who at the same time happened to be the king of England, was reduced by the end thirteenth century to a few modest holdings in Gascony, having lost Normandy already in 1204 to Philip Augustus. By the thirteenth century, the French king could claim a right to hear appeals from decisions made in baronial courts—a right which he sometimes even exercised. In all of this, local legal practices might still vary greatly, but royal power was steadily expanding and bringing a certain degree of uniformity. At the same time, the lines between secular and ecclesiastical jurisdiction were often blurred, providing a multilayered aspect to the everyday experience of law that continued until the end of the ancient regime.

By the close of the thirteenth century, much of the blueprint for the institutions and processes of French law that would last until the eighteenth century—and would make it possible for scholars today to argue for the presence in late medieval France of an emerging *ius commune*, conceptually distinct if intimately linked to French royal and provincial law—had been more or less drafted. Scholars still argue over whether and when the *ius commune*, understood in its boldest sense as legal practices grounded in the Roman-canon law and common to Europe, ever came to France (or elsewhere). Moreover, even vocal proponents of the *ius commune* acknowledge "there are details in the overall situation in French lands that are difficult to follow and reconstruct."[1]

The ground is more solid for scholars who restrict the meaning of *ius commune* to refer to "a law common to the universities," as such a definition leaves room for the undeniable welter of local legal activity that took place in late medieval France and that is difficult to bring within any meaningful usage of "common law."[2] Such a definition certainly allows France to be brought within discussions of the *ius commune*, as jurists in French universities and law schools played important roles in its intellectual formation, even if legal practices might, in some cases, remain little influenced by it. At the heart of the *ius commune* was a procedural revolution, forged in the law schools of Italy and France in the twelfth and thirteenth centuries and disseminated by papal and secular authority, that envisioned legal processes controlled by learned judges who were granted considerable *ex officio* powers to initiate legal inquiries.

This so-called "inquisitorial model" of litigation depended upon active judges, increasingly armed with university degrees in law, who were invested with broad powers to initiate criminal and civil proceedings, examine witnesses, even under torture, and to act (in principle, at least) as a brake on the adversarial tendencies of earlier medieval legal traditions. These transformations were sufficiently pervasive that, by the end of the thirteenth century, it was possible for one popular and fantastically imagined text that circulated widely in France to portray a litigious demon exclaiming in the middle of a lawsuit he initiated in the court of heaven: "I have asked for nothing except the *ius commune!*"—by which he claimed a right afforded to all God's creatures to defend legal interests under the rules and procedures spelled out in Roman-canon law. However, if the new mode of legal process entailed in the *ius commune* had emerged as a potential unifying feature of French legal culture by the end of the thirteenth century, its emergence had not been entirely foreseeable one hundred years earlier. There were a number of serious impediments to the emergence of a learned law common to France. For example, at the dawn of the thirteenth century, jurists and theologians at the University of Paris (and elsewhere) were still trying to disentangle legal process from the vestiges of the divine ordeal—a Carolingian-era method of establishing legal proof that relied upon burnt flesh or a submerged body to determine guilt or innocence. Although its use had begun to wane throughout much of Europe in the late twelfth century, the ordeal remained a troublesome feature of medieval legal process until papal reforms promulgated in 1215 effectively abrogated its use.

The Ordeal Revisited

Despite its place on the margins of legal practice in the early thirteenth century, the ordeal was a significant barrier to a *ius* common to all of France. The ordeal was an unruly form of trial that did not permit the consistent application of formal substantive rules to similar cases, could not be easily or effectively controlled from centralized royal or ecclesiastical courts, and that produced inscrutable, unreviewable judgments.[3] Although its use had become increasingly marginalized—not least by university elites who for the most part abhorred it—the ordeal remained an available legal process in France at the dawn of the thirteenth century. It remained, for example, one of the primary modes of proof in criminal accusation against serfs.[4] Replete in Carolingian legal sources, the ordeal possessed an impressive legal pedigree. Charlemagne had legislated that "everyone should believe the ordeal without any doubt," simultaneously confirming that the ordeal was authoritative and that it was subject to doubts.[5] Fundamental to the ordeal was a seemingly pervasive belief that elements of the natural world could reveal God's judgment through the flesh of the accused—unworthiness betrayed by festering corruption visible on the flesh itself. We know that in many cases the ordeal was understood to render a spiritual accounting rather than a legal one.[6] Thus, the ordeal might be inscrutable as a factual determination, but it remained intelligible within the teachings of medieval theology.[7]

It is undoubtedly correct that medieval ordeal practices contained an element of penitential discipline and provided local communities with cover in hard cases.[8] But the ordeal also proved to be an effective tool for oppressing marginalized groups within medieval France. One such case occurred at Blois. It illustrates the intractable unruliness of the ordeal as a legal process, and foreshadows the cycle of expulsion and re-invitation that Jews in France would experience over the course of the thirteenth century. In 1171, some members of the Jewish community in Blois were accused of the ritual murder of a Christian boy. Because the accusers lacked sufficient proof for a conviction (i.e., witnesses to the act, or a confession from the perpetrators), a priest suggested that they employ the ordeal to make their case. Jews and free Christians in Blois enjoyed an exemption from the ordeal, but this privilege did not prevent the ordeal from being used against the Jews. The priest proposed that a particular Christian slave be put to the ordeal in order to prove the truth of the accusations. The slave passed the ordeal of cold water, thus "proving" Jewish guilt for the murder. Two Jews were subsequently burned to death for the suspected killing.[9]

The events at Blois illustrate a feature of the ordeal that was also becoming increasingly problematic for ecclesiastical and royal authorities. Because there could be no appeal from it to a higher court (to whom would one appeal the *judicium dei?*), the ordeal was particularly difficult to insulate from the machinations of motivated locals. Just as a determined priest orchestrated an ordeal against the Jews of Blois, a motivated parishioner might offer to prove serious charges against priests or bishops by submitting to an ordeal. As Richard Fraher has shown, charges of simony or concubinage leveled against priests highlighted for the medieval Church the extent to which the ordeal was difficult to control from a political or administrative center, and accounted, in Fraher's view, for the papal opposition to the ordeal.[10] Perhaps unsurprisingly, such attempts at proving by one's own body another's guilt appear to have had high success rates. Whatever the papacy might have thought about the incident at Blois, it recognized the dangers of the ordeal when it was used by agitated parishioners against unpopular clerics.[11] From the papacy's perspective, it was better for ecclesiastical superiors to discipline clerics than to have such matters addressed by unpredictable and unreviewable ordeal processes.

Alongside the administrative and institutional challenges posed by the ordeal, a sentiment had arisen among many theologians at the University of Paris that the ordeal was illegitimate as a theological matter.[12] Coupled with increasing doubts about the ordeal expressed by early thirteenth-century canon lawyers, and the fact that many communities sought to avoid using it where they could,[13] it was possible for Innocent III to move decisively against the ordeal at the Fourth Lateran Council held in 1215.[14] In canon 18 of the council, priestly participation in ordeals was prohibited, effectively removing whatever ecclesiastical sanction the ordeal had enjoyed. Whether Innocent III's prohibition was enough on its own to end the practice is still a matter of debate, but it is clear enough that ordeal practice in Europe withered quickly after 1215.

Quite curiously, at least one prominent figure studying and lecturing at Paris in the middle of the thirteenth century displayed a wistful nostalgia for the ordeal. In 1252, thirty-seven years after the Fourth Lateran Council abrogated the ordeal, Roger Bacon wrote of "certain prayers that were instituted long ago by men of truth, or rather ordained by God and the angels." When these "prayers are made over glowing iron, and over the water of a river" then "innocents are approved, and [the guilty] is condemned of a crime."[15] Bacon had perhaps never actually observed an ordeal. He was born one year before the Fourth Lateran Council prohibited priestly participation in it. But he had witnessed the growing influence of men trained in canon law within the governance structures of the Church, and we might see in his remarks a thinly veiled rebuke of the growing legalism of his day. "At one time," he complained in another place, "the Roman curia was ruled by God's wisdom, but now it is ruined by legal pronouncements derived from lay emperors." Worse, the jurists responsible for this inversion are now "more highly praised than a master of theology."[16] One is tempted to find in these remarks more than a little professional jealousy and indications of fierce competition between the theological and canon law faculties at the University of Paris. Bacon, then at Paris, was not the only theologian to express such opinions about lawyers.[17]

The Growth of Legal Professionalism

The growth of the papal legal bureaucracy that prompted acerbic remarks like Bacon's had begun in earnest in the late twelfth century, and had prompted complaints from the beginning. Already in the 1150s, Bernard of Clairvaux had bitterly remarked on the "litigious prattle" that polluted the papal court and distracted popes from their obligations of prayer and pastoral care. For this unfortunate state of affairs, Bernard did not hesitate to blame renewed interest in the resurgent Roman law. A century later, and feeling beset by the same evils, Bacon could imagine the defunct ordeal as part of a golden age in which righteous prayers and earthly elements revealed imminent divine justice through human flesh. In his own day, law was no longer a ritual of prayer and revelation; it had become a profession, complete with its own priesthood, liturgy, and texts.[18]

The same Lateran Council that effectively ended the ordeal in 1215 had provided directions for replacing it. For example, in canon 8 the papacy tried to find a delicate balance between insulating clerics against false accusations of wrongdoing that might be brought from spite or jealousy and that the

ordeal practice facilitated, and simultaneously increasing the Church's capacity for clerical discipline through legal processes. The solution was a hierarchical arrangement in which ecclesiastics of superior rank could discipline
clerics of a lower rank, yet were themselves insulated from accusations made
by inferiors or by laypersons. Canon 38 placed important checks on judges in
these cases by requiring them to employ "a notary or two competent men" to
record the judicial process. The aim was accountability. The prescribed process required that a judge would "oversee all the acts of the inquiry, namely,
citations and delays, refusals and exceptions, petitions and replies, interroga-
tions and confessions, the depositions of witnesses and presentation of documents, interlocutions, appeals, renunciations, decisions, and other acts which
take place."[19] The scaffolding for modern civil and criminal procedure was
erected. All of these steps in the inquiry were to "be written down in convenient order, the time, places, and persons to be designated."[20]

    The stated purpose of this canon was to provide a record in cases where
someone claimed they were subject to a "dishonest or imprudent" judge.[21]
But it did much more; it mandated the conditions under which all ecclesiastical litigation would be recorded and more significantly, made it subject
to review by superior judges within the ecclesiastical hierarchy, culminating
with the pope who was the *judex ordinarius* of everyone. Judges failing to
comply with the requirement that their proceedings be recorded were liable
to punishment. Taken together, these two canons represented the canon law's
response to the end of the divine ordeal. Judicial inquiries were to follow a
prescribed order—including allegations, responses, interlocutory appeals,
depositions, etc.—and put into a written dossier that could be transmitted
through a judicial hierarchy over which the pope presided. The obligations
of pastoral care were taking on an increasingly juridical character.

    This increased reliance on formalized processes and a written record were
hardly peculiar to canon law. Jurists molded by Roman law education had
been developing inquisitorial legal procedures for decades before the Fourth
Lateran Council. Likewise, Italian cities had traditions of notarial practice
that reached back to the eleventh century, perhaps even earlier. These notarial practices had spread to parts of France in the twelfth century, and were
well in place in many seigniorial courts in southern France. In thirteenth-
century Paris, royal notaries were instituted in an attempt to divert non-
contentious legal matters out of the overburdened royal courts. The iconic
depictions of Louis IX sitting beneath an oak tree in Vincennes issuing oral
judgments to humble petitioners belie a growing and complex royal legal
system in France. Over the course of the thirteenth century, French jurists
exploited a range of Roman and canon law texts—alongside the treatises of
"customary" law that appeared in the 1250s and began to proliferate in the
late thirteenth century—to construct the processes of law that would apply
in the royal domain.[22]

The increasing reach of the learned law in thirteenth-century France coincided with the emergence of a peculiar form of legal literature known as the *coutumiers*. The *coutumiers*, or treatises of customary law, usually attached to a particular region or province, occupy a contested place within French legal scholarship. A venerable tradition of French legal history has generally considered collections of customary law that emerged in the 1250s and proliferated in the latter half of the thirteenth century to be a sort of vernacular bastard child—unworthy of its more distinguished, university-born brother and more than a little embarrassing. At the same time, another scholarly tradition, sharing certain intellectual commitments also found in strands of the English common law, has valorized the *coutumiers* as an expression of autochthonous popular practices emerging independently of the Roman law and its imperial sympathies.

In fact, the *coutumiers* were both more and less than these scholarly caricatures. Some of them were unapologetically copied from earlier, neighboring *coutumiers*, removing any claim that they were authentic local practices existing from time immemorial. At the same time, the *coutumiers* have been unjustly maligned by scholars who see them as feeble imitations of the learned laws. As Ada Kuskowski has recently shown, some of the same textual practices that are extolled as evidence of sophistication in the learned laws (including shameless repetition of texts without attribution) are downplayed as evidence of derivation and inferiority when it comes to the *coutumiers*. Although they operated outside the orbit of the Roman-canonical tradition taught in the universities, the *coutumiers* played an important role in vernacularizing French law and professionalizing French lay courts.[23]

Guido de Collemedio and the *Ius Commune*

The career of Guido da Collemedio, an important but little known bishop of Cambrai from 1296 to 1306, offers a neat window into the intellectual dynamism that marked French law at the end of the thirteenth century. This, despite that fact that Guido was not French and Cambrai was not yet part of France. Guido was from an Italian family that had come to prominence in central Italy by the 1220s. Pascal Montaubin has conclusively shown that Guido was from Anagni, southwest of Rome.[24] Guido's family was already relatively well placed by the early thirteenth century, participating skillfully in the clientelism prominent in central Italy. One of his older relatives, Pietro da Collemedio, was appointed to the Roman curia in 1217 and served as chaplain to Pope Honorius III before being named cardinal by Innocent IV in 1244.[25]

Guido was part of a veritable "colonization" movement undertaken by central Italian clerics in the thirteenth century who established themselves in large numbers in places like England, northern France, and the

Low Countries.[26] He studied Roman and canon law, probably at Bologna as other Collemezzo family members had done. He is also probably the Guido de Collemezzo who became the treasurer of Thérouanne in Calais sometime prior to 1275. In 1275, he asked and received permission to teach law at the University of Naples.[27] In 1276, he became councilor to Charles Anjou, king of Sicily. He also authored an abridgment of Innocent IV's commentaries on the decretals. Two manuscript copies of Guido's abridgement survive.[28] When the episcopal seat at Cambrai became vacant in August of 1296, Boniface VIII quickly appointed Guido as bishop, probably hoping he would bring some stability to an independent diocese that had long been a target of annexation by surrounding powers.

Given his background in teaching law, it is entirely unsurprising that while he was bishop of Cambrai he would have owned manuscripts concerned with law and penitential discipline, as these would have been important resources for the pastoral and judicial roles of his position as bishop of a large diocese. Among his manuscripts was a text described as the *Compilatio episcopi Cameracensis*, a text that was at once a curious sort of *ordo iudiciorum* (a legal process manual) and an account of Marian Theology. The *Compilatio* contained a short heading that explained "[This is] the reason why the Blessed Virgin is called our Advocate," a heading which signaled Mary's role as an actor in a legal process.[29] Indeed, the text presents Mary as the central figure in a lawsuit initiated by Satan, who had sent a demon to sue in the court of heaven for possession of all human souls.[30] Guido sent a copy of the text to the archbishop of Reims as a gift.

The bishop of Cambrai did not compose the text he named the *Compilatio*. We do not know who did. In 1262, an author from the Low Countries named Jacob van Maerlant had included essentially the same text as a small chapter in his popular vernacular Grail cycle, although he claimed only to have copied the text from somewhere else. Earlier than that, we cannot go. Whatever its origins, the text that the Bishop of Cambrai came to possess at the end of the thirteenth century enjoyed wide circulation in Europe. By the fourteenth century, it could be found in manuscripts used in law schools, where it was almost certainly used as a pedagogic device for teaching legal process, as well as in theological manuscripts, where its legal aspects were secondary to its theological import. By the fourteenth century, versions of the text also circulated in several vernacular translations, including French, Catalan, and Italian.

That the spiritual battle between Mary and Satan over the fate of humankind could be portrayed as a lawsuit should not be a surprise. Medieval Christian theology easily understood sacred history in legal or quasi-legal terms, beginning with Original Sin and ending with the Last Judgment. For medieval lawyers, especially but not only canonists, law's relationship to theology was close enough that law, too, could be counted on to narrate the justification and salvation of the *human genus*. Guido, a powerful bishop and a former law professor, might have come across this text when he was teaching law. A version of this lawsuit was used in the classrooms at Bologna, as marginal allegations in a surviving manuscript clearly show.[31]

In any event, the text set hell's complaint against God's perceived injustice within the framework of a lawsuit. Complete with citations to Roman law, canon law, and the Bible, the text portrays the resounding defeat Mary handed to the demon sent by Hell to try the case. Ultimately, and despite her proficiency with legal texts, Mary defeated the demon with an emotional plea. In the trial's climactic scene, she bared her breasts and moved Christ to tears by reminding him of her maternal care for him as an infant.[32] It is not impossible to be somewhat sympathetic to the demon's complaint that he had been shown not celestial justice, but rather the justice of flesh and blood. Mary's dramatic bodily display may have seemed rather ordeal-like by the lights of the learned law on which the demon relied so tenaciously throughout the trial. Indeed, the demon's remark *"Non peto nisi* ius commune *quod nemini denegatur"* ("I ask nothing except the *ius commune* which is denied to no one")[33] must have seemed like the correct response for university-trained lawyers, who had labored so hard to establish such a thing in France over the course of the thirteenth century.

Conclusion

It was possible by the end of the thirteenth century to speak of a *ius* that was sufficiently common that a demon could claim it in a legal process initiated before the heavenly court—at least in a text owned and copied by a law professor *cum* bishop in an autonomous diocese on France's northern border. The situation on the ground in France remained rather short of this idealized notion of a *ius commune*. French royal policies aimed at crown expansion in the early thirteenth century also tended, in some cases, to strengthen local and provincial institutions that were largely allowed to survive so long as royal agents from Paris, rather than local notables, filled important provincial offices. Thus, while it was externally recognized that the king of France had no superior in his realm, variation in custom and law between the provinces remained significant. There were also numerous jurisdictional immunities held by some cities and ecclesiastical bodies that served to preserve overlapping and sometimes conflicting jurisdictions in thirteenth-century France. Still, some deeply entrenched regional differences were starting to erode, and a law common to the French realm was beginning to emerge.

The twelfth-century theological and intellectual assault on the divine ordeal—an assault that was spearheaded at the University of Paris—had been preceded by an intense renewal of lawyerly interest in classical Roman procedure by Italian and French jurists. In the early decades of the thirteenth century, French canon and civil lawyers stood ready to implement modes of trial that they had appropriated from the classical jurists and repurposed for French courts. These new legal processes changed the experience of litigation in France in both royal and provincial courts. In these new modes of trial, judges exercised considerable control over the initiation of legal processes, the leveling of charges against suspects, the acquisition of evidence, and the examination of witnesses. In criminal cases, these new processes even permitted judges to question witnesses and suspects through torture in order to uncover facts that only the guilty could be presumed to know. Obsessively documentary, these new procedures required literate judges and legions of scribes to record the copious testimonies extracted by the inquests. In cases concerned with property rights, the new procedures required skilled lawyers who could steer clients through them.

So there emerged in France as in much of Southwestern Europe a growing body of professional lawyers who, by the early thirteenth century, could expect to make careers exercising judicial functions, providing paid legal advice, and advocating client interests within these new legal processes. These men worked within a common textual world, glossing classical Roman and contemporary legal texts as well as the new legislation that both papal and royal chanceries were producing with newfound vigor and sophistication. They made it possible that even demons might make a claim to the *ius commune* in thirteenth-century France.

Notes

1. Manlio Bellomo, *The Common Legal Past of Europe, 1000–1800*, trans. Lydia Cochrane (Washington, DC, 1995), 106.
2. See, for example, Raoul C. van Caenegem, *European Law in the Past and the Future: Unity and Diversity over Two Millennia* (Cambridge and New York, 2002), 10–21.
3. Karl Shoemaker, "Criminal Procedure in Medieval European Law: A Comparison between English and Roman-Canonical Developments after the IV Lateran Council", *Zeitschrift der Savigny-Stiftung für Rechtsgeschichte* 116 (1999): 174–201.
4. There is a rich literature on the ordeal. John Baldwin, "The Intellectual Preparation for the Canon of 1215 against Ordeals", *Speculum* 36 (1961): 613–636; Rebecca Coleman, "Reason and Unreason in Early Medieval Law", *Journal of Interdisciplinary History* 4 (1974): 571–591; Peter Brown, "Society and the Supernatural: A Medieval Change," *Daedalus* 104 (1975): 133–151; Paul Hyams, "Trial by Ordeal: The Key to Proof in the Early Common Law," in *On the Laws and Customs of England: Essays in Honor of Samuel E. Thorne,* ed. Morris Arnold et al. (Chapel Hill, 1981), 90–126; Robert Bartlett, *Trial by Fire and Water: The Medieval Judicial Ordeal* (Oxford and New York, 1986), Richard Fraher, "IV Lateran's Revolution in Criminal Procedure: The Birth of Inquisitio, the End of the Ordeals, and Innocent III's Vision of

Ecclesiastical Politics in *Studia in Honorem Eminentissimi Cardinalis Alphonsi M. Stickler,* ed. R. I. Castillo Lara (Rome, 1992), 97–111; Finnbar McCauley, "Canon Law and the End of the Ordeal," *Oxford Journal of Legal Studies* 26 (2006): 473–513. My own somewhat polemical contribution to the debates is Shoemaker, "Criminal Procedure in Medieval European Law," 174–201.

5. *Monumenta Germanae Historica, Leges* II, 1, 150.

6. Shoemaker, "Criminal Procedure in Medieval European Law," 179–180; 197–201.

7. Despite Carolingian-era legislation embracing it, the ordeal was not without skeptics. A number of popes had expressed serious doubts about its use, at least in specific cases. Pope Nicholas I, for example, forbade the judicial ordeal in the adultery accusations that Lothair II brought against his wife, Queen Teutberga. Phillipus Jaffe ed. *Regesta Pontificum Romanorum* (Leipzig, 1885), # 2872. Pope Steven V prohibited ordeals of iron or water in an accusation of infanticide (*Decretum,* C.2, q.5, c.20), though as John Baldwin points out, Stephen apparently confused the ordeal with torture designed to elicit a confession. Baldwin, "The Intellectual Preparation", 616–636, n. 9.

8. Coleman, "Reason and Unreason in Early Medieval Law", 571–591; Peter Brown, "Society and the Supernatural," 133–151.

9. Shlomo Eidelberg, "Trial by Ordeal in Medieval Jewish History: Laws, Customs and Attitudes", Proceedings of the American Academy for Jewish Research, 46–47 (1978–79): 105–120, esp. 116.

10. Fraher, "IV Lateran's Revolution," 97–111.

11. Ibid., 99.

12. Baldwin, "The Intellectual Preparation."

13. Hyams, "Trial by Ordeal," 126.

14. Stephan Kuttner and Antonio García y García, "A New Eye Witness Account of the Fourth Lateran Council", *Traditio* 20 (1964): 115–178.

15. *Opera Quaedam Hactenus Inedita Fr. Rogeri Bacon, Vol. 1 containing I. Opus Tertium, II. Opus Minus, III. Compendium Philosophiae,* ed. J. S. Brewer (London, 1859), 526. I am grateful to Nick Jacobson for bringing this passage to my attention.

16. *Compendium Studii Theologicae,* ed. Hastings Rashdall (Aberdeen, 1911, reprint 1966); Translated in *Life in the Middle Ages,* ed. George G. Coulton (New York, 1967), 2:55–62. See also George de Lagarde, *La naissance de l'esprit laïque au declin du Moyen âge* (Paris, 1934), 2:142.

17. James Brundage, "Vultures, Whores and Hypocrites: Images of Lawyers in Medieval Literature," *Roman Legal Tradition* 1 (2002): 56–103; Karl Shoemaker, "When the Devil Went to Law School: Canon Law and Theology in the Fourteenth Century," in *Crossing Boundaries at Medieval Universities,* ed. Spencer E. Young (Leiden, 2011), 255–275.

18. The most recent and authoritative account in English of this process is James Brundage, *The Medieval Origins of the Legal Profession: Canonists, Civilians and Courts* (Chicago, 2010).

19. C. 38. *Constitutiones Concilii quarti Lateranensis una cum Commentariis glossatorum* (MIC, Series A: Corpus Glossatorum 2; Vatican City, 1981), 1–172.

20. Ibid.

21. Ibid.

22. Sophie Peralba, "Des coutumiers aux styles. L'isolement de la matière pro-céduraleaux XIIIe et XIVe siècles," *Cahiers de recherches médiévale* 7 (2000), http://crm.revues.org/887.

23. Ada Kuskowski, "Writing Custom: Juristic Imagination and the Invention of Customary Law," (unpublished PhD, Cornell University, 2012), 272; André Gouron, "Le droit commun a-t-il été l'héritier du droit romain?" *Comptes-rendus des séances de l'Académie des Inscriptions et Belles-Lettres* 142, no. 1 (1998): 292.

24. Pascal Montaubin, "Avec de l'Italie qui descendrait l'Escault: Guido da Collemezzo, Évêque de Cambrai (1296–1396)," in *Liber Largitorius: Études d'histoire médiévale offertes à Pierre Toubert par ses élèves*, ed. Dominique Barthélemy and Jean-Marie Martin (Geneva, 2003), 476–502.

25. Agostino Paravacini Bagliani, *Cardinali di curia e* familiae *cardinalizie dal 1227 al 1254* (Padova, 1972), 1:168–185.

26. Pierre Toubert, *Les structures du Latium médiéval. Le Latium méridional et la Sabine du IX à la fin du XII siècle* (Rome, 1972), 2: 1358.

27. Montaubin, "Avec de l'Italie qui descendrait l'Escault," 482.

28. BnF, lat. 3987 and 4306. Johann F. von Schulte, *Die Geschichte der Quellen und Literatur des Canonischen Rechts. Band 2. Von Gregor IX bis auf das Concil von Trient (1234–1563)* (Stuttgart 1875) 178–179.

29. The *Compilatio* can now be found within BnF Lat. 1093, beginning at folio 22v.

30. I have treated various aspects of this lawsuit elsewhere: Karl Shoemaker, "The Devil at Law in the Middle Ages," *Revue de l'histoire des religions* 228 (2011): 567–586 and Shoemaker, "When the Devil Went to Law School," 255–275.

31. Bologna, Collegio di Spagna, ms. 126, fols. 189r-195r.

32. Shoemaker, "The Devil at Law," 580–586.

33. A slightly more accessible early printed version of the text containing the demon's lament can be found in an incunable under the title *Processus Iudiciarius* (Augsburg, 1473), fol. 4.

CHAPTER 5

BETWEEN *ASHKENAZ* (GERMANY) AND *TSARFAT* (FRANCE): TWO APPROACHES TOWARD POPULARIZING JEWISH LAW

Judah D. Galinsky

Around the year 1420, the famed legal authority, Jacob Molin of Worms (known as Maharil), was asked by a rabbinic colleague and friend, Ḥayyim Tsarfatti of Wiener-Neustadt (previously of Augsburg) regarding his intention to write a book on the laws of family purity in the German-Jewish vernacular, Yiddish (*leshon ashkenaz*), for the purpose of making these laws more accessible to the broader reading public, including women. Maharil's response was a sharp one and revealed his fundamental negative attitude toward all works of popular halakhah:[1]

> And I was astonished that you were considering writing [a handbook] in German – for we are distraught over the previous ones [i.e. legal handbooks written in Hebrew] – because every layman who is able to read Rashi's commentary on the Pentateuch or [one who can read the material] from the *maḥzor*[2] or [those who studied] the interpretation (*shittah*) [i.e. the Tosafist's glosses to the Talmud] in their youth but had ceased [studying] days and years ago, or those who never apprenticed with an established scholar (*lo shimmesh talmidé ḥakhamim*) – all these [readers] joined together in the "valley of the fools" and look to the words of our teachers, the authors [of handbooks] such as *Sha'aré dura, Semak, Turin*[3]...and they determine and implement the law based on these books![4] They are about whom the Talmudic sages referred to...as "*Tanna'im* who bring destruction upon the world" (Sotah 22a), for they do not comprehend the legal reasoning [of the law] and the application of ritual and civil law which can change according to the reasoning of the law...[5]

Maharil's harsh critique of Ḥayyim Tsarfatti's proposed project was not so much directly linked to the language in which he chose to write (Yiddish instead of Hebrew) but rather the result of his having made such a choice—to make halakhah accessible to non-initiates, to people who had no right to determine the law for themselves.[6]

In this sharply formulated response, one can discern a clearly stated argument for rabbinic authority and control over the dissemination of specialized knowledge. The consequence of spreading knowledge of the law to the unqualified was a real concern for this rabbi from the Rhineland.[7] In his opinion, knowledge of the law could only be transmitted orally via scholars "who are proficient in determining the law—and they should teach these laws to the women of their home, neighborhood and city."[8] Maharil implies that the only way to prevent errors in understanding and applying the laws was to have them transmitted to the laity via the mediation of legal specialists or their proxies.[9]

From the above exchange between the two early fifteenth-century scholars—one from Worms in the west of Germany and the other from Wiener-Neustadt in the east[10]—a difference of opinion regarding the merits of popularizing Jewish law emerges.[11] One scholar was considering writing a legal work in the vernacular so that laypeople would have some knowledge of the law, whereas the other bemoaned all accessible works of law, even those written in Hebrew.

In this study, I will explore the possibility that these two approaches were not solely the product of post-black-death realities, perceptions, and society in Germany,[12] but that they had roots in the two major legal cultures among the Jews of northern Europe—France and Germany. My focus will be the thirteenth century, although there are indications that these trends began earlier.[13] The point of departure will be a comparison between the mainstream writings on Jewish law in these two centers, with regard to their literary character and their prospective reading audience.[14] I will suggest that, emerging from this comparison, we can identify in France, from the beginning until the end of the century, a sustained interest among the scholarly class in producing accessible legal works for an audience that is less knowledgeable than the rabbinic elite (i.e., Talmudic scholars, judges or students). In Germany, however, no parallel concern can be detected among mainstream scholars until the last quarter of the century. I will conclude the study by placing its results within the context of broader scholarly discourse on the subject.

Halakhic Literature in Thirteenth-Century France

The first book written in the thirteenth century and completed ca. 1202–1204, *Sefer ha-terumah* (Book of Offering), was written by Barukh ben Isaac. He was a student of the famous French Tosafist Isaac of Dampierre.[15] The external structure of the work was organized topically and not according to the order of the Talmud.[16] Barukh ben Isaac's work begins with the laws of ritual slaughter, laws relating to food preparation, and includes laws regarding family purity, divorce, idolatry, and various other areas of halakhah. It concludes with the laws of Sabbath.[17] To a large extent, the internal structure of each of the sections, in contrast to the external structure, is organized according to the Talmudic tractate that it is commenting on.[18] The content of the work, written in the Aramaic-Hebrew mix, is scholarly and follows the Franco-Jewish dialectical method known as Tosafot.[19] All of this indicates that Barukh ben Isaac's primary reading audience was a scholarly one.

There are, however, certain indications that Barukh ben Isaac did wish to make his work more accessible to a wider audience. In addition to the topical arrangement already mentioned, he was selective in treating only Talmudic subject-matter that had practical implications in medieval times, leaving out discussions that were merely exegetical or theoretical. This limitation had the potential of making the work more attractive to readers who were only interested in the practical application of the law. Of even greater importance was his decision to write an abridgment in Hebrew, which served the dual function of being a short practical summary of the larger work as well as a detailed table of contents. He prefaced his work with a brief introduction that describes the abridgment's dual function:

> I Barukh the son of R. Isaac have explicated this book so that anyone looking at these references *(simanim* that are *remazim)* [i.e. table of contents] may find [an answer to] what he seeks. For there [i.e. in these *simanim*] he can find many a time clarification [of the law] in brief *[be-kotser]* together with some of the sources, in short *[derekh ketsara]*. However, in the book itself, in the place where the reference will direct to go and look – there, all can be found, explicated, with its sources and its reasoning, at length as is needed.[20]

In these *simanim*, the author did away with much of the learned discussion found in the body of the work and presented his reader with the practical conclusions and legal innovations of the Tosafist school. In this context, it is also worth emphasizing that, in composing his abridgment, Barukh ben Isaac chose to write in Hebrew, whereas the language he used in the body of the work was the more complex rabbinic mix of Hebrew and Aramaic of the Talmud.

Having a book arranged topically and focused on the practical, the learned reader could find the specific law in which he was interested with relative ease, via the *simanim* that served as the table of contents. More importantly, even a less than learned reader could utilize the same *simanim* in order to gain direct access to the law. A non-specialist who would hesitate before studying a complex Talmudic-Tosafistic discussion as found in the body of the work might consider reading an accessible Hebrew summary.[21] These three interrelated features—practical focus, topical structure, and, most important, the abridged version appended to the beginning of the work—reveals an author with an awareness of a varied reading audience and one who was motivated to reach out to them.

The next stage in the development of accessible works of law in France was significant and it influenced all subsequent legal writing in that area. A comprehensive legal work, *Sefer ha-mitsvot* (Book of Commandments) or *Semag*, which covered all aspects of the law, was completed by Moses of Coucy ca. 1250.[22] It was heavily influenced by the great Maimonidean code, *Mishneh torah*.[23] The author, to a large extent, followed the logical (non-Talmudic) structure of that work as well as its internal structure. He also adopted classic Rabbinic Hebrew as the language of his work, eschewing the Talmudic mix of Aramaic and Hebrew that was much more prevalent among medieval Talmudic scholars.[24] Moreover, although Moses of Coucy, in contrast to Maimonides, cited the Talmudic source of the law, at times at great lengths, and included alternate legal opinions in his discussion as well, he still made an effort to simplify his treatment.

The contrast between Moses of Coucy's simplified version and the in-depth discussion found in Barukh ben Isaac's work is striking. Seemingly, Moses of Coucy, to a certain extent, internalized the Maimonidean ethos of producing a simplified comprehensive code to be read without constant recourse to the Talmud.[25] Whereas in the *Sefer ha-terumah* it was the abridgment that demonstrated the author's desire to reach out to a more inclusive reading audience, in *Sefer ha-mitsvot* one can see how Moses of Coucy's entire program was motivated by a wish to make the law more accessible for a readership that was not necessarily engaged with high-level Talmudic discussion. In this context, it is worth noting that a number of years before he wrote his legal work, Moses of Coucy was active as an itinerant preacher who traveled to various Jewish diaspora communities.[26]

Nonetheless, despite the great advances made by Moses of Coucy in making the laws accessible to various types of French Jews, there remained three features of the *Sefer ha-mitsvot* that made his work less appealing than it might have been. The first factor, one that he shared with Maimonides, was the inclusion of entire sections of law that were irrelevant to medieval Jews living outside the land of Israel. The second and third factors were the inclusion of lengthy Talmudic citations and of conflicting post-Talmudic legal opinions. Altogether, these three features rendered the work longer, more complex, and less user-friendly than warranted and, therefore, limited its appeal among the non-elite readers.[27]

The final stage in the French trend toward accessible legal works may be traced to the authors' realization that they could dispense with or at least modify those very features that burdened Moses of Coucy's work of law. The two authors who wrote such works were Abraham ben Ephraim and Isaac ben Joseph of Corbeil. Abraham ben Ephraim completed his work, *Sefer ha-simanim* (the Book of Reference), ca. 1260, quite soon after Moses of Coucy's work was circulated.[28] He chose the title because he wanted to emphasize that his book was primarily an abridgment of Moses' book. In fact, the overall structure of the work and its content are deeply influenced by the *Sefer ha-mitsvot*, so much so that he encourages the reader of his work to actually copy the original work of Rabbi Moses as well. In one of the versions of his introduction, he even included a warning that one should not decide the law without first consulting Moses of Coucy's work.[29]

Isaac of Corbeil completed his work, entitled *'Ammudé golah* (Pillars of the Exile), ca. 1276–1277. Although the author never referred to his work as a shortened version of Moses of Coucy's book, and its overall structure differed radically from it, nevertheless its legal content was primarily abridged from the *Sefer ha-mitsvot*.[30] Over time, his book became known as *Semak*—an acronym for *Sefer mitsvot katan*, that is, the Small or Short Book of Commandments.

These two works—Abraham ben Ephraim's *Simanim* and Isaac of Corbeil's *Semak*—abridged Moses of Coucy's weighty tome in three significant ways. They removed all the sections irrelevant to a medieval Jew in the diaspora. They shortened or eliminated the lengthy Talmudic citations (usually retaining a reference to the source) and did the same regarding the citation of conflicting legal opinions. In addition, both authors did not feel obligated to treat all the hypothetical aspects of the law relevant to medieval Jews as found in the *Sefer ha-mitsvot*. Laws rarely implemented and discussions that were too complex were simply removed. The final product of both these works was a more user-friendly and portable work than the bulky *Sefer ha-mitsvot*. It is no wonder that by the end of the thirteenth century people were referring to Moses of Coucy's work as *Sefer mitsvot **ha-gadol*** (or its acronym *Semag*)—the Large Book of Commandments.

It is worth noting that Isaac of Corbeil had no qualms about having his readers gain knowledge of the law directly from his work, and in this he differs from Abraham ben Ephraim. He never warned them, as did Abraham ben Ephraim, to consult Moses of Coucy's work before deciding the law. Moreover his plan, as outlined in his introductory letter, was to promote obligatory communal study of his work for both the learned and unlearned members of the community.[31] He even encouraged women to study his work as well.[32] The only concern that Isaac of Corbeil voiced dealt with the common occurrence of the text being corrupted due to copyist errors. In order to overcome this very real problem, he instructed his non-elite readers not to decide the law from his work on the basis of it unless they were certain that it was reviewed by a scholar well versed in the law or if they knew that a scholar had previously studied from their copy.[33] The agenda formulated by Isaac of Corbeil in his introductory letter was to improve the commitment and religious observance of the laity by introducing them to the law via his accessible legal handbook.[34]

The preceding pages have illustrated the gradual development of accessible halakhic works in France during the thirteenth century, beginning with the useful abridgment that Barukh ben Isaac appended to his work that could be read even by the less than learned and concluding with the popular handbook by Isaac of Corbeil, which he expected to be studied daily by all members of the community—learned and lay people alike. Although the various works treated in this brief survey differ in many ways, I believe that common to these authors was a desire to spread knowledge of Jewish law to the non-elite. This impulse is what binds all these authors together despite the vast distance that separates their distinct reading audiences.[35] Evidently, they felt a certain affinity with the popularization effort of Maimonides, even if they did not embrace the Andalusian content of his halakhah.[36]

Halakhic Literature in Thirteenth-Century Germany

In Germany, the development of halakhic literature took a different trajectory from that of France. An examination of the central halakhic works produced in Germany and eastward during the first three quarters of the thirteenth century does not reveal a serious interest in simplifying the law or making it accessible.[37] The primary works of that time were those authored by Eliezer b. Joel ha-Levi (Ra'avyah) of Cologne, Simḥah of Speyer, Barukh of Mainz, and Isaac b. Moses of Or Zarua' Vienna.[38] The first of these three scholars was active in the Rhineland until approximately 1225 and the last, although a product of the Rhineland schools, as he studied with both Eliezer ben Joel and Simḥah of Speyer,[39] was active in the east, mainly in Vienna, until approximately 1250.[40] All four authors composed their works in basically the same format. This can be determined by examining their books, *Avi ha-'ezri* of Ra'avyah and *Or Zarua'* of Isaac b. Moses,[41] and the meticulous reconstruction by Simha Emanuel of the lost works of both Simḥah of Speyer and Barukh of Mainz.[42] All of them loosely followed the order of the Talmud and included within their works legal responsa and court rulings, in addition to their learned interpretations of the Talmud and legal decisions that emerged from the text.[43] In short, these influential works included everything a scholar and a judge would be interested in having at his disposal when studying the Talmud, that is, learned material important both for study and for applied law.[44] These works were essentially closed books for anyone not proficient with the Talmudic text. To put matters in perspective, none of the authors of these works even bothered to pen an abridgement similar to the *Sefer ha-terumah* by Barukh ben Isaac.[45] It is hard to envision a non-scholar finding interest in these weighty books and opening them in order to study materials in them. In short, in seeking to identify the reading audience of these Rhineland works it would seem that they were targeted for the elite: the judge, the scholar of the law, and his students.

There is, however, one book of law from this time period that was written with a broader reading audience in mind—Eleazar of Worms' *Rokeaḥ*.[46] It was meant to be read independently of the Talmud and it largely avoided complex Talmudic discussions. In other words, it was meant even for the non-Talmudic reader—a point the author makes explicit in his introduction.[47] It is worth noting that despite living in the same geographic area and being a contemporary of the other three legal authorities from the Rhineland, Eleazar was not part of the mainstream; he belonged to the movement known as *Ḥasidé Ashkenaz*—the German Pietists.[48] He studied with Judah the Pious in Speyer and may also have joined his teacher later on in Regensburg.[49] As Haym Soloveitchik and Israel M. Ta-Shma have demonstrated, a major theme of the Pietist religious-social agenda was an emphasis on practical religious law and its popularization among all members of society.[50] The *Rokeah* is, therefore, an outgrowth of his Pietistic agenda and so did not create any sort of traction within the mainstream rabbinic class in Germany toward the production of accessible works of law.[51]

In addition to Eleazar of Worms' work, it is worth mentioning two semi-legal works—*Perushim u-fesakim* by Avigdor Katz of Vienna, a student of Simḥah of Speyer and *Kol bo* by Shemarya, the son and student of Simḥah—both from the mid-point of the century. The two works are closely related, but the exact nature of that relationship is not clear. Neither of these works is extant and their medieval existence has only recently been revealed thanks to the efforts of Simcha Emanuel.[52] For the purpose of this study, it is worth noting that both works are structured according to the verses of the Torah and both include popular sermonic-midrashic content as well as halakhic materials, making the work attractive to a broader audience.[53] It would seem that these books were conceived with a broader reading audience in mind, yet cannot be described as works of law.

During the last quarter of the thirteenth century however, one can detect a certain shift within the rabbinic class in Germany, linked to the figure of the famous Meir of Rothenburg (Maharam).[54] He himself authored a number of accessible monographs on practical matters of the law such as the laws of blessings on food, laws of *'eruvin*,[55] laws of mourning, and laws of ritual slaughter.[56] Maharam choice to deal with topics such as blessings and mourning, relevant to all Jews, using a topical format and a relatively accessible presentation; in particular, the monograph on blessings may indicate that the author was reaching out to an audience other than the scholarly. More significant, however, were the works of his colleague Isaac of Dura in his *Sha'aré dura* on the laws relating to preparation of kosher foods and family purity[57] and that of Maharam's student Samson ben Tsadok in his *Tashbets*, an accessible collection of his teacher's customs and legal decisions.[58] Both of these works survived in numerous medieval manuscripts which attest to their wide circulation. Also worthy of mention is the written "sermon" of another student of Maharam, Ḥayyim b. Isaac, Or Zarua' published under the title *Derashot u-fiské halakhot*. This text was clearly meant to be read by or at least read to the layman.[59] This scholar also penned an abridgement to the Or Zarua', written by his father Isaac Or Zarua', mentioned above.[60] Ḥayyim's accessible work circulated widely, in contrast to that of his father. The difference between father and son is, I believe, emblematic of the change that took place during the last quarter of the thirteenth century.[61]

From this brief survey of German halakhic literature, it emerges that the authors' primary reading audience in the first three quarters of the thirteenth century was the scholarly class. Not until the latter part of the century, particularly in the school of Meir of Rothenburg, do we identify a shift in orientation. In this context, it is worth noting that Meir was not a typical product of the Rhineland; his advanced Talmudic studies took place mainly in northern France, in the area of Paris and its environs, not in Germany.[62]

The contrast between the gradual but consistent development of accessible works in France and the lack of any real movement in Germany in that direction suggests that Maharil's negative stance toward popular halakhic literature in the early fifteenth century did not begin with him but was deeply rooted in the Rhineland. Although I have not found such a position articulated by any of the early thirteenth-century scholars mentioned above, such a voice is heard at the end of the century.

Asher ben Yeḥi'el, the famous Rosh, was the primary legal authority of Germany during the late thirteenth century, following Meir of Rothenburg's imprisonment in the year 1286, and an important communal leader there, until he immigrated to Spain in the year 1304. His family hailed from Cologne in the Rhineland and he was active in Worms, Mainz, and possibly Erfurt for a short period of time.[63] His negative attitude toward the reliance on legal handbooks without consulting the primary Talmudic sources is well known and is usually cited in the context of criticism of the Maimonidian code, *Mishneh torah*.[64]

One of Rosh's strongest statements against the use of secondary legal works was penned in relation to Isaac of Corbeil's *Semak*. In one of his responsa, Asher ben Yeḥi'el expresses his strong reservations of unlearned people who rely on legal handbooks for their halakhic knowledge:

> And death unto those (literally "their spirit should be exhaled [from their body]") who decide cases according to books and codes of the great ones, while being completely ignorant of Mishnah and Talmud. For at times the copyist errs between "obligated [to pay]" and "exempt [from payment]", between "prohibited" and "permitted". In addition, due to their lack of intelligence they do not fully comprehend the author's words and err.[65]

Rosh differentiates between two types of errors that are liable to confound the unschooled reader—one due to mechanical errors that routinely crept into texts during the copying process and the other simply due to a lack of understanding.[66]

Rosh seems to be saying that the law is too serious a matter to be decided by those not intimately acquainted with the primary sources. Despite being a student of Meir of Rothenburg, Rosh's position is apparently representative of the traditional Rhineland legal culture, which neither produced nor promoted accessible halakhic works, especially not for the lay reading public. Indeed, Rosh and his predecessors saw too clearly the dangers of misunderstanding and misapplying the law, and this fear overshadowed the potential benefits of educating the public through the written word. In fact, Rosh's own legal work, the *Pesakim* (legal decisions) or *Piské ha-Rosh*, composed while residing in Spain, was much closer to that of Eliezer b. Joel (Ra'avyah) and other Rhineland scholars[67] rather than to that of the French, Moses of Coucy or Isaac of Corbeil.[68] Moreover, like his Rhineland ancestors, he did not feel the need to write an abridgment to his collection of laws—this was left for his son Jacob to accomplish.[69]

Considering the above, I would suggest that there was a fundamental difference between the French attitude toward accessible legal works and the one expressed by Maharil at the opening of this study. The French Tosafist Isaac of Corbeil's endeavor to introduce the laity to the law via accessible legal works was exactly what the fifteenth-century rabbi bemoaned and regretted. The lack of interest on the part of mainstream German scholars during the course of the thirteenth century in producing such accessible works and the explicit statement by Rosh are indications that Maharil was not alone in his negative attitude toward the popularization of the law, and may reflect long-standing Rhineland rabbinic values. Whereas the French rabbis emphasized the spread of knowledge and the education of the laity, with a view to promoting religious observance among the people, the Germans were more interested in protecting the integrity of the halakhah and ensuring its proper implementation. The French Rabbis were willing to relinquish a degree of control for the greater religious edification of the people, whereas the Rhineland rabbis felt it was vital that all legal knowledge be facilitated via experts in the law.

Concluding Thoughts

In two separate studies, Israel M. Ta-Shma suggested that the growth in halakhic literature in Germany and France during the thirteenth century was due to the influence of *Ḥasidé Ashkenaz* (the German Pietists), students of Judah the Pious, who incessantly preached the need to link study to practice—in contrast to the prevailing view of the Tosafists in France and Germany who envisioned study as the ultimate value. Alternatively, he theorized that even if one could not point to a causal relationship, it was clear to him that the religious-social problems to which the Pietists were reacting were the same as those that motivated both French and German scholars to write their works of law.[70]

The two main issues that troubled the Pietists according to Ta-Shma, were caused by the overemphasis on dialectics by the French Tosafist movement. In his opinion, this intellectual orientation led to a downgrading of simple religious observance among the elite and Jewish society as a whole. In addition, it alienated those unable to study in the Tosafist scholastic mode to the degree that they withdrew from Torah study. It was to counter these societal ills that the Pietists decided to emphasize practical halakhah and the importance of studying halakhic handbooks.

Although the Ta-Shma's thesis, especially the modified one, is fascinating and thought-provoking, I believe that in light of the results of the study presented here, a second look at these thirteenth-century literary developments is warranted. As I have shown, there are strong grounds to differentiate between developments that occurred in thirteenth-century France and in Germany in the non-Pietistic circles.[71] Moreover, the general impression one derives from reading the halakhic works composed in these two areas is that the German authors wrote for a local audience of rabbinic scholars, judges, and their students in Germany, whereas the French authors wrote for the Jews of France and the broader diaspora Jewry.[72]

In short, the character of the literary output of each legal culture is quite distinct. It appears that we have before us a fascinating story of conflicting ideals and values, which led to the fundamentally differing views of Ḥayyim Tsarfatti, whose family name indicates a French origin, and of the Maharil from the Rhineland, at the outset of the fifteenth century but whose roots can be traced to an earlier time, at least as early as the thirteenth century. Whereas the French placed a premium upon spreading knowledge and thus promoting observance, the Germans sought to retain the integrity of the law and ensure its proper implementation.

My description of French and German Jewish legal culture leads us to another issue which demands further exploration: what brought about this divergence between these two great northern European Talmudic cultures and what historical context can help us understand it? This inquiry deserves a study of its own,[73] yet it is worth noting here that the "French" approach of the thirteenth-century Jewish scholars runs parallel, to a certain extent, to changes occurring in the Christian world at this time, such as the increasing interest by the Church in the religiosity of its laypeople, the preaching activities of the mendicants, and the development of "pastoral care" literature.[74]

Notes

*   The research for this study was supported by the Israel Science Foundation (grant no. 1474/12).

1. See Israel J. Yuval, *Ḥakhamim be-doram* (Jerusalem, 1989), 311–318. To a large extent, my understanding of this exchange and its significance has been shaped by Yuval's treatment. See as well Agnes Romer-Segal, "Yiddish Works on Women's Commandments in the Sixteenth Century," *Studies in Yiddish Literature and Folklore* (Jerusalem, 1986), 37–59; Edward A. Fram, *My Dear Daughter: Rabbi Benjamin Slonik and the Education of Jewish Women in Sixteenth-century Poland* (Cincinnati, 2007), 12–15.

2. Maharil is most probably referring to the relatively straightforward halakhic materials found in some medieval prayer books such as the classic twelfth-century *Maḥzor Vitry*.

3. *Sha'aré dura* was a work that focused on prohibitions relating to food preparation and family purity. The work was authored in Germany by Isaac of Dura

during the last quarter of the thirteenth century. *Semak* or as its author titled his work *'Ammudé golah* is a popular legal handbook (discussed below) covering all relevant laws to a Jew living in medieval Europe. The work was completed in France by Isaac of Corbeil around the years 1276–1277. Turin should be read *Turim* is the work known as *Arba'ah turim*, a four-volume work that treats in depth all aspects of the law relevant to a medieval Jew. It was authored in Toledo by a German émigré to Spain, Jacob b. Asher ca. 1320–1340. For brief descriptions of all these works see Menahem Elon, *Jewish Law–History, Sources, Principles* (Philadelphia, 1994), 3: 1248–1249 (*Sha'aré dura*); 1263–1265 (*Semak*); and 1277–1302 (*Turim*).

4. Manuscript evidence backs up Maharil's claim, all of the aforementioned works have survived in numerous medieval copies, a strong indication of their broad appeal.

5. *She'elot u-teshuvot Maharil ha-ḥadashot*, Isaac A. Satz, ed. (Jerusalem, 1977), 93, 92–93.

6. See Yuval, *Ḥakhamim*, 317.

7. See studies cited above n. 1.

8. Later on in the responsum, Maharil offers an alternative model of how to disseminate the knowledge of these laws. He writes that every scholar should teach the women directly so that they avoid the prohibition of prohibited sexual relation or that he should instruct the female members of his household and they should inform their female friends.

9. See as well *She'elot u-teshuvot Maharil*, Isaac A. Satz, ed. (Jerusalem, 1980), 199, 315–316 and Yuval, *Ḥakhamim*, 316.

10. He previously resided in Augsburg, see Yuval, *Ḥakhamim*, 311–312.

11. See as well Yuval, *Ḥakhamim*, 313 and Fram, *My Dear Daughter*, 14–15.

12. One may also add the professionalization of the rabbinate at this time. On these events and their impact see Yedidya A Dinari, *Ḥakhmé ashkenaz be-shalhé yemé ha-benayim* (Jerusalem, 1984), 56–63 and Mordechai Breuer's "Prologue: The Jewish Middle-Ages," in *German-Jewish History in Modern Times,* ed. Michael A. Meyer (New York, 1996), 1: 54–57; Eric Zimmer, *Harmony and Discord: an Analysis of the Decline of Jewish Self-government in Fifteenth Century Central Europe* (New York, 1970), 118–123.

13. I intend to treat these earlier indications in a separate study.

14. This basic distinction was already noted by Ephraim Kanarfogel in his recent book. See Ephraim Kanarfogel, *The Intellectual History and Rabbinic Culture of Medieval Ashkenaz* (Detroit, 2013), 5–6.

15. See Ephraim E. Urbach, *Ba'alé ha-tosafot* (Jerusalem, 1980), 347–354; Simcha Emanuel, "'Ve-ish al mekomo mevo'ar shemo': le-toldotav shel R. Barukh b. Yitsḥak," *Tarbiz* 69 (2000), 423–440 and recently, Yoel Friedman, "*Sefer ha-terumah le-Rabbenu Barukh b. R. Yitsḥak: Megammot mivne ve-nusaḥ,*" (PhD dissertation, Hebrew University of Jerusalem, 2013).

16. It is worth noting that the scope of the book is fairly limited especially in comparison to the works that followed his.

17. The complete list of topics treated in *Sefer ha-terumah* as it appears in most manuscripts and in the printed version is the following: 1. *Sheḥita, terefot and issur ve-hetter*; 2. *Ḥalla* and *nidda*; 3. *Gittin* and *ḥalitsa*; 4. *'Avodah zarah* and *yen nesekh*; 5. *Sefer torah* and *tefillin*; 6. *Erets yisra'el*; 7. *Shabbat*. It is worth noting that

in the earliest dated mss. (1254) London–British Library Harley 5684 (catalogue Margoliyot 518), which seems to preserve an earlier authorial version of the work the order is: *1. shehita, terefot and issur ve-hetter; 2. 'avodah zarah and yen nesekh; 3. shabbat; 4. gittin and halitsa; 5. halla and nidda; 6. sefer torah and tefillin; 7. erets yisra'el.* See Friedman, "*Sefer ha-terumah*," 14–15.

18. Urbach, *Ba'alé ha-tosafot*, 349.

19. For a description of the Tosafist scholastic approach to the Talmud, see Haym Soloveitchik, *Collected essays* (Oxford, 2013), 1: 3–10.

20. In the standard printed edition the introduction can be found in Barukh b. Isaac, *Sefer ha-terumah* (Warsaw, 1897), 196 and I utilized Vatican—Biblioteca Apostolica ebr. 145 order to correct the text.

21. It is worth noting that many medieval manuscripts of the abridgement survived independently of the work itself, see Friedemann, "*Sefer ha-terumah*," 271.

22. The best concise study of Moses of Coucy, his life and works remains that of Ephraim E. Urbach, *Ba'alé ha-tosafot*, 465–479. See as well Elon, *Jewish Law*, 1261–1263, and Judah D. Galinsky, "The Significance of Form: R. Moses of Coucy's Reading Audience and his *Sefer ha-Mitsvot*," *AJS Review* 35 (2011): 293–321.

23. See Isadore Twersky, *Introduction to the Code of Maimonides (Mishneh Torah)* (New Haven, 1980), esp. 188–195, 259–272.

24. Once again following Maimonides' lead, see Twersky, *Introduction*, 325–336.

25. For a more in-depth discussion of Moses aims and goals see Galinsky, "Significance of Form."

26. See Urbach, *Ba'alé ha-tosafot*, 466–471 and Judah D. Galinsky, "R. Moshe mi-Coucy ke-hasid, darshan u-fulmusan," MA thesis, Bernard Revel Graduate School (New York, 1993), and Galinsky, "The Significance of Form," 298–299.

27. It would seem that Moses of Coucy was not willing to concede any group of potential readers. He wanted his book to appeal both to the scholar and to the educated layman who may have studied Talmud in his youth but was no longer seriously engaged with the material. It was this ambition that may have caused his book to be too unwieldy for the interested layperson.

28. See Urbach, *Ba'alé ha-tosafot*, 488–490, and Israel M. Ta-Shma, *Keneset mehkarim* (Jerusalem, 2004), 4: 264–268.

29. Avraham Y. Havazelet, "Sefer simane mitsvot le-Rabbenu Avraham b. Efrayim," in *Sefer ha-zikaron li-khevodo u-le-zikhro shel R. Yitshak Yedidya Frankel,* ed. David B. Lau and Yosef Buksbaum (Tel-Aviv, 1992), 281–304, see especially 288, n. 14.

30. See Urbach, *Ba'alé ha-tosafot*, 571–574; Ta-Shma, *Keneset mehkarim,* 265; Elon, *Jewish Law*, 1263–1265; Ephraim Kanarfogel, "German Pietism in Northern France: The Case of R. Isaac of Corbeil," in *Hazon Nahum; Studies in Jewish Law, Thought, and History Presented to Dr. Norman Lamm*, ed. Yaakov Elman and Jeffrey S. Gurock (Hoboken, 1997), 207–227.

31. Isaac is explicit about this in the letter he appended to his work. The letter serves as an introduction in all standard printed editions of the book. See *Sefer 'ammudé golah…ha-nikra semak* (Jerusalem, 2005), 1. For Isaac's program in its medieval context and a partial translation of this introduction, see Sarit Shalev-Eyni, *Jews among Christians: Hebrew Book Illumination from Lake Constance* (London, 2010),

14–16, and Shimon Schwarzfuchs, *Yehudé tsarfat be-yemé ha-benayim* (Tel Aviv, 2001), 265–266.

32. See *Sefer 'ammudé golah, 2* and Judith R. Baskin, "Some Parallels in the Education of Medieval Jewish and Christian Women," Jewish History, 5 (1991), 41–51, esp. 43. He most probably had in mind study with the help of a learned male.

33. Ibid. Note that Elon's partial translation of this source, *Jewish Law*, 1265 is not accurate.

34. This emerges most clearly from his letter. See Urbach, *Ba'alé ha-tosafot*, 571–572 and Schwarzfuchs, *Yehudé tsarfat,* 265–266.

35. Within this context see Moses of Coucy's praise of Maimonides' success in popularizing the law, *Sefer mitsvot gadol ha-shalem* (Jerusalem, 1993), 12.

36. See Soloveitchik, *Collected Essays*, 31–38 where he emphasizes the insularity of French legal thought.

37. There is one exception to this observation, the *Rokeah* of Eleazar of Worms, which I will address below.

38. The basic biographic and bibliographic information of all these scholars can be found in Urbach, *Ba'alé ha-tosafot*, 378–388 (Eliezer ben Joel); 411–420 (Simha of Speyer); 425–429 (Barukh of Mainz); 436–447 (Isaac Or Zarua'). For a thorough description of these scholars' legal works and for updated biographical information, see the recent study of Simha Emanuel cited below.

39. As Urbach has shown (ibid., 436–439) Isaac was born in Bohemia and studied in his youth with local scholars there and in addition to studying in the Rhineland, Isaac traveled to Paris to study under the great Tosafist Judah Sir Leon and travelled to Regensburg where he studied with famous Judah the Pious (He-hasid). On the French aspect of Isaac's career, see Avraham (Rami) Reiner, "From Rabbenu Tam to R. Isaac of Vienna: The Hegemony of the French Talmudic school in the twelfth century," in *The Jews of Europe in the Middle Ages (Tenth to Fifteenth Centuries)*, ed. Christoph Cluse (Turnhout, 2004), 273–282.

40. His son Hayyim followed his example and studied in Germany (with the great Meir of Rothenburg) and spent time throughout his life in various cities in Germany and cities in the east, see Noah Goldstein, *Rabbi Hayyim Eliezer ben Isaac Or Zarua: his life and work, and a digest of his responsa*, D. H. L. dissertation, Yeshiva University, (1959), 23–26.

41. For basic biographic information on all these scholars and for a description of the works by Eliezer ben Joel and Isaac Or Zarua', see Urbach's *Ba'alé ha-tosafot*. However for a description of Eliezer's lost book see Simcha Emanuel, *Shivré luhot: sifré halakhah avudim shel ba'alé ha-tosafot* (Jerusalem, 2006), 86–103.

42. For a description of Simhah's and Barukh's lost works (with additional updated biographic information) see Emanuel, *Shivré luhot*, 154–161 and 104–127, especially 123–127.

43. This emerges quite clearly from Emanuel's description. See as well Kanarfogel, *The Intellectual History*, 5–6. This is not to claim that there are no differences at all between the works, especially between the earlier works and the later one such as Or Zarua'. However they all do have in common the traits outlined above.

44. See Kanarfogel, *The Intellectual History*, 37–84.

45. Although one can find a table of contents in these works, the abridgement of Isaac Or Zarua's was written later on by his son, see below n. 60.

46. In general see Urbach, *Ba'alé ha-tosafot*, 388–411 for a more in-depth description of some of his works see Simha Emanuel's introduction to his edition of R. Eleazar of Worms, *Derasha le-fesaḥ* (Jerusalem, 2006), 1–66.

47. See Urbach, *Ba'alé ha-tosafot*, 397–399.

48. Much has been written on this unique group and its impact upon Franco-German Jewry. The group's beginning can be found in Speyer (and later in Regensburg) toward the end of the twelfth century. In general, see Ivan G. Marcus, *Piety and Society: the Jewish Pietists of Medieval Germany* (Leiden, 1981), 36–41, and "The Historical Meaning of Hasidei Ashkenaz: Fact, Fiction, or Cultural Self-Image?" in *Gershom Scholem's Major Trends in Jewish Mysticism 50 Years After*, ed. Peter Schäfer and Joseph Dan (Tübingen, 1993), 103–116. See as well H. Soloveitchik, "Piety, Pietism and German Pietism; 'Sefer Ḥasidim I' and the Influence of 'Ḥasidei Ashkenaz,'" *Jewish Quarterly Review* 92 (2002), 455–493 and the JQR volume (Forum: *Sefer Hasidim*) devoted to this article, *Jewish Quarterly Review* 96 (2006). As to the difference between mainstream German scholars and those belonging to the Pietist group during the thirteenth century, see, for example, Ephraim Kanarfogel, *Peering through the Lattices: Mystical, Magical, and Pietistic Dimensions in the Tosafist Period* (Detroit, 2000), 45–50, 214–217.

49. Urbach, *Ba'alé ha-tosafot*, 390.

50. See Haym Soloveitchik, "Three Themes in the Sefer Ḥasidim," *AJS Review* I (1976), 339–344 and Israel M. Ta-Shma, "*Mitsvat talmud torah ke-ba'aya ḥevratit-datit be-sefer ḥasidim,*" in his *Halakhah, minhag, u-metsi'ut be-ashkenaz, 1000–1350* (Jerusalem, 1996), 112–129.

51. This conclusion differs substantially from that of Ta-Shma, Ta-Shma, "*Mitsvat talmud torah ke-ba'aya ḥevratit-datit be-sefer ḥasidim,*" 120–121 and see "Concluding Thoughts."

52. See Emanuel, *Shivré luḥot*, 166–175.

53. See Kanarfogel, *The Intellectual history*, 360–361.

54. See Urbach, *Ba'alé ha-tosafot*, 521–564.

55. Laws that allowed the Jew to carry on the Sabbath in the public domain via the construction of "fictitious" walls that convert the public into private space, see recently Micha Perry, "Imaginary Space meets Actual Space in Thirteenth-century Cologne: Eliezer ben Yoel and the Eruv," *Images* 5 (2011) 26–36.

56. See Ephraim Kanarfogel, "Preservation, Creativity, and Courage: The Life and Works of R. Meir of Rothenburg," Jewish Book Annual, 50 (1992), 249–259.

57. See Ta-Shma, *Keneset meḥkarim*, 1: 175–178, 328–336.

58. See Urbach, *Ba'alé ha-tosafot*, 561.

59. See Kanarfogel, *The Intellectual History*, 361.

60. See Urbach, *Ba'alé ha-tosafot*, 442–445.

61. One may wish to consider the seeming embrace of the Maimonidean code, Mishneh Torah in this study-hall, see Urbach, *Ba'alé ha-tosafot*, 251, 554–555 and Soloveitchik, *Collected Essays*, 37–38.

62. See Urbach, *Ba'alé ha-tosafot* and Kanarfogel, *The Intellectual History* as well as Susan L. Einbinder, *Beautiful Death: Jewish Poetry and Martyrdom in Medieval France* (Princeton, 2002), 70–80.

63. The best biographical sketch of the Rosh remains that of Abraham H. Freimann, "Ascher ben Jechiel, sein Leben und Wirken," *Jahrbuch der Jüdisch-Literarischen*

Gesellschaft 12 (1918), 237–317. Freimann wrote about the Rosh's family in a separate paper, "Die Ascheriden (1267–1391)," *Jahrbuch der Jüdisch-Literarischen Gesellschaft* 13 (1919–1920), 142–254. The two articles were translated into Hebrew by Menahem Eldar, *Ha-Rosh: Rabbenu Asher b. R. Yeḥi'el ve-tse'etsa'av* (Jerusalem, 1986); for corrections to the Freimann account, see Israel M. Ta-Shma, "Between East and West: Rabbi Asher b. Yehiel and his son Rabbi Yaaqov," in *Studies in Medieval Jewish History and Literature III*, ed. Isadore Twersky and Jay M. Harris (Cambridge, MA, 2000), 179–196.

64. See Elon, *Jewish Law*, 1226–1229 and Judah D. Galinsky, "Ashkenazim in Sefarad: The Rosh and the Tur on the Codification of Jewish Law," *Jewish Law Annual* 16 (2006), 3–23, especially 4–12.

65. *She'elot u-teshuvot ha-Rosh*, ed. Isaac Yudlov (Jerusalem, 1994), *kelal* 43 *siman* 12b, 185b.

66. It is worth contrasting Rosh's statement with that of Isaac of Corbeil cited above. Isaac, in contrast to Rosh, expressed concern only about copyist errors.

67. See Galinsky, "Ashkenazim," 11. One would also have to compare his work to the *Halakhot* of Isaac Alfasi of Spain and North Africa. See Judah D. Galinsky, "Ha-Rosh ha-ashkenazi bi-sefarad: '*tosafot ha-Rosh*', '*piské ha-Rosh*', yeshivat ha-Rosh," *Tarbiz* 74 (2005), 404–409.

68. Although one could argue that his attitude was not a reflection of the classic Rhineland approach but was formed purely as a reaction to the social-legal reality, which he encountered in Castile, that is, the complete reliance on the Maimonidean code and the disregard of the Talmud and its commentators.

69. See Galinsky, "*Ha-Rosh*," 408.

70. See Israel M. Ta-Shma, "*Mitsvat talmud torah*," especially 119–124 and his *Keneset meḥkarim*, 1: 317–344, especially 331–336.

71. In my opinion, it would be difficult to argue that the French developments outlined above were due to the influence of the German Pietists. The only French scholar surveyed above who shows any kind of awareness of the Pietist's teachings is Isaac of Corbeil. See Kanarfogel, "German Pietism in Northern France" and his *Peering through the Lattices*, 59–92, and Soloveitchik, "Piety, Pietism and German Pietism," 480–484.

72. This can be seen by their emphasis on local customs and the inclusion of responsa and court decisions in their works. All of these elements add much local color to their presentation. In the French legal works all of the above is either completely absent or very much downplayed. A similar point has recently been made by Ivan Marcus with regard to the French Talmudic culture, see Ivan G. Marcus, "Why Did Medieval Northern French Jewry (*Tsarfat*) Disappear?" in *Jews, Christians and Muslims in Medieval and Early Modern Times: A Festschrift in Honor of Mark R. Cohen*, ed. Arnold E. Franklin et al. (Leiden, 2013). I thank Micha Perry for calling my attention to the relevance of Marcus' study for my thesis.

73. See Judah Galinsky "Rabbis, Readers and the Paris Book Trade: Understanding French Halakhic Literature in the 13th Century" to be published in Elisheva Baumgarten, Katelyn Mesler, and Ruth Karras eds., *Entangled Histories: Knowledge, Authority, and Transmission in Thirteenth-Century Jewish Cultures* (Philadelphia, 2015).

74. For a broad overview of these developments and a select bibliography see Lesley Smith, "The Theological Framework," in *The Cambridge History of Christianity, vol. 4, Christianity in Western Europe, c.1100–c.1500,* ed. Miri Rubin and Walter Simons (Cambridge, 2009), 75–88, especially 78–81, as well as her study in this volume (chapter 1) and Joseph Goering, *William de Montibus (c. 1140–1213): The Schools and the Literature of Pastoral Care* (Toronto, 1992), 58–99. See as well chapter 2 in this volume.

CHAPTER 6

AUTHORITY, CONTROL, AND CONFLICT IN THIRTEENTH-CENTURY PARIS: CONTEXTUALIZING THE TALMUD TRIAL[1]

Yossef Schwartz

In the thirteenth century, Paris became a laboratory for experimentation with power, where the political, religious, and scholarly elite began to develop institutional means of exercising authority.[2] As a result, Paris became not only the most prominent European intellectual center of that time, but also the most organized, centralized, and scrutinized. This process emerged from an early medieval culture in Christian Europe that lacked coordinated mechanisms for inhibiting intellectual dissent: from the cases of Johannes Scotus Erigena and Berengar of Tours to Roscelin, Abelard, and Gilbert of Poitiers, we can trace a well-known and comparatively well-documented chain of events that demonstrates the inefficiencies that characterized institutional responses to the challenges posed by clerics belonging to the intellectual elite.[3] This study analyzes the Talmud Trial and related events in Paris during the 1240s to describe the forms of control that became possible once intellectual restrictions and censorship traversed their academic boundaries and became integrated with clerical and political power. Such synchronized pressures were absent from other thirteenth-century Christian-Jewish confrontations, but became commonplace in the early fourteenth century (e.g., in prosecutions of the Talmud by inquisitors such as the Dominicans, Bernard Gui, and Jacques Fournier) and continued well into the early modern period.[4] In this article, I present a twofold argument: first, that the triumvirate of monarchic, papal, and academic authority—normally identified as an early fourteenth-century political development—was already operative in the mid-thirteenth century, at least in the context of the Talmud

Trial; and second, that a nuanced understanding of this trial must incorporate the perspective of this shared exercise of authority.

This is not to say that heresy was an unknown concept prior to this medieval turning point; on the contrary, from its earliest stages, Christian polemic literature is punctuated with a range of external and internal arguments and, certainly, heterodoxy is a subject of intense interest in Latin patristic writings. Indeed, twelfth- and thirteenth-century Catholic investigations of heresy were typically anchored in patristic concepts, although they were often anachronistically used to describe contemporary phenomena. Therefore, the consolidation of powers that will be explored below was preceded by a set of strongly established procedures, particularly in complicated and ambiguous instances where the opponent was neither an outsider nor a political enemy (such as Saracens or Cathars) but a privileged individual or community that held a claim to orthodoxy and was sheltered by patronage.

The case of Peter Abelard is illustrative: having been captured between the Council of Sens (Pentecost 1140) and the papal curia in Rome (July 16, 1140), namely between Cistercian and papal powers, he secured a place of refuge with the Cluniac abbot Peter the Venerable who, if we accept his own testimony (the only extant evidence from the final phase of this affair), was able to reconcile Abelard and Bernard, effectively disarming the condemnation that had been leveled against Abelard only after protracted and complex machinations.[5] This case was framed by two others that echo similar patterns: the more than 20-year effort to condemn and silence Berengar of Tours, which preceded the Abelard affair by several decades, and the unsuccessful trial of Gilbert of Poitiers, that took place soon after the events involving Abelard.[6]

In this study, I trace the emergence of an authoritative mechanism for making decisions in doctrinal matters, while comparing it with contemporaneous measures against rabbinic writings. The procedures enacted in reaction to Jewish texts were no less ambitious and complicated than their intra-Christian parallels. This analysis will examine one of the major events from the thirteenth century, the Talmud Trial of 1240, along with the subsequent burning of the Talmud in 1241 (and, possibly, in 1244 and 1248) in Paris and the continuing series of acts relating to the Talmud until 1248.

A second major event from this time, worth noting but not explored here, that may be related to (and has certainly been associated with) the Talmud Trial, was the Maimonidean controversies in the area of Montpellier and the inquisitorial acts that allegedly occurred in the city of Montpellier in 1232 (or 1233). These events may be related as well to the anti-Aristotelian interdictions of 1228–1231, as initiated by Pope Gregory IX.[7]

The Talmud Trial in Paris was an outcome of two conterminous enterprises: the translation into Latin of newly discovered Hebrew materials (primarily sections of the Babylonian Talmud and commentaries by Rashi on biblical and talmudic passages) and decisive acts to censor these freshly translated sources. A decade earlier, a series of less documented events seems to embody this same twofold mechanism: at that time, major writings by Maimonides (e.g., *Guide of the Perplexed* [*Moreh nevukhim*] and *Sefer ha-mitsvot* [*Book of the Commandments*]) were translated into Latin[8] and Maimonides's Hebrew writings were allegedly condemned and burned in 1233 by certain Latin authorities in Montpellier. Any comparison must be preceded by an assessment of what transpired, where, and by whom; alas, the information needed for a robust description of these events remains a desideratum.[9]

In order to contextualize the events relating to the Talmud Trial that took place in Paris, I will outline additional instances of censorship, investigation, and condemnation, involving all or some of the same agents, in Paris and elsewhere. Whereas each of these topics encompasses some degree of interaction between political and social elements, they all involve learned elites that draw from more formal sources of power (e.g., the pope and bishops, royalty and chancellors, and Jewish communal leadership).

Placing the Parisian Talmud Trial in Context

The Parisian censure of the Talmud in the 1240s has been a topic of scholarly interest since the mid-nineteenth century.[10] In Jewish historiography, Paris (1240) and Barcelona (1263) represent two types of, and perhaps trends in, the anti-Jewish polemic that emerged in Christian Europe during the late Middle Ages. Despite having been promoted by Jewish apostates—Nicholas Donin in Paris and Pablo Christiani in Barcelona—they differed ideologically as well as institutionally in their strategies for converting Jews and their narratives about Judaism.[11]

Among the few biographic details that have been transmitted about the enigmatic Nicholas Donin, the primary catalyst for papal initiation of this trial is the fact that he was condemned by the Jewish community 15 years earlier (in 1225), shortly before the eruption of the Maimonidean controversy.[12] Considerable speculation has been devoted to the cause of Donin's excommunication and his subsequent motivations. With Chen Merchavia and Görge Hasselhof, I tend to assume that Donin was influenced by Maimonidean rationalists, which might suggest another link between his rejection by the Jewish community and his actions in Paris during the 1240s. Given our current evidence, this connection remains hypothetical.[13]

The trial of the Talmud in Paris encompassed a distinctly inquisitorial combination of elements. I concur with William Jordan's assessment[14] that such proceedings did not yet have a stable format; therefore, the kinds of assertions made by Baer concerning how the trial "should" have been conducted are not applicable to this period.[15] On the other hand, especially now that scholars have access to the Moscow and Vatican manuscripts of *Vikkuah Rabbenu Yeḥi'el mi-Paris* (*The Disputation of R. Yeḥi'el of Paris*),[16] there is no longer reason to doubt the Jewish narrative details of juridical negotiations that were held between Jewish community representatives, Queen Mother Blanche of Castille, and an appointed inquisitorial committee (and, perhaps, even King Louis IX); this documentation has been synthesized by Judah Galinsky in his meticulous, scene-by-scene reconstruction of this trial, drawn from a comparative analysis of the corpus of extant Hebrew manuscripts.[17] The Christian documentation, such as the materials gathered in the codex in the Bibliothèque Nationale de France that records these proceedings (MS lat. 16 558), that has recently undergone intensive scholarly analysis[18] also provides unambiguous proof of their inquisitorial qualities. Furthermore, as we shall see (below), its similarities with a series of thirteenth-century events that took place in Paris, particularly with respect to the participation of the highest levels of academic, royal, and clerical leadership, renders it a typical, if perhaps extreme, expression of a new method of intellectual control, capturing a stage in its formation.[19]

The general definition of inquisitorial proceedings (mentioned above) encompasses a broad spectrum of possibilities on which the trial of the Talmud falls closer to the actions taken to censor university masters and/ or their writings than to those waged against popular heretical movements. That is to say, it more closely resembles the first investigation of Amalric of Béne in 1204 than the action against the Amalricians in 1210, namely, the condemnation of ideas versus the execution of those who promulgated them. As Thijssen observes regarding this pair of cases, it is no coincidence that the concepts being condemned originated with a prominent scholar who had taught the king, whereas the local clerics who spread these ideas in their preaching were punished for having committed a capital offense.[20] It is no less significant that, in the Talmud Trial in Paris, neither Jewish witnesses nor the Jewish community were being prosecuted or at risk of punishment. This case cannot be extricated from its threat to the Jewish texts that were ultimately burned, as the writings of John Scotus Erigena had been nearly twenty years earlier.

As Thijssen rightly claims,[21] no other thirteenth-century university initiated mechanisms of intellectual control with the intensity reflected by the censorial and inquisitorial efforts exercised in Paris. While papal involvement in university affairs at this time was largely unremarkable, the degree of foreign involvement in parochial matters at the University of Paris was exceptional. After all, the players who were active in the Talmud Trial—king, bishop, pope, scholars, and mob—also took part in a variety of university proceedings. The sources gathered by Denifle in *Chartularium Universitatis Parisiensis*[22] reveals many such thirteenth-century incidents. Table 6.1 provides a chronological listing of well-known examples, with summaries that give special attention to the functionaries involved in each. This presentation highlights the parallel nature of the proceedings that addressed academic heresy and those taken against the Talmud.[23] These 20 entries are divided

Table 6.1 Inquisitorial and Censorial Acts in Thirteenth-Century Paris

I. 1200–1231

1200—A royal decree from King Philippe Auguste ensures a place for professors and students in Paris.

1204—The first trial of Master Amalric of Bène (d. 1206) is initiated by the Parisian Faculty of Theology and later involves Pope Innocent III.[24]

1210—The final sentence for heresy is decreed by the Council of Paris against Amalric and his followers, together with the writings of David of Dinant and Aristotle's *libri naturales*.[25] Ten convicted heretics are publicly executed.

1215—Papal regulation of studies in Paris is enacted (via Cardinal Legate Robert de Courçon). The condemnation of Amalric and David is reaffirmed, together with "Mauricii hyspani" and Aristotle's works on metaphysics and natural philosophy, in original or summary form.[26]

1219—Pope Honorius III proclaims a bull on the study of medicine, law and theology in Paris,[27] providing papal support for the university in its struggle against the bishop and the chancellor.

1225—Pope Honorius III condemns the teachings of Erigena, followed by the public burning of Erigena's writings.[28]

1228—Pope Gregory IX prohibits Paris theologians from incorporating philosophy into their teaching.[29]

1229—Treaty of Paris signed. Count Raymond VII commits to the establishment of the University of Toulouse.

1229–1231—Papal support extended toward the university masters' strike (waged against the bishop's failure to support them).

1231—The papal bull *Parens scientiarum* (April 13, 1231) issued by Pope Gregory IX[30] to affirm earlier university statutes. The pope asserts the need to reexamine Aristotle's prohibited books. Committee appointed on April 24, 1231.[31]

II. 1239–1256

June 1239—Pope Gregory IX issues letters to the Bishop of Paris and (through him) to the kings of France, England, Aragon, Navarre, Castile, Leon and Portugal, ordering the confiscation and examination of Jewish books.

June 1240—The trial of the Talmud is held in Paris.

1241 – (and again in 1244) Condemnation "by Bishop William of Auvergne, Chancellor Odo of Châteauroux and all the regent masters of theology" of the Dominican Friar Stephen ("frater Stephanus," who may be Etienne de Venizy) and the ten erroneous teachings[32] (*reprobate a cancellario Parisiensi Odone et magistris theologie Parisius regentibus*[33]). Censure repeated by Dominican general chapter of June 1243.[34] The ten articles are publicly refuted in January 1244.

June (?) 1241—Burning of the Talmud.

Continued

Table 6.1 Continued

May 1244—Letter from Pope Innocent IV dispatched to King Louis on the enforcement of anti-talmudic rulings: "Our beloved son, the Chancellor of Paris, and the Doctors Regent of Holy Writ in Paris" (*dilectus filius concellarius Parisiensis, et doctores regentes Parisiis in sacra pagina*) carried out the orders of Pope Gregory by burning the Talmud and other books that "were condemned by those same doctors" (*reprobatos per doctores eosdem*).

1247–1248—Letter sent by Papal Legate Odo of Châteauroux to Pope Innocent IV, summarizing the reexamination of the Talmud Trial proceedings. It is followed by a signed document from Parisian clergy and university masters confirming the condemnation (May 1248).

1254—Pope Innocent IV condemns thirty-one errors by the Franciscan Master Gerardo of Borgo San Donnino, *Introductorium in evangelium aeternum*,[35] and ultimately excommunicates him.[36]

1256—Pope Alexander IV condemns William of St. Amour, *De periculis novissimorum temporum*.[37] A Dominican petition against William is sent to the king.[38] Papal reassurance of the Dominican and Franciscan mandates issued,[39] supporting the conclusions of committee of cardinals (Odo of Châteauroux, Hugh of Saint Cher OP, Stefan of Vansca).

III. 1270–1277

1270—Étienne Tempier, Bishop of Paris and former Chancellor (1263–1268), and Master of Theology condemns thirteen philosophical errors[40] (papal vacancy).

1277—Tempier condemns 219 theses,[41] exceeding (or independent of) his original papal mandate.

---

into three phases: the period from 1200 to 1231 is normally associated with the formal development of the university and the increasing integration of Aristotelian science despite its inclusion in at least one early inquisitorial proceeding; general studies of thirteenth-century intellectual history rarely discuss the period from 1239 to 1256, which tends to receive scholarly attention in local histories of the university and its inner tensions; and, 1270–1277 is probably the most celebrated time, for its dramatic developments within the history of philosophy and science.

　　While these entries include manifold details that merit further attention and investigation, this list surveys the most intensely documented mechanism for intellectual control in operation during the thirteenth century. It also offers a glimpse of the kaleidoscopic interactions between the hierarchies involved in this dynamic power play. Earlier historiographies tend to concentrate on the exercise of authority concerning Aristotelian *libri naturales* in the first half of the thirteenth century (1210, 1215, and 1231) and radical Averroistic thought during the 1270s, with less attention to the purely theological debates that dominated mid-century concerns. It was during the 1240s and 1250s that complex alliances and competing interests within and around the University of Paris became clearly manifest. For our discussion, this second period—which includes both stages of the Talmud Trial and the theological refutations of the teachings of Dominican Friar Stephen in 1241 and 1244—is most relevant.

A central figure in these two affairs, Odo (Eudes) of Châteauroux, was at the mid-point of his long and illustrious career.[42] After becoming a Magister of Theology in 1230, Odo was appointed Canon at Notre Dame in 1234, Chancellor of the University of Paris in 1238, Cardinal in 1244, Papal Legate to France in 1245, and then he accompanied King Louis as Apostolic Legate to the Holy Land, Egypt, and North Africa from 1248 to 1254. While Odo may have been successful in the purely academic, theoretical realm, he apparently excelled in the administrative and political spheres. While his name rarely appears in studies of intellectual history, his role is critical for our study of the entanglement between intellectuals and society in Paris.

In the procedure that was devised by the Parisian Faculty of Theology, the locus of "inquisition" as a general investigation was distinct from—while being intimately connected with—its core legal decisions. This new method operated on the basis of a list of errors;[43] as is vividly demonstrated by the Talmud Trial, which employed a list that had been prepared by Donin for the Pope, to guide the examination and interrogation of the rabbis until the Cardinal Legate and the Parisian masters reached their verdict. As well-known cases from the early fourteenth century clearly demonstrate (e.g., Marguerite Porete and Meister Eckhart), this became the standard method for inquisitorial trials of intellectuals and books.[44]

The unusually high level of royal involvement in the clerical inquisitorial process—a pattern that was repeated in Barcelona—can best be explained on the grounds of the juridical issues involved. As *Iudei nostri*, Jews could not be approached by Church officials without royal approval.[45] Thus Pope Gregory IX's directive that Bishop William address the kings of France, England, Aragon, Navarre, Castile, Leon, and Portugal.[46] Here Louis IX, the only king to approve the papal initiative, provides a counter example, within the same theo-political framework, to Frederick II, who was not even contacted by the papal representative, but who promoted his own investigations in Germany and Sicily.[47]

Many scholars have theorized about the motives behind Louis's embrace of the papal call, and each explanation captures certain key aspects.[48] I would like to underscore an essential, contextualizing element: the university in Paris enjoyed a great deal of papal and royal attention throughout the thirteenth century.[49] It must be noted that royal engagement in university conflicts and investigations was not unique to the Talmud Trial, as attested by the cases against the Amalricians of 1210 and William of Saint Amour in 1256. At the University of Paris, royal efforts were added to enduring papal involvement with the Faculty of Theology to constitute the unique triad of Church authority, a centralized monarchy, and a leading theological academic institution, necessary to achieve the radical departure from the earlier "social contract" between Christian authorities and Jewish communities in Latin Christendom. This consolidation of power may explain why the Bishop of Paris was selected to distribute the papal letter to the European bishops and monarchs, and why Paris was the sole locus for full implementation of this papal initiative.[50]

A number of questions must be addressed to accurately define the mechanism that was created in Paris. First, there seems to be some uncertainty regarding the Christian actors involved in the first trial (in 1240), whether the masters of theology were actually participants? Second, even if royal permission were necessary at the confiscation stage and, perhaps, prior to book burnings, how shall we explain royal involvement in the trial itself?[51] Finally, can the mere existence of such a new instrument of control convey the motivations for taking this action against the Talmud? Let us now consider each of these issues.

While we cannot fully resolve the question of Christian interlocutors, convincing evidence does exist. Although no contemporaneous records of the trial have been transmitted, we have three documents that were composed within a decade of this event. The report of the trial in the Parisian codex, which (at least in its final form) is also the latest composition,[52] makes no mention of masters of theology as participants, noting only higher clerics, including the University Chancellor. The two others, written by Pope Innocent IV in 1244 and by Odo in 1248, explicitly cite the involvement of masters of theology.

While no significant role is ascribed to the Parisian masters of theology in the "records" of 1240, the papal reconstruction of these events depicts their instrumental positions. In a letter from May 9, 1244, Pope Innocent IV wrote to Louis IX that "our beloved son, the Chancellor of Paris and the Doctors Regent in Holy Writ in Paris" (*dilectus filius cancellarius Parisiensis, et doctores regentes Parisiis in sacra pagina*) followed the orders of Pope Gregory by burning the Talmud and other books that "had been condemned by those same doctors" (*reprobatos per doctores eosdem*).[53]

This description is echoed in a letter written by Odo, then Cardinal and Papal Legate to Pope Innocent IV,[54] providing us with the most comprehensive overview of this near decade-long affair. Toward the end of this correspondence,[55] Odo boldly threatens that a scandal could be expected if the papacy withheld support from the decisions taken by the university masters, clergy, and *populus* of Paris. This warning completes the circle that began with the papal initiative, which was sent to the Bishop of Paris and ultimately took the form of a demand presented by Paris against the Pope.[56]

In May 1248, a sizeable representation of clergy and professors of theology and law assembled to authorize the verdict of the committee that had been appointed, here too by a papal directive, to reexamine prior decisions concerning the Talmud. The document, as edited by Denifle,[57] was signed by: four high clergy officials—Bishop William of Auvergne, two abbots from St. Victor, and Lucas, *decanus Parisiensis*; eleven professors of theology[58]—including Albertus Theutonicus (i.e., Albert the Great), Galterus/Gualterus (of Château-Thierry), *cancelarius (universitatis) Parisiensis*, and Robert Coton/Cocon; fourteen professors of decretal law; and, twelve *alii boni viri* from the clergy—among them, again, Dominicans Theobald de Sezanne and Henry of Cologne (Henricus Teutonicus). According to Thomas de Cantimprè, the latter was the main prosecutor during the first proceeding in 1240.[59]

Therefore, only one of these three documents makes no mention of the theology masters. The failure of the Parisian trial report to cite these university representatives might reflect the fact that its final version was edited as part of a Parisian propaganda campaign that aimed to convince the papacy of the authority and legitimacy of the original decision, where the highest ranking clergy carried greatest significance, and thus merited inclusion. Moreover, given that the Paris codex, including the trial record, was copied and edited by a single hand ca. 1248, this entire volume should be viewed as a single source (irrespective of the prior versions of its contents) where the role of the masters, who translated and commented on the Hebrew sources, is unambiguously presented.

On the issue of royal involvement, I would compare royal policy in the Talmud Trial to two other cases from the middle third of the thirteenth century: in 1236, Frederick II summoned a similar combination of political and clerical powers in Hagenau and Augsburg to discuss the blood libel against the Jews of Fulda;[60] twenty years later, in 1263, King James I of Aragon instigated a disputation in his palace in Barcelona. In each case, a monarch took an active role in preparing and conducting an investigation of Jewish Scriptures and beliefs, thereby coordinating an effort that involved lay nobles, Church officials, Jewish apostates, and Jewish community representatives. None of these proceedings could be described as outstanding with regard to their subject matter: anti-talmudic rhetoric and accusations of sacrilege and hostile behavior by Jews toward Christians had already become widespread to such an extent that these actions could be almost described as routine. On the institutional plane, however, they were indeed innovative, by striving to forge an unprecedented constellation of powers that could reconfigure generations-long stable and predictable structures of authority. Royal engagement was essential to this emerging configuration and it reflected the self-image, aspiration, and vision of each of these kings.

The amalgamation of power that took shape during the Talmud Trial, despite its similarities to contemporaneous proceedings at the University of Paris (as listed above), differs on one crucial point: while the other cases might be viewed as internal university matters,[61] during the trial of the Talmud the masters became involved in a political and legal issue that extended beyond academic affairs. This distinction has not yet received serious consideration among the historians who study the changing roles that masters of theology played in external matters. The following selection from William J. Courtenay's discussion of the Parisian Faculty of Theology prior to the reign of Philip the Fair (1285–1314) provides a case in point:

> The reign of Philip the Fair marks a turning point in the relationship of king and university, and especially that of king and masters of theology. Before Philip, the king of France did not call upon members of the University of Paris or of its faculties to help implement royal policy. Nor were masters of theology asked by the king to prepare a learned opinion on a matter of church doctrine or law, or to judge persons outside the university community. All the cases in the thirteenth century, including 1270 and 1277, concerned persons and positions that arose within the faculties of the university, and even the case of the disciples of Amaury de Béne at the beginning of the thirteenth century included persons connected with the university. A new and very different chapter thus begins with Philip the Fair, one that set important precedent.[62]

Remarkably, this passage makes no mention of the extensively documented Talmud Trial. A comparison of the changing roles of pope, king, and masters in the case against the Talmud in 1240 and the 1308 proceeding against the Templars might prove fruitful. While a detailed analysis goes beyond the scope of this chapter, one major contrast is immediately apparent: if the Talmud Trial is marked by cooperation between monarchy and papacy, the action against the Templars—an international and privileged Christian group—is characterized by conflict between these same seats of authority. This factor might explain why the masters of Paris unanimously signed the condemnation of the Talmud whereas, as Courtenay shows, in the case of the Templars, the king was only able to recruit a discrete group of masters to his position.

From a Jewish perspective, this innovative strategic shift in tactics was no less alarming than its possible outcomes; therefore, the early stage of the Paris trial, according to both Hebrew and Latin accounts, was a negotiation on authority and jurisdiction. Rabbi Yehi'el refused to take an oath and negotiated to transfer these proceedings to the papal authority in Rome (the first of his two attempts was successful). Therefore, in the Christian-Jewish context, if the Barcelona event of 1263 strives to make practical use of the old-new scholastic method of public *disputatio*, the Paris event was a catalyst for the new mechanism of inquisitorial control, then starting to take root in Christian society. As Galinsky convincingly demonstrates, the author of the *Vikkuah* desperately attempted to bring the Paris trial in line with long-standing Jewish expectations—namely, a public debate[63]—placing this challenge in the more familiar, less threatening paradigm encountered in Barcelona.

Conclusions: Intellectuals and Power

In this chapter, I have aimed to prove that mid-thirteenth century Paris was uniquely positioned to provide the groundwork for the consolidation of powers whose emergence made possible the new and ominous reception of Judaism by Christian intellectuals. Medieval academic institutions in general, and specifically the thirteenth-century University of Paris, as McLaughlin compellingly argues, "not only claimed freedom but exercised control."[64] Another key to the unique position of Paris is derived from the character of its university, with its complex relationship to both religious and royal lines of authority. King Louis immediately consented to the papal call because he, more than any of his counterparts, had the tools to execute this task. I suggest that his position can best be understood when compared with the two other mutual efforts carried out against Jews by the Church and royal powers during the mid-thirteenth century: Hagenau and Augsburg in 1236 and Barcelona 1263. Furthermore, I posit that the events in Paris relate more closely to the situation in Augsburg than to those in Barcelona.

The most compelling question, which will likely remain unresolved, concerns the potential relationship between the internal Jewish Maimonidean controversy of the 1230s mentioned at the beginning of this study and the anti-talmudic measures in Paris a decade later. In his writings from the 1280s, the Italian Jewish author Hillel of Verona, was the first to suggest a link between these two events.[65] I refer here to his well-known claim that Maimonides's *Guide of the Perplexed* and *Sefer ha-madda'* (*Book of Knowledge*) were burned in Paris, an incident that was directly followed by the burning of the Talmud. Hillel reported that the latter event was interpreted as an expression of divine wrath; and, in response, ashes from both incidents were then mingled.[66]

Hillel's view of Paris as an apt setting for the burning of both Maimonides's writings and the Talmud is surely related to the famous trial of the Talmud and its first documented burning, but it might also be related to his familiarity with the anti-Averroistic acts that took place in Paris during the 1270s, shortly before he composed these letters. If this is accurate, then by pointing out the structural similarities between acts of censorship against the writings of Maimonides versus those against the writings of Aristotle and his Arab interpreters, both of which originated in Paris—the primary locus of intellectual control—he anticipated the intuition of the modern historian Heinrich Graetz[67] by six centuries.

In that light, I would like to add a nuance to the well-known assertions of Amos Funkenstein,[68] Jeremy Cohen,[69] and many others.[70] Rather than positing that the Church made a radical turn during the thirteenth century by bringing intra-Jewish heresies as well as intra-Christian heresies under its jurisdiction, I would assert that the Church was developing systematic mechanisms for intellectual control while expanding its intellectual authority to include all normative groups under Christian dominion, inclusive of Jewish writings. To some degree, until this threatened the most elementary practices of learning and of daily life, European Jewry adjusted quite readily to these new dynamics of intellectual control, as reflected by the intra-Jewish controversies. At the same time, these altered relationships between Christian institutions shattered the established order by creating mechanisms that would remain dominant for centuries, well into the early modern era.

Notes

1. An earlier version of this chapter was presented during a conference at the Center for Advanced Judaic Studies at the University of Pennsylvania, December 2012. At that time, I received many helpful comments from conference participants, including other Fellows at CAJS. I extend special thanks to William Jordan, Sara Lipton, Judah Galinsky, Piero Capelli, Elisheva Baumgarten, and the anonymous readers of this article.

2. For the most detailed descriptions of those mechanisms of control, see Luca Bianchi, *Censure et liberté intellectuelle à l'université de Paris (XIIIe-XIVe siècles)* (Paris, 1999). However, Bianchi seems to pay less attention to royalty as an element in the development of Parisian methods of intellectual control, certainly during the thirteenth century. Two recently completed dissertations provide important analyses of the early thirteenth-century Parisian masters of theology, each focusing on different social and intellectual perspectives. In her study of the theory of knowledge, among other distinctive arts of academic self-reflection, Ayelet Even Ezra significantly contributes to our understanding of Paris as a locus for blurred hierarchies in part due to the masters' own intellectual and religious priorities; see *The Discourse of Knowledge in the Faculty of Theology, Paris, 1220 – 1240* (PhD dissertation, Tel Aviv University, 2011), esp. 26–43. Slightly earlier, Spencer Young submitted his dissertation on this same theological community in Paris, though with an emphasis on different intellectual and social aspects. See *Queen of the Faculties: Theology and Theologians at the University of Paris, c. 1215–c. 1250,* (PhD dissertation, University of Wisconsin-Madison, 2009). William Courtenay's general observations on the early development of academic inquiry raise some crucial issues on the relationship between academic institutions and inquisitorial mechanisms but he seems to overlook the unique role played by Parisian masters. See his "Inquiry and Inquisition: Academic Freedom in Medieval Universities," *Church History* 58 (1989): 168–181.

3. See Jürgen Miethke, "Theologenprozesse in der ersten Phase ihrer institutionellen Ausbildung: Die Verfahren gegen Peter Abaelard und Gilbert von Poitiers," in Jürgen Miethke, *Studieren an mittelalterlichen Universitäten. Chancen und Risiken* (Leiden, 2004), 275–312; R. I. Moore, *The War on Heresy* (Cambridge, MA, 2012), 29–31. Of particular relevance to this question is Peter Godman, *The Silent Masters. Latin Literature and Its Censors in the High Middle Ages* (Princeton, 2000). Although Godman's perspective differs in many respects from the one presented here, his conclusions largely concur with my own, and see note 6.

4. See Y. H. Yerushalmi, "The Inquisition and the Jews of France in the Time of Bernard Gui," *Harvard Theological Review* 63 (1970): 317–376; Jeremy Cohen, *The Friars and the Jews: The Evolution of Medieval Anti-Judaism* (Ithaca, 1982), 78–81; Kenneth Stow, "The Fruit of Ambivalence: Papal Jewry Policies Over the Centuries," in *The Roman Inquisition, the Index and the Jews: Context, Sources and Perspectives,* ed. Stephan Wendehorst (Leiden, 2004), 3–17.

5. For a detailed description of Abelard's process in the context of contemporaneous heresy trials, cf. M. T. Clanchy, *Abelard: A Medieval Life* (Oxford, UK and Cambridge, MA, 1999), 288–325; For Peter's testimony, see Letter 98 in Giles Constable ed., *The Letters of Peter the Venerable* with introduction and notes (Cambridge, MA, 1967), I, 258f.

6. Both the continuity with and break from the twelfth-century methods, which encompassed an ideology of intellectual power that had not yet developed a mechanism for its implementation, and the system of control that was actualized during the thirteenth century reflects the evolution of the institutional corporation of masters described in detail by Godman, *The Silent Masters.* Godman rightly points out that this control mechanism "arose from problems often posed but never solved by the intellectuals of the twelfth [century]" (p. 344). Analyzing the shift toward university learning in the early thirteenth century, Godman asserts that: "Divided among themselves, each of these scholars had only a limited authority of his own; and it was not until after the *magistri*, as a group or a faculty, had learned to collaborate with the authority of the church that conditions existed in which the masters of theology, during and after the 1240s, could function as a semi-synodal body to define doctrine and condemn error." (p. 339 f.).

7. On the relationship between the Maimonidean controversy and the Talmud Trial see Heinrich Graetz, *Geschichte der Juden* (Leipzig, 1894³), VII: 52–54; for a detailed analysis of Gregory's Aristotelian politics, see Bianchi, *Censure et Liberté*, 110–116.

8. For a general overview of the reception of Maimonides's *Guide* in the Latin West, see Jacob Guttmann, *Die Scholastik des dreizehnten Jahrhunderts in ihren Beziehungen zum Judenthum und zur jüdischen Literatur* (Breslau 1902; New York, 1970); Jacob Guttmann, "Der Einfluß der maimonidischen Philosophie auf das christliche Abendland," in Wilhelm Bacher et al., *Moses ben Maimon. Sein Leben, seine Werke und sein Einfluss* (Leipzig, 1908), I: 135–230. Guttmann's description has been revised and updated by Görge K. Hasselhoff, *Dicit Rabbi Moyses. Studien zum Bild von Moses Maimonidesim lateinischen Westen vom 13. bis 15. Jahrhundert* (Würzburg, 2005).

9. I intend to treat this topic in the near future, meanwhile see Azriel Shohat, "Berurim be-farashat ha-pulmos ha-rishon 'al sifré ha-Rambam," *Zion* 36 (1971): 27–60 [Hebrew] and Joseph Shatzmiller, "Li-temunat ha-maḥloket ha-rishona 'al kitvé ha-Rambam," *Zion* 34 (1969):126–144. I recommend Jeremy Cohen's description and annotated bibliography on the variety of scholarly opinions on this topic, see Cohen, *The Friars and the Jews,*52–60.

10. Recently, the various texts related to this event were translated and published together with a comprehensive overview by Robert Chazan, see *The Trial of the Talmud Paris, 1240* (Toronto, 2012). See also Judah Galinsky, "The Different Hebrew Versions of the 'Talmud Trial' of 1240 in Paris," in *New*

Perspectives on Jewish-Christian Relations: In Honor of David Berger, ed. Elisheva Carlebach and Jacob J. Schachter (Leiden, 2012), 109–140; I thank Piero Capelli for allowing me to read his yet unpublished paper, "Jewish Converts in Jewish-Christian Intellectual Polemics in the Middle Ages."

11. It is noteworthy that Paris witnessed both approaches since Pablo later moved from Barcelona to Paris and attempted to apply that same method of disputation there as well, and see Joseph Shatzmiller, *La deuxième controverse de Paris. Un chapitre dans la polémique entre Chrétiens et Juifs au Moyen Age* (Paris-Louvain, 1994).

12. For an enumeration of Donin's charges against the Talmud and a survey of his involvement in the Parisian Talmud controversy in 1240, see Chen Merchavia, *Ha-talmud bi-re'i ha-natsrut* (Jerusalem, 1970), 227–290. For the biographical sources on Donin, see Solomon Grayzel, *The Church and the Jews in the XIIIth Century* (Philadelphia, 1933), 339f. For further discussion, see William Chester Jordan, *The French Monarchy and the Jews: From Philip Augustus to the Last Capetians* (Philadelphia, 1989), 137–141; Israel J. Yuval, *Two Nations in Your Womb: Perceptions of Jews and Christians in Late Antiquity and the Middle Ages* (Berkeley, 2006), 280–284; Yossef Schwartz, "Images of Revelation and Spaces of Knowledge, the Jew, the Christian and the Christian-Jew: Jewish Apostates as Cultural Mediators in Medieval Spain," ed. A. Fidora and Matthias M. Tischler, *Christian North—Moslem South* (Münster, 2011), 267–287, esp. 278f. Judah Galinsky recently drew my attention to a late thirteenth-century legal Hebrew writ of divorce found in many medieval copies of the *Semak* in which one of the persons involved is named "Mattityah who is nicknamed (*ha-mekhunne*) Donin." This may hint at Donin's Jewish name, prior to changing it to Nicholas at the time of his conversion.

13. For a summary of scholarly hypotheses on this subject, see Cohen, *The Friars and the Jews*, 61, n. 19. See also the thesis put forth by Israel M. Ta-Shma, "Rabbi Yehiel de Paris," Ecole pratique des hautes études (Section des sciences religieuses), *Annuaire* XCIX (1990–1991): 215–219.

14. William Chester Jordan, "Marian Devotion and the Talmud Trial of 1240," *Wolfenbütteler Mittelalter-Studien 4.* (Wiesbaden, 1992): 61–76 [reprint in William C. Jordan, *Ideology and Royal Power in Medieval France* (Aldershot, 2001): XI].

15. Fritz I. Baer, "Le-vikkoret ha-vikkuḥim shel R. Yeḥi'el mi-Paris ve-shel R. Moshe ben Naḥman," *Tarbiz* 2 (1931): 172–187, at 172–177.

16. MS Moscow-Guenzburg 1390; Vatican ebr. 324.

17. Galinsky, *Different Hebrew Versions*, 127.

18. Gilbert Dahan, ed., *Le brûlement du Talmud à Paris 1242–1244,* (Nouvelle Gallia Judaïca [1]) (Paris, 1999).

19. The very same mechanism is described by Jürgen Miethke, "Papst, Ortbischof und Universität in den Pariser Theologenprozessen des 13. Jahrhunderts," in Jürgen Miethke, *Studieren an mittelalterlichen Universitäten. Chancen und Risiken* (Leiden, 2004), 313–359. The king is also an actor in some of the cases described by Miethke, and see ibid., pp. 338f., 342.

20. J. M. M. H. Thijssen, "Master Amalric and the Amalricians: Inquisitorial Procedure and the Suppression of Heresy at the University of Paris," *Speculum* 71 (1996): 43–65.

21. J. M. M. H. Thijssen, *Censure and Heresy at the University of Paris, 1200–1400* (Philadelphia, 1998), ix. Despite the chronology indicated in the title of this volume, most of Thijssen's study is dedicated to the condemnation of 1277 and fourteenth-century developments; for an account of earlier acts of censorship cf. Mary M. McLaughlin, *Intellectual Freedom and its Limitations in the University of Paris in the Thirteenth and Fourteenth Centuries* (New York, 1977), 17f.

22. Henricus Denifle, ed., *Chartularium Universitatis Parisiensis* (Paris, 1894–1897) (henceforth CUP).

23. On Jews being linked to philosophy and heresy in popular Christian imagery (e.g., preaching and visual images) from Paris during the first half of the thirteenth century, see Sara Lipton, *Images of Intolerance. The Representation of Jews and Judaism in the Bible moralisée* (Berkeley, 1999), 61, 70–77, 94–111.

24. Miethke, "Papst," 314–317; Thijssen, "*Master Amalric,*" 43–65.

25. CUP, I, 70–72, n. 11–12.

26. CUP, I, 78–80, n. 20.

27. CUP, I, 90–93.

28. CUP I, 106–107, n. 50.

29. CUP, I, 114–115.

30. CUP, I, n. 79, pp. 136–139.

31. CUP, I, n. 87, pp. 143f.

32. Miethke, "Papst," 63–67.

33. CUP, I, n. 128, pp. 170f:

34. CUP, I, n. 130, p. 173; McLaughlin, *Intellectual Freedom*, 211, 424f., n. 181; F. Pelster,"Die Pariser Verurteilung von 1241. Eine Frage der Datierung," *Archivum Fratrum Praedicatorum* 18 (1948): 405–417; William J. Courtenay, "Dominicans and Suspect Opinion in the Thirteenth Century: The Cases of Stephen of Venizy, Peter of Tarentaise, and the Articles of 1270 and 1271," *Vivarium* 32 (1994): 186–195, here 187–189.

35. CUP, I, n. 243, pp. 272–275; McLaughlin, *Intellectual Freedom*, 186f.

36. CUP, I, n. 257, p. 297; n. 277, pp. 315–316.

37. CUP, n. 288, pp. 331–333; 289, pp. 333–335; McLaughlin, *Intellectual Freedom*, 188f.

38. CUP, I, n. 282, pp. 324–326.

39. CUP, I, n. 290, pp. 335–337.

40. CUP, I, n. 432, pp. 486f.

41. CUP, I, n. 473, pp. 543–558.

42. David Behrman, "Volumina vilissima, a Sermon of Eudes de Châteauroux on the Jews and their Talmud," in *Le brûlement du Talmud,* ed. Dahan, 191–209, esp. 191–193; Miethke, "Papst," 328f.

43. Miethke, "Papst," 344.

44. Joseph Koch,"Philosophische und theologische Irrtumlisten von 1270–1329," in Joseph Koch, *Kleine Schriften,* I (Rome, 1973), 423–450.

45. Robert Chazan, "Trial, Condemnation and Censorship: The Talmud in Medieval Europe," in *The Trial of the Talmud Paris, 1240*: 1–93, here 18. This reality is also negatively reflected in the case of Raymond of Toulouse, who is repeatedly blamed for protecting heretics and employing Jews, and see Moore, *War on Heresy*, 241–273.

46. Grayzel, *Church and the Jews*, n. 95, pp. 238–241.

47. Although this conflict is usually portrayed, in less romantic terms, as the consummate struggle between papal "conservative" and royal "liberal" attitudes, it is noteworthy that, before coming into conflict with the papacy, Frederick defined his role as a Catholic king in the Melfi constitution (*Liber Augustalis*) of 1231 in terms that resemble the Capetians' self-perception; see Moore, *War on Heresy*, 268f.

48. Lipton, *Images of Intolerance,* 184, n. 74; Jordan, "Marian Devotion; Jacques Le Goff, "Saint Louis et les juifs," in *Le brûlement du Talmud*, ed. Dahan, 39–46.

49. On the Faculty of Theology's intensified hostility toward philosophy during the first decades of the thirteenth century, its influence at the royal court (esp. via the *Bible moralisée*) and its gradually developing involvement with Jews, see Lipton, *Images of Intolerance*, 97f.

50. And see a similar hypothesis that was recently raised by Chazan, *Trial, Condemnation and Censorship*, 18f.

51. These questions emerged from my discussions with colleagues at the Center for Advanced Judaic Studies in Philadelphia (n. 1 above). I am deeply indebted to Sara Lipton, Talya Fishman, and, especially, to William Jordan for the constructive remarks that helped me to refine my thesis on these points.

52. Despite its appearance as a "protocol" that was recorded as a single work, this codex is actually a compilation that was completed in its current form after 1248, as attested by the reference to Odo, "now the Bishop of Tusculum and the Legate of the Apostolic See to the Holy Land;" and see Isidore Loeb, "La controverse de 1240 sur le Talmud," *Revue des etudes juives* 3 (1881): 39–57, here 55, quoting MS BNF lat. 16558, fol. 230d: *"cancelarium Parisiensem, nunc autem Tusculanum episcopum et apostolice sedis legatum in Terra sancta."*

53. For the Latin text and an English translation, see Grayzel, *Church and the Jews*, 250–253; for a new English rendering by Jean Connell Hoff, based on the Simonsohn translation (*The Apostolic See and the Jews*, I, no. 171), see *The Trial of the Talmud, 1240*, 93–125, here 96.

54. CUP, I, n. 173, 202–204; Grayzel, *Church and the Jews*, 275–278.

55. CUP, 204, 27–30.

56. Stow, *Fruit of Ambivalence*, asserts: "This was a local Parisian affair. And it was moved by the rebellious secular clergy, far more than by the mendicants, as is attested by the mostly secular signatures on the condemnation of 1248" (p. 11). This seems to be an overly bold formulation and, reflecting on the whole process, I am unsure that such a sharp division between papacy, mendicants and seculars can be presumed; nevertheless, this comment accurately depicts a genuinely Parisian initiative.

57. CUP I, n. 178, 209–211; Grayzel, *Church and the Jews*, 278f.

58. Young, *Queen of Faculties*, 60–62; 240f. Young emphasizes that this document is unique, not only for mentioning the involvement of all masters of theology but by recording their names as well. Young therefore uses this list to reconstruct a comprehensive list of faculty members.

59. Tomae Cantipratani OP, *Bonum universale de apibus*, I, 3, Douai, Ex Typographia Baltazaris Belleri 1627, 17–18. The Dominican records describe this as an encounter between the King of France and the Dominicans (here represented

by Henry of Cologne), without acknowledging any involvement from the Pope or the Bishop of Paris and depicting other church authorities (here represented by Walter de Cornut, Archbishop of Sens) in a wholly negative light. See Paul Lawrence Rose, "When Was the Talmud Burnt at Paris? A Critical Examination of the Christian and Jewish Sources and a New Dating: June 1241," *Journal of Jewish Studies* 62 (2011): 324–339, here 329f.; Chazan, *Trial, Condemnation and Censorship*, 22. It is noteworthy that Tomas's exemplum is part of an allegorical portrayal of the sins committed by the higher clergy that makes no attempt to accurately depict these events.

60. On the investigation sponsored by Frederick, see Robert Chazan, *Church, State and Jew in the Middle Ages* (Ann Arbor, 1980), 123–126; Ernst Kantorowitz, *Frederick the Second* (New York, 1957), 413f.; Yuval, *Two Nations*, 278.

61. The case of the Amalrician could be viewed as exceptional but, in fact, it indirectly involved teachings by a formerly prominent university figure.

62. William J. Courtenay, "Learned Opinion and Royal Justice: The Role of Paris Masters of Theology during the Reign of Philip the Fair," in *Law and the Illicit in Medieval Europe*, ed. Ruth Mazo Karras, Joel Kaye, E. Ann Matter (Philadelphia, 2008), 149–163, esp. 150, 155, 159, here 162. This same description also appears in his article in the volume of *Miscellanea Mediaevalia* on the theme, "A Historical Topography of 1308," and see, William J. Courtenay, "The Role of University Masters and Bachelors at Paris in the Templar Affair, 1307–1308," in *1308. Eine Topographie historischer Gleichzeitigkeit [Miscellanea Mediaevalia 35]*, ed. Andreas Speer and David Wirmer (Berlin and New York, 2010), 171–181. See also Jürgen Miethke's article in the same volume, pp. 182–198.

63. Galinsky, *Different Hebrew Versions*, 139f.

64. McLaughlin, *Intellectual Freedom*, 22; this element in McLaughlin's argument effectively modifies Luca Bianchi's criticism, positioning her (and Haskins) to be depicting a romanticized medieval university, as a place of intellectual freedom, and see Bianchi, *Censure et liberté intellectuelle*, 53.

65. Cohen also draws heavily on these passages by Hillel, see Cohen, *The Friars and the Jews*, 59f.; cf. recently Reimund Leicht, "Miracles for the Sake of the Master of Reason. Hillel ben Samuel of Verona's Legendary Account of the Maimonidean Controversy," *Micrologus* 21 (2013): 579–598.

66. Hillel of Verona, *Letter to Maestro Gaio*, fol. 19a-b. Most scholars tend to discount Hillel's evidence as either a highly manipulative polemic or a source that was written too late to be relevant (some fifty years after the events being described). Such dismissal of his writings overlooks the fact that Hillel relies on information that he received in Barcelona, directly from his teacher Jonah Girondi. Hillel's encounter with Jonah has erroneously been dated to the 1260s; however, we have clear evidence that Jonah left Barcelona far earlier, during the early 1240s or early 1250s at the latest. According to this revised timeframe, whatever Hillel learned from Jonah would have been conveyed within a decade of the burning of these Jewish texts in Paris and, thus, might reflect the initial shock among the Jewish leadership. I am indebted to Judah Galinsky for the fruitful dialogue that led me to this realization. For the dates of Jonah's residence in Barcelona, cf. Israel M. Ta-Shma, *Ha-nigle she-banistar: le-ḥeker sheki'é ha-halakhah be-sefer ha-zohar* (Tel Aviv, 2001), 70; Judah D.

Galinsky, "*Sefer arba'ah turim ve-ha-sifrut ha-hilkhattit shel sefarad ba-me'a ha-14: hebbetim historiyyim, sifrutyyim ve-hilkhattiyyim,*" (PhD dissertation, Bar Ilan University, 1999), 18, n. 18. The calculation that Hillel studied with Jonah during the 1260s comes from a misreading of information in this same letter: immediately after stating that he stayed with Jonah in Barcelona until his master left for Toledo, Hillel mentions Jonah's death in Toledo. These contiguous comments led scholars to assume that Jonah had moved to Toledo just before his death (ca. 1264).

67. Above, n. 7.

68. Amos Funkenstein, "Changes in Christian Anti-Jewish Polemics in the Twelfth Century," in *Perceptions of Jewish History* (Berkeley, 1993), 172–201.

69. Cohen, *Friars and the Jews*; Cohen Jeremy, "Scholarship and Intolerance in the Medieval Academy: The Study and evaluation of Judaism in European Christendom,,in *Essential Papers on Judaism and Christianity in Conflict. From Late Antiquity to the Reformation*, ed. Jeremy Cohen (New York and London, 1991), 310–341.

70. Anna Sapir Abulafia, "Jewish-Christians Disputations and the Twelfth-Century Renaissance," *Journal of Medieval Studies* 15 (1989): 105–125; Gilbert Dahan, *La polémique Crétienne contre le Judaïsme au moyen âge* (Paris 1991); Yvonne Friedman, "Anti-Talmudic Invective from Peter the Venerable to Nicolas Donin (1144–1244)," in *Le brûlement du Talmud*, ed. Dahan, 171–189.

PART 2

POLEMICS, PERSECUTIONS, AND
MUTUAL PERCEPTIONS

CHAPTER 7

JOSEPH BEN NATHAN'S *SEFER YOSEF HA-MEKANNÉ* AND THE MEDIEVAL JEWISH CRITIQUE OF CHRISTIANITY

Daniel J. Lasker

One of the major differences between medieval, northern European, Jewish anti-Christian polemic (written in France and Germany) and similar literature written in southern Europe (Iberia, Provence, and Italy) is the almost total lack of philosophical argumentation in the former. In a previous discussion of this phenomenon, I argued that northern European Jewish polemicists were familiar with philosophical argumentation against Christianity, but they generally eschewed its use in their polemical treatises. I used the following formulation: "Most Ashkenazic Jews were not familiar with 'Greek wisdom'; even the intellectuals among them were generally not fluent in philosophy. There is no reason to believe that a polemicist, addressing his book to a Jewish audience which itself was not philosophically sophisticated, would use arguments which even he would regard as foreign."[1] In a second article, I gave a reason why Ashkenazic polemicists eschewed philosophical polemics, asserting that they acted not so much out of their own mindsets or ignorance of these arguments but because their audiences would not have been receptive.[2]

David Berger was critical of my conclusions, responding that both the "polemicists and their audience inhabited the same cultural world," and, therefore, "the philosophical arguments in question did not resonate with the [Ashkenazic polemicists] any more than with their audience." He also claims that these authors were not the intellectual elite (they "stood a cut or more below" them), and the audiences might have been more intellectually sophisticated than the authors were.[3]

In the following, I will revisit northern European polemics a third time with a view to reevaluating my claim that their authors were knowledgeable of southern European rationalist polemics and decided, for one reason or another, to eschew them. I will do this by an analysis of *Sefer Yosef ha-Mekanné* (*The Book of Joseph the Zealous*) by Joseph ben Nathan Official, written in northern France apparently in the second half of the thirteenth century.[4] What I will argue is: (1) the polemical genre, which is almost invariably intimately connected to philosophy, is foreign to northern Europe and was imported from southern Europe; (2) Joseph ben Nathan was a professional polemicist who had more than a passing acquaintance with southern European philosophical or rational argumentation; and (3) northern European polemicists adapted the polemical genre to meet Ashkenazic traditions and modes of thought, thereby almost entirely ridding it of its philosophical connections.

First, an introductory comment: When we say Ashkenazic or northern European polemical treatises, we are referring to three interrelated sources, *Sefer Yosef ha-Mekanné*, *Nitsahon yashan*, or *Nitsahon Vetus* (*The Older Book of Polemic*),[5] and the texts in Rome Hebrew manuscript 53.[6] We should probably count the additions to Joseph Kimhi's *Sefer ha-berit* (*Book of the Covenant*) that seem to have affinity with this material[7] and the few pages of a work called *Teshuvot ha-minim* (*Responses to the Heretics*).[8] The account of the Disputation of Paris, *Vikkuah Rabbenu Yehi'el mi-Paris* (*The Disputation of Rabbi Yehiel of Paris*), apparently also composed by Joseph ben Nathan Official, can be read as a polemic, but it is better seen as a Jewish spin on the proceedings in Paris in 1240 and as a defense of the Talmud; it has no argumentation against Christianity per se (in contrast, for instance, to Nahmanides' account of Barcelona).[9] We also have an account of what Joseph Shatzmiller calls the second Paris disputation.[10] Members of the Prague school of polemicists— Yom Tov Lipmann Muhlhausen, Avigdor Kara, and Menahem Shalem— are not classical northern European polemicists, since these authors are both Central European and obviously influenced by the Sephardic type of philosophical argumentation that had now made its way to the northeast.[11] Their early fifteenth-century dates separate them from the other northern European polemics by over hundred years. Perhaps we could include Isaac ben Abraham Troki, but as a Karaite who spoke a Turkic language, he was certainly not an Ashkenazi. His work does share some aspects with earlier northern European polemics, but the context is very different, since late sixteenth-century Poland/Lithuania was not thirteenth-century France-Germany.[12] In his bibliography of medieval Jewish polemical literature, Judah Rosenthal has quite a number of authors listed under Tsarfat (France), but the vast majority of these authors made the list because of possible polemical material in their non-polemical compositions, such as French exegetes, or because they came from places which are now in France but were not part of France in the Middle Ages, such as what Jews called Provence.[13] Thus, except for *Yosef ha-Mekanné*, *Nitsaḥon yashan*, Rome 53, and perhaps the additions to *Sefer ha-berit*, we really have no more purely northern European polemical treatises. The following conclusions about northern European polemics are based, therefore, on a very small database. The first conclusion is that the polemical genre is non-native to northern Europe. The earliest Jewish anti-Christian polemics were written in Judaeo-Arabic in the ninth century, just as Jews under Islam started experimenting with new literary genres.[14] These genres included halakhic monographs, books of grammar, philosophical treatises, biblical exegesis, epistles, poetry, and more. Jews in Iberia, first Muslim and then Christian, adopted these genres, and, in turn, passed them on to Provence. It was in twelfth-century Iberia that ninth-century Judaeo-Arabic polemics were rendered into Hebrew—both the full translation of *Qiṣṣat mujādalat al-usquf* (*The Account of the Disputation of the Priest*), which became *Sefer Nestor ha-komer* (*The Book of Nestor the Priest*), and two of the anti-Christian chapters of Daud al-Muqammaṣ's '*Ishrūn maqālah* (*Twenty Treatises*), which were included in Judah ben Barzilay al-Bargeloni's *Perush sefer yetsira* (*Commentary on Sefer yetsirah*). It was only natural, then, that the first original Hebrew polemics were written either in northern Spain or in Provence as part of the transfer of Andalusian culture to the Midi, and those polemics, Jacob ben Reuben's *Milḥamot ha-Shem* (*Wars of the Lord*) and Joseph Kimḥi's *Sefer ha-berit* are suffused with Andalusian content.[15]

We should also remember that polemics and philosophy go together. As I have tried to demonstrate for over 35 years, these two areas have influenced each other decisively, including questions of epistemology, the nature of the Divinity, and theodicy.[16] Many polemical authors were also philosophers or rationalist thinkers, from al-Muqammaṣ to Rabbi Hasdai Crescas, Rabbi Joseph Albo, and Don Isaac Abravanel; and many philosophers included anti-Christian passages in their philosophical treatises, such as Rav Saadia Gaon and Rabbi Judah Halevi. In the early modern period, when Moses Mendelssohn participated in anti-Christian polemics, he did so as a philosopher. The dialogical style, going back to Plato, occurs in both philosophical treatises, such as Judah Halevi's *Kuzari* and Solomon ibn Gabirol's *Mekor ḥayyim* (*Fons Vitae/Fountain of Life*), and polemics such as *Sefer ha-berit* and Shem Tov Ibn Shaprut's *Even boḥan* (*Touchstone*).

What about northern Europe? Without entering into a full discussion of which genres are present in Ashkenaz, it is obvious that the polemic was not originally one of them. When Jewish scholars had anti-Christian comments or sentiments, as they assuredly did, they expressed them in commentaries, poetry, and chronicles. I do not believe, as some others do, that Ashkenazic biblical commentaries are replete with polemical comments, but I do not deny that such comments exist.[17] And yet, even the most polemical of the commentators, Joseph Bekhor Shor, did not see fit (as far as we know) to write a polemic; he was satisfied with writing a commentary into which he fit his anti-Christian remarks.[18] Furthermore, I know of no northern European treatises written as dialogues. Thus, when Joseph ben Nathan Official wrote his account of the Paris Disputation, *Vikkuaḥ Rabbenu Yeḥi'el mi-Paris,* and his own *Sefer Yosef ha-Mekanné,* he was doing something revolutionary on the northern European Jewish scene. And it is not unlikely that the origin of this new idea of writing a treatise devoted specifically to polemic in the form of a dialogue came from the family homeland—Provence.[19]

This leads to a second point: the role of Joseph ben Nathan Official the Zealous. Joseph was the brother of Elijah and Asher, the son of Nathan, the son of Joseph, the son of Nathan, the son of Meshulam, the son of Nathan, the son of Todros. And Todros was a Jew from Narbonne. The family became French in the mid-twelfth century when Meshulam moved to Melun, but afterwards Meshulam maintained contact with Provence, just at the time the first original Hebrew anti-Christian polemics were being written there. So, although by Joseph ben Nathan's day, the family had been in northern France for five generations, *Yosef ha-Mekanné* includes Provençal polemical traditions, perhaps passed down inside the Official family. Joseph's citations of arguments offered by various family members would indicate that anti-Christian polemics was the family business.[20]

This fits into my statement that Joseph was what I would call a professional polemicist. I do not mean that he earned his living by polemics, but rather that he did not engage in polemics in a haphazard or superficial manner. He trained himself for his role of zealous defender of Judaism. He records extensive discussions with Christian clergy and apostate Jews, and even if not all of these accounts are reliable, they must represent some sort of actual interchanges. He also consulted with Christian converts to Judaism; these proselytes feature prominently in *Yosef ha-Mekanné* despite what must have been their small numbers in northern Europe.

Furthermore, unlike the overwhelming majority of his contemporary Jews, even the most learned of them, Joseph knew Latin, as we can see in the extensive transcriptions of New Testament verses into what I would call Judaeo-Latin and Kirsten Fudeman would probably call Hebraico-Latin.[21] Perhaps Joseph was assigned the job of writing up the Jewish account of the Paris Disputation, *Vikkuaḥ Rabbenu Yeḥi'el mi-Paris,* specifically because of his knowledge of Latin since the proceedings were apparently conducted in that language. We know this because the Jewish narrative records that the talmudic story of Jesus's fate in what R. Travers Herford euphemistically translates as "boiling filth" was recited in the vernacular so that the Queen would understand it.[22] If this passage was read in the vernacular, the rest of the disputation must have been conducted in Latin, and Joseph's knowledge of that language and of Christianity would have been of much value to Rabbenu Yeḥi'el and his Jewishly learned, but perhaps Christianly challenged, colleagues.

What else did Joseph know? Passages in his book seem to have been borrowed from the three twelfth-century Hebrew polemics all of which have Sephardi or Provençal provenance: *Sefer Nestor ha-komer, Sefer ha-berit,* and *Milḥamot ha-Shem.* He quotes at length Saadia's proofs in his *Emunot ve-de'ot* (*Opinions and Beliefs*) that the Messiah had still not come. He also cites Saadia in the context of the correct interpretations of Gen. 1:26 ("Let us make man") and Gen. 18 (the three men who visit Abraham), and in one manuscript there is a reflection of Saadia's refutation of those who believe in abrogation of the commandments. All of these arguments are found in the anti-Christian sections of *Emunot ve-de'ot.* This means that Joseph also had access to Saadia's philosophical refutation of the Christian trinity in book two of *Emunot ve-de'ot,* but that he chose not to use it.[23] Furthermore, in the context of the correct interpretation of Genesis 18, Joseph also mentions Nissim Gaon, Solomon ibn Gabirol, and Abraham ibn Ezra.[24] This list of authorities indicates that Joseph was well acquainted with Christian doctrines and with a wide range of southern European Jewish refutations of those doctrines including rational ones employing philosophical terminology. Nevertheless, Joseph did not use any of that argumentation or terminology. In light of the literature with which Joseph had familiarity, the absence of such terminology or argumentation could not have been from ignorance of southern European Hebrew treatments of Christian theological doctrines.

This point is reinforced by a passage in Rome Ms. 53 that may or may not have been authored by the same Joseph ben Nathan Official. After the similar polemic which we find in *Sefer Yosef ha-Mekanné,* near the end we suddenly have a passage which reflects philosophical polemic—God is said to be three, the father, the son and the "spirit of impurity."[25] The father is the governing power of the Creator; the son is life since he lives, and the spirit is wisdom. Furthermore, the trinity is compared to the sun which is the sun itself, its light and the combination of the two of them.[26] The polemicist's answer is not very impressive—the sun's power is much greater than the light on the Earth, and, therefore, they are not equal, and besides God's wisdom is not separate from Him. In addition, Jesus could not have been a son, despite Ps. 2:7 ("You are my son; I have given birth to you today"), because Exod. 4:22 says that Israel is God's son. What begins as a philosophical argument quickly changes into an exegetical one.[27]

And that leads to a third point: if the idea of a polemical treatise was imported from the south, and if Joseph ben Nathan was the importer, why is his book so different from its prototypes? The answer is that he adapted southern European models to the northern European mentality. Thus, some things remained the same, such as the large number of exegetical arguments and the book by book account of Christian arguments. This is because exegesis is a northern European specialty; after all, the commentary is *the* classical northern European genre. But notice how Jacob ben Reuben begins his exegetical chapters with a theological infrastructure that goes back to Gilbert Crispin (a northern European but whose works obviously made it to the south);[28] all of that is missing in *Yosef ha-Mekanné*. Exegesis is merely exegesis.

The vulgar language of *Yosef ha-Mekanné* is also characteristic of northern Europe. It is true that there is no dearth of vulgarity in the south and in materials which were written in Judaeo-Arabic—Mary's filthy innards and genitals were a favorite subject of Jewish polemicists under Islam and in southern Europe[29] (as they were of the Islamic refuters[30] and the Christian defenders of incarnation, such as Odo of Tournai in his *Disputation with Leo the Jew*[31]). But it is only in the north that Mary is consistently referred to as "Ḥarya" (namely, "excrement"); that the "Holy Spirit" is the "Spirit of Impurity"; that the cross is the warp and woof; that the apostle Peter turns into the "firstling of the donkey" (*peter ha-ḥamor*); and so on.[32] No southern European Jewish polemicist records his father's urinating on a cross in the presence of a bishop as does Joseph Official.[33] Northern European Jews were used to employing coarse epithets when referring to Christians and Christian sancta and that style becomes part of this new genre of polemics.

Furthermore, the dialogic style is replaced by insulting references to the holders of the Christian views, such as those who "bark." In the Paris Disputation, *Vikkuaḥ Rabbenu Yeḥi'el mi-Paris*, presumably recorded by Joseph ben Nathan Official, Nicholas Donin, the apostate initiator of the accusations against the Talmud, is alternately called a heretic, an ass, despicable, foolish, a rebellious son, wild donkey, malignant thorn, scoundrel, and the enemy, among other choice phrases used to describe Donin, "may his bones rot."[34] Joseph makes similar insulting comments about the interlocutors in *Sefer Yosef ha-Mekanné*. Rabbi Yeḥi'el, in contrast, is the angel of the Lord, the man of God, he who counsels miraculously. Even when Jacob ben Reuben tells his Christian challenger that the latter would accept Jacob's words if he had a brain in his skull, Jacob still praises him as a learned philosopher.[35] Northern Europeans make no such concessions to their Christian adversaries.

The arguments adduced herein indicate that Joseph ben Nathan Official the Zealous was well familiar with southern European Jewish rationalist arguments against Christianity and, yet, he almost completely ignored them in his book. It is unlikely that he did not understand them, and while they were undoubtedly foreign to his world outlook, that need not have stopped him from adapting them if he thought they would be convincing arguments. We must conclude that he eschewed these arguments as they would not have been convincing to an audience which was unfamiliar with the rationalistic mindset. Unlike Joseph ben Nathan, his potential readers had not been exposed to southern European polemics. Therefore, Joseph had to adapt those polemics to northern European needs. He was writing for an audience which would appreciate exegesis and insults, and that is what he gave them. I reiterate, therefore, my previous statements that northern European polemicists, indeed, knew philosophical arguments but they did not use them because of their audiences. But why write a polemic at all? Northern European Jews had lived under Christianity for centuries without a perceived need for treatises that were dedicated solely to a refutation of the majority religion. They had exegetical literature that gave authoritative Jewish interpretations of problematic verses. They had poetry and historical chronicles that insulted Christians and berated their behavior. Why did Joseph suddenly adopt a southern European genre?

As one who rejects any necessary connection between Christian pressure and the Jewish critique of Christianity,[36] I think in this case the answer is indeed the tenuous position of the Jewish community of France following the Disputation of Paris and in light of the blood libels. Joseph cites the words of quite a number of Jewish apostates in his book, some of whom argue that Jews no longer have hope of redemption, perhaps one of the reasons for their apostasy. In this situation, Joseph must have felt that the old genres were no longer efficacious. He wrote up the account of the Paris Disputation, *Vikkuah Rabbenu Yehi'el mi-Paris*, and then he went and wrote the first northern European full-fledged anti-Christian polemical treatise. The author of *Nitsahon yashan* followed his lead. But the polemical genre never really caught on in northern Europe. Without a rationalist infrastructure, northern European polemic remained a collection of exegetical comments and insults. For the full flavor of a sophisticated, sustained ongoing critique of Christianity, one has to look to southern Europe, not to the north.

Notes

* Research on this paper was conducted while I was the Corcoran Visiting Professor in the Center for Christian-Jewish Learning at Boston College.
1. Daniel J. Lasker, "Jewish Philosophical Polemics in Ashkenaz," in *Contra Iudaeos: Ancient and Medieval Polemics Between Jews and Christians*, ed. Ora Limor and Guy Stroumsa (Tübingen, 1996), 195–213.
2. Idem., "Popular Polemics and Philosophical Truth in the Medieval Jewish Critique of Christianity," *Journal of Jewish Thought and Philosophy* 8:2 (1999): 243–259.
3. See David Berger, "Polemic, Exegesis, Philosophy, and Science: On the Tenacity of Ashkenazic Modes of Thought," *Simon Dubnow Institute Yearbook* 8 (2009): 29–32.
4. Ed. Judah Rosenthal (Jerusalem, 1970). For a recent overview of this work, see Harvey J. Hames, "Urinating on the Cross: Christianity as Seen in the *Sefer Yoseph Ha-mekaneh* (ca. 1260) and in Light of Paris 1240," in *Ritus Infidelium. Miradas interconfesionales sobre las prácticas religiosas en la Edad Media*, Collection de la Casa de Velázquez (138), ed. José Martínez Gázquez and John Victor Tolan (Madrid, 2013), 209–220.

5. See David Berger, *The Jewish-Christian Debate in the High Middle Ages: A Critical Edition of the Nitsahon Vetus with an Introduction, Translation, and Commentary* (Philadelphia, 1979).

6. Ephraim Elimelekh Urbach, "Etudes sur la literature polèmique au Moyen-Age," *Revue des études juives* 100 (1935): 49–77.

7. Joseph Kimḥi, *Sefer ha-berit u-vikkuḥé Radak 'im ha-natsrut*, ed. Ephraim Talmage (Jerusalem, 1974), 56–68. The French provenance of the book can be seen by the author's mention of his grandfather, apparently Eliezer of Metz, and the citation from Rabbi Joseph Kara (p. 57). See also Joseph Shatzmiller, *La deuxième controverse de Paris* (Paris-Louvain, 1994), 56, n. 187.

8. Judah Rosenthal, ed., *Meḥkarim u-mekorot* (Jerusalem, 1967), 1: 368–372. The author mentions Isaac of Troyes, but the date of the work is unknown.

9. The attribution of the account of the Paris disputation to Joseph Official is based on a colophon in the Paris manuscript of the disputation; see *Sefer Yosef ha-Mekanné*, 141. There is no adequate edition of the Disputation of Paris. See S. Grünbaum, ed., *Vikkuaḥ Rabbenu Yeḥi'el mi-Paris* (Thorn, 1873); *Vikkuaḥ Rabbenu Yeḥi'el mi-Paris*, ed. Reuven Margaliot (Lvov, [n.d.]). Piero Capelli is preparing a critical edition of the *Disputation*, and I thank him for sharing his work with me. For the possibility that the Moscow manuscript is superior to the Paris manuscript, see Judah Galinsky, "The Different Hebrew Versions of the 'Talmud Trial' of 1240 in Paris," in *New Perspectives on Jewish-Christian Relations: In Honor of David Berger*, ed. Elisheva Carlebach and Jacob J. Schacter (Leiden and Boston, 2012), 109–140.

10. Joseph Shatzmiller, *Deuxième controverse*. There are some southern European aspects of this account but they seem to be there since they were introduced by Pablo (Christiani?), such as *personas* and "rational commandments."

11. See Lasker, "Jewish Philosophical Polemics in Ashkenaz."

12. *Ḥizuk emunah* (*Strengthening of Faith*), ed. David Deutsch (Sohrau/Breslau [s.n.], 1873); on the work and its context, see, for example, Golda Akhiezer, "The Karaite Isaac ben Abraham of Troki and his Polemics against Rabbanites," in *Tradition, Heterodoxy and Religious Culture: Judaism and Christianity in the Early Modern Period*, ed. Chanita Goodblatt and Howard Kreisel (Be'er Sheva, 2007), 437–468.

13. Judah Rosenthal, "Sifrut ha-vikkuaḥ ha-'anti-notsrit 'ad sof ha-me'ah ha-shemoneh-'esreh," *Areshet* 2 (1960): 130–179.

14. See Daniel J. Lasker, "The Jewish Critique of Christianity Under Islam in the Middle Ages," *Proceedings of the American Academy for Jewish Research*, 57 (1991): 121–153. For a discussion of the impact of Arabic literature on the new Jewish genres, see Rina Drory, *Models and Contacts. Arabic Literature and its Impact on Medieval Jewish Culture* (Leiden, Boston, Köln, 2000), esp. 126–146.

15. Daniel J. Lasker, "The Jewish-Christian Debate in Transition: From the Lands of Ishmael to the Lands of Edom," in *Judaism and Islam: Boundaries, Interaction, and Communication*, ed. Benjamin Hary, et al. (Leiden and Boston, 2000), 53–65.

16. See, for example, Daniel J. Lasker, "The Impact of Interreligious Polemic on Medieval Philosophy," in *Beyond Religious Borders: Interaction and Intellectual Exchange in the Medieval Islamic World*, ed. David M. Freidenreich and Miriam Goldstein (Philadelphia, 2012), 115–123; 200–203.

17. Idem., "Rashi and Maimonides on Christianity," in *Between Rashi and Maimonides: Themes in Medieval Jewish Thought, Literature and Exegesis*, ed. Ephraim Kanarfogel and Moshe Sokolow (Jersey City, 2010), 3–21.

18. Bekhor Shor was also the French exegete most influenced by French rationalism; see Meir (Martin I.) Lockshin, "Ha'im Yosef Bekhor Shor pashtan?," in *Iggud; mivḥar ma'amarim be-madd'é ha-yahadut*, 1 (2007): 161–172; and see Avraham Grossman, *Ḥakhmé tsarfat ha-rishonim* (Jerusalem, 1995), 472.

19. Both Jacob ben Reuben's *Milḥamot ha-Shem* and Joseph Kimḥi's *Sefer ha-berit* are in the form of dialogues. On the connection between dialogue and philosophy, see Aaron W. Hughes, *The Art of the Dialogue in Jewish Philosophy* (Bloomington and Indianapolis, 2008).

20. On Joseph's lineage and family, see *Sefer Yosef ha-Mekanné*, xx–xxiv, based on Zadoq Kahn, "Etude sur le livre de Joseph le Zélateur," *Revue des études juives* 1 (1880): 234–246. On Provençal traditions in northern European polemics, see Joel E. Rembaum, "A Reevaluation of a Medieval Polemical Manuscript," *AJS Review* 5 (1980): 81–99.

21. See Kristen Fudeman, *Vernacular Voices* (Philadelphia and Oxford, 2010). The connection between the Provençal background of the Official family and the arrival of the polemical genre in northern Europe is also suggested by Jeremy Cohen, "Towards a Functional Classification of Jewish anti-Christian Polemic in the High Middle Ages," in *Religionsgespräche in Mittelalter*, ed. Bernard Lewis and Friedrich Niewöhner (Wiesbaden, 1992), 103.

22. *Vikkuaḥ Rabbenu Yeḥi'el mi-Paris*, 15; See Hyam Maccoby, *Judaism on Trial* (Rutherford, NJ, 1982), 156 (who mistranslates the passage). See Daniel J. Lasker, "Latin into Hebrew and the Medieval Jewish-Christian Debate," in *Latin-into-Hebrew. Volume 1: Studies*, ed. Gad Freudenthal and Resianne Fontaine (Leiden and Boston, 2013), 333–347. For a new discussion and translation of the disputation, see *The Trial of the Talmud: Paris, 1240*. Hebrew texts translated by John Friedman; Latin texts translated by Jean Connell Hoff; historical essay by Robert Chazan (Toronto, 2012).

23. Saadia's work was available to Joseph in a paraphrastic translation; see Ronald C. Kiener, "The Hebrew Paraphrase of Saadia Gaon's *Kitāb al-amānāt wa'l-i'tiqādāt*," (PhD dissertation, University of Pennsylvania, 1984). Saadia's theory of attributes, refutation of the trinity and discussion of the Christian interpretations of Biblical verses 2:5–7, Saadia Gaon, *The Book of Beliefs and Opinions*, trans. Samuel Rosenblatt (New Haven, 1948) 103–110 is on 92–100. His discussion of abrogation (3:7–9, Rosenblatt, 157–173) is on 145–157; and see *Yosef ha-Mekanné*, 37, n.3. The discussion of the Messiah (8:7–9, Rosenblatt, 312–322) is not included in Kiener's edition (which includes Books 1–5 only); see *Yosef ha-Mekanné*, 3–6. This latter passage is found in Jacob ben Reuben's *Milḥamot ha-Shem*, ed. Judah Rosenthal (Jerusalem, 1963), 157–161. If the evidence from Rosenthal's editions is correct, Joseph did not just copy from Jacob in which case he had the paraphrase in front of him. Prof. Kiener's full edition of the paraphrase is scheduled to be published by the Israel Academy of Sciences and Humanities; I would like to thank him for sharing the text with me before publication.

24. *Yosef ha-Mekanné*, 33.

25. For this type of vulgarity, see below.

26. The identification of the persons of the trinity with divine attributes and the use of example of a natural phenomenon as an image of the trinity are characteristics of philosophical polemics; see Daniel J. Lasker, *Jewish Philosophical Polemics against Christianity in the Middle Ages* (New York, 1977; 2nd ed., Oxford and Portland, OR, 2007), 63–76, 93–103.

27. Judah Rosenthal, "Divrei vikkuaḥ mi-tokh sefer *Yosef ha-Mekanné* (nusaḥ ktav-yad roma 53)," *Kovets al yad* 8 (1976): 322.

28. *Milḥamot ha-Shem*, 23–40; and see David Berger, "Gilbert Crispin, Alan of Lille, and Jacob ben Reuben," *Speculum* 49 (1974): 34–47 (reprinted in David Berger, *Persecution, Polemic, and Dialogue. Essays in Jewish-Christian Relations* [Boston, 2010], 227–244).

29. See, for example, Daniel J. Lasker and Sarah Stroumsa, *The Polemic of Nestor the Priest*, vol. 1 (Jerusalem, 1996): 53, 57, 59, 63, 67, 68, 98, 114–115.

30. See, for example, Dominique Sourdel, "Un pamphlet musulman anonyme d'époque 'abbāside contre les chrétiens," *Revue des études islamiques* 34 (1966): 1–33.

31. Odo of Tournai, *On Original Sin: and A Disputation With the Jew, Leo, Concerning the Advent of Christ, the Son of God; Two Theological Treatises*, translated with an introduction and notes by Irven M. Resnick (Philadelphia, 1994), 95.

32. Berger usually glosses over these usages in his translation of *Nitsaḥon yashan*; see *Debate*, 302. For a list of vulgarities in the work, see Mordechai Breuer, ed., *Sefer nitsaḥon yashan (Nitsahon Vetus)* (Ramat-Gan, 1978), 195.

33. *Yosef ha-Mekanné*, 14.

34. On the image of Donin in the account of the Disputation of Paris, see Saadia R. Eisenberg, "Reading Medieval Religious Disputation: The 1240 'Debate' Between Rabbi Yeḥiel of Paris and Friar Nicholas Donin" (PhD dissertation, University of Michigan, 2008), 81–88.

35. *Milḥamot ha-Shem*, 5, 13. And 200 years later the Iberian, Shem Tov ibn Shaprut thought that Jacob's tone was too acerbic to be copied; see José-Vicente Niclós, *Šem Ṭob Ibn Šapruṭ. "La Piedra de Toque" (Eben Bohan). Una Obra de Controversia Judeo-Cristiana* (Madrid, 1997), 7.

36. A good example of this is the proliferation of Jewish anti-Christian polemics in Islamic countries in the absence of a missionary threat. In general, see my "The Jewish Critique of Christianity—In Search of a New Narrative," *Studies in Christian-Jewish Relations* 6 (2011): 1–9.

CHAPTER 8

HOW, WHEN, AND TO WHAT DEGREE WAS THE JEWISH-CHRISTIAN DEBATE TRANSFORMED IN THE TWELFTH AND THIRTEENTH CENTURIES?

David Berger

Discussions of transformations—or lack thereof—in Jewish-Christian polemic in the High Middle Ages traditionally begin with reference to Amos Funkenstein's 1968 article in *Zion*, which then appeared in abridged form in *Viator* and with various modifications in his 1993 book, *Perceptions of Jewish History*.[1] Thus, in 1982, Jeremy Cohen set the stage for his own analysis by expressing reservations about Funkenstein's thesis;[2] in 1996, the first paragraph of Daniel Lasker's assessment of the twelfth century as a turning point in polemic addresses Funkenstein's argument;[3] and Ora Limor's recently published article[4] contrasting the Barcelona and Majorca disputations also begins with Funkenstein although the thrust of her concerns lies elsewhere.

I cannot help but defer to the judgment of such distinguished scholars, and so I too will approach the question before us with initial reference to Funkenstein's thesis. Funkenstein argued that old-fashioned polemics resting primarily on biblical proof-texts were joined in the twelfth century by works emphasizing unaided reason as a means of establishing the truth of Christianity. The prime text here is Anselm's *Cur Deus Homo*. This is not itself a polemical work, but Anselm probably influenced Gilbert Crispin[5] and may have had an impact on the polemic of Odo of Tournai (or Cambrai) on the incarnation[6] as well as the *Dialogus* attributed to William of Champeaux.[7] In addition to the new emphasis on *ratio*, says Funkenstein, we begin to encounter arguments based on the Talmud asserting that it is blasphemous and, more important, that it constitutes heresy—a set of diabolical Jewish secrets. The primary evidence here comes from Peter the Venerable,[8] although Petrus Alfonsi's citation of Talmudic anthropomorphisms has also been presented in John Tolan's study as an assertion that it is a heretical work.[9] The other approach to the Talmud—to wit, its use to demonstrate the truth of Christianity—also makes its first appearance in the twelfth century in Alan of Lille's *De Fide Catholica Contra Haereticos*.[10]

Some scholars, most notably Jeremy Cohen, have argued that the real watershed belongs in the thirteenth century. Needless to say, an assessment of continuity and change in thirteenth-century polemic depends on one's evaluation of the depiction by Funkenstein and others of the Jewish-Christian debate in the twelfth. Moreover, as Lasker's article emphasizes, assessing the impact of new Christian approaches requires an examination of Jewish works as well. On both counts, we need to recognize several methodological constraints. First, there is the elementary consideration that the boundary between centuries is arbitrary. If we see Petrus Alfonsi or Peter the Venerable as bearers of a significant new message with an uninterrupted history, we can surely speak of the twelfth century as the source and incubator of that message. Alan of Lille, on the other hand, wrote his relevant work between 1185 and 1195; this, to be sure, is the twelfth century, but had he written in 1201, our periodization for the Christological use of the Talmud would hardly have changed.

This point also bears on a second methodological concern associated with the paucity of sources. Alan's use of the Talmudic assertion that the world will last 6,000 years—2,000 chaos, 2,000 Torah, and 2,000 the messianic age—introduced what was to become a central weapon in the Christian polemical arsenal, but this citation is the only example of such Christian utilization of the Talmud before the third quarter of the thirteenth century.[11] (I regard this use of the Talmud as considerably more striking than the few other allegedly similar citations that scholars have noted, and so I follow Funkenstein by placing it in a category of its own.) On the one hand, Alan's lack of familiarity with the Talmud means that this argument had gained enough currency to have come to his attention through other channels; on the other, it is difficult to attribute great historical significance to a lone quotation. Similarly, if the argument that the Talmud is a heretical, satanic work appears in Peter the Venerable and nowhere else (or hardly anywhere else), we can see the reference as the harbinger of future developments but not as an indication of a deep change or even as a key influence on the later phenomenon. The more time that passes between the work in question and the later development, the more wary we must become about drawing a direct line between the two. And so we come to the paucity of Jewish polemics. Lasker had precisely two twelfth-century polemics to work with—Jacob b. Reuben's *Milḥamot ha-Shem* (*Wars of the Lord*) and Joseph Kimhi's *Sefer ha-berit* (*Book of the Covenant*)—both written around 1170 in southern France. They are surely valuable in revealing aspects of polemical interchange in that narrow time and space, but we must be careful not to extrapolate beyond the area that we can assess in a reasonably informed fashion.

We shall eventually have to address issues that Funkenstein did not engage, but his typology serves as a convenient means of organizing the discussion. Let us begin, then, with the innovative Christian use of reason. There is no question that many twelfth-century Christian works are suffused with references to *ratio* as a means of demonstrating Christian truth. Anna Sapir Abulafia has devoted the better part of an entire book to an exploration of this theme, arguing that some Christians—here again Peter the Venerable is the primary figure—had begun to question the degree to which Jews, who were after all impervious to reason, were fully human.[12] The rhetoric and even the substance of arguments from *ratio* appear already in Crispin's late eleventh-century work, and Lasker has noted that both twelfth-century Jewish polemics stress the resort to reason.

Nonetheless, I believe that Gilbert Dahan was correct in a very brief passage in his work on Christian polemic against Judaism to note the non-philosophical nature of most of the arguments from reason in pre-fourteenth-century works.[13] That the terminology of "reason" was sometimes invoked for purely Scriptural arguments did not escape the notice of Sapir Abulafia either and, in such cases, we must markedly discount its importance. Of course, the use of the term tells us something, but substance matters, to put the point moderately, at least as much as language. If we are to trust Bernhard Blumenkranz—and he certainly deserves the presumption of trustworthiness—the first person to assert explicitly that he was going to use an argument based on reason without recourse to Scripture was hardly an arch-rationalist. Peter Damian, writing as early as the mid-eleventh century, declared, "With the prophetic passages having been set forth, it pleases us to contend with you by reason alone."[14] However, as I noted in my very first publication, the argument itself—that the interminable Jewish exile can be explained only by the sin of the crucifixion—was very far from novel and does not appeal to *ratio* in any innovative sense.[15] When Avraham Grossman sought to provide an example of the new Christian emphasis on *ratio* (*tevunah sikhletanit*), he also fixed on the argument from the Jewish exile.[16] This striking choice of the very same point made by Damian serves to underscore the lack of novelty in many arguments labeled rational.

The next level of *ratio* is philosophical, but here again we need to be sensitive to the use to which such arguments are put. On quite rare occasions, Christians maintained that a disputed doctrine could be demonstrated by reason alone, but, for the most part, philosophy was mobilized only to show that an apparently unreasonable doctrine is possible. To the degree that specific arguments of this sort appear for the first time in the twelfth or thirteenth century, the fact that they do not directly challenge Jewish belief does not diminish their novelty, but it does diminish their danger to Jews and, therefore, their ultimate significance. Moreover, some of these arguments are, in fact, not novel but go back to the patristic age and are reflected in philosophical discourse in the Islamic world preceding our period.

If we look at the one late twelfth-century Jewish polemic that cites Christian philosophical contentions characterized as arguments based on "*sekhel*," we find that Jacob ben Reuben's interlocutor does begin with a very strong declaration: "I will show you from the wisdom of the intellect that everyone with understanding should truly believe in the worship of the trinity."[17] The continuation, however, presents what Lasker has characterized as an "image" of the trinity—to wit, a glowing coal consisting of matter, fire, and flame—and the argument ends in a fashion guaranteed to disappoint the expectations raised by the opening promise: "When you see this among one of the created entities, you are obligated not to express wonderment with respect to the Creator, for everything is in accordance with his will. Thus, I believe and strengthen myself in the worship of the trinity."[18]

The next argument from reason alone reported by Jacob also proffers a strong assertion—that God recognized that the world cannot be saved without His entering the womb of a woman who was and would remain a virgin. However, although Jacob provides a refutation, the contention is presented almost as an aside, and, in the final analysis, all the Christian argues is that it is possible for divinity to enter a womb without contamination. Following this, we are presented with various scenarios imagining a king's forced or voluntary degradation, with the Christian maintaining and the Jew denying that some of them render the incarnation plausible, but once again (despite the longstanding availability of *Cur Deus Homo*), there is no argument from reason that even purports to demonstrate that God in fact became or had to become man.[19]

Thus—the *language* of *ratio* as distinct from *auctoritas* or of *sekhel* as distinct from *ketuvim* appears and even becomes standard in some Christian works and in Jewish circles familiar with more sophisticated Christian polemics, but its polemical force leaves much to be desired. The Christian formula, we recall, was 100 years old by the time we get to *Milḥamot ha-Shem* and *Sefer ha-berit*. After all this time, it manifests itself in the former work in the relatively weak fashion that we have just examined. As to *Sefer ha-berit*, Lasker notes that it uses the rhetoric of *sekhel* constantly but does not contain a section devoted to rational arguments; it surely presents no argument designed to provide a philosophical proof of the validity of a Christian doctrine.

As I have already noted, the use of the term reason for Scriptural arguments is, from a substantive perspective, window dressing, even if it is revealing window dressing. Arguments for the christological interpretation of biblical verses are arguments from *auctoritas* par excellence, and they do not change one whit if they are described as so compelling that any reasonable person will be persuaded by them. It is true that such an assertion can lead to a more hostile perception of the unreasonable Jew, which is manifestly a matter of deep seriousness, but the consequences do not follow from any innovation in the argumentation itself.

In the thirteenth century, by far the most sophisticated philosophical polemic by a Jew was that of Moses of Salerno. The twenty pages of the printed edition consist almost entirely of Jewish arguments directed against fundamental Christian doctrines as well as refutations of Christian responses to those arguments. At one point, Moses says clearly that he does not need to deal with efforts at affirmative demonstration of the doctrines in question. "It is known," he writes, "that Christians have no proof for the unity of the threefold God other than the analogies with the sun, fire, and the soul."[20] Toward the very end, however, we finally encounter one argument that actually attempts a philosophical demonstration of a Christian doctrine. Since God can be shown to be intellect, one who engages in intellection, and the object of intellection, he is thus triune (pp. xviii–xix).[21] Setting aside this exceptional argument, and keeping in mind the unusually philosophical character of Moses' polemic, we can assert with some confidence that *ratio* in the strong, philosophical sense did not pose a major threat to Jews in the twelfth or thirteenth centuries. To a significant degree, Aquinas's position—noted by Funkenstein—that the mysteries of the faith can be shown to be consistent with reason but not demonstrable by reason underscored the Jewish advantage in this portion of the polemical arena and helped to undermine further the already meager efforts to provide such demonstrations. At the same time, there is no denying that Jewish self-confidence was greatly reinforced by the conviction that Christian beliefs were logically indefensible, and from that perspective, arguments that they were in fact within the realm of possibility decidedly mattered.

In thirteenth-century France, we have two major polemical works: Meir of Narbonne's *Milḥemet mitsvah* (*Religious War*) in the South[22] and *Sefer Yosef ha-Mekanné* (*The Book of Joseph the Zealous*) in the North.[23] As we might expect, the former contains some philosophical material, but the latter does not; neither does the *Nitsaḥon Vetus* (*Nitsaḥon yashan*, *The Older Book of Polemic*), the other major polemic from the Ashkenazic orbit, in this case from Ashkenaz proper,[24] nor—with one exception—does the material in Rome manuscript 53, a mélange of Ashkenazic polemic. This characteristic underscores the point about geography and culture rather than periodization. Not only do these works not utilize or react to *ratio* in the strong sense; they do not even use the rhetoric of *ratio*. Whatever importance we may wish to ascribe to arguments from reason, we must keep in mind their restriction to limited cultural contexts.[25]

Such context is relevant to another consideration as well. *Milḥamot ha-Shem* and *Sefer ha-berit* are relatively restrained in their characterization of Christianity and Christians. *Sefer Yosef ha-Mekanné* and the *Nitsahon Vetus* are not. If we confined our attention to the polemical genre alone, we would be tempted to say that the thirteenth century gave birth to the use of profoundly insulting rhetoric or at least that polemic was transformed in that century by its utilization of such rhetoric. But it is obvious that the thirteenth century has nothing to do with this development, which is found in northern Europe almost from time immemorial. It is the product of a culture, not of a century or a genre. Once Ashkenazic Jews began writing polemical works—which happened in the thirteenth century—they naturally incorporated the tone that marked their discourse about Christianity in the eleventh and twelfth.[26]

While it is hardly necessary to demonstrate this, I point out a remarkably uninformed passage in the prefatory section added by Funkenstein to the version of his article published in *Perceptions of Jewish History*.[27] Here, he recognizes the existence of such rhetoric as a characteristic of Ashkenazic popular culture but inexplicably maintains that it is not to be found in formal polemics. By the time Funkenstein's book appeared, convenient editions of *Sefer Yosef ha-Mekanné* and the *Nitsahon Vetus* had long been available. Nonetheless, here is what we are told:

> Religious polemics…hardly reflects…the whole gamut of attitudes of one religion towards the other. For one thing, the written treatises seldom reflect the situations and arguments of a live altercation. And then, written polemics focuses, overemphasizes dogmatic issues; it tends to reflect the normative, official stand of each camp. Officially, as we shall see, both Judaism and Christianity developed a doctrine of relative tolerance towards each other. Judaism (in Christian terms) was to remain as a testimony to the veracity of Christianity until the end of days. Christianity (in Jewish terms) was eventually classified as a monotheistic religion of sorts—at least removed from the category of idolatry. How different though were the less official voices! The very language of the *tossafists* (sic) deciding that Christians are not idolatrous testifies to the rift between reason and sentiment: "As to today's idolaters, we hold it that they do not worship idolatry." [28]
>
> An entire semantics of hatred towards each other was part of the everyday attitude that seldom comes to the fore in the stylized polemical tracts.[29] Nor does it reflect the considerable fascination of each to the other.

Then, in a postscript to the article, he recapitulates the key assertions in this passage: "From the twelfth century onwards, the legal and philosophical classification of Christianity as a monotheistic religion prevailed. But the gap between the normative position and the popular sentiment was considerable."[30]

I begin my comments with an aside: The Tosafists did not write the word "idolaters" ('*akum*) in the sentence "As to today's idolaters, we hold it that they do not worship idolatry." The term '*akum* is an artifact of later censorship.

The Tosafists surely wrote that today's *gentiles* do not worship idolatry, so that "the rift between reason and sentiment" disappears, at least in this passage. As to more critical matters, the Tosafists are no less "official" than whatever works Funkenstein had in mind. Indeed, since "Judaism" never "officially" removed Christianity from the category of idolatry, surely not in the Middle Ages, it is difficult to imagine to what works he was alluding. The legal and philosophical classification of Christianity affirmed by Funkenstein did not "prevail" and can by no means be characterized as normative.[31] And, of course, the "semantics of hatred" comes very much to the fore in the "stylized polemical tracts" of Ashkenaz that Funkenstein appears not to have read. But to return to our concerns, the material to which he points underscores the fact that the presence of invective in thirteenth-century polemic has little to do with the polemical genre and nothing to do with the thirteenth century.

Ashkenazic culture is also a critical factor in matters that go beyond the virtual absence of philosophy and the presence of vitriol. There is an aggressiveness that appears to invite confrontation. Polemical works are not structured with care once the biblical order—whether of the Hebrew Bible or the New Testament—ceases to govern. This was a culture attuned—often brilliantly—to ad hoc exegesis and analysis; it was not suited to architectonic literary composition. This exegetical bent may also be responsible for one of the important contributions of thirteenth-century northern polemics—to wit, a major expansion of the Jewish critique of the New Testament. Unlike the later work of Profiat Duran, the Ashkenazic critique is unsystematic and does not strive for overall coherence, but it is marked by the sharp apercus and sensitivity to contradiction that one expects of the bearers of this culture. Thus, as I have argued elsewhere, approaches to Jesus himself are a mélange of whatever points appear useful in a particular context with little or no effort to establish a coherent picture.[32]

And so we turn to the Talmud, where something critically important decidedly took place in the thirteenth century. Nicholas Donin's attack on the Talmud came almost a century after the attack by Peter the Venerable. Donin appears to have known the Talmud well and there is no evidence of his reliance on the earlier work. While I have doubts about the impact that the "Talmud as other law" argument had on the actual treatment of Jews in the thirteenth century, I am convinced by Jeremy Cohen's thesis that it was Donin's intention to undermine the toleration of Jews through the use of that argument—to wit, that the Jews are not really governed by the Hebrew Bible and, therefore, do not serve as witnesses to its authenticity. Others have emphasized Donin's assertion that the Talmud contains blasphemies against Jesus as well as R. Yeḥi'el's proposal that the Jesus of the Talmud is not the Jesus of Christianity. But I am inclined to think that the most dangerous argument of all was Donin's collection of Talmudic laws that discriminate against gentiles. Here the assertion that *aggadah* is not binding accomplished nothing, so the Jews responded—both in Paris and later in southern Europe—by affirming that Christians have a legal status different from that of the gentiles of the Talmud, who were, of course, ancient pagans. For Ashkenazic Jews, these assertions were never internalized to the point of concluding that Christianity is not 'avodah zarah, but it is likely that they ultimately had some effect on the classification of Christians in Jewish law.

At this point, we come to the second and final public disputation in thirteenth-century France, where Pablo Christiani of Barcelona fame made another appearance.[33] This article does not analyze the Barcelona disputation precisely because its significance is so well known and it has been so thoroughly studied and debated that the departure that it represents can be taken for granted.[34] In a word, Pablo is known for his introduction of a different approach to the Talmud—the one adumbrated in Alan of Lille's citation about the threefold division of history—that uses it to prove the truth of Christianity. In Barcelona, Pablo neither articulated a hostile attitude toward the Talmud, nor did he argue for a revocation of the toleration of Jews. In Paris, however, he is depicted as asserting that he will prove that Jews are without faith just like the *Bougres* and are deserving of destruction. Cohen, who had argued that even in Barcelona Pablo saw the Talmud as a book that deviates from biblical religion and has no legitimate place in Christian society, naturally saw the discovery of the manuscript of the second Paris disputation as vindication, although he does concede that Pablo's attitude could have undergone some development between 1263 and 1270.[35] There is no question in my mind that Pablo never had a positive evaluation of the Talmud, but there does appear to be significant development, certainly on the rhetorical level and, probably, even in substance.

Two explanations for this change come to mind. If we see the change as rhetorical, then it may result from the fact that James I of Aragon was not likely to have been receptive to calls for the destruction of the Jews; the thirteenth-century French monarchy was rather different. If we see it as substantive, it may well result from the radicalization engendered by failure to achieve the intended objective at Barcelona and even the bitterness engendered by this failure. Since I have argued for the general accuracy of Naḥmanides' account of his disputation and, therefore, for his relative success in deflecting—temporarily to be sure—the impact of Pablo's efforts, I am entitled to make this argument more readily than those who are skeptical.[36] In any event, when Pablo says that he will prove that Jews have no faith, he may mean, as Cohen understands him, that the Talmud is a heretical work, but he may also mean that since the Jews do not believe what he will prove is taught in their own sacred works—whether the Bible or the Talmud—it follows that they believe in nothing at all.

It is of no small interest that the Jewish protagonist R. Abraham ben Samuel sees Pablo's attack on the Jews' "Torah," which here means Talmud, as a continuation of Donin's although the content of the argumentation is very different. It is of great interest indeed—and of considerable historical importance—that he sees the long-term result of the Paris disputation as the discrediting of Donin despite the fact that its immediate result was the burning of the Talmud:

> There was a heretic in the time of R. Yehi'el about twenty years ago who chattered and collected the *aggadot* and the story of Jesus and all his stench and sought to destroy our entire remnant. At the end of the affair, you perceived in light of the rabbi's words that there was no substance to the assertions of the heretic, and he was vanquished. He was fearful and provided no further answers. Thus, you should have honored precedent and reviled this heretic whose words are of no use. The little finger of the first heretic was thicker than the loins of this one (cf. I Kings 12:10), who would not have been valued in comparison to his predecessor as the skin of garlic, for all his days he has not understood anything properly.[37]

Although such an assertion was in R. Abraham's interest, it would have been bereft of credibility if French Jewry did not feel that in the long run the Talmud had been protected. This passage allows us to conclude with a high degree of confidence that, approximately one generation after the first Paris disputation and the subsequent burning of the Talmud and related works, the availability of such works in France was sufficient to enable the rabbinic leadership to see the outcome of the disputation as a Jewish victory. Thus, the oft-expressed speculation that the relative decline in French Jewry's leading role in the rabbinic constellation of Ashkenazic Jewry resulted from a shortage of books stemming from the events of the early 1240s appears implausible.[38] Moreover, for all the long-term dangers of the attack on the Talmud, it is striking that the encyclopedic *Nitsahon Vetus* contains precisely one paragraph—the very last one in the book—on the subject,[39] Meir of Narbonne's work also contains a single discussion (once again at the end),[40] and *Sefer Yosef ha-Mekanné* contains nothing at all.

There is much more to be said about the second Paris disputation. A very brief comment by R. Yehi'el marginalizing *aggadah*[41]—perhaps unexpected in an Ashkenazic work—is echoed by R. Abraham. Despite the precedent in the earlier disputation, the language here is striking to the point where it would elicit surprise even if it came from a philosophically oriented Spanish or Provencal Jew: "This Friar Paul has come to bring proofs to us on the strength of the *aggadah*, which contains neither Torah not fear [of God] and in many places was formulated only to attract the hearts of the people in accordance with the meaning of biblical verses, just as your archpriest Jerome did for you."[42] A remark by R. Moses Taku in a very different context distinguishing the authoritative *aggadot* of the Babylonian Talmud from those in other collections also reappears, as R. Abraham chastises Pablo for "setting aside the Talmud and bringing us proofs from *midreshé aggadah*—even though they too will do you no good."[43]

Alan of Lille's talmudic passage about the ages of chaos, Torah, and the Messiah appears at the very end.[44] As I noted in a recent article, this placement helps explain the otherwise puzzling absence of that passage from the Barcelona disputation. The assertion that the world would last 6,000 years—2,000 chaos, 2,000 Torah, and 2,000 the messianic age— purportedly confirmed two crucial Christian contentions: that the Messiah has already come, and that the messianic age will not be (or is not) an age of Torah. Thus, it could have been used at Barcelona to support the Christian position regarding the first item on the agenda (whether or not the Messiah has already come), but it is overwhelmingly likely that Pablo was saving it, as he did in Paris, for the final item ("that the laws and ceremonials ceased and should have ceased after the advent of the...Messiah"). But because the Barcelona disputation was cut short, that final topic was never discussed.[45]

Finally, in light of the argument that I made many years ago that twelfth-century Christians were not committed to a serious missionary effort aimed at Jews,[46] Pablo's activities in both Spain and France reflect a very different reality. That this disputation reflects a missionary and not just a persecutory objective is evident from the following passage about royal intentions:

> This is what the king commanded us: Whenever Paul the heretic wants to debate with you, you must all gather, old and young. Perhaps there is among you an individual who will understand his responses and his proofs and will decide to turn to the Torah of Jesus, and I will thus take from you "one from a city and two from a family" (Jeremiah 3:14).[47]

Since the literary—not merely polemical—output of northern European Jewry was largely interrupted by expulsion and other forms of persecution in the late thirteenth and early fourteenth century, the reaction of this Jewry to the Christian use of the Talmud was never fully developed. No less important, northern Christians did not develop that approach to a point that exploited its full potential. What that potential was became all too clear in late medieval Spain.

Notes

1. Amos Funkenstein, "Ha-temurot be-vikkuaḥ ha-dat she-bein yehudim le-notsrim ba-me'ah ha-yod-bet," *Zion* 33 (1968): 122–144; Amos Funkenstein, "Basic Types of Christian Anti-Jewish Polemics in the Later Middle Ages," *Viator* 2 (1971): 373–382. The final version appears as the major component of chapter 6 of Amos Funkenstein, *Perceptions of Jewish History* (Berkeley, Los Angeles and Oxford, 1993), 169–219.
2. Jeremy Cohen, *The Friars and the Jews: the Evolution of Medieval anti-Judaism* (Ithaca, 1982), 25–32.

3. Daniel Lasker, "Polemics at the Turning Point: Jewish Evidence from the Twelfth Century," *Harvard Theological Review* 89 (1996): 161–173.

4. Ora Limor, "Polemical Varieties: Religious Disputation in 13th Century Spain," *Iberia Judaica* 11 (2010): 55–79.

5. *Disputatio Judei et Christiani*, in *The Works of Gilbert Crispin, Abbot of Westminster*, ed. Anna Sapir Abulafia and G.R. Evans (London, 1986), 9–61.

6. Odo of Tournai, *On Original Sin: and A Disputation With the Jew, Leo, Concerning the Advent of Christ, the Son of God; Two Theological Treatises*, translated with an introduction and notes by Irven M. Resnick (Philadelphia, 1994).

7. *Dialogus inter Christianum et Judaeum de Fide Catholica, Patrologia Latina* (henceforth *PL*) 163: 1045–1072.

8. Yvonne Friedman, ed., *Petri Venerabilis Adversus Iudaeorum Inveteratam Duritiem* (Brepols, 1985).

9. John Tolan, *Petrus Alfonsi and His Medieval Readers* (Gainesville, 1993), 19, 22–25.

10. *PL* 210: 410.

11. I have discussed the role of this passage in medieval and early modern Jewish-Christian polemic in "Torah and the Messianic Age: The Polemical and Exegetical History of a Rabbinic Text," in *Studies in Medieval Jewish Social and Intellectual History: Festschrift in Honor of Robert Chazan,* ed. David Engel, Lawrence Schiffmann, and Elliot Wolfson (Leiden, 2012), 169–187.

12. Anna Sapir Abulafia, *Christians and Jews in the Twelfth-Century Renaissance* (London and New York, 1995).

13. Gilbert Dahan, *La polémique chrétienne contre le Judaisme au Moyen Age* (Paris, 1991), 115–116.

14. *Dialogus inter Judaeum Requirentem et Christianum e Contrario Respondentem, PL* 145: 64. Blumenkranz noted this in *Juifs et Chrétiens dans le monde occidental, 430–1096* (Paris, 1960), 217–218.

15. See my "St. Peter Damian: His Attitude toward the Jews and the Old Testament," *Yavneh Review* 4 (1965): 80–112, reprinted in David Berger, *Persecution, Polemic, and Dialogue: Essays in Jewish-Christian Relations* (Boston, 2010), 261–288, at 275–276.

16. Avraham Grossman, "Ha-metah ben torah le-'hokhmah' be-ferush Rashi le-sifrut ha-hokhmah she-ba-mikra," in *Teshurah le-'Amos : asufat mehkarim be-farshanut ha-mikra muggeshet le-'Amos Hakham,* ed. Moshe bar Asher et al. (Alon Shevut, 2007), 13–27, at 23. For my reaction to Grossman's overall thesis, see David Berger, "Polemic, Exegesis, Philosophy, and Science: Reflections on the Tenacity of Ashkenazic Modes of Thought" in *Jahrbuch des Simon-Dubnow-Instituts* 8 (2009): 27–39, reprinted in David Berger, *Cultures in Collision and Conversation: Essays in the Intellectual History of the Jews* (Boston, 2011), 152–166.

17. Jacob ben Reuben, *Milhamot ha-Shem*, ed. Judah Rosenthal (Jerusalem, 1963), 7. The relevant chapter of this work has now been translated into English in Wendy Schor-Haim, *Jacob ben Reuben's Sefer Milhamot Hashem, Chapter One: A Jewish Philosophical Critique of Christianity*, (PhD dissertation, New York University, 2012).

18. Ibid., 8.
19. Ibid., 11–20.
20. Ta'anot (Arguments), ed. Stanislaus Simon, Mose ben Salomo von Salerno und seine philosophischen Auseinandersetzung mit den Lehren des Christentums (Breslau, 1932), xi.
21. Ibid., xviii–xix. An additional brief but highly sophisticated philosophical polemic to which no attention has been paid is to be published shortly in 'Iyyun by Israel Netanel Rubin. The two manuscripts of this anonymous polemic provide different titles; Rubin has chosen "She'elot ha-pilosof." The work, like Moses of Salerno's, was composed in Italy—and at virtually the same time (1264 for the former, 1270 for the latter.) Here too the Christian aims to refute an important Jewish philosophical argument against Christianity but does not pose arguments demonstrating the truth of Christian dogmas.
22. Parma manuscript 2749. Substantial sections of the work have been transcribed or published in William K. Herskowitz, Judaeo-Christian dialogue in Provence as reflected in "Milhemet Mitzva" of R. Meir Hameili (D.H.L. dissertation, Yeshiva University, 1974), and Moshe Blau, Shittat ha-kadmonim 'al massekhtot nazir, zevaḥim, 'arakhin, u-temurah, ve-sefer milḥemet mitsvah (New York, 1973).
23. Judah Rosenthal, ed., Sefer Yosef ha-Mekanné (Jerusalem, 1970).
24. David Berger, The Jewish-Christian Debate in the High Middle Ages: A Critical Edition of the Nitzzahon Vetus with an Introduction, Translation, and Commentary (Philadelphia, 1979).
25. In chapter 7 of this volume ("Joseph ben Nathan's Sefer Yosef ha-Mekanné and the Medieval Jewish Critique of Christianity"), Daniel Lasker defends his position that Ashkenazic polemicists omitted philosophical arguments only because they did not believe that their audience could absorb them. As he indicates, I had argued that this is unlikely and that the absence of such polemic in northern Europe results from the fact that such arguments were alien to the mentalité of the authors themselves. Despite Lasker's characteristically well-formulated presentation, I remain unpersuaded. Let me note the following: (1) Lasker's argument refers to the very specific circumstances of Joseph Official's background and lineage and cannot be applied directly to the unknown author of the Nitsahon Vetus, though one who is persuaded by it could be open to an expanded application. (2) Lasker concedes that philosophical arguments were "undoubtedly" foreign even to Joseph Official's "world outlook." (3) He asserts that Joseph would not have withheld effective arguments from his audience unless he was convinced that they could not absorb them. The argument that a polemicist would not have withheld effective arguments from his Jewish audience was precisely my argument for the position that the problem lay with the author. I asserted that a particular philosophical argument that the author of the Nitsahon Vetus was likely to have known but failed to transmit was hardly so complex as to be incomprehensible to an Ashkenazic audience. "A Tosafot passage of average difficulty," I wrote, "is considerably more daunting." Thus, it is far more likely that the utilization of a much less sophisticated version of the argument reflects the fact that the philosophical formulation did not resonate with the author himself. If it had, he would not have withheld it from his most capable readers. It

is, of course, the case that once we assume that such arguments were alien to the thought pattern of the authors, there is every reason to believe that this was also true of their readers even though they, like the authors, were capable of understanding them in purely intellectual terms. In the final analysis, Lasker too agrees, indeed insists, that philosophical arguments did not speak to Ashkenazic Jews. Consequently, our disagreement about the authors of these works does not affect the larger point.

26. Mordechai Breuer published a one-page appendix to his edition of the *Nitsahon Vetus* (*Sefer nitsahon yashan: sefer vikkuah neged ha-notsrim* [Ramat Gan, 1978], 194) in which he listed 33 of these pejorative terms. See too Anna Sapir Abulafia, "Invectives against Christianity in the Hebrew Chronicles of the First Crusade," in Anna Sapir Abulafia, *Christians and Jews in Dispute: Disputational Literature and the Rise of Anti-Judaism in the West (c. 1000–1150)* (Aldershot, Hampshire and Brookville, Vermont, 1998).

27. P. 171.

28. Funkenstein's footnote: "B.T. *'Avoda Zara* 2a and the *tossafot* (sic) ad locum: *nir'eh de-ta'am ha-hetter mi-shum de-'akum she-beineinu kim lan de-la palhu la-'avodat kokhavim*. On this issue, see Jacob Katz, *Exclusiveness and Tolerance: Studies in Jewish-Gentile Relations in the Middle Ages* (Oxford, 1961), 24–47."

29. Funkenstein's footnote: "A cursory reading of the tossafists (sic) or early responses (sic)—e.g., the tossafists (sic) on *'Avoda Zara*—reveals a whole network of semantic substitutions to everything sacred to Christians. Christ was referred to as 'the hanged one' (*ha-talui*), an allusion to the biblical verse 'for the hanged one is a curse of God.' Churches were not houses of prayer (*tefila*) but of vain (sic) (*tifla*). Relics were 'the filth of their bones' (*rekev 'atsmoteihem*). Saints (*kedoshim*) were prostitutes (*kedeshim*). The cross was *sheti va-'erev*, an illicit mixture. Maria was *Haria*, and so on." (*Tefila, tifla, kedoshim,* and *kedeshim* are Funkenstein's transliterations; the other Hebrew words appear in Hebrew typeface.)

30. P. 200.

31. This matter is not central to our concerns here, and a full discussion would take us far afield. Let me say the following with ruthless brevity: The only medieval authority of stature who is very likely to have taken the position that Christianity is not to be considered *'avodah zarah* (usually translated "idolatry," though the English term is really inappropriate for Christianity) was R. Menahem ha-Me'iri, and even in his case some scholars dissent. A tosafist passage (*Sanhedrin* 63b and parallels) affirms that *shittuf*, or association, is permissible for non-Jews. Many early modern and modern authorities took this to mean that Christian worship is permitted to non-Jews, though it is unlikely that this understanding is correct. Other Tosafist passages clearly presuppose that Christianity is *'avodah zarah* even for non-Jews; see *Tosafot 'Avodah Zarah* 14b, *s.v. hatsav kashba* and *Tosafot 'Avodah Zarah* 50a *s.v. ba'einan ke'ein penim ve-lekka*. During R. Yehi'el of Paris's disputation, he was placed in a very difficult position and reluctantly allowed that Christians might be saved through their faith, but it is perfectly clear that he did not want to say this; see my discussion of this passage in David Berger, "On the Image and Destiny of Gentiles in Ashkenazic Polemical Literature," in *Cultures in Collision and Conversation*, 118–120. There are passages in *Tosafot* and related

literature suggesting that ordinary medieval Christians may not for various
reasons be treated as worshippers of *'avodah zarah*, but this is not a judgment
about the Christian religion itself.

32. David Berger, "On the Uses of History in Medieval Jewish Polemic against
Christianity: The Search for the Historical Jesus," in *Jewish History and Jewish
Memory: Essays in Honor of Yosef Hayim Yerushalmi*, ed. Elisheva Carlebach,
John M. Efron, and David N. Myers (Hanover and London, 1998), 25–39,
reprinted in David Berger, *Persecution, Polemic, and Dialogue*, 139–157, at
142–146.

33. See Joseph Shatzmiller, *La deuxième controverse de Paris: Un chapitre dans la
polémique entre chrétiens et juifs au moyen âge* (Paris and Louvain, 1994).

34. The major book-length treatment is Robert Chazan, *Barcelona and Beyond:
The Disputation of 1263 and Its Aftermath* (Berkeley, 1992). For my approach
to some of the issues, see my assessment of the book in "The Barcelona
Disputation: Review Essay," *AJS Review* 20 (1995): 379–388, reprinted in
David Berger, *Persecution, Polemic, and Dialogue*, 199–208.

35. "Vikkuaḥ Paris ha-sheni ve-ha-pulmos ha-yehudi–notsri shel ha-me'ah
ha-shelosh 'esreh," *Tarbiz* 68 (1999): 558–579, at 567–570.

36. Berger, "The Barcelona Disputation."

37. Shatzmiller, *La deuxième controverse*, 45.

38. I completed this article just before the appearance of *The Trial of the Talmud,
Paris, 1240*, Hebrew texts translated by John Friedman, Latin texts translated
by Jean Connell Hoff, historical essay by Robert Chazan (Toronto, 2012). In
his valuable essay, Chazan notes this "somewhat strange" passage and suggests that despite the repeated condemnations of the Talmud by the French
monarchy after the 1240's, these "condemnations had not in fact impinged
on the actual practice of the Oral Torah by French Jewry" (p. 84) and that
they did not cause a decline (to the extent that there was a decline) in Jewish
intellectual activity (p. 87). The difference between our assessments is that
I consider it difficult to account for this passage unless even written versions of the Talmud and the literature surrounding it remained more or less
available.

39. Berger, *The Jewish-Christian Debate* # 245, Hebrew section, 163–164, English
section, 230.

40. Parma ms., 214aff.

41. *Vikkuaḥ R. Yeḥi'el mi-Paris*, ed. S. Gruenebaum (Thorn, 1973), 2; English
translation in *The Trial of the Talmud*, trans. Friedman and Hoff, 131.

42. Shatzmiller, *La deuxième controverse*, 51. I have translated *peshat ha-mikra'ot* as
"the meaning of biblical verses" even though *peshat* can signify "straightforward meaning." It is difficult for me to accept the assumption that even
an Ashkenazic Jew would regard aggadic interpretation of biblical verses as
straightforward. I am grateful to Prof. Mordechai Cohen for confirming that
R. Abraham could have used the term *peshat* in this sense.

43. Ibid. I consider it unlikely that R. Abraham meant that Pablo was setting
aside the legal material in the Talmud. The earlier passage is in Taku's *Ketav
tamim*, Paris ms. fol.7b (facsimile published by Joseph Dan [Jerusalem, 1984],
Ozar Neḥmad 3, 63).

44. Shatzmiller, *La deuxième controverse*, 57.

45. Berger, "Torah and the Messianic Age", 172, n.8. Even before the discovery of the manuscript of the second Paris disputation, I had speculated (orally but not in writing) that this is the likely explanation. I would like to think that this speculation is now close to being confirmed.

46. "Mission to the Jews and Jewish-Christian Contacts in the Polemical Literature of the High Middle Ages," *American Historical Review* 91 (1986): 576–591, reprinted in David Berger, *Persecution, Polemic, and Dialogue*, 177–198.

47. Shatzmiller, *La deuxième controverse*, 47. It cannot be ruled out that this was a Jewish misperception of the king's intention, but there appears to be no concrete reason to reject the report.

CHAPTER 9

OF MILK AND BLOOD: INNOCENT III AND THE JEWS, REVISITED

John Tolan

Much of the past century of scholarship devoted to the history of medieval European Jewry has attempted to trace and explain the waning of Christian tolerance and the rise of anti-Jewish prejudice and violence, as measured by a number of macabre indices: increasing legal restrictions, host desecration and ritual murder accusations, massacres, and expulsions. Various key turning points have been suggested: the first crusade, for Bernhard Blumenkranz; the missionary preaching of the Franciscan and Dominican friars, for Jeremy Cohen; the anti-talmudic polemics of Latin authors in the twelfth century, for myself and others. But key among the culprits blamed for the rise of anti-Judaism has been one of the most powerful and charismatic popes of the Middle Ages: Innocent III. Nineteenth-century historian Heinrich Hirsch Graetz, in his monumental *Geschichte der Juden,* makes Innocent into the principal culprit for the ills of European Jews. Innocent represents "The Church at war against Jewry." He was "an embittered enemy of Jews and Judaism, and dealt severer blows against them than had any of his predecessors."[1] Although more recent historians have been more sanguine in their assessment, many have agreed on the central importance of Innocent's anti-Jewish policies: Edward Synan devotes a full chapter of his *The Popes and the Jews in the Middle Ages* to Innocent: "For many reasons, the pontificate of Pope Innocent III has been taken as the central instance of the medieval confrontation of popes and Jews. With his reign, all the major principles have been formulated and reduced to practice;...the main lines had been drawn by the time this most powerful of popes died."[2] For Robert Chazan, "the pontificate of Innocent III represents both a hardening of Church policy towards the Jews and a sharpening of anti-Jewish rhetoric."[3]

Innocent indeed manages to confirm traditional papal policy toward Jews while simultaneously affirming a harder anti-Jewish line and stepping up anti-Jewish rhetoric. His issuance of the *Constitutio pro Judeis* is highly instructive. The *Constitutio* is the traditional text guaranteeing papal protection for Jews, specifically assuring that they may practice their religious rites, be free from undue pressure to convert, and have synagogues and cemeteries; violence against their persons and property is punished by excommunication. Innocent reissues the same privilege that several of his predecessors had issued, citing five of them by name. Yet he adds two brief paragraphs that change the tone considerably: first, an introduction in which he provides a theological justification for the limited and conditional tolerance offered to Jews: "Although in many ways the disbelief of the Jews must be reproved, since nevertheless through them our own faith is truly proved, they must not be oppressed grievously by the faithful."[4] And at the end of his *Constitutio*, he adds a sentence which makes these traditional guarantees precariously conditional: "We desire, however, that only those be fortified by the guard of this protection who shall have presumed no plotting for the subversion of the Christian faith."[5] The implication is that some Jews plot against Christianity and, for them, there is no papal protection against violence.

In this article, I look at one aspect of Innocent's Jewish policy that has evoked little comment: I argue that, compared with earlier popes and legislators (lay or ecclesiastical) he shows a marked concern for questions of purity and of the dangers of pollution from contact with Jews (and for that matter, with heretics and Muslims, although that will not be our concern here). I base my case on three letters which the Pope sent to France (thus, my justification for broaching this topic in a volume devoted to continuity and change in thirteenth-century France): a letter to King Philip II Augustus (January 16, 1205), a mandate to the Archbishop of Sens and the bishop of Paris (July 15, 1205), and a letter to the Count of Nevers (January 17, 1208). In these missives, Innocent expresses not only a mistrust of Jews who mock Christianity and bear violent designs against Christians, he worries about the polluting effects of contact transmitted physically through wet nurses and through consumption of Jewish meat and wine, particularly as the latter could be used for the Eucharist.

Up until the twelfth century, bodily purity seems to have little preoccupied canon law regarding Jews. When popes, church councils, and other church authorities ruled on relations between Christians and Jews, concerns of bodily purity—of "pollution" from contact with infidels—is rarely, if ever, a concern. Early Christian legislation sought to keep Christians out of synagogues and to prevent Jews from mocking Christian rites or symbols (e.g., from burning a crucified image of Haman on Purim), but the dangers were not expressed in terms of corruption or pollution coming from physical contact with Jews. Interreligious marriage was, of course, prohibited, but the danger is not seen as physical contact but *contumelia creatoris* (insult to the creator): they are worried about blasphemy, not pollution. This is all the more striking given that, in other areas, physical pollution was a real issue: a number of authors address the question, for example, of whether a man who has had a wet dream can participate in the Eucharist.[6] Jews might be seen as a theological threat to Christians, but not as a physical one.

By the end of the Middle Ages, of course, Jews were often portrayed as a real physical threat to Christians: this is seen most dramatically in the host-desecration accusations and, above all, in the ritual murder accusations (or blood libel). Moreover, by the end of the Middle Ages and the early modern period, numerous texts present physical contact with Jews (and increasingly, in the Iberian Peninsula, *conversos*) as dangerous and impure, a "pollution" that often involved contact with fluids: water poisoned by Jews that Christians unwittingly introduced into their bodies, or the blood, milk, and semen of Jews. To cite one example among many, Vincente de Costa Mattos, in his *Breva discurso contra a heretica perfidia da judaismo* (Tolosa, 1696): affirms that children of Old Christians should not be suckled by "Jewish vileness because that milk, being of infected persons can only engender perverse implications."[7]

It is in the early thirteenth century that one sees the first signs of the emergence of this preoccupation with the "polluting" contact of Jews, and one sees it clearly in these three texts of Innocent III. Innocent is not the first to express such fears and concerns, but he is the first pope to give them wide credence and authority. We shall see that it is probably not mere coincidence that these concerns emerge concurrently with the establishment of the doctrine of the transubstantiation, which affirmed the real, physical presence of God in the Eucharistic species. Let us first look at each of the three bulls in context.

On January 16, 1205, Innocent sent a letter to King Philip II Augustus of France. In this bull, *Etsi non displiceat Domino,* the pope complains of the privileged status that the king accords to Jews that unconscionably places them above Christians.[8] The Jews of the kingdom of the French have become "insolent," claims the pope. He attacks, in particular, the practice of moneylending, which inverses the normal power relationships between Christians and Jews: Jews abscond with the property of Christians and of the Church. Particularly unacceptable, for the pope, is the trampling of traditional jurisprudence based on oral testimony (in which Christian witnesses were accorded more authority than Jews). Here, on the contrary, more credence is given to signed documents (contracts in the Jews' possession), inverting traditional hierarchies. The letter is a bitter (if implicit) criticism of the aid and abetment that the king and his officers grant to Jewish lenders, to the detriment of Christian debtors. Beyond the question of usury, the pope lambasts what, for him, are other examples of Jewish "insolence": they construct new synagogues (one of which is taller than the neighboring church); they have Christian servants, in clear violation of church law; and they openly mock Christians and make jest of veneration of the cross during Holy Week. The pope accuses the Jews of being accomplices to thieves and even of killing Christians: he cites the example of a student found dead in a latrine (while some historians have seen this as an accusation of ritual murder, in fact the pope does not claim that there was any ritual or liturgical dimension to this murder, which is simply seen as a product of the Jews' implacable hatred of Christians). The final lines of this bull are a barely veiled warning to the king and an exhortation to restrain the Jews and to punish their "blasphemies."

Before analyzing this bull in greater detail, let me briefly present the two other bulls that interest us here. Innocent sent the second one, *Etsi Iudeos,* to the Archbishop of Sens and the Bishop of Paris on July 15, 1205[9]: Innocent returns to the themes of *Etsi non displiceat Domino,* to which he refers; he also refers to similar letters that he sent to the Duke of Burgundy and the Countess of Troyes. The bull concerns the practice of Christian servants (*seruientes*)[10] working in Jewish homes—clearly a common occurrence (well attested in Latin and Hebrew documents[11])—a point that the pope had addressed (as we have seen) in *Etsi non displiceat Domino.* The pope reiterates the prohibition of employment of Christian *seruientes* by Jews. Unlike the king, the bishop and archbishop have no legal authority over Jews. The pope thus exhorts them to use the sentence of excommunication against those Christians who have commerce with Jews who continue to employ Christian domestic servants. The pope is clearly attempting to go further than a principled condemnation, seeking to find efficacious remedies against a practice that had been frequently outlawed and remained widely practiced.

Innocent sent the third bull, *Ut esset Cain,* to Count Hervé IV de Donzy of Nevers on January 17, 1208.[12] He here takes up the same themes he had already addressed in his *Etsi non displiceat Domino.* His main goal is to put an end to "the exaction of usury" by Jews who benefit from the complicity and help of the count and his officers. These practices have dire consequences, according to the pope: widows and orphans are stripped of their possessions; Christians are imprisoned, while the Jewish lenders who extort exorbitant usurious interest occupy castles and palaces and refuse to respond to ecclesiastical courts (concerning cases, presumably, which involve clerics and ecclesiastical goods). This situation is made possible by the complicity and support of the count, whom Innocent enjoins to cease giving his aid to these Jewish lenders. As in *Etsi non displiceat Domino,* Innocent here evokes, in a second section of the letter, a whole series of Jewish practices that create "scandal." First of all, Jewish butchers kill animals "according to the Jewish rite" and sell the remaining meat (all that is inedible according to kosher restrictions) to the Christians. The pope is clearly bothered by the impression that the Jews consider themselves superior to Christians to whom they sell things that they themselves judge unfit for consumption; like the undue power of the moneylenders, this inverses the hierarchy that God established between Christians and Jews. The same principle applies to Jewish women who sell milk "publicly for the nourishment of children." Is he referring to wet nurses? Elisheva Baumgarten thinks that this is improbable, since the Hebrew documentation frequently mentions Christian wet nurses in Jewish employ, but never the reverse. Were these women selling the milk of their domestic animals? In any case, the pope's impression, once again, is that they are selling to Christians what they judge to be not good enough for their families. As for wine, it is even worse, because they keep the best for themselves and sell the inferior-quality wine to the Christians; this "Jewish" wine, at times, is even consecrated in the Eucharist.

What do these three bulls tell us about Innocent's vision of Jews' proper place in Christian society and about how and why he thought they should be restricted to that place? I would like to focus on three elements apparent in these documents: Innocent's theology of Jewish slavery, his fear of the consequences of the "insolence" of Jews who do not accept their subservient place in Christian society, and the fears of pollution and sacrilege—notably stemming from contact between Jews and the Eucharistic species.

Theology of Jewish "Slavery"

In the three bulls, Innocent justifies his exhortations to lay and ecclesiastical authorities to restrict Jewish "insolence" through the claim that Jews have submitted to slavery by rejecting and killing Christ. While Innocent is, of course, presenting well-worn themes, commonly found in anti-Jewish polemics and in other theological treatises, the bulls present an uncommonly clear and uncompromising legal argument founding Jewish social inferiority on theological principles.

In the three bulls, Innocent presents his action as a defense of divinely ordained hierarchies merited by Jewish sins. In the opening words of *Ut esset Cain*, he compares the Jews to Cain. Just as Cain was a murderer and an untouchable, despised and rejected by humanity because he killed his brother Abel, the Jews, guilty of murdering their Lord, are vagabonds on the face of the Earth; their perpetual exile punishes and recalls their crime. But just as the sign of God prevented Cain from being killed, so we must let Jews live among us. The Jews are the enemies of Christ and utter blasphemies against his name. They should be tolerated but must be kept in a position of social inferiority; they must be prevented from exercising power over Christians. Innocent affirms that they have been reduced to slavery as punishment for the crime of having killed their Lord who had come to free them. In *Etsi non displiceat Domino*, he develops another Old Testament prefiguration: the story in Genesis of the two sons of Abraham: Isaac, "the son of the free woman" (Sarah), who prefigures the Christians, and Ishmael, the "son of a servant" (Hagar), who represents the Jews, whose destiny is eternal servitude. Moreover, the Jews themselves implicitly accepted their status as slaves: when Pontius Pilate washed his hands of his responsibility for the death of Jesus, Jerusalem's Jews cried out, according to Matthew: "His blood is on us and on our children!" [Mt. 27:25; cited in two of the three bulls]. The Son's blood still cries out to the ears of the father, says Innocent in *Etsi non displiceat Domino*: thus, any prince who fears divine wrath must make sure that the Jews remain subservient to Christians. This continuity of punishment is natural because of a continuity of guilt: Jews are and remain agitated by their rabid hatred of their Christian benefactors, and they delight when their affairs cause divisions and conflicts among Christians, the pope affirms in *Ut esset Cain*.

The Consequence of the "Insolence" of Jews

Having laid out the theological principles of Jewish servitude to Christians, Innocent is on a moral and theological high ground from which he can denounce those Jews and Christians who attempt to upset this divinely ordained hierarchy. The fact that Jews have Christian servants and that they exercise undue power over Christians and over cult objects because of usurious loans inverses this divinely decreed order and constitutes so many proofs, for the pope, of the "insolence" of the Jews. Christians who accept or even encourage such insolence are accused of aiding the Lord's enemies.

In *Etsi Iudeos,* Innocent affirms that "even our enemies, the Saracens, cannot stand the insolent Jews and expel them from their territory." He is probably referring to the emigrations provoked by the Almohads' anti-Jewish (and anti-Christian) policies in North Africa and the Iberian Peninsula. The Jews are intolerable because of their "insolence," while they should humbly recognize their status as slaves in Christian society. Yet, instead, they seek to harm their Christian hosts. To illustrate this Jewish hostility, he cites a proverb which we find in other sources as early as the twelfth century, for example, in the sermons of Peter of Blois[13]: the Jews are "like the mouse in a pocket, like the snake around one's loin, like the fire in one's bosom." He returns to this proverb at the end of the bull, emphasizing the animal imagery attributed to the Jews, whom he accuses of already having begun "to gnaw in the manner of a mouse, and to bite in the manner of a serpent."

Philip Augustus had all the Jews of his royal domain arrested, confiscated their property, and then expelled them in 1182. His biographer, Rigord, praises the king for this expulsion, affirming that the Jews, through their usurious moneylending, had obtained half of Paris, had locked up countless Christian debtors as prisoners in Jewish homes, and had converted their Christian servants to Judaism. These things clearly justified their expulsion, claims Rigord, for whom this is a singular proof of the king's piety. But, in 1198, the king allowed the Jews to return to the royal domain and those Jews who settled there (no doubt far fewer than the number that had been expelled in 1182) seem to have specialized in moneylending. Thus, when Pope Innocent III writes this letter to the king in 1205, he catalogues (just as Rigord had) the abuses caused by Jewish usury, emphasizing that goods belonging to the Church were now in Jewish hands. This bull has been studied by historians in particular as a testimony of the practice of money-lending by Jews of the Île de France and of the tensions caused both by the subsequent debt and by the fact that royal agents participated in the coercive enforcement of the loans: particularly in the arrest and imprisonment of debtors. This was one of the causes of the 1182 expulsion and it continued to create problems for Philip and his successors, some of whom took measures to reduce the risks run by debtors and to limit the role played by royal agents in collection and enforcement. These tensions, nevertheless, continued until Philip IV the Fair expelled the Jews from the French Kingdom in 1306. This expulsion involved a much larger territory and many more Jews than from the royal domain of 1182.

The situation in 1205–1208 is one of renewed tensions for the now quite small Jewish community whose principal economic activity appears to be moneylending. The resentment expressed by Rigord before 1182 is born anew, all the more so as some prominent lay and ecclesiastical authorities in the king's entourage (including Rigord himself) were not happy to see Jews readmitted in 1198. Some of them were, no doubt, the pope's source of information; they must have painted to him an alarming portrait of Jewish "insolence" and its dire consequences, and, clearly, Innocent was ready to accept their point of view with little hesitation. In the two bulls where he deals with the question of usury, Innocent paints a very dark picture indeed, insisting on the most dramatic examples of a world turned upside down: sacred vessels and other church property in hock to Jews, widows and orphans coldly disinherited, and a perverted justice system in which Jewish witnesses are preferred to Christians.

Yet the symptoms of this "insolence," for the pope, go well beyond the issues of usury. He cites, as we have seen, numerous examples showing how Jews refuse to accept their subservient place in Christian society. Some involve direct challenges to Christian practice: a synagogue, taller than the neighboring church, where Jews pray so loudly that mass cannot be held next door. Some Jews, claims the pope, openly mock Christian devotion to the crucifix during Holy Week processions. This "insolence" is seen in commercial operations as well, where Jews sell what they consider not good enough for them (be it meat, milk, or wine) to Christians, as if to their inferiors. Numerous texts, indeed, attest to collaboration between Jewish and Christian butchers in cities throughout Europe: as the hind legs of even properly slaughtered animals were not kosher, it made eminent sense to sell the non-kosher meat to Christians. Various Christian writers had addressed this issue before Innocent, most affirming that it was licit to buy such meat from Jews (arguing that Christian willingness to eat all that God has given us was a testimony to the superiority of the new Christian covenant over the old Jewish one); others, like Innocent, frowned on such consumption or prohibited it.[14]

One of the principal preoccupations of the pope in these bulls, as we have seen, is the presence of Christian servants in Jewish homes. Jews' employment of Christian servants overturns the hierarchy that must prevail, for Innocent, between the "sons of the crucifiers" and those of the Crucified. This had long been an object of legislation in both lay and canon law: various laws of the *Theodosian code* prohibited Jews from owning Christian slaves *(serui);* these prohibitions were subsequently oft repeated.[15] The Pope observes that numerous Jews have Christian servants in their homes, performing domestic chores and taking care of their children. This, indeed, seems to be a widespread phenomenon throughout contemporary northern European Jewry, as we see in both Latin and Hebrew sources.[16] As with the collaboration between Christian and Jewish butchers, Innocent is fighting deeply entrenched and widely accepted practices, trying to paint them as scandalous in order to justify their abolishment.

Transubstantiation and Ritual Purity

Most of what we have examined so far is fairly standard in writing and legislation concerning Jews in the late twelfth or early thirteenth centuries: as we have seen, Innocent addresses these issues more forcefully and with greater hostility to Jews than his predecessors, but the general outlines of his Jewish policies are not new. There is one exception to this: Innocent seems to show a preoccupation with purity and with the dangers of pollution that close daily contact with Jews represent to the body of Christendom. It is perhaps no accident that the two passages in these bulls that most clearly evoke such fears both have to do with the Eucharist. It is under Innocent III's pontificate that the Fourth Lateran Council (in 1215) establishes the doctrine of the transubstantiation, according to which the bread and wine of the Eucharist are physically transformed into the flesh and blood of Christ. The doctrine provoked much debate and dissension within the Church and clearly some unease that is reflected here in passages concerning milk and wine.

We have seen that Innocent railed against the employment of Christian servants in Jewish homes. While other churchmen had worried about the spiritual dangers of such cohabitation, which could lead to apostasy, Innocent, in *Etsi non displiceat Domino,* intones darkly of the "abominations" that Jews inflict on their wet nurses. He explains this more fully in *Etsi*

Iudeos, where he denounces what he presents as a common practice: Jews oblige their Christian wet nurses to extract some milk into the latrines for three days after they have taken communion. Did some Jews, in fact, make their wet nurses perform such a humiliating rite, to mark their contempt for the Eucharist? Or is the pope (or more likely one of his sources of information) making a false accusation that he knows will provoke the ire of his readers? In any case, it is quite unlikely that this was a common practice, as the pope insinuates. Given the difficulties that families had in finding wet nurses in Medieval Europe, it is hard to believe that Jewish parents would deliberately humiliate a woman who provided nourishment to their infants.[17] Moreover, Innocent's accusation presupposes, on the part of Jews, a strong disdain for their Christian servants; this does not correspond with the image we find in the Hebrew documentation; on the contrary, we find rabbis arguing about whether, for example, to give a gift to one's Christian servant during Purim[18]. Finally, it seems that the emergence of such rumors, and the fact that they were widely accepted (even, here, at the Lateran), has little to do with real-life Jewish practice; it is the fruit of the Christian clerics' theological preoccupations. The supposed fact that Jews oblige their wet nurses to express their milk into the latrines after they have taken communion shows (for the pope) that Jews recognize the power of the Eucharist—a power present even in the milk of these Christian women. It also suggests hostility toward the sacrament: this milk, imbued with the Divine presence, is tossed away in a filthy place. In the same way, host desecration stories will, starting in the thirteenth century, relate that Jews put hosts in latrines or on refuse heaps.[19] In a perverse logic, it is believed that Jews recognize Christ's presence in the consecrated host (and, here, even in the milk of women who have taken communion) and that this presence provokes their implacable, eternal, and violent hatred. Here again, one is struck by the harsh language in this bull and by the Pope's tendency to spread anti-Jewish rumors: in *Etsi non displiceat Domino*, he accused them of complicity with thieves and with the murder of innocent Christians.

We have seen how, in *Ut esset Cain*, Innocent denounces the practice of Jewish winemakers to keep the good wine and sell the rest to Christians: "and with this, now and again, the sacrament of the blood of Christ is performed." Here again, the pope expresses his fears concerning the potentially sullying effects of contact between Jews and the species of the Eucharistic sacrament. In both cases, these preoccupations are to be understood in the context of contemporary debates on the doctrine of the transubstantiation, which is subsequently adopted by the Fourth Lateran Council in 1215. This preoccupation, which might seem paradoxical, highlights the hesitations and uncertainties provoked by these debates: why should the purity (or impurity) of the wine matter if the sacrament truly transforms it into the blood of Christ, which by definition should be immune to any corruption?

Conclusions

These three bulls confirm the portrait that a number of historians paint of Innocent as an uncompromising advocate of reducing contact between Jews and Christians. He is dealing here with themes common among Christian authors who write on Judaism and Jews, but he does so with a vehemence and an aggressiveness rare in earlier papal correspondence. These texts represent a hardening of pontifical rhetoric concerning the Jews, to whom Innocent attributes an implacable hostility toward Christianity and Christians, whom they mock and—given the opportunity—kill.

I would, nevertheless, fall short of agreeing with Heinrich Graetz's portrayal of Innocent as the chief culprit for the degeneration of Christian-Jewish relations in medieval Europe. Indeed, to search for a "turning point" between an age of tolerance and one of persecution is simplistic and perhaps pointless. What we do see here, clearly, is the fear and disgust caused by everyday physical interactions between Jews and Christians that had been, and remained, frequent. The fear of the corruption of the Eucharistic species by contaminating contact with Jews is present in these letters, as we have seen—and, to my knowledge, for the first time. While Innocent makes no accusations of host desecration per se, we see reflected in these letters some of the same concerns that will later lead to full-blown stories of host desecration—the first and most influential of which will come some eighty years later, in 1290, in Paris. In these stories, as Miri Rubin has shown, supposed Jewish hostility toward the host serves as "proof" of the transubstantiation. This imagined hostility confirms that Jews are the eternal and constant enemies of Christians. This poisonous idea, responsible for the loss of thousands of lives in Jewish communities throughout Europe in the fourteenth and fifteenth centuries, is not yet fully blown in Innocent's bulls. But we see the seeds from which such ideas will sprout.

Notes

This publication is part of the research project RELMIN "The Legal Status of Religious Minorities in the Euro-Mediterranean World (5th–15th centuries)." The research leading to this publication has received funding from the European Research Council under the European Union's Seventh Framework Programme (FP7/2007–2013)/ERC grant agreement n°249416.

1. See Heinrich Graetz, *Geschichte der Juden von den ältesten Zeiten bis auf die Gegenwart aus den Quellen neu bearbeitet*, vol.7, *Von Maimunis Tod (1205) bis zur Verbannung der Juden aus Spanien und Portugal* (Leipzig, 1890; reprint Darmstad, 1998), 1–10; translation Bella Löwy, *History of the Jews, From the Earliest Times to the Present Day* (London, 1904), 3: 512. He calls Innocent "Das Papsttum in Kampfe gegen das Judentum" and states: "Dieser papst Innocenz III. war ein erbitterter Feind der Juden und des Judentums und hat ihnen tiefere Wunden geschlagen, als sämtliche vorangegangenen Widersacher."

2. Edward Synan, *The Popes and the Jews in the Middle Ages: An Intense Exploration of Judaeo-Christian Relationships in the Medieval World* (New York, 1965), 15.

3. Robert Chazan, "Pope Innocent III and the Jews," in *Pope Innocent III and his World*, ed. John Moore (Aldershot, 1999), 187–204.

4. Translated by Synan, *The Popes and the Jews,* 230.

5. Ibid., 232.

6. Dyan Elliott, "Pollution, Illusion, and Masculine Disarray: Nocturnal Emissions and the Sexuality of the Clergy," in *Constructing Medieval Sexuality,* ed. Karma Lochrie (Minneapolis, 1997), 1–23.

7. Quoted in David Biale, *Blood and Belief: The Circulation of a Symbol between Jews and Christians* (Berkeley, 2007), 115.

8. For the full Latin text of the bull, with English and French translations, commentary and bibliography, see John Tolan, "Etsi non displiceat Domino," Notice n° 30385, RELMIN project, http://www.cn-telma.fr/relmin/extrait30385/.

9. See John Tolan, "Etsi Iudeos," Notice n° 30352, RELMIN project, http://www.cn-telma.fr/relmin/extrait30352/.

10. While in the previous bull he had spoken of Christian *serui* working for Jews, here he uses the term *seruientes*. Indeed, *serui* generally refers to slaves, emphasizing their non-free legal status, while *seruientes* refers to their functions rather than their legal status. Innocent here distinguishes between the two terms, repeatedly using the word *serui* to designate the servile status imposed on Jews as punishment for the killing of Christ.

11. See Elisheva Baumgarten, *Mothers and Children: Jewish Family Life in Medieval Europe* (Princeton, 2004).

12. See John Tolan, "Ut esset Cain," Notice n° 30493, RELMIN project, http://www.cn-telma.fr/relmin/extrait30493/.

13. See Samuel Singer, *Thesaurus proverbiorum medii aevi* (Berlin, 2000), 129–130.

14. See David Freidenreich, *Foreigners and their Food: Constructing Otherness in Jewish, Christian, and Islamic Law* (Berkeley, 2011). I thank David Freidenreich for letting me see his manuscript before publication.

15. For examples, see http://www.cn-telma.fr/relmin/resultats/?typeRecherche=extraits&MOT_CLE[]=slaves.

16. See Baumgarten, *Mothers and Children.*

17. On the difficulties of finding wet nurses in medieval Europe, see Christiane. Klapisch-Zuber, "Parents de sang, parents de lait: La mise en nourrice à Florence (1300–1500)," *Annales de démographie historique* 19 (1983): 33–64; Baumgarten, *Mothers and Children.*

18. See Baumgarten, *Mothers and Children.*

19. Miri Rubin, *Gentile Tales: The Narrative Assault on Late Medieval Jews* (New Haven, 1999).

CHAPTER 10

THE IMAGE OF CHRISTIANS IN MEDIEVAL ASHKENAZIC RABBINIC LITERATURE

Ephraim Kanarfogel

R ecent scholarship has sought to characterize the way that Jews perceived Christians during the medieval period, focusing especially on polemical texts in which Jews shared their understanding of Christianity.[1] During the trial of the Talmud in 1240, Yeḥi'el of Paris was asked whether the restrictive talmudic legislation that was directed toward Gentiles includes Christians. He responded in the negative, a response to which we shall return.[2]

In his groundbreaking work on the relationship between Jews and Christians in medieval Europe, Jacob Katz provides evidence from talmudic interpretations and halakhic literature. He maintains that Ashkenazic legists, who sought to justify ongoing economic interactions between Jews and Christians on days or with commodities proscribed by talmudic law due to affinities with idolatry (*'avodah zarah*), did not mean to suggest that Christianity or its adherents were non-idolatrous. Rather, these authorities provided narrow casuistic arguments to allow the economic interactions to continue.

The Talmud (*'Avodah zarah* 6a) limits commerce with Gentiles on their festivals for two related reasons: the idolater will give thanks during his worship for these transactions, and the commodities or funds that the non-Jew acquires will allow him to offer items in the service of idolatry that might otherwise have been unavailable. During the medieval period, as Katz notes,

> Jews did business with non-Jews on the latter's holy days and dealt in any commodity that had value. So far as economic dealings were concerned, the talmudic prescriptions had fallen into almost complete abeyance …The exact meaning of such passages requires careful scrutiny before we arrive at any far-reaching conclusions as to the real opinion of the halakhists concerning the nature of the Christian religion.[3]

Among the texts adduced by Katz to support his approach is a responsum by Gershom b. Judah of Mainz (960–1028) that permits business dealings with Christians on their festivals, and allows accepting clerical vestments as collateral for loans. Rabbenu Gershom invokes a teaching of R. Yoḥanan (*Ḥullin* 13b), that "Gentiles outside the land [of Israel] are not idolaters; they are merely following the practice of their forefathers." Katz comments that

> the application of the above pronouncement to this particular point did not imply that Christians were not idolaters for all religious purposes...for here [Rabbenu Gershom] clearly assumes that the Gentiles in question, i.e., the Christians, do worship idols, but that their actions do not count as such in its strict halakhic sense. It was by a juridical formula that he made his case, and not by a distinction based on historical or theological considerations. The same applies to all the other authorities who have cited this decision without mentioning its originator.[4]

Katz notes a brief passage from a lengthy *Tosafot* at the beginning of '*Avodah zarah* (2a, s.v. *asur*) as representative of the "other authorities who have cited this decision without mentioning its originator." Elsewhere, he cites a formulation of Rashi—preserved by his grandson Rashbam (Samuel b. Meir)— that permits business transactions with Christians on their festival days, indicating that the talmudic prohibition was meant to include only devout idolaters. Katz concludes that for Rashi as well, there was no intent to "absolve the Christians of his day from the taint of idolatry" through the positing of a theological principle about Christianity. Rather, the suggestion that Christians were less devout was sufficient to allow for the relaxation of the rabbinic prohibition against doing business with them on their festivals.[5] Nonetheless, David Berger has suggested that these justifications "serve to mitigate the most pejorative evaluation of the status of its worshipers," and do go "some moderate distance toward mitigating the image of medieval Christians as idolaters."[6]

Although Katz points to several *Tosafot* as further support, he does not discuss them in detail.[7] Moreover, other texts that have become available suggest that this situation was more fluid than imagined. A single, overarching attitude in Ashkenaz concerning the religious nature and halakhic status of Christians cannot be sustained. A number of Tosafists held that not all Christians were idolaters, whereas others suggested new ways to localize this designation within Christian society.[8]

Twelfth-Century Initiatives

The *Tosafot* to '*Avodah zarah* that includes Rabbenu Gershom's formulation (without attribution) judges it insufficient to permit doing business with Gentiles on their festivals.[9] Two of the accepted solutions are attributed (by others) to Rashi or Rashbam: "we know that the Gentiles among us do not worship '*avodah zarah*,"[10] and engaging in commerce with the Gentiles on these days cannot be avoided, because this would give rise to potentially damaging enmity (*evah*).[11] The latter reason ostensibly does not say anything about the nature of Christianity.

Tosafot then presents the approach of Rashbam's younger brother, Rabbenu Jacob Tam (d. 1171). Rather than arguing that "times had changed," which allowed leniencies to be proposed, Rabbenu Tam suggests an innovative interpretation of the opening Mishnah in '*Avodah zarah*: only the sale of items that an idolater can offer as part of his worship service (*tikrovet*) is prohibited. Rabbenu Tam explains that although the Mishnah also prohibits moneylending on these days, only money lent without interest is intended, since this would provide the idolater with "free funds" to purchase worship items. If interest is charged, however, the idolater's gain is significantly reduced, as is the impact of the Jewish lender on the idolater's worship.

Indeed, for Rabbenu Tam, money was the only common commodity that should not be given freely to Christians, as it could be used to procure worship objects. *Tosafot* asserts that if a Christian asked to borrow money in order to make an offering to the Church, a Jew should refuse. Elhanan, son of Isaac of Dampierre (Isaac, known by the acronym Ri, was Rabbenu Tam's nephew and leading student), allows this, because the monies collected typically went to feed the officiants and not to support the worship service, for which other funds were available. Similarly, Ri's student, Barukh b. Isaac, maintains in his *Sefer ha-terumah* that the small amounts contributed by individual Christians, even if derived from transactions with Jews, could have been provided by other sources and are, therefore, insignificant. Ri notes, however, that if the money from a particular transaction was earmarked for worship services, those funds should be redirected.[12]

Although Rabbenu Tam's larger aim has been debated,[13] a passing remark in *Tosafot* suggests that Rabbenu Tam proposed his explanation in order to downplay the possibility that Christians were not idolaters: "According to Rabbenu Tam's interpretation, there is no reason to wonder about the widespread practice (*minhag ha-'olam*) to conduct business with them on their festival days, even if they are considered to be idolaters." The implication is that, while Rabbenu Tam's solution preserves this assumption about Christians, the other approaches presented by *Tosafot* do not.

Eli'ezer b. Nathan (Ra'avan) of Mainz applies the allowance that "we know that they do not worship '*avodah zarah*" only to those Christians "who sometimes work on their festivals and do not even go to houses of worship," and thus do not give thanks for their transactions at those times. Jews cannot transact business with Christians who attend worship services regularly, and especially on their festivals. Although Ra'avan adds a broader allowance, that these business transactions are also "vital for continued Jewish existence (*kedé hayyenu*)," he concludes "that it is better to be stringent and avoid them entirely."[14]

Rashbam is also cited as advocating that one should not rely on the allowance of *evah* (enmity) to conduct transactions on the day of a festival.[15] Israel

Ta-Shma has suggested that these calls for personal stringency were not meant to detract from the halakhic viability of the allowances that were promulgated by Tosafists, but rather to encourage the merchants to consider the specific business circumstances in which he finds himself (including the inclinations of the non-Jew with whom he is about to interact), and to conduct himself accordingly.[16]

Nonetheless, Ra'avan of Mainz recommends additional stringencies that were adopted by other German Tosafists. With regard to selling garments or coverings that were to be placed on or near the altar, he asserts that "one who is stringent will be blessed," even as he allows the selling of clerical vestments, coats (lit. *duslas*, dossals) and other ornaments worn by the priests, and to receive these objects and other church vessels as securities for loans. Clerical vestments were worn by priests to meet kings and rulers and not only during the worship service. There is no such justification, however, for the sale of garments used exclusively for the altar.[17]

Focusing again on the need to be aware of the actual practices of Christians, Ra'avan notes, with regard to renting a home to a Christian in light of certain talmudic restrictions concerning Gentiles, that "in eastern Europe and Byzantium, they are surely devout (*vaddai adukim*), since they place objects of '*avodah zarah* in the gates, doorways and walls of their homes."[18] Although Ra'avan's grandson, Eliezer b. Joel ha-Levi (Ra'avyah, d. ca. 1225), generally endorsed the allowances for doing business with Christians on their festivals, he concludes that "it is best not to do business involving worship objects on their festival with those who are known to be fully invested in idolatrous worship (lit. *minim*, heretics) such as priests."[19] Jacob Katz also suggests that *Sefer ḥasidim*—the guidebook of German Pietism during the early thirteenth century—rejected the French Tosafists' casuistic solutions and justifications for dealing with these kinds of items.[20]

Ra'avyah's teacher, Eliezer of Metz (d. 1198; Eli'ezer taught in the Rhineland for a period and had been a student of Rabbenu Tam),[21] was emphatic about the weakness of a key Tosafist legal strategy. The leniency of potential enmity (*evah*) was rather limited, as there are forms of commerce that will not engender enmity if briefly curtailed; this leniency is, thus, best avoided.[22] Barukh b. Isaac held similarly, preferring instead the approach that "we know that the [Christians] do not give thanks to their deity."[23] Moses b. Jacob of Coucy (ca. 1240), on the other hand, limits the allowance favored by Barukh, maintaining that it is effective "only when we know that the Gentile is not linked with idolatry and does not go to give thanks."[24]

Isaac b. Moses Or Zarua' (d. ca. 1250) studied with Tosafists in both northern France and Germany (including Ra'avyah). He attributes several anonymous opinions in the *Tosafot* on '*Avodah zarah* to Rashbam and even records Rashbam's hesitation about one of them. Isaac also rejects the view of Rabbenu Tam for not providing a sufficiently plausible explanation of the underlying talmudic texts, and concludes that the only approach that does not pose any interpretational difficulties is the one of minimizing enmity (which, as noted, does not impinge on the essential question of whether Christianity is idolatrous).[25]

However, the rabbinic support expressed for various allowances in both northern France and Germany during the late thirteenth century suggests that these became widely accepted. Perets b. Elijah of Corbeil (d. 1297), among others, brings together and endorses those allowances that maintain contemporary Christians were not complete idolaters.[26]

The Halakhic Status of Clerical and Ritual Objects

As noted by Jacob Katz, *Tosafot* on *'Avodah zarah* (50a-b, s.v. *ba'inan*), along with parallel passages citing Ri of Dampierre and Rashbam, permits commerce in certain church items. These include candles and wax, loaves of bread (or cakes) that were typically brought as gifts for the priests and other officiants (but were not offered up as part of the worship service), and priestly vestments and ritual items such as chalices.

The designation of an idolatrous offering (*tikrovet*) from which a Jew cannot benefit according to talmudic law depends on whether an analogous item or process was part of the sacrificial service in the Temple. Candles are not in this category, since the *menorah* in the Temple was not connected to the sacrificial offerings. Moreover, as candles and wax are considered *meshammeshé 'avodah zarah*—items that enhance the Christian worship service rather than items that were actually offered—the extinguishing of the candles by a priest or layman constitutes a sufficient act of nullification (*bittul*) that allows them to be sold to a Jew or given as collateral. Priestly garments were provided for the use of the officiants (and were considered to be their personal property, as was the chalice), just as the loaves of bread that were given to the priests were not part of the actual church service. Indeed, the only item prohibited by these *Tosafot* passages is the incense pan or censer-bearer.[27]

Similar formulations were offered by Ra'avan and Ra'avyah, who allowed the priests' vestments and dossals(as noted above), as well as their goblets and other ornaments, to be sold by Jews and to be accepted as collateral for loans. They too prohibited only censer-bearers and the incense itself. Ra'avyah adds a tradition received from his father, Joel b. Isaac ha-Levi (d. ca. 1200), that while candles and wax could be sold to and purchased from Christians, these materials should not be used in the performance of Jewish ritual precepts that required the lighting of candles; further, Ra'avan adds that the statues and icons found in the church should also not be sold or accepted as pawns.[28] The leniencies noted were reproduced in *Sefer or zarua'*, and in other thirteenth-century Tosafist sources.[29]

At the same time, however, a strongly held opinion developed among northern French Tosafists that restricted dealing with almost all priestly and church objects, even if laymen were the ones selling or buying them.[30] One such restrictive passage appears in *Tosafot* on *'Avodah zarah* (14b, s.v. *ḥatsav*), in the name of "R. Barukh ben R." (with the name of R. Barukh's father unidentified), which corresponds to a section from Barukh b. Isaac's *Sefer ha-terumah*.[31]Barukh prohibits buying or selling a priest's chalice, even if it had been slightly damaged as an intended act of nullification, since it could still be used by the priest, as well as books of Christian liturgy and scripture (referred to as *sefarim pesulim*). The Venice edition of *Sefer ha-terumah*, along with three manuscripts, attributes this view to the *Tosafot* of Eliezer of Metz to *Nedarim* (62b).[32]

Eliezer of Metz' *Tosafot* to *Nedarim* are not extant, but he writes in his *Sefer yere'im* that dealing in these clerical commodities (chalices, censer-bearers, priestly coats and other garments, and decorated covers to beautify the altar) is prohibited.[33] Indeed, while Eliezer was willing to be lenient regarding candles,[34] his student, Eleazar of Worms, notes that Eliezer wanted to prohibit them at some point because the *menorah* was found in the inner precincts of the Temple and candles are, thus, a significant aspect of the worship service.[35] Indeed, it was against this claim that Ri of Dampierre maintained that candles should be viewed in the lenient way that Rashbam did.[36]

Moreover, Eliezer of Metz' comment to *Nedarim* 62b can be reconstructed. The Talmud relates that Rav Ashi sold woodlands to idolaters. Ravina wonders why he was unconcerned that the idolaters would then use the wood to fashion objects of idolatry. Rav Ashi responds that since "most trees are used to provide heat," this is the (permitted) purpose of the sale. As recorded in the mid-thirteenth-century Italian compendium, *Shibbolé ha-leket*, Eliezer of Metz derives from this talmudic discussion that it is prohibited to lend or sell objects to Christians that are typically used for idolatrous purposes—such as priests' chalices, censer-bearers, and church liturgies—or to lend money to Christians (even at interest) if their intent was to purchase these and related items. Eliezer concludes that whoever is able to observe these restrictions "will merit God's salvation."[37]

As noted above, Eliezer of Metz also wished to limit the justification for doing business with Christians on their festivals because of enmity (*evah*), although few followed him.[38] His stringencies, however, with regard to selling church and clerical materials and objects were adopted not only by his younger colleague in northern France, Barukh b. Isaac, author of *Sefer ha-terumah*, but also by Moses b. Jacob of Coucy (d. ca. 1250), author of *Sefer mitsvot gadol*.[39]

The Position of Moses of Coucy

Jacob Katz concludes that as opposed to *Sefer ḥasidim*, Moses of Coucy permitted dealing in Christian ritual objects, noting that although some prohibitions remained, "his method…is casuistic and he accepts the exemptions authorized by his predecessors."[40] In fact, however, Moses of Coucy cites restrictive passages from both *Sefer yere'im* and *Sefer ha-terumah* (without attribution). Indeed, the only area of leniency in *Sefer mitsvot gadol* involves candles and wax, and perhaps certain priestly garments. As we have seen, these religious objects were more easily permitted for commerce, since their connection to idolatrous worship is somewhat tenuous.

Recent research has shown that Moses of Coucy composed a first version of *Sefer mitsvot gadol* that he subsequently revised. The best manuscripts of *Semag* are divided between these versions, while the first edition (Venice, 1547) appears to be a melange.[41] Moses follows the stringent view of Eliezer of Metz in the earlier version, even employing the language of *Sefer yere'im*. He disallows accepting a pawn from objects of worship and clerical accoutrements, including "goblets, incense pans and coats that are worn during the service."[42] The later version of *Semag* adds *mitronot*, a type of priestly garb, to the list of prohibited items, subsequently citing an allowance for them in the name of Rashbam along with an allowance for candles in the name of (Moses' teacher) Judah Sirleon (in the name of Ri), provided there is nullification.[43]

After discussing the allowances for doing business with Christians on their festivals (and expressing concern with one of the key justifications, as noted above), *Semag* returns to the issue of buying and selling prohibited objects. Here, both versions follow the passage from *Sefer ha-terumah* (Venice, 1523) referred to above,[44] and they conclude in accordance with *Sefer ha-terumah* and *Sefer yere'im*.[45] Moreover, at least one manuscript of *Semag* includes the restrictive passage from *Tosafot R. Eli'ezer mi-Metz* to *Nedarim* 62b.[46] In sum, Moses of Coucy features the stringent views of *Sefer yere'im* and *Sefer terumah*, with only a small degree of Rashbam's and Ri's leniencies, although to be sure, other thirteenth-century Tosafists who cite the position of Eliezer of Metz balance or reject it by presenting the more lenient northern French approach.[47]

Just before citing the *Tosafot* of Eliezer of Metz, which also prohibits the selling of Christian books and liturgies, *Shibbolé ha-leket* presents the view of Avigdor b. Elijah Katz of Vienna (in the name of Eliezer of Verona) that selling these is permitted.[48] At the same time, however, other passages in *Shibbolé ha-leket* suggest that Isaiah di Trani (Rid, d. ca. 1240) was stringent in these matters in the way that Eli'ezer of Metz and his northern French followers (Barukh b. Isaac and Moses of Coucy) were. Several passages among the writings of Isaiah, who studied in Germany with the Tosafist Simḥah of Speyer (and had access to the talmudic writings of Rabbenu Tam and his German students),[49] confirm this assessment.[50]

Changes in Christendom during the Thirteenth Century

Bringing together the two issues that have been discussed until this point, it is clear that the Tosafist views are not nearly as monolithic as Jacob Katz had maintained; there is no single mindset among the Tosafists about the status of

Christians and their worship objects. It is possible to suggest that the lenient Tosafist position about benefiting from Christian ritual objects held that because contemporary Christians were not considered to be unmitigated idolaters (at least regarding the economic restrictions indicated by talmudic law), one may benefit even from worship items that were under the control of the church offi-ciants, provided that these items did not represent recognized images or symbols of Christianity and were not instrinsic to the worship service. Those Tosafists who were decidely less lenient, beginning with Eli'ezer of Metz, may have been inclined to overall stringency in dealing with Christians (as idolaters), although the approaches of Barukh b. Isaac in *Sefer ha-terumah* and Moses of Coucy in *Sefer mitsvot gadol* do not easily support such a simple reading.

Indeed, while there are other halakhic issues that may have impacted these considerations,[51] it is possible to contextualize the (heretofore unnoticed) devel-opment of the stringent position on the part of Barukh b. Isaac and Moses of Coucy that did not allow for deriving economic benefit from church and ritual objects[52] by focusing on the increased clericalization of the church during the late twelfth and early thirteenth centuries.[53] As noted above, Barukh and Moses also sought to monitor the effectiveness of the approach that "we know that the [Christians] do not give thanks to their deity," as a means of allowing Jews to do business with Christians on their festivals.[54]

Moses of Coucy and other like-minded Tosafists understood that a shift was occurring within Christendom. Clerics were being given greater responsibility for the affairs of Christian society. As such, clergymen were now seen, at least by the rabbinic elite, as more devoted Christians than laymen, and the practice of *'avodah zarah* could be localized among the clergy and their closest followers. This distinction is also evident in another formulation of *Sefer ha-terumah* (and *Sefer mitsvot gadol*), that distinguishes between healing performed by a Gentile doctor (from which a Jew may benefit), and healing done by someone from among the *minim*, (clerics), who invokes "an idolatrous formula" (*laḥash shel 'avodah zarah*) that is prohibited according to talmudic law.[55]

This development may also explain Moses of Coucy's insistence that Jews not deceive Christians in economic interactions: "We have already explained concerning the remnant of Israel that they are not to deceive anyone, whether a Christian or a Moslem."[56] Based on another passage in *Sefer mitsvot gadol*, in which Moses emphasizes that the "remnant of Israel" will remain in the Diaspora as long as injustices are commited against others, Jacob Katz suggests that Moses' appeal "is wedded to the messianic expectation which once again became intense at this period in Jewish history."[57] Judah Galinsky maintains that this directive is part of a larger program to ensure that absolute truthfulness should be practiced in all instances, occasionally even beyond the stated dictates of talmudic law.[58]

In light of Moses of Coucy's awareness of clericalization and its impact, he perhaps preached moral behavior toward Christians because he held that non-clerical Christians were not so intimately involved with idolatry. In addition, in using the phrase "the remnant of Israel," Moses wished to indicate that, among the Jews, no such distinction existed between the rabbinic leadership and the larger community in terms of moral or religious beliefs and commitments.

At the same time that Moses of Coucy composed his *Sefer mitsvot gadol*, his Tosafist colleague, Yeḥi'el of Paris, indicates during the trial of the Talmud that there is a possibility for Christians to be saved. The only impediment appears be the issue of *'avodah zarah*, which Gentiles cannot practice if they wish to be considered proper followers of the Noachide laws.[59] Shortly before this, however, Yeḥi'el was asked about the restrictions that the Talmud placed on non-Jews, which medieval Jewry supposedly applied to Christians; he responds that this was not the case. Part of his proof stems from the fact that while "according to the Mishnah, business may not be done with non-Jews for three days before their festivals, if you were to go right now to the *rue de Juifs*, you would see how much business we do [with Christians] even on the very day of the festival(s)."[60]

As a French Tosafist, Yeḥi'el of Paris was undoubtedly aware of the leniencies and justifications that extended back to Rashi and Rashbam.[61] As has been noted, several of the formulations put forward by French Tosafists stopped short of identifying contemporary Christians as complete idolaters. Although Rabbenu Tam and a number of German Tosafists argued against this softer perception, the more lenient view largely won the day.

Moreover, unlike Moses of Coucy, who was firmly committed to the more restrictive approaches of Eli'ezer of Metz and Barukh b. Isaac concerning the status of the clergy and their religious implements, Yeḥi'el was free to suggest that if Christians could move further in the direction that had already led to the dissolution of business restrictions on their festivals, salvation might indeed be possible. Yeḥi'el's intention is reflected in his use of the phrase, "let me tell you a way that you can be saved even through your faith," which can also be translated according to the Hebrew original as "a way that you can be saved even according to your belief."[62]

For Yeḥi'el of Paris and those Tosafists whose approach he supported, Christianity could not easily be removed from the halakhic category of *'avodah zarah*. However, individual Christians were perceived as not fully idolatrous, just as Moses of Coucy and the Tosafist approach that he favored held that Christians who were not members of the clergy were also somewhat removed from idolatrous worship. These nuanced Tosafist perceptions had important ramifications for economic and social practices and interactions, if not for larger theoretical reassessments or reimaginings.[63]

Notes

1. See Ivan Marcus, "Jews and Christians Imagining the Other in Medieval Europe," *Prooftexts* 15 (1995), 209–217; Anna Sapir Abulafia, "Invectives against Christianity in the Hebrew Chronicles of the First Crusade," in *Crusade and*

Settlement, ed. Peter W. Edbury (Cardiff, 1985), 66–72; David Berger, "On the Image and Destiny of Gentiles in Ashkenazic Polemical Literature," in *Persecution, Polemic and Dialogue* (Boston, 2010), 117–138; David Berger, "Medieval Christians and Jews: Mutual Perceptions and Attitudes," in *Cambridge History of Judaism*, vol. 6, ed. Robert Chazan (in press).

2. See *Vikkuaḥ R.Yeḥi'el mi-Paris*, ed. Reuven Margoliyot (Lemberg, 1888), 21; and below, n. 60.
3. See Jacob Katz, *Exclusiveness and Tolerance* (Oxford, 1961), 29–32.
4. See Ibid., 33–34. See also Jacob Katz, *Ben yehudim le-goyim* (Jerusalem, 1960), 43, 116; David Berger, "Jacob Katz on Jews and Christians in the Middle Ages," in *The Pride of Jacob*, ed. Jay Harris (Cambridge, MA, 2002), 41 n. 1, 60–61; Berger, *Persecution, Polemic and Dialogue*, 169–170.
5. See Katz, *Halakhah ve-kabbalah* (Jerusalem, 1986), 284, which cites the Rashbam passage from *Toldot adam ve-ḥavvah* by Yeroḥam b. Meshullam (d. ca. 1350). It is found already in Asher b.Yeḥi'el, *Piské ha-rosh al massekhet 'avodah zarah*, 1:1 (Asher was a teacher of Yeroḥam), and in *Tosafot R. Elḥanan*, ed. Aaron Kreuzer (Bnei Brak, 2003), fols. 1b-2a, which Ephraim E. Urbach, *Ba'alé ha-tosafot* (Jerusalem, 1980), 1:254, dates to 1182. See also Israel Elfenbein, ed., *Teshuvot Rashi* (New York, 1943), sec. 327 (on deriving benefit from Christian wine:"they are not well-versed in the worship of idols,") cited by Katz, *Exclusiveness and Tolerance*, 34, n. 2; *Sefer or zarua'*, piské 'avodah zarah, secs. 95–96, ed. Machon Yerushalayim (Jerusalem, 2010), 3:582.
6. See Berger, "Medieval Christians and Jews," (above, n. 1), at n. 25.
7. See Katz, *Exclusiveness and Tolerance*, 29 (n. 3); Katz, *Bein Yehudim le-Goyim*, 40 (n. 20); and below, n. 27.
8. Menaḥem ha-Me'iri of Perpignan (d. 1315) considered Christianity to be excluded from 'avodah zarah, although the motivation and scope of Meiri's approach has been debated. See Katz, *Exclusiveness and Tolerance*, 114–128; Katz, "Od 'al savlanuto ha-datit shel R. Menaḥem ha-mei'ri," *Zion* 46 (1981): 243–246; Berger, *Persecution, Polemic and Dialogue*, 293–294; Israel Ta-Shma, *Halakhah, minhag, u-metsi'ut be-ashkenaz, 1000–1350* (Jerusalem, 1996), 251–261; Israel Ta-Shma, *Ha-sifrut ha-parshanit la-talmud* (Jerusalem, 2000), 2: 167–170; Moshe Halbertal, *Ben torah le-ḥokhmah* (Jerusalem, 2000), 80–108.
9. Urbach, *Ba'alé ha-tosafot*, 2:654–657, identifies the editor of *Tosafot 'avodah zarah* as a student of Rabbenu Perets b. Elijah of Corbeil (d. 1297). Prior strata include those from Elḥanan b. ha-Ri and Samuel of Falaise (based on the *Tosafot* of his teacher, Judah Sirleon, a student of Ri). Passages from the halakhic works *Sefer ha-terumah*, *Sefer mitsvot gadol*, and *Sefer or zarua'* are also cited in these *Tosafot*; on these Tosafist works and authors, see below, nn. 12, 24, 25.
10. See Kreuzer, *Tosfot R. Elḥanan*, above, n. 5. Passages in *Tosfot R. Elḥanan* and *Tosfot Rash mi-Shantz* also assert that the Christians in their day did not express gratitude to their deity as a result of the business transactions that they did with Jews. See Ta-Shma, *Halakhah, minhag, u-metzi'ut be-ashkenaz*, 248 (n. 22).
11. See *Sefer or zarua'*, secs. 95–98 (3:582, col. 2); *Sefer Ra'avyah 'al massekhet 'avodah zarah*, ed. David Deblitzky (Jerusalem, 1976), 23 (sec. 1051); and the precis to Barukh b. Isaac, *Sefer ha-terumah*, hilkhot 'avodah zarah, sec. 134 (Jerusalem, 2003), 23.

12. See *Sefer ha-terumah, hilkhot 'avodah zarah*, sec. 134, fol. 47b-c; Urbach, *Ba'alé ha-tosafot*, 1:350–351; Kreuzer, *Tosfot R. Elhanan*, fol. 5a; and *Sefer Mordekhai 'al massekhet 'avodah zarah*, sec. 795. See also *Piské ha-Rosh 'al massekhet 'avodah zarah*,1:1; *Hiddushé ha-Ritva 'al massekhet 'avodah zarah*, ed. Moshe Goldstein (Jerusalem, 1982), 6, s.v. *le-halvotan*; and *Piské R. Yesha'yah di-Trani le-massekhet 'avodah zarah*, ed. A. Y. Wertheimer et al. (Jerusalem, 2006), 167; and below, n. 50.

13. See, for example, Shalom Albeck, "Yahaso shel Rabbenu Tam le-va'ayot zemanno," *Zion* 19 (1954): 106–112, 123–126, 141; Urbach, *Ba'alé ha-tosafot*, 1:62–66, 89–93; and Haim Hillel Ben-Sasson, "Hanhagatah shel Torah," *Behinot be-vikkoret ha-sifrut* 9 (1956): 46–48.

14. See *Sefer Ra'avan – even ha-'ezer* (Jerusalem, 1975), sec. 288, fol. 124b. The twenty-first canon of the Fourth Lateran Council of 1215 requires every Christian who had attained the age of reason to confess his sins at least once a year and to receive communion at least at Easter. See also Solomon Grayzel, *The Church and the Jews in the XIIIth Century* (New York, 1966), 115, for the letter by Innocent III (1205) to the Archbishop of Sens and the Bishop of Paris.

15. See *Sefer or zarua', piské 'avodah zarah*, sec. 99 (end), 3:584.

16. See Ta-Shma, *Halakhah, minhag u-metsi'ut*, 249.

17. See *Sefer Ra'avan*, sec. 289. See also Deblitzky, *Sefer Ra'avyah 'al massekhet 'avodah zarah*, 24 (sec. 1051); *Sefer ha-asufot*, ms. Montefiore 134, fol. 130c (sec. 450), and below, 28. See also Joseph Shatzmiller, "Church Articles: Pawns in the Hands of Jewish Moneylenders," *Wirtschaftgeschichte der mittelalterichen Juden*, ed. Michael Toch (Munich, 2008), 98–99; Joseph Shatzmiller, *Cultural Exchange* (Princeton, 2013), 28–33. Rabbenu Tam and Rashbam also allowed Jews to sell priestly garments, as noted by their nephew Ri, who nonetheless recommended stringency because of the confusion that might ensue. See *Shittat ha-kadmonim 'al massekhet 'avodah zarah*, (*Teshuvot u-fesakim le-Ri ha-Zaken*), ed. Moshe Blau (New York, 1991), 3: 245 (sec. 137). See also *Shibbolé ha-leket—ha-helek ha-sheni*, ed. Simha Hasida (Jerusalem, 1988), 41 (sec. 9).

18. See *Sefer Ra'avan*, sec. 291, fol. 125a; Shlomo Eidelberg, "Tseror he'arot," *Tarbiz* 52 (1983): 647–648; Israel Ta-Shma, *Keneset mehkarim* (Jerusalem, 2000), 1: 224–229, 245–249.

19. See Deblitzky, *Sefer Ra'avyah 'al massekhet 'avodah zarah*, 22–23. Ra'avyah rejects the innovative approach of Rabbenu Tam because "it does not reflect the simple sense of the Talmud," but he ends up following it *de facto*. See Ta-Shma, *Halakhah, minhag u-metsi'ut*, 248.

20. See Katz, *Exclusivness and Tolerance*, 97–102 (based on *Sefer hasidim*, ed. Judah Wistinetski [Frankfurt, 1924], secs.1233, 1349–1350, 1359). See also Shatzmiller, "Church Articles" 97–98; and Ephraim Kanarfogel "R. Judah he-Hasid and the Rabbinic Scholars of Regensburg: Interactions, Influences and Implications," *Jewish Quarterly Review* 96 (2006): 17–37.

21. See Rami Reiner, "Rabbenu Tam: rabbotav (ha-tsarfattim) ve-talmidav bené Ashkenaz," (MA thesis, Hebrew University, 1997), 111–113 and compare with Urbach, *Ba'alé ha-tosafot*, 1:156–158.

22. See *Sefer yere'im ha-shalem* (Jerusalem, 1973), sec. 270, fol. 129a; and above, n. 14. Eliezer's position is also found (nearly a century later) in the (halakhic) *derashot* of

Ḥayyim b. Isaac Or Zarua'; see *Piské halakhah shel R. Ḥayyim Or Zarua': derashot Maharaḥ*, ed. Y. S. Lange (Jerusalem, 1972), 39 [ed. Abbitan, sec. 11, p. 15, col. 2], to *parashat va'era*. Ta-Shma, *Halakhah, minhag u-metsi'ut*, 250, suggests that this perhaps reflects an approach akin to that of the German Pietists, one of whose principals, Eleazar of Worms, also studied with Eliezer of Metz; see below, n. 35. As we shall see, however, there was also a tendency toward strictness in northern France during the thirteenth century.

23. See *Sefer ha-terumah, hilkhot 'avodah zarah*, sec. 134 (fol. 47a). *Tosafot 'avodah zarah* 2a also notes this limitation.

24. See Moses b. Jacob of Coucy, *Sefer mitsvot gadol (Semag), lo ta'aseh* 45 (Jerusalem, 1993), 1: 78.

25. See *Sefer or zarua'*, secs. 95–99, 3:582–584. See also above, n. 15; and *Piské halakhah shel R. Ḥayyim Or Zarua'*, ed. Lange, above, n. 22. Isaac b. Moses rejects the allowance of "we know that they do not worship idolatry," because the talmudic case on which it was based assumes that the former idolater now had the status of a *ger toshav* (an assertion that had been rejected by *Sefer ha-terumah*, above, n. 23), although he also rejects the allowance of *evah* in a situation "where it is certain that the Gentile is an idolater," as his teacher Ra'avyah did (above, n. 19).

26. See, for example, *Sefer ha-dinim le-Rabbenu Perets*, ms. Vienna (National Library) 180, fol. 366r. This manuscript passage has been blurred, undoubtedly due to censorship. Rabbenu Perets' view is recorded clearly, however, in *Sefer kol bo*, ed. David Avraham (2001), 5: 895, (sec. 97), and is also found in the parallel *Orḥot ḥayyim le-R. Aharon ha-Kohen (mi-Lunel)*, ed. Moshe Schlesinger (Berlin, 1899), 2: 226 (sec. 21). On the surviving manuscript fragments of R. Perets' *Sefer ha-dinim*, see Ismar Elbogen, "Les 'Dinim' de R. Pereç," *REJ* 45 (1902), 99–111, 204–217 (and esp. 104). Asher b. Yeḥi'el (*Piské ha-Rosh 'al massekhet 'avodah zarah*, 1:1) presents a formulation similar to that of Rabbenu Perets (in the names of Rashi and Rashbam; above, n. 5), although he also records the allowance of *mishum evah*. *Sefer Mordekhai 'al massekhet 'avodah zarah*, sec. 795, cites each of the leniencies.

27. See Katz, *Exclusiveness and Tolerance*, 44, where he also cites *Tosafot 'Avodah zarah* 14b, s.v. *ḥatsav*, although this passage represents a rather different Tosafist view; see below, nn. 31, 44. See also *Shittat ha-kadmonim 'al massekhet 'avodah zarah*, ed. M. Blau (New York, 1969), 2:251–252; Aaron. Kreuzer, "Tosfot Ri ha-Zaken 'al massekhet 'avodah zarah," *Moriah* 33:1–3 (B'nei B'rak, 2013): 4–5. See *Semak mi-Tsirikh*, ed. Isaac J. Har-Shoshanim (Jerusalem, 1979), 1:139 (sec. 211: the chalice is merely a receptacle and does not require nullification).

28. See *Sefer Ra'avan*, sec. 289; Katz, ibid., 45; Deblitzky, *Sefer Ra'avyah*, 24 (sec. 1051); and above, n. 17. At the end of this section (p. 26), Ra'avyah cites the (lenient) rulings of Rashbam in his name. See also *Sefer ha-asufot*, ms. Montefiore 134, fol. 130c (sec. 450). R. Meir of Rothenburg (d. 1293) ruled similarly that priestly garments should not be fashioned into a *tallit* or used for any other *mitsvah*, nor should jewels worn by priests be used to adorn a *tallit*. See *R. Meir b. Barukh mi-Rotenburg: teshuvot, pesakim u-minhagim*, ed. Isaac Z. Kahana (Jerusalem, 1957), 1: 227–228 (secs. 123–125). Dr. Pinchas Roth was kind enough to provide Provençal rabbinic material on the loaves given to priests. While almost all Ashkenazic authorities considered these loaves to be gifts for the priests, several Provencal halakhists considered them to be a *tikrovet*, perhaps because they were presented in tithing baskets. See, for example, Samuel ben

Mordekhai's commentary on *Mishneh torah* (to *hilkhot 'avodah zarah*, 7:15), in ms. Paris 355, fol. 42a; Zeraḥyah ha-Levi, *Sefer ha-ma'or* to *'Avodah Zarah* (chapter four), fol. 23b in the pagination of the Rif (*Sefer ba 'al ha-ma'or*, ed. Daniel Bitton [Jerusalem, 2005], 3:422). See also Yeroḥam b. Meshullam, *Toldot adam ve-ḥavvah*, 17:4 (fol. 128). Ra'avad of Posquières disagrees with Zeraḥyah ha-Levi; for his (lenient) position and an Ashkenazic view that prohibited these breads (since *bittul* cannot be accomplished), see below, n. 36.

29. See *Sefer or zarua'*, *piské 'avodah zarah*, sec. 209, 636 a-b. See also Ḥasida, *Sefer shibbolé ha-leket*, 39 (sec. 9), who cites Rashbam extensively ibid., 41, and below, n. 37, for his citation of the stringent view of Eliezer of Metz. *Sefer Mordekhai*, secs. 842–843 (=ms. Vercelli C235, fols. 117b-c) cites the allowances of both Rashbam and Ra'avyah (and rejects the position of Eliezer of Metz). In his *Sefer ha-dinim*, ms. Vienna 180, fols. 374r-v (*Kol bo*, 945, and *Orhot ḥayyim*, 230–231, sec. 6), Rabbenu Perets cites various French allowances mentioning both Rashi and Rashbam. However, he considers the priest's chalice to be a genuine *'avodah zarah* accessory, just like the censer-bearer; see also *Piské ha-Rosh*, 4:1. See also *Bayit ḥadash* to *Arba 'ah turim*, *Yoreh de 'ah*, sec. 139, s.v. *va-ḥatikhot*; and the position attributed to R. Meir of Rothenburg in *Semak mi-Tsirikh* (above, n. 27), expressed also by R. Meir's student, R. Ḥayyim b. Isaac Or Zarua', in his *Derashot*, ed. Lange (above, n. 22), 38, that the chalice can hold materials that were integral to the church service. See also Perets's glosses to Isaac of Corbeil's *Sefer mitzvot katan (Semak)*(sec. 68, and ms. Hamburg-Levi 70); and *Orhot ḥayyim*, 2:230–231. On the citation of Eliezer of Metz' view by *Tosfot Rabbenu Perets* (to *Nedarim*), see below, n. 37. Note also (above, n. 9) the role of Rabbenu Perets and his students as editors of *Tosafot* on *'Avodah zarah*, in which many of the French leniences are found.

30. An ordinance whose attribution to Rabbenu Tam is uncertain, prohibits buying church vessels and vestments or accepting them as security, a position that is not associated with him elsewhere as far as I can tell. Moreover, a version of this *takkanah* specifies that it refers to the purchase of stolen church items; the restriction is due to the possible peril involved, rather than to distinctly halakhic considerations. See Louis Finkelstein, *Jewish Self-Government in the Middle Ages* (New York, 1964), 171–175, 178, 188–189, 211. See also Shatzmiller, "Church Articles," 97.

31. See *Sefer ha-terumah* (Venice, 1523), *hilkhot 'avodah zarah*, sec. 138; and Urbach, *Ba'alé ha-tosafot*, 1:354 (n. 65).

32. See Simha Emanuel, *Shivré luḥot* (Jerusalem, 2006), 295 (n. 337); ms. Parma [de Rossi] 617, fols. 190c-d; ms. Paris BN Heb. 359, fols. 132r-v; ms. JTS Rab. 1115, fols. 153v-154r; and see also *Piské haRrosh*, 1:15. See also Shatzmiller, *Cultural Exchange*, 26–27. On the linkage with *Nedarim* 62b, see below, n. 37.

33. See *Sefer yere'im*, sec. 102 (fols. 37a-b); sec. 270 (fol. 129a); sec. 364 (fol. 197a); and see the next note. Although the word *kippot* in this passage perhaps refers to a priestly head-covering, the version of *Sefer yere'im* cited in *Sefer Mordekhai* (which is otherwise identical to *Sefer yerei'im*, sec. 102) reads *ve-kaps she-lovshim ha-shammashim*, suggesting that this refers to some kind of cape-like garment. Compare *Haggahot maimuniyyot*, *hilkhot 'avodah zarah*, 7:2; and below, n. 43; *Teshuvot rabbenu gershom*, ed. Shlomo Eidelberg (New York, 1955), 75 (and Katz, above, n. 27). Rabbenu Gershom maintains that the priests' garments are akin

to the garments that *kohanim* wore during their Temple service (which were an instrinsic part of the service). He therefore based his own allowance to sell or accept priests' garments as collateral on R. Yoḥanan's principle that Gentiles outside of Israel were not considered to be idolaters.

34. See *Sefer yere'im ha-shalem*,sec. 101 (end*)*. See also ms.Vercelli C235, fol. 117b.

35. See R. *El'azar mi-Vermaiza, ma'aseh rokeaḥ 'al pi ketav yad "sefersinai"* Berlin *ha-muze'on ha-yehudi* (VII.262.5), ed. Emese Kozma (Jerusalem, www.imhm. blogspot.com, entry for 2/08/10), 74 (sec. 600; top). See also Simha Emanuel, *R. El'azar mi-Vermaiza: derashah le-fesaḥ* (Jerusalem, 2006), 25 (n. 89). In the previous section in Eleazar's work (sec. 599, about eating milk and meat at the same table), Eliezer of Metz is cited by name, and earlier within sec. 600, Eleazar of Worms cites the lenient viewof Rashbam with regard to candles and wax (above, n. 27). See also *Sefer or zarua'*, *piské 'avodah zarah*, secs. 208–209, and below, n. 50.

36. See Blau, *Shittat ha-kadmonim 'al massekhet 'avodah zarah*, (above, n. 17), 3:265, sec. 161 (end). See also ms. Mantua 30, fol. 245v. Ra'avad of Posquières, *Katuv sham* (to *'avodah zarah*), ed. Haim Freiman (Jerusalem, 2003), 213, also prohibits the wax and candles as *tikrovet*. See also *Ḥiddushé ha-Ramban* to *'Avodah zarah* (51b), ed. Chaim D. Chavel (Jerusalem, 1970), 202. After citing the allowance for candles according to Rashbam, Naḥmanides notes that an unnamed figure prohibited them, concluding, however, that this view is mistaken (since the *menorah*, although lit in the inner sanctum of the Temple, was not part of the sacrificial service). See Ta-Shma, *Halakhah, minhag u-metsi'ut be-ashkenaz*, 250–251; and Ephraim Kanarfogel, "Between Ashkenaz and Sefarad: Tosafist Teachings in the Talmudic Commentaries of Ritva," in *Between Rashi and Maimonides*, ed. Ephraim Kanarfogel and Moshe Sokolow (New York, 2010), 246 (n. 30).

37. See Hasida, *Shibbolé ha-leket*, (above, n. 17); and without attribution in *Tosfot ha-Rosh 'al massekhet nedarim*, ed. Bezalel Deblitzky (Jerusalem, 2001), 87; *Tosfot Rabbenu Perets ha-shalem 'al massekhet nedarim*, ed. MordekhaiY.Weiner (Jerusalem, 2006), 150; and *Tosafot* on *Nedarim* 62b, s.v. *ha'ikka* (in truncated form). See also *Ḥiddushé ha-Rashba 'al massekhet nedarim*, ed.Yaakov Salomon (Jerusalem, 1991), 250; ms. Vatican 144 (below, n. 46); and Urbach, *Ba'alé ha-tosafot*, 1:162–163, 2:635.

38. See above, nn. 22–26. Note also Eliezer's concern about the idolatrous nature of saint worship, and those who might encounter public displays or processions involving saint veneration, in *Sefer yere'im*, sec. 270 (fols. 128a–b). See Katz, *Exclusiveness and Tolerance*, 45; and below, n. 51. Here too, Eliezer's approach does not seem to have impacted Ashkenazic halakhic literature. See *Ḥiddushé ha-Ran 'al massekhet sanhedrin*, ed.Yisrael Sklar (Jerusalem, 2004), 445 (s.v. *yak-hol afillu*); *Semak*, sec. 29; and Judah Galinsky, "Gishot shonot le-tofa'at mofté ha-kedoshim ha-notsrim be-sifrut ha-rabbanit shel yemé ha-benayim," *Ta-Shma: meḥkarim le-zikhro shelYisra'el M.Ta-shma*, ed. Moshe Idel et al. (Jerusalem, 2011), 1:195–200.

39. Citing one passage from *Sefer yere'im*, Katz (*Exclusiveness and Tolerance*, 44, n. 2) considers Eliezer of Metz to be the lone holdout, preventing the lenient northern French Tosafist view regarding Christian ritual objects from being

"universally accepted." See also idem., *Ben yehudim le-goyim*, 52 (n. 25). Compare with Isaac b. Moses, *Sefer or zarua', piské 'avodah zarah*, sec. 130, 3:597, who ratifies a stringency endorsed by Eliezer b. Isaac of Prague (or Bohemia) prohibiting a Jew to sell writing tablets and ink to priests lest they record their teachings on them. See, *Haggahot maimuniyyot, hilkhot 'avodah zarah*. 7:2; *Haggahot asheri*, 1:15; and below, n. 48. On Eliezer of Prague, see Urbach, *Ba'alé ha-tosafot*, 1:212–215; *Sefer or zarua'*, pt. 1, *she'elot u-teshuvot*, sec. 113, 1:107–108); *hilkhot netilat yadayim*, sec. 75 (1:81); and *hilkhot se'udah*, sec. 155 (1:146).

40. See Jacob Katz, *Exclusiveness and Tolerance*, 102–103; Moses b. Jacob of Coucy, *Sefer mitsvot gadol* (Venice, 1547), *lo ta'aseh* 45 (fols. 10a-b); and above, n. 27.

41. See *Semag*, vol. 1 (*mitsvot lo ta'aseh*), editor's introduction, 17–24; and vol. 2 (*mitzvot lo ta'aseh*), editor's introduction, 17–24.

42. See *Semag, lo ta'aseh* 45, 77 and see above, n. 33.

43. See ibid., 77–78. Compare *Haggahot maimuniyyot, hilkhot 'avodah zarah*, 7:2. A rabbinic commentary suggests (*Semag*, ibid., n. 45) that *me'ilim* connotes garments that serve as coverings for the religious implements or for the altar, while *mitronot* refers to priestly garb. However, the simple meaning of the term *me'il* in Ashkenazic texts is priestly clothing. Since the word *mitronot* may connote a cape, it is possible that *me'ilim* refer to the basic service garments of the priest, while *mitronot* are outerwear. This distinction is found in one version of Eliezer of Metz' formulations (above, n. 33). Outerwear may be more easily permitted since it was worn publicly, outside the church service. However, it is more likely that the later version of *Semag* simply includes a more lenient view concerning priestly garments generally (like that of Rashbam), and the two terms mean the same thing.

44. See ibid., 79; and above, n. 31.

45. Ibid.

46. See ms.Vatican 144, fol. 112d; and above, n. 37.

47. See above, n. 29. See also *Kitsur sefer mitsvot gadol le-R. Avraham ben Efrayim*, ed. Yehoshua Horowitz (Jerusalem, 2005), 145, which cites the various French leniences of Rashi, Rashbam, Ri and R. Judah Sirleon, along with perhaps the only leniency associated with Eliezer of Metz: if certain ritual objects had already reached the hands of a Jew, they could be nullified by a Christian at that point so that the Jew would not now have to forego benefit.

48. See Hasida, *Shibbolé ha-leket*, (above, n. 17). Eliezer of Verona was a student of Ri of Dampierre. He composed *Tosafot* to *Bava Batra* and was apparently a teacher of Avigdor Katz' teachers. See Urbach, *Ba'alé ha-tosafot*, 1:433–36. Yosef Karo, *Shulḥan 'arukh, Yoreh de'ah*, sec. 139:15, rules in accordance with the view of Eliezer and Avigdor, while Moses Isserles rules stringently, following *Sefer ha-terumah* and *Semag* (above, nn. 44–45). Note that the leading fifteenth-century Austrian rabbinic authority, Israel Isserlein (*Terumat ha-deshen, pesakim*, #112, cited by Isserles) rules that selling *sefarim pesulim* to priests is prohibited if these books discuss matters of Christian faith (*sefer yir'atam*). If, however, the contents of a book are not known (seemingly due to a language barrier), it is possible to be lenient since the majority are works of "law, medicine, astronomy, mathematics and music."

49. See Israel Ta-Shma, *Keneset meḥkarim* (Jerusalem, 2005), 1: 9–48.

50. See Ḥasida, *Shibbolé ha-leket*, 40 (sec. 9). See the references to these formulations in Rid's *tosafot* and *pesakim*, Ḥasida, *Shibbolé ha-leket*, nn. 28, 29, 33, 36, 39, 42; and see above, n. 12.

51. Note, for example, the acceptance of a Christian oath for business transactions. See Katz, *Exclusiveness and Tolerance*, 34; Berger, "Jacob Katz on Jews and Christians," 60–61; idem., *Persecution, Polemic and Dialogue*, 170, 294; and Galinsky, "Gishot shonot," 195–196. For Ra'avyah's stringent view, see Deblitzky, *Sefer ra'avyah 'al massekhet 'avodah zarah*, 28 (sec. 1053); *Sefer Mordekhai 'al massekhet 'avodah zarah*, sec. 809.

52. Compare, Urbach, *Ba'alé ha-tosafot*, 1:176–177, 351–352, 474–475.

53. See, for example, Caroline Bynum, *Jesus as Mother: Studies in the Spirituality of the High Middle Ages* (Berkeley, 1982), 9–21, 53–58, 236–241, 247–262; Richard William Southern, *Scholastic Humanism and the Unification of Europe* (Oxford, 1995), 134–137; Richard William Southern, *Western Society and the Church in the Midde Ages* (Harmondsworth, 1970), 36–41; and Jeremy Cohen, *The Friars and the Jews* (Ithaca, 1982), 33–44.

54. See above, nn. 23–24.

55. See *Sefer ha-terumah, hilkhot 'avodah zarah*, sec. 153; *Semag, lo ta'aseh* 45 (and ms. Berlin Or. Phillip 1392, fol. 189r); Galinsky, "Gishot shonot," 215–216, who notes the presence of this passage in Rabbenu Peretz' *Sefer ha-dinim*. See also *Semak*, sec. 13 (end); above, n. 31; and Ya'akov Fuchs, "Ketav yad Mantua ha-kehilah ha-yehudit 30 u-terumato," *Tarbiz* 79 (2011): 402–408. The German Tosafist Simḥah of Speyer (d. ca. 1230), and his student, R. Bonfant (Samuel ha-Levi of Worms), indicate that the penance (of immersion) for a reverting apostate was meant to atone for sins committed while living among Christians such as consuming non-kosher foods; no mention is made of atonement for the worship of idolatry. See *Teshuvot u-fesakim*, ed. Efraim Kupfer (Jerusalem, 1973), 290–91 (sec. 71), and see Ephraim Kanarfogel, "Returning to the Jewish Community in Medieval Ashkenaz: History and Halakhah," in *Turim: Studies in Jewish History and Literature Presented to Dr. Bernard Lander*, ed. Michael A. Shmidman (New York, 2007), 1: 69–97.

56. See *Sefer mitsvot gadol* (ed. Venice), *mitsvat 'aseh* 82 (fol. 167d).

57. See Katz, *Exclusiveness and Tolerance*, 104–105.

58. See Judah Galinsky, "R. Moshe mi-Coucy ke-ḥasid, darshan u-folmosan: hebbetim me-'olamo ha-maḥshavti u-fe'iluto ha-tsibburit," (MA thesis, Yeshiva University, 1993), 43–50. See *Semag, mitsvat lo ta'aseh* 152 (fol. 58b); *lo ta'aseh* 170 (fol. 61a); and Jeffrey Woolf, "Some Polemical Emphases in the *Sefer Mitswot Gadol* of Rabbi Moses of Coucy," *JQR* 89 (1998): 98.

59. See Margaliyot, *Vikkuaḥ R. Yeḥi'el*, 22–23 (translated in David Berger, *Polemic, Persecution and Dialogue*, 119): "The rabbi responded: let me tell you a way that you can be saved even through your faith. If you observe the seven commandments that you have been commanded, you will be saved through them. The bishops rejoiced and responded: indeed we have ten! The rabbi replied: that is fine with me."

60. See Margaliyot, *Vikkuaḥ R. Yeḥi'el*, 21 (and above, n. 2). See also Woolf, "Some Polemical Influences," 99 (n. 84); and Katz, *Exclusiveness and Tolerance*, 108–109, 122–123; and Katz, *Ben yehudim le-goyim*, 113 (n. 15a), and 123 (n. 43).

61. For the full range of Yeḥi'el's intellectual activities and literary productivity, see Simha Emanuel, "R.Yeḥi'el mi-Paris: toldotav ve-zikkato le-erets yisra'el," *Shalem* 8 (2008): 86–99, and Ephraim Kanarfogel, "R. Tobia de Vienne et R.Yehiel de Paris: La creativité des Tosafists dans une periode d'incertitude," *Les cahiers du judaïsme* 33 (2011): 4–17.

62. See above, n. 59.

63. Fuchs, "Ketav yad Mantua" (above, n. 55).

CHAPTER 11

JEWS "FEIGNING DEVOTION": CHRISTIAN REPRESENTATIONS OF CONVERTED JEWS IN FRENCH CHRONICLES BEFORE AND AFTER THE EXPULSION OF 1306

Jessica Marin Elliott

Around 1330, a chronicler from Egmond Abbey in the county of Holland recorded the story of an image desecration that was said to have been committed by a converted Jew four years earlier, near France.[1] The chronicler described a Jew who converted to Christianity under false pretenses, "hurrying to the baptismal bath through perverse deceit," solely to gain access to a nearby church where images of Christ and the Virgin Mary were displayed. He attacked the icons, "provoking" them with "various and unlimited mutilations." In order to correct "this wickedness," the Virgin Mary appeared in a dream to a blacksmith and demanded that he defend her honor in a duel against the Jew. The blacksmith was able to defeat the Jew with a single blow, and the "wretched man" was "devoured by flames."

As this story suggests, by the mid-fourteenth century, Christian chroniclers in France and in neighboring counties with Francophone rulers worried about the status and sincerity of converted Jews. Under what circumstances was a conversion valid? How could you tell a "true" convert from someone who had sought baptism for malicious purposes? How could you identify a lapsed convert who had returned to Judaism, and what dangers might that individual pose to the Christian community?

Based on increased persecution of Jews in the high Middle Ages, some scholars have posited a crucial change in Christian attitudes toward Jewishness as early as the twelfth century.[2] Scholars such as Robert C. Stacey, Lauren Fogle, and Paola Tartakoff have shown that, by the mid-thirteenth century in certain areas of Europe, baptism could not entirely erase a convert's Jewishness.[3] Other historians, such as Jeremy Cohen, Jonathan Elukin, and Chaviva Levin, have drawn on evidence from across medieval Europe to argue that Christian suspicions about Jewish immutability made it very difficult for converted Jews to assimilate into Christian society throughout the Middle Ages, and especially, from the twelfth century on.[4]

This essay will argue, however, that prior to the expulsion of 1306, French chroniclers did not express concerns about a retained Jewishness that lingered after baptism. Although the persecution of Jews clearly intensified in northern Europe in the twelfth and thirteenth centuries, Christian chroniclers in France tended to depict converted Jews in ways that either glossed over the possibility of insincere conversion or emphasized the potential for sincere, spontaneous conversion through the end of the thirteenth century. The most detailed stories often described Jews who had been led to Christianity by a miracle and who persevered in their new faith. Although some narratives did present accounts of individual lapsed converts before 1306, these stories neither generalized from the single example to the category of converts as a larger group, nor went as far as later chronicles would in depicting the dangers that insincere conversion could pose to the wider Christian community.[5] Only after the mass expulsion of French Jews in 1306 did Christian chroniclers in France and the neighboring counties begin to warn readers about Jews who might seek baptism with malicious intent.

Over 100,000 Jewish men, women, and children fled France in the summer of 1306.[6] It is likely that only a small number of Jews chose to convert in 1306 in order to avoid the expulsion.[7] Many French Jews fled to the south and resettled in Provence, Spain, and Italy. Some resettled in the Rhineland; others went to the Low Countries. Some may have returned to France in 1315, but it is likely that the number of returnees was relatively low.[8] Those who returned were forced to leave again during the 1320s, not to return until 1359.[9] The final medieval expulsion of Jews from the Kingdom of France occurred in 1394.[10]

This essay will examine stories that associate conversion with the desecration of Christian spaces and objects, focusing on accounts from eight major chronicles of three alleged acts of desecration: a host desecration in Paris in 1290, an image desecration in Paris in 1310, and an image desecration in Cambron in 1326. The chronicles were composed in Latin and French in France and the neighboring counties with Francophone rulers between the late thirteenth and late fourteenth century.[11]

In addition to the chronicles discussed in this essay, four other French chronicles from before 1306 mention converted Jews, although not in connection with stories of desecration: one describes converts in connection with executions at Blois in 1171; two others discuss converts in connection with the expulsion of 1182; a fourth discusses a lapsed convert in Paris in the

1260s.[12] None of these stories—even that of the lapsed convert—suggest that their authors doubted the possibility of sincere Jewish conversion or worried about the status of converted Jews as a group. Three additional French chronicles refer to converted Jews after 1306: all three describe the forced baptism of Jews during the Shepherds' Crusade of 1320; one also reports a small number of conversions associated with the expulsion of 1306, while another refers to the forced baptism of Jewish infants in 1321.[13] Additionally, two of the chronicles discussed in this essay also mention lapsed converts in Paris in 1307 and the Shepherds' Crusade of 1320, events that are beyond the scope of the essay.[14]

The total number of Christian chronicles that discuss converted Jews is not large—fifteen of the major French chronicles composed between 1175 and 1400—and there is much that we cannot know based solely on chronicle evidence. Nonetheless, examining the stories that link conversion with acts of desecration suggests that Christian attitudes toward converted Jews in thirteenth-century France did not simply reflect declining Christian attitudes toward Jews. The stories that Christian chroniclers chose to tell about converts—and the ways in which they revised those stories over the fourteenth century—suggest that attitudes toward converted Jews were more nuanced, with chroniclers directing their suspicions at converts as a group only after professing Jews had been expelled from France in 1306.

The two earliest accounts of the alleged Paris host desecration date to the 1290s.[15] One version, which appears in the annals of the Abbey of Saint-Denis, notes that several of the Jews involved in the desecration converted after witnessing the resulting miracle. Another version, composed in Flanders by John of Thilrode, claims to be based on the eyewitness testimony of a Jew who converted after witnessing the miracle in Paris. After the turn of the fourteenth century, French chroniclers put less faith in the possibility of conversion. Only one fourteenth-century Christian chronicle, a section of the *Grandes chroniques de France*, associates the 1290 host desecration with conversion. In this version, the Jewish culprit is executed, and only his daughter is baptized. Two other fourteenth-century French chronicles discuss the event without making any reference to conversion in response to the miracle.[16]

In the fourteenth century, Christian chroniclers began to tell a new type of story about converted Jews in France. Three chronicles from the Abbey of Saint-Denis describe an image desecration that allegedly took place in Paris in 1310. None of the three accounts associate the event with a miracle or with the baptism of Jews; in each case, the culprit is a Jew who had been baptized but renounced the faith and publicly spit on images of the Virgin Mary.

Similarly, three fourteenth-century Christian chroniclers from counties outside of France that were under the control of Francophone rulers told a story involving a convert who desecrated images of Christ and the Virgin Mary in 1326. Each version identifies the perpetrator as a Jew who sought baptism in order to gain access to holy images. The evolution of the story during the fourteenth century highlights the growth of Christian fears about converted Jews and the dangers that Christians believed converts could pose to Christian society.

The Short Chronicle of the Church of Saint-Denis

The Short Chronicle of the Church of Saint-Denis, which comprises two series of historical notes recorded in Latin in the margins of the Abbey of Saint-Denis's paschal cycle, contains the oldest account of the Paris host desecration case of 1290.[17] Although this version of the story makes it clear that all the Jews who converted as a result of the miracle had initially been participants in the act of desecration, the chronicler does not suggest that their conversions were inauthentic or that they might pose a threat to the Eucharist in the future.

This account of the host desecration emphasizes the eucharistic miracle, declaring that around Easter, "great proof of our faith was revealed to us." The chronicle claims that multiple Jews obtained a consecrated host from a "certain wicked man." Once the Jews had the host in their possession, they threw it in hot water and pierced it with a knife, so that blood "poured forth copiously" from the wounded host, turning all the water red. No explanation is provided as to how the crime/miracle was discovered. Rather, this account skips directly from the bloodied water to the conclusion of the story, at which point the villains have been captured and have confessed. Although later versions of the story will focus on the civil and ecclesiastical proceedings as the case unfolds, the *Short Chronicle* is mainly concerned with the miracle, which only some of the Jews were able to understand: of the culprits, some remained "confused," while others were baptized.

In this, the earliest of the accounts, the only Jews associated with the incident are the culprits themselves. Later versions suggest that the miracle leads non-participating Jewish witnesses to convert. By the time the event is recorded in the *Grandes chroniques* in the mid-fourteenth century, conversion is no longer sufficient to eliminate Jewish culpability; in the *Grandes chroniques*, the Jew's daughter is baptized, but her father is executed.[18] For later chroniclers, the satisfactory resolution of the story demands the execution of every Jewish culprit: their guilt and "blindness" prevent them from understanding the miracle, and none are inspired by the sight of the miraculous host to convert.[19]

But in Paris in the 1290s, the miracle was enough. At the end of this story, no matter how perfidious their behavior may have been at the beginning of the tale, many of the culprits are so moved by the miracle that they are converted to Christianity and seek baptism. Although the focus could easily have been on the threat that Christians believed Jews posed to holy objects, the emphasis here is on the resolution. For the monks of Saint-Denis who described the event at the end of the thirteenth century, the violent attack was simply the means by which Christ chose to bring a group of Jews to the Christian faith.

The Chronicle of John of Thilrode

The Chronicle of John of Thilrode, written at the end of the thirteenth century at the monastery of Saint-Bavo of Ghent, in Flanders, also presents an enthusiastic view of conversions following the alleged host desecration in 1290.[20] This Latin chronicle, compiled between 1294 and 1295, claims that its account of the host desecration was based on the eyewitness testimony of a certain Johannes, who, along with his entire family, had converted to Christianity after witnessing the miracles at Paris.

John of Thilrode's narrative differs from the *Short Chronicle* in several notable ways. Here, the crime is said to have been instigated by only one Jew, who offered ten *livres* to his Christian maidservant to bring him the consecrated host. Only after receiving the host from his maid did the alleged villain summon other Jews to his home. He then proclaimed, "Surely foolish Christians do not believe in this host?!" and the Jews who had gathered in his home joined him in trying to destroy the host with various tools. One of the Jews seized a large penknife and used it to pierce the host, which divided into three pieces, causing blood to flow "continuously." As a result of this miracle, "many" were moved to convert to Christianity. The story continues: someone again attempted to destroy the host, this time by boiling it in a cauldron full of water, and the host thus turned itself into flesh and blood. After seeing these miracles, the eyewitness, Johannes, converted to Christianity, along with his entire family. As in the *Short Chronicle,* this version of the story ends with multiple conversions, although here some, and perhaps all, of the converted Jews were witnesses to the crime, not the perpetrators. The chronicler highlights the fact that the event came to him through the testimony of one of these converts, which he considers highly authentic and reliable.[21]

John of Thilrode's account demonstrates that by 1294/1295, word of the alleged host desecration had spread from Paris to Ghent, highlighting the movement of stories about Jews and converts between France and the neighboring lands of French-speaking counts.[22] In the mid-1290s, it was conceivable to John of Thilrode's audience both that "many" Jews would be led to spontaneous conversion by witnessing a miracle and that converted Jews would travel between Paris and the major cities of Flanders and Hainaut. This traffic would only increase during the early fourteenth century, as many French Jews fled from their homes and settled in neighboring lands.

Continuations of the Chronicles of William of Nangis and Gerard of Frachet

Continuations of the chronicles of William of Nangis and Gerard of Frachet, important chroniclers from the Abbey of Saint-Denis, make several significant references to converted Jews in the years immediately following the expulsion of 1306.[23] The continuation of William of Nangis, composed around 1315, includes the earliest reference to a lapsed convert who was accused of desecrating images of the Virgin Mary and was executed on the same day that the French mystic Marguerite Porete was burned as a heretic in Paris in 1310.[24] The continuator identifies the lapsed convert as a man who had converted to the Christian faith "a little while ago" and then returned to Judaism "like a dog turned back again to its vomit."[25] The chronicler writes that "in contempt of the blessed Virgin, [the man] strove to spit on her images," and thus "in that very place [where Marguerite was burned], he was completely consumed by fire." Gerard's mid-fourteenth-century continuator generally follows the narrative composed by William's earlier continuator, although he does remove the comparison of the relapse to the turning back of a dog to its own vomit.[26] By the mid-fourteenth century, perhaps there was no need to belabor the point.

The Grandes chroniques de France

In the section of the *Grandes chroniques de France* that was composed between 1328 and 1380, the account of the Paris host desecration of 1290 mentions the baptism of only a single witness to the miracle—the Jew's daughter.[27] Although earlier versions of the story had made it clear that at least some of the Jews who converted were guilty of the desecration, by the mid-fourteenth century, the satisfactory resolution of the story demanded the execution of the Jewish culprit.

Here, the chronicler identifies the villain as a Jew of Paris and writes that a Christian woman "took the body of Jesus Christ in a sacred host," which she had received at Mass during Holy Week, and gave it to the Jew, who threw it in boiling water and stabbed it with a knife. The authorities learned of the crime, and on the advice of the regents of theology and canon law at the University of Paris, the Jew was condemned to death. The chronicler notes that the Jew's wife was named Bellatine and that her daughter, who was approximately twelve years old, was baptized by the bishop of Paris and sent to stay at the convent of the Filles-Dieu. The chronicler does not give the fate of Bellatine.

This section of the *Grandes chroniques* also presents an account of the image-desecrating convert in 1310.[28] According to Jules Viard's edition of the chronicle, a Jew had converted to Christianity "not very long ago" but had then "renounced the faith a little while later and was even worse than he had been before." Out of "scorn" for the Virgin Mary, he "spit on her images everywhere he found them." Without naming the specific authorities involved, the chronicler concludes the tale by stating that the Jew "was sentenced to be burned" and was executed in Paris. The edition of the text that appears in the *Recueil des historiens des Gaules et de la France* generally follows the same narrative, with one notable difference: here the culprit is a Jewess.[29] Although all of the descriptions of the 1310 incident are extremely negative, none of them suggest that the Jew or Jewess converted to Christianity for the purpose of desecrating images of the Virgin Mary, which will be a crucial element of descriptions of the 1326 image desecration written in the mid- to late fourteenth century.

The Chronicle of William the Monk

Around 1330, the chronicler William of Egmond Abbey, which was in the county of Holland and thus under the control of William I of Hainaut, recorded the first account of an image desecration that was said to have been discovered in 1326—an event that would later come to be known as the "Cambron image desecration."[30] William describes "a certain Jew," near France, who converted to Christianity under false pretenses, "hurrying to the baptismal bath through perverse deceit, [showing himself through both] deed and demeanor to be eager to unite himself with the faithful." William suggests that the Jew's true purpose was to gain access to the church, where he attacked an image of Christ, attempting "various and unlimited mutilations," although the image of Christ's body remained "without harm."

In this tale, the culprit is identified as "a certain Jew," rather than as a convert who lapses for one reason or another. This is a significant departure from earlier stories about converts who committed acts of desecration: the chronicler takes particular care to emphasize the fact that, in this instance, the culprit's motive was always to gain access to the holy objects in the church. This is not a case of a convert who later regrets his baptism and commits a desperate act of desecration. For William, this is the story of a Jew who feigned the desire to convert and of the ease with which false converts could infiltrate Christian society.

William continues the story, writing that when "the wickedness of the man offended God, and various mutilations of her image likewise provoked the Virgin Mary," the Virgin took action.[31] She appeared in a dream to a blacksmith, whom William notes was "clearly a simple man." In the dream, the Virgin encouraged the smith to challenge the Jew to single combat in her defense. After the smith ignored several similar requests, the Virgin warned him, "Unless you avenge me and the offense done to my son, exactly as I have repeated to you many times now in dreams, you will be forbidden to enter our temple. Therefore, hurry, acting with manly vigor, and draw the Jew to single combat, since Christ, my son, will help you in these things, and he will make the aforementioned Jew fall subject to you with the lightest blow." Convinced by the Virgin's plea for help, the smith insisted that the Jew be "dragged to the field, where soon he was knocked down not only by the mallet of the smith, but in truth, by the mallet of God." While he was "begging for pardon and confessing wickedness," the Jew was asked why he had not defended himself. He replied that his adversary, the smith, had appeared "as if he had a thousand soldiers helping him." "And so," William concludes, "the wretched man was led to the gibbet, where he was indeed devoured by flames."

William of Egmond, writing in the wake of the influx of French Jews into Flanders and Hainaut in the first quarter of the fourteenth century, had a heightened sense of the threat that he believed this posed to the security of the Christian community. For William, Christendom could no longer protect itself even by converting the Jews. His story warns readers that baptized Jews could prove even more dangerous than professing Jews, since Jews were all too willing to accept baptism in order to have the opportunity to desecrate Christian spaces and sacred objects.

John of Beka's Chronicle of Utrecht and Holland

In the 1350s, twenty years after the first account of the Cambron image desecration, John of Beka recorded another account of the alleged desecration.[32] He writes, "A certain Jew, near Hainaut, asked to become a catechumen and was received from the sacred baptismal font by William, the count [of Hainaut], as an adopted son." This is the first time that the culprit of the story is identified as the count's godson or that the county of Hainaut is mentioned as the setting.

After an unspecified period of time passed, the convert, "feigning devotion, secretly entered the church of a certain monastery." In the church, he "saw an image of the glorious Queen of Heaven, the Virgin Mary, depicted most beautifully, whom he stabbed in her red cheeks with the sharp point of a lance." The convert hurried, undetected, from the church, returning to his "usual activities" as a stream of blood began to flow from the wounded image. Here, John adds a new element to the story, noting that the crippled and sick were healed by the miraculous image. As before, the story concludes with the Virgin Mary appearing to a smith in a dream, asking "urgently" that he "provoke the faithless Christian to a duel." With the Virgin's help, the smith was able to defeat the culprit, and the "wretched Hebrew was strung up, publicly displaying his guilt."

John of Beka shares William of Egmond's concern that the growth of Jewish communities in the lands controlled by the counts of Flanders and Hainaut meant that Christian spaces and sacred objects were increasingly threatened. For John, however, the most serious danger—one far more difficult to detect—came from the baptized Jews who had infiltrated almost all levels of Christian society. The culprit in this version of the tale is not simply a Jew who sought baptism in order to access sacred objects; here he is the godson of the count, and this relationship gives him the opportunity to wreak even more havoc on Christian society.

John of Outremeuse's Mirror of Histories

John of Outremeuse presents another account of the Cambron image desecration in the *Mirror of Histories*, composed in French between 1395 and 1399.[33] He writes that, in 1326, in the county of Hainaut, in the abbey called Cambron, there was a Jew who had been baptized, who was named William. The count had "raised him from the holy baptismal font" and had made him the forester of Mons. One day, as William went through the county, "exercising his office," he came to the Abbey of Cambron. He stayed in an inn, where he found an image of the Virgin Mary, which he struck with a small arrow, causing the picture to bleed. As in the earlier versions of the story, the Virgin appeared to a smith and asked him to fight the Jew for her. The smith, whom John notes was "very sick," went to the judge and said that he "wanted to prove the Jew to be false and a traitor by his body on a field, for he had made the wound with an arrow." In the end, the smith defeated the Jew on the field, and the Jew "died a bad death."

Here the dangerous potential suggested by John of Beka has come to fruition. John of Outremeuse makes it clear that William has received a position in the comital administration through his relationship with the count and that William actually has the opportunity to commit his crime while he is on official comital business. For John of Outremeuse, writing in Flanders at the turn of the fifteenth century, the danger was not simply that Jewish communities had appeared throughout the French-speaking lands of northern Europe over the previous hundred years. By the year 1400, for some French (and French-speaking) intellectuals, the greatest threat came from Jews who were able to seek baptism, form relationships with the leaders of Christian society, gain positions in the civil administration, and then betray that trust by using those very positions to commit crimes against the society that they had infiltrated.

Conclusion

There was a crucial change in the way converted Jews were represented by Christian chroniclers after the expulsion of 1306. Before the expulsion, French chroniclers emphasized stories in which Jews were inspired to convert after witnessing a miracle. Stories of desecration were still told after 1306, but the Jewish culprits were executed, not baptized, at the end. After the expulsion, chroniclers tended to focus on stories in which adult Jews sought baptism, feigning devotion, so that they could desecrate the sacred objects of Christians. This transformation occurred during the first half of the fourteenth century, as the Jews of France were repeatedly expelled and readmitted. As displaced French Jews resettled in other regions of northern Europe, they were followed by stories that urged particular suspicion of converted Jews.

David Nirenberg has argued that, in Spain, the mass conversion of Jews to Christianity in 1391 led to a fundamental change in Christian understandings of Jewishness.[34] By "[raising] the possibility of a world without Jews," the conversions created a "crisis of identification" for Christians at the same moment that it suddenly became very difficult—yet critical—to distinguish Christian from Jew.[35] By the mid-fifteenth century, Spanish Christians had focused this anxiety on converted Jews, with some eventually articulating views of converts as "hybrid monsters," carrying dangerous, immutable Jewish blood.[36]

It is possible that the chroniclers discussed here reflect a similar "crisis of identification" in France in the fourteenth century.[37] Through the end of the thirteenth century, while France was home to a large and robust Jewish population, Christian chroniclers noted the existence of individual lapsed converts, but each lapse was treated as an isolated incident. When chroniclers recorded the earliest versions of the Paris host desecration accusation of 1290, they emphasized the role of the event in inspiring Jews to convert, spontaneously and sincerely, to Christianity. Evidence from other contemporary sources, such as tax records, suggests that converted Jews, as a group, were well integrated into the Parisian working world through the end of the thirteenth century.[38]

When fourteenth-century chroniclers explored the relationship between conversion and desecration, they no longer told stories about Jews who converted after witnessing a miracle. Instead, chroniclers focused on converts who committed acts of violence against icons of Christ and the Virgin Mary, sometimes seeking baptism solely for the purpose of accessing these holy objects. The absence of professing Jews in France after 1306 might have led to heightened speculation about the immutability of Jewishness, as certain French intellectuals turned their gaze to converted Jews. Recognition of the expulsion as official acknowledgment of the failure of French conversionary policies could certainly have contributed to the development of a view that Jews were in some way unconvertible. It is possible that increasing anxiety about Jewish access to Christian sacred spaces—in conjunction with heightened eucharistic and Marian devotion—found an outlet in a newly urgent need to warn French readers of the dangers that fourteenth-century chroniclers feared converted Jews might pose to Christian society, sacred spaces, and holy objects.

Notes

Earlier versions of this chapter were presented at the California Medieval History Seminar (May 15, 2010) and the Historical Society of Israel Medieval Graduate Workshop (February 13, 2011). I would like to thank the conference organizers for the opportunity to present my work and the other participants for their comments and suggestions. I am also grateful to Susan Einbinder for her valuable comments on an earlier version of this material, to Paola Tartakoff for her generous suggestions on a draft of this chapter, and especially, to my dissertation advisor, Sharon Farmer, for her ongoing support and encouragement for this project.

1. "Willelmi Chronicon Monachi, et Procuratoris Egmondani," in *Veteris aevi analecta seu vetera monumenta hactenus nondum visa,* ed. Antonius Matthaeus (Hague, 2nd ed., 1738), 2:642. The count and countess of Holland at this time, William I of Hainaut and Jeanne de Valois, were part of a common northern Francophone courtly culture: Malcolm Vale, *The Princely Court: Medieval Courts and Culture in North-West Europe, 1270–1380* (New York, 2001).
2. Robert Chazan, *Medieval Stereotypes and Modern Antisemitism* (Berkeley, 1997); Gavin I. Langmuir, *Toward a Definition of Antisemitism* (Berkeley, 1990); R. I. Moore, *The Formation of a Persecuting Society: Power and Deviance in Western Europe, 950–1250* (New York, 1987).
3. Robert C. Stacey, "The Conversion of Jews to Christianity in Thirteenth-Century England," *Speculum* 67 (1992): 263–283; Lauren Fogle, "Jewish Converts to Christianity in Medieval London" (PhD dissertation, University of London, 2005); Paola Tartakoff, *Between Christian and Jew: Conversion and Inquisition in the Crown of Aragon, 1250–1391* (Philadelphia, 2012). Other scholars have posited different chronologies for this development in certain regions. Danièle Iancu-Agou, for example, has argued that converted Jews were able to achieve social and religious integration in early sixteenth-century Provence: Iancu-Agou, "Provence: Jewish Settlement, Mobility, and Culture," in *The Jews of Europe in the Middle Ages (Tenth to Fifteenth Centuries),* ed. Christoph Cluse (Turnhout, 2004), 175–189.
4. Jeremy Cohen, "The Mentality of the Medieval Jewish Apostate: Peter Alfonsi, Hermann of Cologne, and Pablo Christiani," in *Jewish Apostasy in the Modern World,* ed. Todd M. Endelman (New York, 1987), 20–47; Jonathan Elukin, "From Jew to Christian? Conversion and Immutability in Medieval Europe," in *Varieties of Religious Conversion in the Middle Ages,* ed. James Muldoon (Gainesville, 1997), 171–189; Chaviva Levin, "Jewish Conversion to Christianity in Medieval Northern Europe Encountered and Imagined, 1100–1300" (PhD dissertation, New York University, 2006).
5. See Léopold Delisle, "Notes sur quelques mss. du musée britannique," *Mémoires de la Société de l'Histoire de Paris et de l'Ile-de-France* 4 (1877): 189; *E Visitationibus Odonis Rigaudi, archiepiscopi Rothomagensis,* in *Recueil des historiens des Gaules et de la France,* ed. M. Bouquet et al., 24 vols. (Paris, 1738–1904), 21:591.
6. William C. Jordan, "Administering Expulsion in 1306," *Jewish Studies Quarterly* 15 (2008): 241–250.

7. *Excerpta e memoriali historiarum Johannis a Sancto Victore,* RHGF 21:647. The 1306 expulsion has been interpreted by some scholars as official recognition of the failure of French conversionary efforts. See Susan Einbinder, *No Place of Rest: Jewish Literature, Expulsion, and the Memory of Medieval France* (Philadelphia, 2009), 1, 15.

8. William C. Jordan, "Home Again: The Jews in the Kingdom of France, 1315–1322," in *The Stranger in Medieval Society,* ed. F. R. P. Akehurst and S. C. Van D'Elden (Minneapolis, 1997), 28.

9. See Roger Kohn, *Les Juifs de la France du Nord dans la seconde moitié du XIVe siècle* (Louvain, 1988).

10. See Gilbert Dahan, ed., *L'expulsion des juifs de France, 1394* (Paris, 2004).

11. On the flight of French Jews to the Low Countries after 1306, see Jean Stengers, *Les Juifs dans les Pays-Bas au Moyen Âge* (Brussels, 1950).

12. Richard Howlett, ed., *The Chronicle of Robert of Torigni, Abbot of the Monastery of St. Michael-in-Peril-of-the-Sea* (Nendeln, 1964), 250–251; Henri-François Delaborde, ed., *Oeuvres de Rigord et de Guillaume le Breton, historiens de Philippe-Auguste* (Paris, 1882), 1:28; Jules Viard, ed., *Grandes chroniques de France* (Paris, 1927), 4:111; Delisle, "Notes sur quelques mss.," 189.

13. *E Floribus chronicorum seu Catalogo Romanorum pontificum, necnon e Chronico regum Francorum, auctore Bernardo Guidonis, episcopo Lodovensi,* RHGF 21:730–31; *Excerpta e memoriali historiarum Johannis a Sancto Victore,* RHGF 21:647, 672; *Continuatio Chronici Guillelmi de Nangiaco (1301–1327),* RHGF 20:626, 628–629. The last is a later continuator of William of Nangis than the one discussed in this chapter.

14. *Continuatio Chronici Guillelmi de Nangiaco,* RHGF 20:596–597; *Chronicon Girardi de Fracheto et anonyma ejusdem operas continuatio,* RHGF 21:29–30, 54–55.

15. On the host desecration accusation, see Miri Rubin, *Gentile Tales: The Narrative Assault on Late Medieval Jews* (New York, 1999); Susan Einbinder, *Beautiful Death: Jewish Poetry and Martyrdom in Medieval France* (Princeton, 2002), 155–179.

16. Another version of the story, which includes the baptism of the Jew's wife and children, survives in sermon form and is therefore beyond the scope of this chapter. See Joanie Dehullu, "L'affaire des billettes: Une accusation de profanation d'hosties portée contre les Juifs à Paris, 1290," *Bijdragen* 56, no. 2 (1995): 133–155; Einbinder, *Beautiful Death,* 155–179; Rubin, *Gentile Tales,* 40–48.

17. My translation is based on *E brevi chronico ecclesiae S. Dionysii ad cyclos Paschales,* RHGF 23:145–46. On the *Short Chronicle,* see Élie Berger, "Annales de Saint-Denis, généralement connues sous le titre de *Chronicon sancti Dionysii ad cyclos-paschales,*" *Bibliothèque de l'école des chartes* 40 (1879): 261–95. Dehullu suggests that this account was likely recorded within several years of 1290: Dehullu, "L'affaire des billettes," 136.

18. The punishment of crimes committed before baptism is addressed by Henry of Ghent, among others, in reference to the hypothetical baptism of a host desecrator. In a quodlibetal question from before 1292, Henry concludes that such a person could not be judged by the civil authorities nor put to death, since his guilt was eliminated by baptism. See Gilbert Dahan, "Juifs

et judaïsme dans la littérature quodlibétique," in *From Witness to Witchcraft: Jews and Judaism in Medieval Christian Thought,* ed. Jeremy Cohen (Wiesbaden, 1996), 223–236.

19. See especially the *Anonymous French Chronicle Finishing in 1308: Extraits d'une chronique anonyme française finissant en M. CCC. VIII,* RHGF 21:130–136, in which the villain's "Jewish blindness" is so extreme that he desecrates the host, fails to recognize the resulting miracle, attacks the host again, and still fails to understand what is happening. The only thing that he is said to "perceive" perfectly is the arrival of the sergeants coming to arrest him: Dehullu, "L'affaire des billettes," 137.

20. My translation is based on "Iohannis de Thilrode Chronicon," in *Monumenta Germaniae Historica, Scriptores* 25, ed. J. Heller (Hanover, 1880), 578. For the dating of this text, see Dehullu, "L'affaire des billettes," 138.

21. For other ways that the testimony reported by John of Thilrode varies from the *Short Chronicle,* see Dehullu, "L'affaire des billettes," 143–144.

22. Ibid., 138.

23. The continuator of William of Nangis also provides the earliest account of the inquisitions of two lapsed converts in Paris in 1307: *Continuatio Chronici Guillelmi de Nangiaco,* RHGF 20:596–597, 601. This incident, which did not involve host or image desecration and is therefore beyond the scope of this essay, was taken up again in the mid-fourteenth century by Gerard of Frachet's continuator: *Chronicon Girardi de Fracheto,* RHGF 21:29–30.

24. My translation is based on *Continuatio Chronici Guillelmi de Nangiaco,* RHGF 20:601. For the dating of this section of the chronicle, see William C. Jordan, *The Great Famine: Northern Europe in the Early Fourteenth Century* (Princeton, 1996), 197, n. 14; Gabrielle Spiegel, *The Chronicle Tradition of Saint-Denis: A Survey* (Brookline, 1978), 107. For the incidents in 1307 and 1310, see Sean Field, *The Beguine, the Angel, and the Inquisitor: The Trials of Marguerite Porete and Guiard of Cressonessart* (Notre Dame, 2012), 82–83, 161–162; for Field's translation of chronicles that describe the executions in 1310, see 233–237.

25. For the use of this phrase, taken from Prov. 26:11, by other Christian authors in reference to lapsed converts, see David Malkiel, "Jews and Apostates in Medieval Europe—Boundaries Real and Imagined," *Past and Present* 194 (2007): 30–31.

26. My translation is based on *Chronicon Girardi de Fracheto,* RHGF 21:29–30. For the dating of Gerard's continuators, see Spiegel, *The Chronicle Tradition of Saint-Denis,* 108–112.

27. My translation is based on Jules Viard, ed., *Grandes chroniques de France* (Paris, 1934), 8:144–145. For the dating of this section of the chronicle, see Dehullu, "L'affaire des billettes," 237.

28. My translation is based on Viard, *Grandes chroniques de France,* 8:277–278.

29. "Une juyve, navoit gaire de temps, sestoit convertie a la foy; mais un pou de temps après renia la foy et fu pire que elle navoit esté avant": *Chronique de saint Denis, depuis l'an 1285 jusqu'en 1328,* RHGF 20:687. The *Chronique de saint Denis* is identified as the French translation of the *Grandes chroniques: Chronique de saint Denis,* RHGF 20:654. See Anne D. Hedeman, *The Royal Image: Illustrations of the Grandes Chroniques de France, 1274–1422* (Berkeley, 1991); Spiegel, *The Chronicle Tradition of Saint-Denis.*

30. Matthaeus, "Willelmi Chronicon Monachi," 642. My translation is primarily based on Matthaeus's edition of the text, although I follow Hordijk's alternate reading of the fifth sentence: C. Pijnacker Hordijk, ed., *Willelmi, capellani in Brederode, postea monachi et procuratoris Egmondensis, Chronicon* (Amsterdam, 1904), 166–167.

31. "Cum autem temporis curriculo dicti nequitia Deum offenderet, beatissimam quoque virginem varia sue ymaginis mutilatione provocaret": Hordijk, *Willelmi, capellani in Brederode,* 166–167. Matthaeus has "dum" instead of "dicti": Matthaeus, "Willelmi Chronicon Monachi," 642.

32. My translation is based on Hans Bruch, ed., *Chronographia Johannis de Beke* (The Hague, 1973), 287.

33. My translation is based on Stanislas Bormans, ed., *Ly myreur des histors, chronique de Jean des Preis dit d'Outremeuse* (Brussels, 1880), 6:276.

34. See David Nirenberg, "Conversion, Sex, and Segregation: Jews and Christians in Medieval Spain," *The American Historical Review* 107 (2002): 1065–1093; Idem., "Enmity and Assimilation: Jews, Christians, and Converts in Medieval Spain," *Common Knowledge* 9 (2003): 137–155.

35. Nirenberg, "Conversion, Sex, and Segregation," 1088; Nirenberg, "Enmity and Assimilation," 145.

36. Nirenberg, "Conversion, Sex, and Segregation," 1078.

37. On the polarization of Jew and Christian in thirteenth-century French *Bibles moralisées,* see Sara Lipton, *Images of Intolerance: The Representation of Jews and Judaism in the Bible Moralisée* (Berkeley, 1999).

38. See Jessica Marin Elliott, "The Changing Status of Converted Jews in Thirteenth- and Fourteenth-Century Northern France" (PhD dissertation, University of California, Santa Barbara, 2014), Chapter 3.

CHAPTER 12

WOMEN BEHIND THE LAW: LAY RELIGIOUS
WOMEN IN THIRTEENTH-CENTURY FRANCE
AND THE PROBLEM OF TEXTUAL RESISTANCE

Anne E. Lester

On June 1, 1310, Marguerite Porete and the spiritual treatise she authored known as *The Mirror of Simple Souls* were burned in the Place de Grève in Paris. The event was noted in many fourteenth-century chronicles, although the authors often differed in their characterization of Marguerite. The English Master John Baconthorpe—writing a decade later—noted that "a certain beguine [*beguuina*], who had published a little book against the clergy, was burned near Paris, with a certain Jewish convert who – as they say – apostatized."[1] The continuers of the chronicles of William of Nangis and Gerard of Frachet referred to her as a "pseudo-woman [*pseudo-mulier*]," while the monks of St.-Denis in the *Grandes chroniques de France* styled her "a learned beguine [*beguine clergesse*]." Sometime later, John of Outremeuse (d. 1400) understood her to be "a beguine very sufficient in learning [*en clergrie mult suffissant*]."[2] By contrast, when the chronicles take note of the Jewish convert, they relate the same story: "On the same day, in the same place, a certain Jew expired in the fire. Having a while ago converted, he then reverted. He was of such great perversity that, in contempt of the Blessed Mary, he was trying to spit on an image of her."[3]

Scholars have rarely commented on the connection between these events. Most who have worked on Porete never mention the fate of the "certain Jew," but rather focus on the trial of the Templars that unfolded at precisely the same moment.[4] Sean Field has suggested that Marguerite and the unnamed Jew may have been burned on the same day because both were cases of "relapse."[5] Cases of reversion were viewed, as Field notes, as "acts of 'apostasy' [and could have been] perceived as an attack on royal policy and prestige."[6] Although death at the hands of inquisitors was fairly rare, it did occur often enough to provoke fears and rumors. Moreover, what we know of Marguerite's life emphasizes the disproportionate knowledge we have of clerical attitudes and representations of lay religious women compared to references to their social reality.[7]

Marguerite's story resonates with that of many other lay religious women of the previous century. These women pose a fascinating and complex problem of textual resistance. This can be partly overcome through a close analysis of archival texts. But these challenges are also suggestive of the broader experiences of marginal groups in France during the thirteenth century. In this way, Marguerite Porete is the endpoint of a longer story that unfolded over the course of the High Middle Ages. By examining the labels and terms applied to religious women between 1210 and 1310, it is possible to trace the ways that clerics began to categorize women who remained outside of formal religious vows.[8] And yet, as in the case of Marguerite, sources that offer labels for these women rarely reveal what the women themselves thought, believed, or attempted to create. Documents of practice, like charters and testaments, offer other ways of reading behavior and provide evidence of the projects that lay religious women undertook, offering a window onto the subjective qualities of women as actors in their own right. Finally, the process of labeling and classifying certain religious laywomen has parallels with the perception and persecution of Jewish communities under Capetian rule. Analyzing the experience of persecution across confessional lines offers new insights into how the clerical-state apparatus worked during the thirteenth century and gives a sense of the interconnected experiences of Jewish and Christian men and women; a connection that is emphasized in the conjoined fate of Marguerite and the "certain Jew."

Mulierculae/Mulieres Religiosae: Power and Classification

By the middle of the thirteenth century, informal groups of religious women flourished in northern France.[9] Unlike nuns, or formal communities of beguines, these women often remained in their homes and, thus, were part of local communal and familial networks. Some dedicated their houses as informal institutions to be used to serve the poor and sick. Beyond these decisions, however, it is nearly impossible to know what their intentions or ambitions were in cultivating this lifestyle. We know much more about vowed women and wives, many of whom left records or were written about in longer narratives, like hagiography. By using the term lay religious women, I mean women who took up a more studied and devoted Christian life along an apostolic model. In addition to regular rounds of prayer and singing of the Psalter (although probably not a formal office, a practice reserved for monastic communities), they took on a life of piety expressed through charity and personal humility. Much of what they did and believed was never committed to texts. Indeed, many women deliberately resisted the kinds of formal relationships and institutions that appear in written records (such as affiliation with specific monastic orders or the formal acquisition of properties and rents), preferring a more flexible religious life that kept them within their local communities, cultivating a (Christ-like) humble persona that eschewed the permanence of the textual record.[10]

From the perspective of legal texts, lay religious women first emerge in the French historical records in local diocesan councils, especially the councils of Paris in 1212, and Noyons and Rouen in 1214 convened in preparation for the Fourth Lateran Council in Rome in 1215. The decrees stipulated that women working in hospitals and hospices and caring for lepers, the infirm, and for pilgrims ought to wear religious habits—that is, to act and have the bearing of professed nuns. These were laywomen who resembled nuns in their behavior but who had not taken formal vows. The idea that laywomen could be tolerated in this context only if they wore habits and conformed to specific norms of regulated behavior betrays the fact that, by 1212, it was primarily women who engaged in active charity of this sort.[11]

As was borne out in the French provincial legislation, laywomen continued to be the primary group providing this kind of active charity during the thirteenth century.[12] Councils held in Rouen in 1231 and 1235, in Tours in 1236, in Sens in 1239, in Paris in 1248, and in Provins in 1251 all displayed a similar set of concerns about the activities of women: professed nuns and religious women should not leave their cloisters to beg, nor were they to visit the sick and poor, nor should they bring children, students, or the infirm into their houses lest it result in scandal and the corruption of the religious life.[13] The repetition of this legislation acknowledges that these were precisely the activities that religious women pursued, even when censured.

By the first quarter of the thirteenth century, as religious poverty and mendicancy assumed a greater spiritual significance, distinguishing pious and knowledgeable religious women from those who could easily be led into false belief and thus pervert the church became one of the major concerns of the ecclesiastical hierarchy.[14] Whereas urban and aristocratic women who renounced their possessions as an expression of their spiritual commitments were lauded, poor women were increasingly constructed as a group apart, as "wretched little women (*mulierculae*)." In the 1230s, *mulierculae* emerged as the favored term for lay religious women in northern France, especially for those women who, in their unwillingness to take up formal vows, refused some aspects of the authority of the institutional church and, thus, appeared to verge on heresy. In 1231 the Cistercian abbots assembled for the annual General Chapter meeting forbade conversation between *mulierculae* and the order's monks, grange managers, and *conversi*.[15] In the same year, a group of lay religious women living outside of Troyes, known for their charity and for intoning the Psalms, were described as *mulierculae* in a complaint made by neighboring monks to the Pope.[16] During the northern inquisitions of 1231 and 1235, Philip the Chancellor (d.1236) used the term to describe women persecuted for heresy in northern France.[17] And when the Cistercian chronicler Aubry of Trois-Fontaines wrote of the trials conducted under the authority of the Dominican inquisitor Robert le Bougre in Champagne and Langres, he too referred to the women under suspicion as *mulierculae*.[18]

Mulierculae was a powerfully loaded and carefully chosen label. The word echoed the language of Paul's Second Epistle to Timothy, where Paul described "silly (or wretched) little women"—using the diminutive not according to size, but to social degree—who were easily led astray by men of false piety.[19] Inherent in this term was the connotation of marginal status; women who were suspect and of ill-repute, associated with moral corruption and whose social position, often one of poverty, meant that they lacked discernment and were easily beguiled. They were not proper aristocratic daughters or matrons, but little women of a lower class and lesser learning. When Thomas Aquinas commented on this passage from 2 Timothy, he made the distinction between "little women" and great ladies; the latter had spiritual advisors who kept them from error, whereas little women were without such aid.[20]

The second half of the thirteenth century saw no new legislation pertaining to nuns and religious laywomen, yet clerics continued to write about their behavior. The *vitae* of holy women like Mary of Oignies and Elisabeth of Spalbeek, while outside the scope of this article, were composed in part to demonstrate the admirable qualities of holy women. On the other side, those women who were accused of heresy were called upon to prove their orthodoxy, whether through bodily mortification or before an inquisitional tribunal. In those trials and in the texts of episcopal officials, papal legates, and royal councilors, the term *mulierculae* persisted.[21] When the council of Lyon convened in 1274, those in attendance revisited the topic of lay religious women when they renewed the Fourth Lateran Council's condemnation of "the excessive diversity of religious orders" by "perpetually forbid[ding] absolutely all forms of the religious life and the mendicant orders founded after the said council which have not merited the confirmation of the apostolic see, and...suppress[ed] them in so far as they have spread."[22]

In preparation for the council, the Franciscan commentator, Gilbert of Tournai, wrote a treatise, *Collection of the Scandals of the Church* (ca. 1273), offering inductive comments for the prelates in attendance at Lyon.[23] Gilbert proffered biting critiques of the various orders in the church, of the secular and regular clergy alike. After a brief description of Cistercian nuns, he admits that there are also "other women at this time for whom we do not know whether to call them secular or nuns, for they partly follow the rite of seculars and partly those of nuns."[24] Toward the end of his text, after glossing the role and behavior of different lay groups, he reserved some of his harshest criticisms for the beguines and lay religious women.

He used Elisabeth of Spalbeek as his main example of the ambiguous status these women exhibited, noting that "there is one among these wretched little women [*inter huiusmodi mulierculas una*] and the public rumor already arose that she is signed with the stigmata of Christ. Yet if this is true," he continued, "it should not be fostered in hidden places, but should be known openly; if it is not true, the hypocrisy and pretense should be confounded."[25]

Guibert's language drew from earlier precedent. By the 1270s, *mulierculae* had become a favored term used by the papacy in its attempts to distinguish regulated women from those who lived outside the sanction of the church. In northern Italy, even as communities of laywomen were joined to the order of St. Damian—living with possessions and following a prescribed monastic rule—other groups continued to live outside the strictures of regulation, following the example of Saint Clare, some even calling themselves *sorores minores*, although that name had never been approved or sanctioned by the church or the Franciscan order. Such behavior was "denounced as absolutely irregular," first by Gregory IX on February 21, 1241 and again nine years later by Pope Innocent IV.[26] Innocent IV's pronouncement condemned these women as "certain little women (*quaedam mulierculae*), internally burdened with sins, but outwardly pretending a specious sanctity."[27] They were—in the minds of the papacy and many within the hierarchical church—pretenders, capable of deception and corruption of the true religious life.

The papal language applied to the Italian case echoed that used earlier in the north. Legislation from the Council of Mainz, held in 1233, addressed women who took "personal and private vows of chastity without entering a convent or professing a rule," stating that "such women called *mulierculae* and women vowed to chastity (*voventes continentiam*) [and] virgins who have offered their virginity to God (*virgines, deo virginitatem suam offerentes*)" must "live in their houses from their own resources. If they were poor they should earn their livelihood by manual labor or in service to others." They were to "submit to their parish priests and be governed by their counsel."[28] By the close of the thirteenth century, however, in the Rhineland a new term came to eclipse the reliance on *muliercula*: *beguine*.

The first major ecclesiastical council to direct specific attention to the question of semi-religious women was the Council of Vienne, convened in 1311–1312.[29] The pertinent decree drew from Pope Clement V's bull known as *Cum de quibusdam* that first circulated at the council and was later published in 1317. In it the Pope explained that "[s]ince certain women commonly known as beguines neither promise obedience to anyone, nor renounce personal property, nor profess any approved rule, they are by no means considered religious, although they wear a so-called beguine habit and attach themselves to certain religious…with special affection." The text continued, noting that some of the women, "as if led into insanity, dispute and preach about the highest Trinity and the divine essence and introduce opinions contrary to the catholic faith…They lead many simple people who are deceived in such things into various errors, and they do and commit much else under the veil of sanctity which occasions danger to souls."[30]

The ambiguities littered through this description are conveyed by the indefinite phrases employed: *"quibusdam mulieribus" "quamquam habitum"* and *"earum aliquae, quasi."* The decree was rendered even more opaque by the inclusion of its final clause, often known as the saving-clause: "Of course, by the preceding we in no way intend to forbid any faithful women, whether or not they promise chastity, from living honestly in their dwellings (*in suis hospitiis*), doing penance, and serving the Lord in a spirit of humility, this being allowed to them as the Lord inspires them."[31] Canon law on the point of lay religious women remained tangled in contradictions and imprecise language.

And yet, as powerful as papal and conciliar legislation could be, as recent scholarship on the beguines has shown, there were limits to labels. Lay religious women continued to flourish after the Vienne Decrees. As Jennifer Deane has shown, in the context of Würzburg, by eschewing the name *beguine* women's communities thrived under a diversity of other titles including: *mulieres devotae, Klausnerinnen, geistliche Schwestern, Jungfrauen, Nonnen,* and *Zugehöringe.*[32] Likewise, in France, as Tanya Stabler Miller has argued, after Louis IX founded the Grand Béguinage in Paris, the beguine life was esteemed as it had become associated with the close cooperation between the secular clergy of Paris and well-respected religious women.[33]

Nevertheless, in France in the circle of reform-minded bishops with ties to the papacy and the university, the label *mulierculae* proved immensely useful and was readily employed.[34] This was the terminology these clerics knew and understood, it was the language of their training and it shaped their agendas for reform. Moreover, it offered a biblical language for understanding the Christian hierarchy and the place of women within it.[35] To speak of *mulierculae* was to speak in the language of Saint Paul. There was also great semantic freedom with a term like *mulierculae*; room for interpretation and movement, condemnation or acceptance as the political and social mood required. In northern France, by avoiding the label *beguine*, clerics allowed for the option of reforming and regulating *mulierculae* under a monastic rule within an established order. When left without oversight to live independently, however, *mulierculae* could be deceived, fall into error, and risk condemnation for heresy. But, as Miller has noted, "the way of life" pursued by lay religious women like the beguines "represented a symbolically important contested ground."[36] Part of what was contested was who determined the definition of a religious life and how those ideas were expressed. To glimpse these competing claims, we must move beyond the categories devised by clerical authors and ask after what occurred behind the labels of the law.[37]

Religious Women and the Acting Subject

There was another side to the *muliercula* identity that existed separate from— and deliberately beyond—clerical comment. There were many women who chose that identity for themselves: who sought to become *mulierculae* and to live as humble, devout poor women, much like the women of the Gospels who had welcomed Christ and cared for him. These were women who generally neither authored their own texts, nor sought to be the subject of comment or hagiographical renown. And it is not clear that they would have taken *muliercula* as a negative term. Women who converted to lay religiosity often created a life outside the textual record, in small houses and hospices, among the poor and sick, and in prayer with female kin, like-minded women, and (occasionally) clerics and local priests.[38] To find individuals who have attempted to efface themselves from the public record, we must look beyond what Sherry Ortner has called "the reified and romanticized subject."[39] Rather, we need to seek evidence of actions, projects, and processes. As Ortner explains, "it is in the formulation and enactment of those projects that [these individuals] both become and transform who they are, and that they sustain or transform their social and cultural universe."[40]

The projects initiated by lay religious women in northern France emerge in the archives in sparse and tantalizing detail. They appear in routine records of property transactions drawn up before episcopal officials, like bills of sale, donations, and testaments. In 1248, for example, Margue le Lens drew up her final testament before the episcopal official of her native St.-Quentin, offering bequests to the poor beguines of the town, to Cistercian nuns, friars, for the care of lepers, the sick, poor women, and abandoned children. But she also decided to give over her own house for use for twenty years as a hospice for the poor (*domum suam ad hospitandum pauperes per viginti annos*). She provisioned this *ad hoc* institution with eight upholstered beds and ten measures of wheat paid annually. Three women— who she names as her friends—were given custody of the house and lived there to care for the poor. She offered them an additional 200 pounds to maintain the domestic hospice and to provide for their needs. After twenty years had elapsed, she conceded that the house was to revert to her heirs.[41] With this gift Margue created a very small informal religious community under the control of women and looking somewhat like a beguinage yet never labeled as such in the sources. Rather, she and the episcopal official who made the record saw this temporary institution as separate and distinct from the beguine way of life.

Archival records from Douai, Lille, Ypres, and Saint-Omer in the area of French Flanders offer similar examples of this lifestyle. Here single women and widows, like Agnes of Corbie, followed the model of Margue le Lens and donated their houses for similar purposes. As Penelope Galloway found, "Agnes made provision in her will in 1265 for a foundation in her home for 'poor beguines, women and the elderly.'"[42] In Mons, several female relatives were documented living together in small informal religious communities founded in individual houses.[43] Galloway notes that these women "were not distanced from the local community by monastic vows or devotion to a centralized order. This helped to ensure the maintenance of a link between the religious women and their families, the existence of which is evident from the fact that many smaller beguine communities were founded and patronized by members of a single family, from whose ranks the majority of recruits often came."[44] Working on networks of poor women in Paris, Sharon Farmer found similar arrangements of care and planning, although in some cases the Parisian houses became permanent institutions for the provision of poor single women and widows.[45] For the most part, however, these arrangements have confounded scholars who work on beguines precisely because they are so ambiguous and rarely employ the terminology of the clerical elite.[46]

Although this lifestyle was less common (or less commonly documented) south of Picardy and the Ile-de-France, it is present in projects that surface in the archives. In 1268, Pope Clement IV approved the petition of the poor woman (*pauper mulier*) Egidia, who "wanted to build a house for religious women (*volenti domum religiosam construere).*" The pope conceded that this was a favorable idea and an honest desire on her part, quite in line with the great multiplication of religious houses then in evidence.[47] We learn nothing more of Egidia or what she had in mind when conceiving of a house for religious women. Was she a poor woman with reference to her social class, or was this a newly adopted lifestyle, a socio-religious identity created by giving up her home and possessions for the creation of this community? Was the house intended for beguines or penitents, or simply laywomen who had taken on a new commitment to the religious life outside of formal monastic vows? By 1268, a poor woman's intentions received the positive notice of bishops, archbishops, and popes alike. Margue and Egidia were neither nuns, nor beguines; they were laywomen of the bourgeois or lesser class who sought to implement an understanding of the apostolic ideal in their own local worlds, and in turn, to articulate through its practice—and through their religious projects—a vision of social reform in their own modest contexts.

The protean nature of such religious houses was part of their design. Most of these foundations were created with the expressed intent of existing as religious and charitable communities only for a generation, after which time they would revert to designated inheritors. They were never meant to be, or to become, permanent religious institutions or to seek affiliation with an established religious order.[48] They provided a setting where women could live together in small groups in a humble and devout manner, and they were meant to be places that humbled their residents in ways that deliberately imitated the humility of Christ and the women who attended him. In this sense, Ortner's term "projects" captures the imperfect nature of these women's endeavors. This was not about permanence in the landscape, or institutionalization, but about process. These houses were spaces where lay religious women could practice charity and pray communally, yet still live in the world, still enjoy the spiritual benefits of mobility and mendicancy, still buy, sell, and donate when needed, and thus take part in the social and familial networks that were and had always been integral to their lives.

It is perhaps not at all surprising that the northern French clergy responded to such women in variable ways: praising some, while labeling or even persecuting others. These were women who tried to exist beyond the law, neither regulated by monastic rules, nor benefiting from ecclesiastical procedures about gifts, donations, and incorporation. To some bishops and archbishops and to the local officials who knew these women and their families, they were laudable examples of apostolic ideals in line with religious impulses animating much of Europe. Yet, to others, especially learned masters in the university and clerics in the royal administration charged with creating policies about religious behavior, such women could upset the order of things and were worthy of suspicion, in need of identifying labels, and potentially deserving of persecution. The Christian men of the clerical-state apparatus understood well the power of such ambiguity, which could lead to acceptance or persecution—a distinction they wielded when the climate called for a robust statement of clerical or royal authority.

Communities of Persecution: Religious Women, Jews, and Capetian-Clerical Power

I would like to close with an observation and to echo some of the suggestions for future research that other scholars have recently offered. First, the observation: throughout the thirteenth century, one experience (and there were certainly others) that lay Christian religious women and Jewish communities shared was that they were targeted at specific moments for persecutions that were not always part of a larger move against one group or another, but rather constituted local displays of power that reified the authority of the church and state.[49] If anything, these localized moments of persecution contributed to the wider and terrifying effects of more totalizing moves to persecute out-groups that occurred in the fourteenth century, particularly during the reign of Philip the Fair (r. 1285–1314). But the local persecutions of the thirteenth century made it clear to clerics and royal officials in northern France that both Jews and lay religious women were in Jennifer Deane's words "good to persecute with."[50] As Deane observed, one of the commonalities of the history of beguines, whether in France, Germany, or Flanders, was that beguines were "integral to tight-knit medieval communities, and they were reliably visible and active within those environments."[51] Persecuting beguines and lay religious women enabled a display of power to reach across communities and into vital nodes at the heart of urban networks, where aristocratic and urban interests met, where social mixing was at its most dynamic, and economic need was most acute. The flexibility of terms like *mulierculae* and the *"quasi"* language of the Vienne Decrees meant that clerics could choose when to apply the mechanisms of persecution and when to pressure communities and networks in ways that rendered the power of the church and crown more explicit. It was the inconsistent application of terminology and by extension of persecutions that was even more powerful and terrorizing.

Jewish communities inhabited a similar integral and integrated space. Although he does not use the same terms, William Chester Jordan has shown that the targeted persecution of Jewish groups in France was highly effective for displaying and reinforcing royal-clerical authority.[52] In this way, the Jews of France, under the dominion of the crown, were a useful group for expressing the power and sovereignty of the king.[53] It is also clear that like beguines and religious women, Jews—both men and women—were intimately knit into the social and economic life of medieval France.[54] To move against the Jews was not just a display of power for elites; it also affected the lives of many in the realm who were made to feel the decision of the sovereign in their midst. Moreover, to move against them inconsistently, as the French rulers did between 1179 and 1328, only further eroded popular perceptions of Jews and, in this sense, joined their experiences of persecution to that of lay religion women.[55] In this way, persecuting both Jews and Christian religious laywomen destabilized community networks and forced Christians in the realm to rely on and recognize the power and presence of the king and his court.

Recognizing the commonalities that lay religious women and Jewish communities shared sharpens our understanding of the state and church and the actors and policies that contributed to the process of categorizing, naming, and persecuting.[56] The men who possessed the authority to classify "good beguines" from "bad beguines," or *mulieres religiosae* from *mulierculae*, were by and large the same men who moved against the Jewish communities of France in terrifying moments designed to make clear the unambiguous power of the royal-clerical apparatus and to reinforce its ideology.[57] These decisions reified sovereign power because they were decisions about the truth or falsehood of belief. They could not be proven, but they had to be plausible (that poor religious women were heretics), or to be proven by virtue of their execution (that the Jews must be expelled from the royal domain). Indeed, as Jordan argued, to understand fully the political history of the medieval state, one must take on the histories of the marginal groups the state created.[58]

I would add to this, as I have tried to suggest here, that the apparatus of the state also created and even (unintentionally) fostered connections between out-groups. What is more, for historians of the state and political history, analyzing the history of women and Jews together may lead to a deeper understanding of how political power was defined and exercised and why it used the mechanisms it did.

Studying the entwined histories of Jews and (often poor) Christian religious laywomen opens up new questions about the nature of medieval communities, particularly urban communities, and the shared affinities that cut across confessional lines. Historiography has not favored this approach. Because Jewish history and women's history were marginalized from the mainstream of political and social narratives, as fields of study they have for decades flourished in very separate scholarly spheres. Bridging these historiographies is hindered by the fact that the two fields have been "so intractably focused on different problems" and have, in turn, suffered from a "mutual indifference" to their separate research agendas.[59] This is unfortunate, for the commonalities are telling.[60] Poor single Christian women often shared the same physical spaces as Jews and other out-groups (e.g., lepers). We can see this in archival records and records of the state that map habitation through tax assessments, but also in the stories communities told that build narrative force and coherence based on shared spaces, objects, and experiences.[61]

Important new scholarship has proceeded in precisely this vein, looking at the "integration of Christian and Jewish" experiences and narratives in deeply revealing ways[62] Elisheva Baumgarten has traced the categories of motherhood and the construction of gender roles within the family to address the common experiences of Christian and Jewish women. In a series of recent articles, she analyzed how the same stories and events appear in both Jewish and Christian sources allowing her to find points of shared knowledge on the part of male Jewish and Christian authors who retold the same stories for different audiences.[63] Other scholars have looked at the social bonds shared by Jewish and Christian women in their experiences of economic and political marginality.[64] Such work reminds us that we must not remain content to comment on and describe the margins, but rather to read the shared experiences of marginality—as a system and identity imposed by and through the clerical-state apparatus—as the very process through which definitions and categories of gender, class, and "otherness" were inscribed and reinforced.[65]

It may be that to look for the workings of projects—when communities come together and act to express their ideas and aspirations—we will see more of these telling interconnections. This means reading the labels and stories of "official" texts very carefully, to peel back distortions, and to probe for the resonances and relations with other out-groups. Stories of host desecrations, for example, that involve poor women (and it is most frequently women in these tales) who had access to hosts and liturgical garments suggest among many things, the imbrication of the social and economic worlds of Jews and Christian laywomen as a site of profound anxiety for the church and state.[66] In Paris at the turn of the fourteenth century, one of the projects that Christian laywomen and Jews as well as recent converts from Judaism engaged in was the pursuit of independent livelihoods, in small houses and apartments, where they attempted to live—often side by side—at levels just above debilitating poverty. The "project" of daily living—paying rents, buying sufficient food, sustaining communal and spiritual networks—in these circumstances was not simple or easy. Moreover, life along the Right Bank, in the parish of St.-Merry and near the Place de Grève not infrequently forced connections and communications among Parisian clerical-intellectual circles, Jewish communities, and Christian religious laywomen.[67] This context, that is, the longer history of labeling, categorizing, and inconsistent persecution may offer more insight into why, on June 1, 1310, Marguerite Porete and her book were burned in the Place de Grève with a "certain Jew." To be sure, as Field notes, both displayed the challenges of "relapse." But their conjoined deaths spoke poignantly to the interactions of these communities in the spaces of Paris where beguines, lay vagabond women, *conversi*, and Jews had lived side by side for decades, creating a complex shared world that we are only beginning to appreciate and that the records—in their silences, ambiguities, and resistance—should make us question all the more ardently.

Notes

I would like to thank Scott Bruce, Jennifer Kolpacoff Deane, and William Chester Jordan for their comments on an earlier draft of this article. Jennifer Deane, Tanya Stabler Miller, and Sean Field all shared copies of their unpublished work on the topic and I am grateful for their insights. I would also like to thank the two anonymous readers for the press for their useful comments.

1. I have followed the translations in Sean L. Field, *The Beguine, the Angel, and the Inquisitor: The Trials of Marguerite Porete and Guiard of Cressonessart* (Notre Dame, 2012), 238. See also Robert E. Lerner, *The Heresy of the Free Spirit in the Later Middle Ages* (Notre Dame, 1972); and Robert E. Lerner, "New Light on *The Mirror of Simple Souls*," *Speculum* 85 (2010): 91–116.

2. Field, *Beguine*, 233–238.

3. Ibid., 235, and Jessica Marin Elliott's chapter in this volume, chapter 11.

4. For the intertwining of the Marguerite's trial and that of the Templars, see Field, *Beguine*, esp. 63–83.

5. Ibid., 161.

6. Ibid. Marguerite was accused of heresy, but remained, as far as we know, silent during her trial and never confessed to the charges.

7. On Marguerite's social and religious context, see the excellent study by John Van Engen, "Marguerite (Porete) of Hainaut and the Medieval Low Countries," in *Marguerite Porete et le Miroir des Simples Âmes: Perspectives*

historique, philosophiques et littéraires, ed. Sean L. Field, Robert Lerner, and Sylvain Piron (Études de philosophie médiévale, 102) (Paris, 2013), 25–68. Unfortunately this article came to my attention too late for me to incorporate its insights into this chapter.

8. See Dyan Elliott, "Women and Confession: From Empowerment to Pathology," in *Gendering the Master Narrative: Women and Power in the Middle Ages*, ed. Mary C. Erler and Maryanne Kowaleski (Ithaca, 2003), 31–51 and her more expansive argument in idem., *Proving Woman: Female Spirituality and Inquisitional Culture in the Later Middle Ages* (Princeton, 2004). See also, Nancy Caciola, *Discerning Spirits: Divine and Demonic Possession in the Middle Ages* (Ithaca, 2003); and Michael D. Bailey, *Battling Demons: Witchcraft, Heresy, and Reform in the Late Middle Ages* (University Park, PA, 2003). In the context of northern France, see also Renata Blumenfeld-Kosinski, "The Strange Case of Ermine de Reims (c. 1347–1396): A Medieval Woman between Demons and Saints," *Speculum* 85 (2010): 321–356.

9. See Bernard Delmaire, "Les beguines dans le Nord de la France au premier siècle de leur histoire (vers 1230 – vers 1350)," in *Les religieuse en France au XIIIe siècle*, ed. Michel Parisse (Nancy, 1989), 121–162; and Penelope Galloway, "'Discreet and Devout Maidens': Women's Involvement in Beguine Communities in Northern France, 1200–1500," in *Medieval Women in Their Communities*, ed. Diane Watt (Toronto and Buffalo, 1997), 92–115.

10. On the complexity and multiple layers of such acts of resistance and subjectification, particularly involving poor women, see Sherry B. Ortner, "Resistance and the Problem of Ethnographic Refusal," *Comparative Studies in Society and History* 37 (1995): 173–193, at 184–186. See also, Ortner, *Making Gender: The Politics and Erotics of Culture* (Boston, 1996), esp. chapter 5, "The Problem of "Women" as an Analytic Category," (116–138); and idem., *Anthropology and Social Theory: Culture, Power and the Acting Subject* (Durham, 2006), esp. chapters 5–6. On the role of women and the mimesis of Christ, see Caroline Walker Bynum, *Fragmentation and Redemption: Essays on Gender and the Human Body in Medieval Religion* (New York, 1992), esp. essays 4–6.

11. J. D. Mansi, ed., *Sacrorum conciliorum nova et amplissima collectio*, 53 vols. (Venice, Florence, Paris, 1759–89, repr.: Paris, 1901–1927), 22: col. 835–836, 906, and 913. The canons of the councils of Paris and Rouen are nearly identical on this matter, though they are listed separately in the manuscript sources: "De iis qui manent in domibus leprosorum et hospitalibus, ut infirmis et peregrinis ministrent," 22: col. 835–836 and 913.

12. On the frequency of these councils and the records of their proceedings, see Richard Kay, "Mansi and Rouen: A Critique of the Conciliar Collections," *The Catholic Historical Review* 52 (1966): 155–185.

13. Mansi, *Sacrorum conciliorum nova*, 23: Rouen 1231: col. 214–215, no. 4, col. 218, no. 35 and 37; Rouen 1235 (concerning corrupt women and miserable women in need of penance), col. 389–92, no. 111 and 109; (on the exclusion of lepers by priests), col. 399–400, no. 144–146. For Sens 1239: col. 509–510, nos. 2–5; Paris 1248: col. 765–768, nos. 6–12; Provins 1251: col. 793–794. A council held in Tours in 1236 noted (canon 13) that it was the bishop's duty to (re)educate heretics and converted Jews and to provide for their needs so that they do not return to their former beliefs (and communities) under the

pretext of poverty. See P. Guérin, *Les Conciles généraux et particulers*, vol 2 (681–1326) (Paris, 1869), 458.

14. Generally, see the comments in Ortner, *Anthropology and Social Theory*, 118–128. On this specific historical context, see Anne E. Lester, *Creating Cistercian Nuns: The Women's Religious Movement and Its Reform in Thirteenth-Century Champagne* (Ithaca, 2011), chapter 3.

15. Lester, *Creating Cistercian Nuns*, 81; Josephus-Mia Canivez, *Statuta Capitulorum Generalium Ordinis Cisterciensis ab anno 1116 ad annum 1786*, 8 vols. (Louvain, 1933–41), 2: (1231) 5.

16. Lester, *Creating Cistercian Nuns*, 15–21.

17. Philip was the chancellor of Notre-Dame in Paris from 1217–1236 and part of the circle of university masters writing on heresy and reform. For his use of the term *mulierculae*, see Lester, *Creating Cistercian Nuns*, 80. On Philip's role in heresy accusations in the north, see David A. Traill, "Philip the Chancellor and the Heresy Inquisition in Northern France, 1235–1236," *Viator* 37 (2006): 241–254.

18. See Lester, *Creating Cistercian Nuns*, 78–80; Aubry of Trois-Fontaines, "Chronicon," ed. P. Scheffer-Boichorst, in *Monumenta Germaniae Historica. Scriptores* (Hannover, 1826–1934), 23: 940.

19. For a discussion of the Vulgate passage [2 Timothy 3:4–6] see Robert E. Lerner, "Vagabonds and Little Women: The Medieval Netherlandish Dramatic Fragment 'De Truwanten'," *Modern Philology* 65 (1968): 301–306, at 304. On the medieval commentaries on Paul's letters, see Theresa Tinkle, *Gender and Power in Medieval Exegesis* (New York, 2010), esp. chapter 2. There is a vast literature on the dating of the Pastoral Letters of Paul, also referred to as the Pseudo-Pauline Epistles. See James W. Aageson, *Paul, the Pastoral Epistles, and the Early Church* (Peabody, MA, 2008); and Peter Walker, "Revisiting the Pastoral Epistles – Part I," *European Journal of Theology* 21 (2012): 4–16 and "Part II," 21 (2012): 120–132.

20. On Aquinas's commentary, see Lerner, "Vagabonds and Little Women," 304, n. 26.

21. Elliott, *Proving Woman*, 119–230. The term also appears in the Cartulary of the bishop of Auxerre in 1271: "in uillam et ecclesias de Karitate, occasione cuiusdam muliercule suspecte de heresi," See *Three Cartularies from Thirteenth-Century Auxerre*, ed. Constance Brittain Bouchard (Toronto, 2012), no. 88 (December 1271), 148.

22. "Second Council of Lyons – 1274," in Tanner, *Decrees of the Ecumenical Councils*, ed. Norman P. Tanner, 2 vols. (London, Washington, DC, 1990), 1: 309–331, at 325–326 (facing Latin-English)

23. Gilbert of Tournai, "Collectio de scandalis ecclesiae," ed. Autbertus Stroick, *Archivum Franciscanum Historicum* 24 (1931): 33–62.

24. Gilbert of Tournai, "Collectio de scandalis ecclesiae," 58.

25. Gilbert of Tournai, "Collectio de scandalis ecclesiae," 62. See also Elliott, *Proving Woman*, 188–189; and on Elisabeth, see Jesse Njus, "The Politics of Mysticism: Elisabeth of Spalbeek in Context," *Church History* 77 (2008): 285–317.

26. Luigi Pellegrini, "Female Religious Experience and Society in Thirteenth-Century Italy," in *Monks and Nuns, Saints and Outcasts*, ed. Sharon Farmer and Barbara Rosenwein (Ithaca, 2000), 119–120.

27. Pellegrini, "Female Religious Experience," 120, n. 80. Strikingly, *muliercula* does not appear to have been used when referring to women suspected of heresy in southern France, although more work on naming and labels in that context is needed. I thank Mark Pegg for his insights on this.

28. As cited in Ernest McDonnell, *The Beguines and Beghards in Medieval Culture: With Special Emphasis on the Belgian Scene* (New York, 1969), 507 and ff. For the Mainz Council of 1233, see Franz J. Mone, "Kirchenverordnungen der Bistüner Mainz und Strassburg aus dem 13. Jahrhundert," *Zeitschrift für die Geschichte des Oberrheins* 3 (1852), 129 and following.

29. See Elizabeth Makowski, *"A Pernicious Sort of Woman": Quasi-Religious Women and Canon Lawyers in the Later Middle Ages* (Washington, DC, 2005). See also the remarks in Field, *Beguine*, 193–207; and Lerner, *The Heresy of the Free Spirit*, 53–84.

30. "Council of Vienne—1311–1312," in *Decrees of the Ecumenical Councils*, 1: 333–401, at 374 (facing Latin-English translation).

31. Tanner, "Council of Vienne," 374.

32. Jennifer Kolpacoff Deane, "From Case Studies to Comparative Models: Würzburg Beguines and the Vienne Decrees," in *Labels and Libels: Naming Beguines in Northern Medieval Europe*, ed. Letha Boehringer, Jennifer Kolpacoff Deane, and Hildo van Engen (Turnhout, 2014), 53–82, at 63–66.

33. Tanya Stabler Miller, "'Love is Beguine': Labelling Lay Religiosity in Thirteenth-Century Paris," in *Labels and Libels*, 135–150; for conflicting clerical attitudes on term "beguine," see Tanya Stabler Miller, "What's in a Name? Clerical Representations of Parisian Beguines (1200–1328)," *Journal of Medieval History* 33 (2007): 60–86. For the French context more broadly, see Sean L. Field, "On Being a Beguine," 117–133.

34. For a similar methodological approach, see Peter Biller, "Words and the Medieval Notion of 'Religion'," *Journal of Ecclesiastical History* 36 (1985): 351–69; see also Miller, "What's in a Name?"; and Lerner's discussion of the label *pseudo* as applied to women accused of heresy in Lerner, *The Heresy of the Free Spirit*, 70–71.

35. See Tinkle, *Gender and Power in Medieval Exegesis*, esp. 1–51.

36. Miller, "'Love Is Beguine,'" 149.

37. See Jo Ann McNamara, "*De quibusdam mulieribus*: Reading Women's History from Hostile Sources," in *Medieval Women and the Sources of Medieval History*, ed. Joel T. Rosenthal (Athens and London, 1990), 237–258.

38. See John Van Engen, *Sisters and Brothers of the Common Life: The Devotio Moderna and the World of the Later Middle Ages* (Philadelphia, 2008), esp. chapters 1–2.

39. Ortner, "Resistance and the Problem of Ethnographic Refusal," 186.

40. Ibid., 187.

41. Her detailed testament [Arch. Mun. de Saint-Quentin, liasse 28, December 17, 1248] is edited in *Testaments Saint-Quentinois du XIVe siècle*, ed. Pierre Desportes (Paris, 2003), no. 44, 124–127.

42. Galloway, "'Discreet and Devout Maidens,'" 103.
43. Ibid., 103–104.
44. Ibid., 103.
45. The communities at Ste.-Avoye in the parish of St.-Merry, just off the rue du Temple and that of the Haudriettes, founded near the Place de Grève for poor widows, are good examples. See Sharon Farmer, *Surviving Poverty in Medieval Paris: Gender, Ideology and the Daily Lives of the Poor* (Ithaca, 2002), 147–151; for networks of poor women, see 151–164; and Sharon Farmer, "Down and Out and Female in Thirteenth-Century Paris," *American Historical Review* 103 (1998): 345–372.
46. See Delmaire, "Les beguines dans le Nord de la France," 122–126.
47. Mathieu Maximilien Quantin, *Recueil de pièce pour faire suite au Cartulaire général de l'Yonne* (Auxerre, 1873), 317, no. 642
48. See Lester, *Creating Cistercian Nuns*, 7–12.
49. See William Chester Jordan, *The French Monarchy and the Jews: From Philip Augustus to the Last Capetians* (Philadelphia, 1989) and Susan Einbinder, *Beautiful Death: Jewish Poetry and Martyrdom in Medieval France* (Princeton, 2002). For the persecution of women as heretics, see Elliott, *Proving Woman*; and R. I. Moore, *The War on Heresy: Faith and Power in Medieval Europe* (London, 2012); see also the comments by Miri Rubin, *Speculum* 65 (1990): 1025–1027 in her review of R. I. Moore, *The Formation of a Persecuting Society: Power and Deviance in Western Europe, 950–1250* (Oxford, 1987).
50. Deane, "From Case Studies to Comparative Models," 76. Deane uses this phrase only with respect to beguines.
51. Deane, "From Case Studies to Comparative Models," 77.
52. William Chester Jordan, "Jews, Regalian Rights, and the Constitution in Medieval France," repr. in William Chester Jordan, *Ideology and Royal Power in Medieval France* (Aldershot, 2001), no. 15, 1–16, at 3.
53. William Chester Jordan, "Princely Identity and the Jews in Medieval France," repr. in Jordan, *Ideology and Royal Power in Medieval France*, no. 13, 257–273, at 259.
54. See Rosa Alvarez Perez, "Next-Door Neighbors: Aspects of Judeo-Christian Cohabitation in Medieval France," in *Urban Space in the Middle Ages and the Early Modern Age*, ed. Albrecht Classen (Berlin and New York, 2009), 209–229.
55. See Jordan, *French Monarchy and the Jews*, 257–259.
56. R. I. Moore, *The Formation of a Persecuting Society: Authority and Deviance in Western Europe 950–1250*, 2nd ed. (Oxford, 2007), 184.
57. See Talal Asad, "Medieval Heresy: An Anthropological View," *Social History* 11 (1986): 345–362, esp. 359–360. See also Yossef Schwartz in this volume, chapter 6.
58. William Chester Jordan, "Jewish Studies and the Medieval Historian," *Exemplaria* 12 (2000): 7–20, at 16.
59. Jordan, "Jewish Studies and the Medieval Historian," 18. More recently, see Monica H. Green, "Conversing with the Minority: Relations among Christian, Jewish and Muslim Women in the High Middle Ages," *Journal of Medieval History* 34 (2008): 105–118, at 107.

60. See Elisheva Baumgarten, "'A Separate People?' Some Directions for Comparative Research on Medieval Women," *Journal of Medieval History* 34 (2008): 212–228.

61. See Farmer, *Surviving Poverty in Medieval Paris*, 136–146; Miri Rubin, *Gentile Tales: The Narrative Assault on Late Medieval Jews* (Philadelphia, 1999), 40–48; and Einbinder, *Beautiful Death*, 155–179.

62. Jordan, "Jewish Studies and the Medieval Historian," 20; and Jordan, "Saving Medieval History: Or, The New Crusade," in *The Past and Future of Medieval Studies*, ed. John Van Engen (Notre Dame, IN, 1994), 259–272, at 261–262.

63. Elisheva Baumgarten, *Mothers and Children: Jewish Family Life in Medieval Europe* (Princeton, 2004); Elisheva Baumgarten, "Shared Stories and Religious Rhetoric: R. Judah the Pious, Peter the Chanter and a Drought," *Medieval Encounters* 18 (2012): 36–54; and Elisheva Baumgarten, "A Tale of a Christian Matron and Sabbath Candles: Religious Difference, Material Culture and Gender in Thirteenth-Century Germany," *Jewish Studies Quarterly* 20 (2013): 83–99.

64. See William Chester Jordan, "Jews on Top: Women and the Availability of Consumption Loans in Northern France in the Mid-Thirteenth Century," *Journal of Jewish Studies* 29 (1978): 39–56; and more recently, the articles in the Special Issue of the *Journal of Medieval History* 34 (2008), especially Victoria Hoyle, "The Bonds that Bind: Money Lending between Anglo-Jewish and Christian Women in the Plea Rolls of the Exchequer of the Jews, 1218–1280," 119–129.

65. On this and on ways of reading, see the comments in Kathleen Biddick, "Genders, Bodies, Borders: Technologies of the Visible," in *Studying Medieval Women: Sex, Gender, Feminism*, ed. Nancy F. Partner (Cambridge, MA, 1993): 87–116.

66. Rubin, *Gentile Tales*; Einbinder, *Beautiful Death*, and Elliott, chapter 11 in this volume.

67. See Palémon Glorieux, *Aux origins de la Sorbonne*, 2 vols. (Paris, 1965–1966); and Léon Cadier and Camille Couderc, "Cartulaire et censier de Saint-Merry de Paris," *Mémoires de la société de l'histoire de Paris et de l'Ile-de-France* 18 (1891): 101–271.

PART 3

CULTURAL EXPRESSIONS AND
APPROPRIATIONS: ART, POETRY, AND
LITERATURE

CHAPTER 13

MIRRORING SAMSON THE MARTYR:
REFLECTIONS OF JEWISH-CHRISTIAN
RELATIONS IN THE *NORTH FRENCH HEBREW*
ILLUMINATED MISCELLANY

Sara Offenberg

Concerning a martyr in Metz, in the Year 1276…I, Benjamin the Scribe, the writer of this maḥzor, composed this poem for the martyr Samson.[1]

These are the opening and closing remarks of a lament composed in memory of Rabbi Samson of Metz. His story has come down to us via this single source, which is the only extant evidence of his martyrdom, composed by Benjamin the scribe and copied by him in the *London Miscellany*, British Library Add. MS 11639, also known as *The North French Hebrew Miscellany*,[2] produced in northern France sometime between 1278 and 1280.[3] Although earlier scholars studied the story of Samson of Metz, they never considered it in relation to other texts in the manuscript or to the images.[4] In this study, I address this lament against the background of the other texts and images in *London Miscellany*, with a specific focus on one of the illuminations in the manuscript, portraying the biblical Samson and the Lion and in light of Jewish-Christian medieval relations.

At the heart of this study stands the image of Samson and the conviction that, when studying any illuminated manuscript, the texts and illuminations should be examined together and not as separate units. For the manuscript's patron, it was an entire corpus ordered for a specific intention. This conviction is especially cogent when the illuminations refer to several texts in the

Figure 13.1   Samson and the Lion, The *London Miscellany*, British Library Add. MS 11639, fol. 520a.

manuscript. In order to understand the connection between Benjamin the scribe's lament and the illumination of the biblical Samson, however, I must first offer some background on the *London Miscellany* and the manuscript's possible patron. Afterwards, we shall return to Samson of Metz and to the illustration of the biblical Samson.

The *London Miscellany* includes eighty-four different texts, presumably chosen to suit one particular patron's needs and tastes.[5] The volume is rather small in size, measuring only 16.5 cm × 12.5 cm, has 739 folios, and includes Hebrew and Aramaic texts written in both French square and semi-cursive script.[6] The scribe wrote his first name, Benjamin, in all three colophons, and he apparently penned all of the central and marginal texts.[7] The volume is rich in marginal illustrations and includes thirty-nine full-page illuminations of Bible stories arranged in five series, some drawn in separate quires. There were several stages in the work on the illuminations, and in the facsimile edition Yael Zirlin mapped the various ateliers and the number of hands that worked on each section of the illumination program.[8] She was not the first to study these stages and their iconography; the manuscript's entire iconographical plan has been explained in different ways by a range of art historians.[9]

From stylistic analyses, Zirlin concluded that the decorations were done in five stages: the first two at the ateliers of Artois, possibly those in Saint-Omer, and the rest in Parisian ateliers from the 1280s until the 1320s. She contends that the artwork was done by Christians, who introduced latent Christian ideas in the images. She concludes that although Benjamin might have been present in the atelier at the time the work was done, even as a learned man he would not have understood the Christian import, as Jews were generally not familiar with Christian imagery.[10] However, Zirlin's contention is not in line with the realities of the period: not only were Jews very much aware of the meaning of Christian art, but they also responded to it.[11] Whereas it is true that the iconography and style of the images in the *London Miscellany* are closely related to French Christian illustrations, we have to explore the context in which these images were created. The implication is not that the illuminations were necessarily done by a Jewish illuminator, but that the patron or a person acting on his behalf (such as the scribe) directed the artist to design and illustrate the scenes in a particular way.[12]

Michel Garel addressed the manuscript's provenances and identified its patron as most likely a merchant from the area of Picardy-Artois,[13] and this fits well with Zirlin's identification of the two ateliers that are identified as being responsible for the first series of full-page illuminations (which includes the scene to be discussed below). He based this assumption on a calendar on fol. 542b, where the Christian saints and their holy days are written with attention to the *marcheque*, which marks the thirteen weeks between Christmas and the day of Archangel Gabriel. The weeks before Christmas are also noted in the calendar and, according to Garel, these weeks all had considerable economic importance; therefore, he concludes that the patron was likely a merchant.[14] Malachi Beit-Arié also addressed the issue of the likely patron, noting that it appears as if the manuscript was made for Benjamin himself, who probably came from Metz. According to Beit-Arié, Benjamin was not only a scholar capable of composing a learned lament, but also a wealthy man able to finance the costs of such a lavish manuscript.[15]

The claim raised by Beit-Arié that Benjamin was also the owner of the manuscript might find support in Garel's research regarding the meaning of two shields among the illustrations. Garel identifies the shields, seen on fols. 333b and 348a, showing a dismembered eagle as reflecting the symbol of the *Jurue* (street of the Jews), the Jewish neighborhood in Metz,[16] as also found on seals remaining from the beginning of the fourteenth century.[17] Whereas Garel argued that this motif alludes to Rabbi Samson of Metz, we might also conclude that this illustration was meant to recall Benjamin's city of origin.[18]

Why was the manuscript's patron interested in a lament in memory of an individual if he did not know him personally? Had it referred to more than one individual, it could have been understood as a general elegy dedicated to martyrs, but this lament mentions only one name—Rabbi Samson from the city of Metz—and Benjamin was a close friend of Rabbi Samson.[19] Thus, if Benjamin copied the manuscript for a patron other than himself, we might have expected him to provide more details, but it does seem to be written for someone who knew Samson (whether Benjamin or another close acquaintance).

Samson of Metz was martyred after being imprisoned for ten years. Doniach noted that he was suspected of being a heretic (after he had converted to Christianity) and his martyrdom was linked to the church's persecution of the Cathars. He associates Samson's execution with Clement IV's bull published in 1267, "*Turbato corde audivimus*," whereby the Inquisition received the authority to interrogate Jews and punish converted Jews who return to their former religion.[20] According to Jordan, it seems that Samson (referred to by Benjamin as Rabbi Samson) was supposed to have been executed in 1269 along with other Jews and lepers who were burned alive, but was not among that group. Jordan contends that Jewish communities or individuals were engaged in an effort to influence the authorities to delay Samson's execution, and that was the reason he was imprisoned for ten years.[21] Considering the use of the phrase "because he was forced" (*'al asher ne'enas*), Einbinder further discusses the possibility that Samson was probably forced to convert to Christianity (as already mentioned by Doniach),[22] and finding a lament that honors the memory of a Jew who submitted to baptism is a significant discovery:[23]

> If, indeed, Samson was imprisoned on false charges in the late 1260s, he may well have succumbed at some point to pressure to convert. And then— otherwise he would not be a *qadosh*, a holy martyr—he decided to revert to the faith of his youth. Unfortunately, once baptized, Samson was subject to the laws governing relapsed heretics, condemned (if he refused to abjure his perverse beliefs) and executed. If this reading is correct, Benjamin's poem is a unique instance of a martyrological lament written for a converted and relapsed Jew.[24]

Einbinder deals with the performance aspect of this lament and the attitude and response of the listeners. She understands the second stanza as referring to the torture tools and notes that Samson was first tortured with hot coals and broken on the wheel prior to before being burned before a crowd of onlookers who chanted hymns or dirges.[25] She finds that the lament's strophic form is suitable for singing in the synagogue, with a soloist performing the verse followed by the congregation. She suggests that we learn from the last stanza that the lament was to be performed in public, but notes that there is no evidence regarding the musical features of liturgical texts.[26] However, I should point out the presence of one melody in this manuscript, although it is probably not entirely in the categories of liturgical poetry that are mentioned by Einbinder. I refer to Raphael Loewe's study of

another unique text in the manuscript: a *piyyut* dealing with Jewish persecution, with a note by the scribe that it should be sung to the melody of a
French *vadurie* (a love song identified as a composition by Moniot de-Paris,
active after 1250); thus, we do have some reference to melody.[27] The importance of this *piyyut* for our purpose here is that we learn that the performance
aspect is very much present in the *London Miscellany*, especially as it comes
in connection with a song dealing with Jewish-Christian relations, and the
manuscript's viewer/reader is taken into account.

The lament's second stanza describes the binding of Samson's hands by
using a citation of a verse referring to the biblical Samson: "Tied in chains,
crowned like the Timnite's bridegroom/So they could break his bones."
Samson is called "the Timnite's bridegroom," based on Judg. 15:6: "Then the
Philistines said: Who hath done this? And they said: Samson, the son-in-law
of the Timnite."[28] This is in line with a convention of pairing an individual's
name with a biblical character (the most common such name in laments
is of course Isaac).[29] Thus, Benjamin's text makes the connection between
Samson of Metz and the biblical Samson.

As mentioned, an illustration of the biblical Samson appears on fol. 520a
where we find an image of Samson and the Lion inside a golden medallion,
on a blue diaper pattern (Figure 13.1). He is pictured with a beard and long
hair, dressed in red, wrestling with the lion, and subjugating him with his
left knee while tearing his jaws apart. This scene of Samson killing the lion
is not a common one in Jewish manuscripts and, as far as I know, this is the
earliest portrayal of the scene.[30] The usual depiction of Samson on the lion's
back is based on Christian portrayals developed from images of Hercules, and
popular in Romanesque and Gothic art.[31] Iconographically, Samson riding
the lion represents Christ conquering the devil in his descent to Hell. Using
Paul's Epistle to the Heb. 11, Isidore of Seville elaborated on the typological
parallel between Samson and Jesus, as the martyrdom of Samson is a typological for Jesus's death for the salvation of the humankind: "*Samson salvatoris
nostri mortem et victoriam figuravit.*"[32] Thus, as with other biblical figures, in
medieval Christian theology and art, the image of Samson is understood in
the lens of Christological interpretation, especially in the images of Samson
riding the lion.

The Hebrew inscription below the medallion, which was added in the
fourteenth century, reads: "This is Samson riding the lion and tearing its
jaws."[33] In the biblical account of Samson rending the lion, there is no hint
in the text of Samson's riding the beast and I could not find any text of this
sort in Rabbinic or medieval Jewish sources.[34] What is particularly interesting in the *London Miscellany* is that the fourteenth-century scribe who added
the inscription had already adopted the convention of "Samson riding the
lion" and described the scene in that way. This could be a later understanding of the image, and not necessarily the original intention of the painter

(i.e., to portray Samson actually riding the lion). Before further examining this scene, we should look at another scene portraying Samson in a Hebrew-French manuscript.[35] We find the Samson portrayal only in the *Mishneh Torah* in the Budapest Library of the Hungarian Academy of Sciences, Kaufmann Collection, A.77, produced in 1296 and also called *Codex Maimuni*, where the scene is illustrated on fol. 90b at the bottom of the opening page of the sixth book

Samson is pictured with long hair, atop the lion, barefoot, dressed in red, and rending the beast, and in this illustration, he does indeed appear to be riding the lion (Figure 13.2). The image is associated with the Nazirite laws, which are found on the same page; Judg. 13 tells that Samson was dedicated to serve God as a Nazirite, so portraying him in this context in the *Mishneh Torah* was quite appropriate.[36] In terms of Jewish-Christian relations in the late thirteenth century and at the beginning of fourteenth-century France, it is interesting to find an image that is so loaded with allegorical and typological meaning in a Hebrew manuscript. For better understanding of this issue, let us now return to the *London Miscellany*.

The Samson scene in the *London Miscellany* is part of a series of full-page illuminations of non-chronological biblical episodes seen on fols. 516b–527b. The series begins with the created universe on fol. 516b, and, opposite it, a scene of the fourth day of the Creation. On the following pages, three eschatological beasts appear: the bird *Bar-yokhani*, which is related to the images on the following pages, Leviathan, and Behemoth (*Shor ha-bar*, wild ox). The series continues to portray biblical scenes: the Judgment of Solomon, Aaron's Budding Rod, Samson (see Figure 13.1), Adam and Eve, Noah's Ark, and the Binding of Isaac. The series ends with a display of the Temple implements, two scenes showing the High Priest, and, finally, David and Goliath. Elsewhere, I have suggested that this series illustrates Yose ben Yose's *piyyut* "*Atta konanta 'olam be-rov hesed*" ("You Established a World with Most Grace"), which was recited on Yom Kippur in medieval France.[37] This *piyyut*, which was probably composed in the fifth century, falls into the category of the *Seder 'avodah* (Order of Worship) liturgy, that is, poetry that describes the rituals performed by the High Priest on Yom Kippur, written as part of the Yom Kippur prayers of the *mahzor* on fols. 412b–416b. The *piyyut* is divided into two parts: the first begins with the Creation and tells the story of the temptation in the Garden of Eden, Noah, Abraham, and the Binding of Isaac, while the second deals with the High Priest's ritual on Yom Kippur.[38] The *piyyut*'s text is based on Psalms 104, 106, 108, on the apocryphal book of Ben Sira (Ecclesiasticus), and on Mishnah *Yoma*.[39] The illuminations correspond not only to the *piyyut*, but also to the relevant *piyyut*'s commentary, which appears near the end of the manuscript on fols. 723b–732a.[40]

The series of images is not located adjacent to the relevant texts: the *piyyut* is written approximately a hundred folios prior to the images (fols. 412b–416b), and the *piyyut*'s commentary is written at the end of the

Figure 13.2 Samson and the Lion, *Codex Maimuni*, Kaufmann Collection, A.77, II, fol. 90a. Courtesy of Library and Information Center of the Hungarian Academy of Sciences.

Source: See the manuscript on the web site: http://kaufmann.mtak.hu/en/ms77/ms77-090r.htm. Gabrielle Sed-Rajna, "The Illustrations of the Kaufmann *Mishneh Torah* (Budapest, Academy of Sciences, Ms.77)," *Journal of Jewish Art* 6 (1979): 64–77.

manuscript (fols. 723b–732a). However, the entire decoration program, aside from the marginal illustrations, is based on a series of images that are not necessarily located adjacent to the relevant texts. Furthermore, the texts are written as part of a larger liturgical corpus of work (*maḥzor* and *piyyut* commentaries), and could not be interrupted in order to contain full-page illuminations next to them. Furthermore, the texts themselves (the *piyyut* and its commentary) are not written one next to the other, but with a separation of over 300 folios. Gérard Genette addressed the issue of the order in which one reads written texts, and refers to jumping between chapters in medieval compilations.[41] In the *London Miscellany*, we find an example of a manuscript that was probably supposed to be read and browsed through, and thus the location of the texts and images on distant folios should not be seen as an obstacle. Rather, we should consider the way in which the manuscript was intended to be used.

The Samson story is not referred to either in the *piyyut* or in the associated commentary, so it is somewhat puzzling to find this illustration as part of the series. However, the image is actually connected to the *piyyut* in one way, as the text of the Book of Judges 13 is written on the margins of fols. 413b–416a, near the *piyyut*. This biblical chapter, which tells the Samson story, is part of the *haftarah* reading on the Sabbath for the pericope *Naso* (Num. 4:21–7:89), which elaborates the dedication of the Tabernacle. Another possible connection might be that this image, which can be associated with the Book of Judges, was included as a reminder to the believer to mend his ways and follow the Lord's law. These connections, by proximity, could be one explanation, but they do not seem to provide a strong enough reason to order an illumination of Samson; thus, we should consider other explanations of the scene.

According to Madeline Caviness, the educated medieval viewer was supposed to see and understand the iconography as multivalent; thus, the image had multiple, overlapping meanings.[42] Therefore, the next suggestions are meant to complement each other as we strive to understand the possible reason for the inclusion of this scene and interpret this image as an allusion to the martyrdom of Rabbi Samson of Metz.[43]

The final verse in the lament for Samson of Metz refers to the Temple cult and offering of redemption: "May God remember on our behalf/ How he [Samson] made his offering to cleanse [our] sin/ When I make offering in the House of the Lord to glorify [Him]."[44] As Einbinder notes: "Since the time of the First Crusade, the Temple cult had provided Jewish martyrological poets with a way of memorializing violence in the language of ritual purity... The same motif is evident in Benjamin's refrain, which focuses on the personal offering of the victim, who, sinless himself, atones for others with his death."[45] Therefore, the martyr is elevated to the status of a cultic offering, as was Isaac, who was supposed to be sacrificed. We should remember that the Binding of Isaac is a central subject in the prayers and *selihot* (pleas for mercy) during the High Holidays[46] and in the context of illuminations for the *Seder 'avodah,* Benjamin might have been referring to a parallel between Samson's martyrdom and the offering in the Temple. Perhaps the inclusion of the Samson illustration juxtaposed with the *Seder 'avodah* was also meant to symbolize Rabbi Samson's righteousness despite his probable forced conversion, and the scene could be depicting an act of redemption for his sins on the Day of Atonement.

There is a strong association between martyrdom and Yom Kippur, for example, the lament for the Ten Martyrs ("These [things] I Remember": *Elleh ezkerah*), which is recited after the *Seder 'avodah* on Yom Kippur; some of the phrases in Benjamin's lament were taken from *Elleh ezkerah*, and we should remember that the biblical Samson was also a martyr.[47] Previously, we found that the allusion to the city of Metz is very prominent in the illustrations of the shields of the *Jurue*; therefore, we can see an awareness to visual reminder of the patron's past,[48] be it his town or his friend Samson of Metz. Therefore, owing to the performance aspect of the lament, it is possible that the image of Samson might well have been intended to serve as a visual reminder of the martyrdom of Samson of Metz.[49]

Notes

1. I am using Susan L. Einbinder's translation, *Beautiful Death: Jewish Poetry and Martyrdom in Medieval France* (Princeton and Oxford, 2002), 105, 107.

2. *The North French Hebrew Miscellany: British Library Add. MS 11639*, ed. Jeremy Schonfield (London, 2003); George Margoliouth, *Catalogue of the Hebrew and Samaritan Manuscripts in the British Museum* (London, 1899), 402–427, sign. 1056; Sara Offenberg, *Illuminated Piety: Pietistic Texts and Images in the North French Hebrew Miscellany* (Los Angeles, 2013). The entire manuscript is available online: http://www.bl.uk/manuscripts/FullDisplay. aspx?ref=Add_MS_11639&index=0.

3. The lament appears on fols. 534a–535b. Israel Davidson, *Thesaurus of Mediaeval Hebrew Poetry*, 4 vols. (New York, 1970), III: 773; Michel Garel, "The Provenance of the Manuscript," in *North French Hebrew Miscellany* 27–37, esp. 34–35.

4. The lament was first published by Adolf Neubauer and in 1932 Nakdimon Doniach published the same text with corrections and a French translation (also correcting the town's name to Metz). Susan L. Einbinder published the lament in Hebrew with an English translation and analyzed the text and Samson's martyrdom. Adolf Neubauer, "Elegie auf den Martyrtod eines Simson in Mainz im Jahre 5036=1276 von Binjamin Ha-sofer," *Israelietische Letterbode* 8 (1882–1883): 36–37; Leopold Zunz, *Literaturgeschichte der Synagogalen Poesie* (Hildesheim, 1966), 487 (first published: Berlin 1865); Nakdimon Shabbethay Doniach, "Le poème de Benjamin le Scribe sur R. Samson le Martyr," *Revue des études juives* 93 (1932): 84–92; Bernhard Blumenkranz, "En 1306: Chemins d'un exil," *Evidences* 13 (1962): 17–23, esp. 20; William Chester Jordan, *The French Monarchy and the Jews: From Philip Augustus to the Last Capetians* (Philadelphia, 1989), 218–219; Einbinder, *Beautiful Death*, 32–34; 100–125; Raphael Loewe, "Description of the Texts," in *North French Hebrew Miscellany*, 188–287, esp. 257–258.

5. The manuscript begins with the Pentateuch, followed by liturgical texts, including the maḥzor in the French rite and commentary on the holiday

prayers. We also find the Passover *Haggadah*, calendar tables, mystical writings, halakhic works and more. Loewe, "Description of the Texts," 188–287. This is the earliest manuscript containing *Sefer mitsvot katan* (*Semak*) composed by Rabbi Isaac ben Joseph of Corbeil in 1277. Ephraim Kanarfogel, "German Pietism in Northern France: The Case of R. Isaac of Corbeil," *Ḥazon Nahum: Studies in Jewish Law, Thought, and History, Presented to Dr. Norman Lamm*, ed. Yaakov Elman and Jeffrey S. Gurock (New York, 1997), 207–227; Ephraim Kanarfogel, *Peering through the Lattices: Mystical, Magical and Pietistic Dimensions in the Tosafist Period* (Detroit, 2000), 81–92. See Judah Galinsky, "Rabbi Isaac Corbeil and his *Amudé Golah* (*Semak*): What Can Manuscripts Teach Us about Their Composition and Intended Audience?" *Paper Delivered at the Center for Jewish History* (November, 2011). I thank the author for generously sharing his papers with me and see as well his study in chapter 5 of this volume.

6. The main text was copied at the first stage, whereas the marginal texts were added later. Malachi Beit-Arié, "The Making of the *Miscellany*," in *North French Hebrew Miscellany*, 62–64. See also Loewe, "Description of the Texts."

7. Beit-Arié, "Making of the *Miscellany*," 70.

8. Yael Zirlin, "The Decoration of the *Miscellany*: Its Iconography and Style," in *North French Hebrew Miscellany*, 75–161.

9. On the illuminations in this manuscript, see George Margoliouth, "An Ancient Illuminated Hebrew MS. at the British Museum," *Jewish Quarterly Review* 17 (1905): 193–197; Zofia Ameisenowa, "The Tree of Life in Jewish Iconography," *Journal of the Warburg Institute* 2 (1939): 326–345; Jacob Leveen, *The Hebrew Bible in Art* (London, 1944), 72–84; Mendel Metzger, "Illustrations Bibliques d'un manuscrit Hébreu du Nord de la France (1278–1340 environs)," *Mélanges offerts à René Crozet à l'occasion de son soixante-dixième anniversaire*, ed. P. Gallais et Y.-J. Riou (Poitiers, 1966), 1237–1253; Bezalel Narkiss, *Hebrew Illuminated Manuscripts* (Jerusalem, 1969), 86; Zofia Ameisenowa, "Die hebräische Sammelhandschrift Add. 11639 des British Museum," *Wiener Jahrbuch für Kunstgeschichte* 24 (1971): 10–48; Joseph Gutmann, *Hebrew Manuscript Painting* (New York, 1978), 78–80; Gabrielle Sed-Rajna, "The Paintings of the *London Miscellany*, British Library Add. Ms 11639," *Journal of Jewish Art* 9 (1982): 18–30; William Chester Jordan, "A Jewish Atelier for Illuminated Hebrew Manuscripts at Amiens?" *Wiener Jahrbuch für Kunstgeschichte* 37 (1984): 155–156; Thérèse Metzger, "Les enluminures du Ms. Add. 11639 de la British Library, un manuscrit Hébreu du Nord de la France (fin du 13e siècle—premier quartier du 14e siècle): Problèmes iconographiques et stylistiques," *Wiener Jahrbuch für Kunstgeschichte* 38 (1985): 59–290; Gabrielle Sed-Rajna, "Ateliers de manuscrits hébreux dans l'occident médiéval," in *Artistes, artisans et production artistique au Moyen Age: Colloque international, Université de Rennes II—Haute-Bretagne, 2–6 mai 1983*, ed. Xavier Barral i Altet, 2 vols. (Paris, 1986), I: 339–352; Offenberg, *Illuminated Piety*; Joseph Shatzmiller, *Cultural Exchange: Jews, Christians, and Art in the Medieval Marketplace* (New Jersey, 2013), 133–137.

10. Zirlin, "Decoration of the *Miscellany*," 124–127, 135–161; Zirlin, "The Jewish Christian Polemic in Pictures: The *North French Miscellany* (BL. Add. MS. 11639)," in *Timorah*, ed. Bracha Yaniv (Ramat Gan, 2006), 61–72.

11. On studies specifically referring to this issue see Marc Michael Epstein, *Dreams of Subversion in Medieval Jewish Art and Literature* (Pennsylvania, 1997); Katrin Kogman-Appel, "Coping with Christian Pictorial Sources: What Did Jewish Miniaturists Not Paint?" *Speculum* 75/4 (2000): 816–858; Shulamit Laderman, "Two Faces of Eve: Polemics and Controversies Viewed through Pictorial Motifs," *Images* 2 (2008): 1–20, esp. 6–7; Sara Offenberg, "*Bittuyim le-hitmodedut 'im ha-sevivah ha-notsrit ba-ommanut u-va-sifrut ha-yehudit bi-yemé ha-benayim*," (PhD dissertation, Ben-Gurion University of the Negev, 2008).

12. On the advisors inside the atelier see: Jonathan Alexander, *Medieval Illuminators and their Methods of Work* (New Haven; London, 1992), 53–54, 63–64.

13. Michel Garel, "Provenance of the Manuscript," in: *North French Hebrew Miscellany*, 27–37.

14. Garel, "Provenance of the Manuscript," 30.

15. Beit-Arié, "Making of the *Miscellany*," 71.

16. On the *Jurue* see: Pierre Mendel, "Les Juifs à Metz," *Annales de l'Est* 31 (1979), 239–57, esp. 243–44; Pierre Mendel, "Les Juifs à Metz avant 1552," *Mémoires de l'academie nationale de Metz* 15 (1971–1972), 77–93, esp. 85–86.

17. Garel, "Provenance of the Manuscript," 34–37. More on Jewish seals from Metz see Daniel M. Friedenberg, *Medieval Jewish Seals from Europe* (Detroit, 1987), 111–114.

18. Metz was an imperial town that became part of France only in the sixteenth century. Henri Gross, *Gallia Judaica: Dictionnaire Géographique de la France d'après les sources rabbiniques; avec une préface de Danièle Iancu-Agou et de Gérard Nahon et un supplément de Simon Schwarzfuchs* (Leuven, 2011), 346–350 (first published Paris, 1897)

19. An acrostic reading spells out "Samson" and another one spells "my brother" (*ahi*). Doniach, " Poème de Benjamin," 85–86; Einbinder, *Beautiful Death*, 107. Perhaps this could be taken literally as his brother.

20. Doniach, "Poème de Benjamin," 85–87. Solomon Grayzel, *The Church and the Jews in the XIIIth Century* (New York, 1966), II, 102–104.

21. Jordan, *French Monarchy and the Jews*, 218–219. See also Blumenkranz, "En 1306," 20.

22. Doniach, "Poème de Benjamin," 86

23. Einbinder, *Beautiful Death*, 33–34, 112–115.

24. Ibid., 33.

25. "They bring wheels upon wheels within wheels and coals hot for blowing." Einbinder, *Beautiful Death*, 32–33, 105, 110, 119 n. 19. On the wheel as a torture device see Mitchell B. Merback, *The Thief, the Cross and the Wheel: Pain and the Spectacle of Punishment in Medieval and Renaissance Europe* (London 1999), chapter 5.

26. Einbinder, *Beautiful Death*, 102, 108–111, 118 n. 5.

27. Raphael Loewe, "A *Piyyut* and a French Love Song" in: *North French Hebrew Miscellany*, 170–187.

28. Einbinder, *Beautiful Death*, 120, n. 31.

29. Simcha Emanuel, *Shivré luḥot: sifré halakhah avudim shel ba'alé ha-tosafot* (Jerusalem, 2006), 256–57. I thank Joel Binder for this reference.

30. It appears in another French manuscript, discussed below. Samson appears in an illuminated *haggadah* (ca. 1300) from Castile but with a strong affiliation with France. In this *haggadah*, London, British Library, Or. 2737, fol. 35b, Samson, dressed in red, is rending the lion, and the Hebrew inscription reads: "The brave Samson." Julie Ann Harris, "Love in the Land of Goshen: Haggadah, History, and the Making of British Library, MS Oriental 2737," *Gesta* 52 (2013), 161–180, esp. 178; Bezalel Narkiss, *Hebrew Illuminated Manuscripts in the British Isles*, 2 vols. (Jerusalem and London, 1982), I, 45–51, esp. 47. On this manuscript and its relation to France, see Leor Jacobi, "Jewish Hawking in Medieval France: Falconry, Rabbenu Tam, and the Tosafists," *Oqimta* 1 (2013), 1–85, esp. 40–46; Katrin Kogman-Appel, *Illuminated Haggadot from Medieval Spain: Biblical Imagery and the Passover Holiday* (University Park, PA, 2006), 42–43. See the manuscript on the British Library website: www.bl.uk/catalogues/illuminatedmanuscripts/ILLUMIN.ASP?Size=mid&IllID=51176. Gabrielle Sed-Rajna discussed four other scenes of Samson from Ashkenazic manuscripts produced in the fourteenth and fifteenth centuries: *The Hebraic Bible in Medieval Illuminated Manuscripts* (Tel Aviv, 1987), 133. To Sed-Rajna's list we can add two more manuscripts: the *Forli Siddur*, London, British Library, Add. 26968, fol. 340b, made in Italy 1385; the *Ulm Maḥzor*, Kaufmann Collection, Budapest, Library of the Hungarian Academy of Sciences, Kaufmann Collection, A383, fol. 189a made in Germany in 1430.

31. On the iconographic development of Samson in medieval sculpture and its Christian meaning see Kirk Ambrose, "Samson, David, or Hercules? Ambiguous Identities in Some Romanesque Sculptures of Lion Fighters," *Konsthistorisk Tidskrift* 74 (2005), 131–147; Vivian Mann, "Samson vs. Hercules: A Carved Cycle of the Twelfth Century," *ACTA* 7 (1980), 1–38; Georg Swarzenski, "Samson Killing the Lion: A Mediaeval Bronze Group," *Bulletin of the Museum of Fine Arts* 38 (1940), 67–74.

32. *Allegoriae Quaedam Sacrae Scripturae*, 81, PL 83.112. Swarzenski, "Samson Killing the Lion," 68. Barbara Nolan, "Promiscuous Fictions: Medieval Bawdy Tales and Their Textual Liaisons," in *The Body and the Soul in Medieval Literature: The J.A.W. Bennett Memorial Lectures, Tenth Series, Perugia, 1998*, ed. Piero Boitani and Anna Torti (Suffolk; Rochester, 1999), 79–105, esp. 94. See also Jonathan Cohen, "On Martyrs and Communal Interests: Rabbinic Readings of the Samson Narrative," *The Review of Rabbinic Judaism* 11/1 (2008), 49–72, esp. 49–52.

33. *Zeh shimshon ha-rokhev 'al ha-'ari ve-korea' pihu*. My translation. Beit-Arié, "Making of the *Miscellany*," 67.

34. I thank Leor Jacobi for this point and for discussing this issue with me.

35. Due to the expulsion of the Jews from France in 1306, very few illuminated manuscripts from France have come down to us and as far as I know only our Miscellany includes includes the prayer service. These are the only illuminated manuscripts with figurative miniature paintings known to me: a Bible made in 1286, now kept in Ms. Paris, Bibliothèque Nationale heb. 4; the *Dragon Haggadah*, Hamburg, Staats-und Universitätsbibliothek, Cod. Heb. 155, (thirteenth century); a Pentateuch made in 1296 and kept in a private collection; and the *Poligny Pentateuch*, Paris, Bibliothèque Nationale,

Cod. Hébr. 36 (Poligny, 1300), which includes only one miniature. Michel Garel, *D'une main Forte: Manuscrits Hébreux des Collections Françaises* (Paris, 1991), 102–103; David Stern, "The Hebrew Bible in Europe in the Middle Ages: A Preliminary Typology," *JSIJ* 11 (2012), 1–88, esp. 48–49 (electronic journal: http://www.biu.ac.il/JS/JSIJ/11-2012/Stern.pdf); Narkiss, *Hebrew Illuminated Manuscripts*; Gabrielle Sed-Rajna, *Les manuscrits hébreux enluminés des bibliothèques de France* (Leuven, 1994). On the expulsion see: Susan L. Einbinder, *No Place of Rest: Jewish Literature, Expulsion, and the Memory of Medieval France* (Philadelphia, 2009).

36. This manuscript was illuminated by a Christian artist. Sed-Rajna, "Illustrations of the Kaufmann *Mishneh Torah*." See also Evelyn M. Cohen, "The Kaufmann *Mishneh Torah* Illuminations," in *David Kaufmann Memorial Volume: Papers Presented at the David Kaufmann Memorial Conference, November 29, 1999, Budapest*, ed. É. Apor (Budapest, 2002), 97–104, esp. 98.

37. Offenberg, *Illuminated Piety*, chapter 1. On this *piyyut* see: Davidson, *Thesaurus of Mediaeval Hebrew Poetry*, I, 8815; Ismar Elbogen, *Studien zur Geschichte des judischen Gottesdienstes* (Berlin, 1907), 49–99, esp. 79–81; Heinrich Graetz, "Die Anfänge der neuhebräischen Poesie," *Monatsschrift für Geschichte und Wissenschaft des Judentums* 9 (1860), 19–29, esp. 20–23; Leopold Zunz, *Die Ritus des synagogalen Gottesdienstes* (Berlin, 1919), 101; Daniel Goldschmidt, *Maḥzor la-yamim ha-nora'im: le-fi minhag bené ashkenaz le-khol 'anfehem: kolel minhag ashkenaz (ha-ma'aravi), minhag polin u-minhag tsarfat le-she'avar*, 2 vols. (Jerusalem, 1970), II, 465–478; Andreas Lehnard, "*Seder yom ha-kippurim kakh hu*": Zur Entwicklung der synagogalen Liturgie des Versohnungstages," in *The Day of Atonement: Its Interpretations in Early Jewish and Christian Traditions*, ed. Thomas Hieke and Tobias Nicklas (Leiden, 2012), 257–269, esp. 262–264; Zvi Malachi, "*Ha-"avodah" le-yom ha-kipurim: ofyah, toldotehah ve-hitpatḥutah ba-shirah ha-'ivrit*," (PhD dissertation, The Hebrew University of Jerusalem, 1974), 20–23; Aharon Mirsky, *Piyyuté Yose ben Yose* (Jerusalem, 1977), 26–31, 178–203; Michael D. Swartz and Joseph Yahalom, *Avodah: An Anthology of Ancient Poetry for Yom Kippur* (University Park, PA, 2005), 1–40, and see the Hebrew text with English translation on 291–341; Joseph Yahalom, "*'Az be-'en kol:*" *seder ha-'avodah ha-erets-yissre'eli ha-ḳadum le-yom ha-kippurim* (Jerusalem, 1996); Zvi Zohar, "*U-mi etaher etkhem – avikhem she-bashamayim: tefillat seder ha-'avodah shel yom ha-kippurim: tokhen, tifkud u-mashma'ut*," *AJS Review* 14 (1989), 1–28.

38. Goldschmidt, *Maḥzor*, II, xviii–xxv.

39. Menashe Raphael Lehmann, "Mi-sefer ben sira u-megillot yam ha-melaḥ la-'avodat ha-mikdash bi-tefilllot yom ha-kippurim," in *Masoret ha-piyyuṭ*, ed. Binyamin Bar-Tikva and Ephraim Hazan (Ramat Gan, 2000), 13–18 (Hebrew); Malachi, "*'Avoda" for Yom Kippur*, 163–71; Mirsky, *Piyyuté Yose ben Yose*, 26–31; Yahalom, "*'Az be-'en kol*," 15, 21–23, 28–30.

40. For the entire text of the *piyyut* commentary see Offenberg, *Illuminated Piety*, 178–197. For more commentaries on this *piyyut* see, Elisabeth Hollender, *Clavis Commentariorum of Hebrew Liturgical Poetry in Manuscript* (Leiden, 2005), 523.

41. Gérard Genette, *Paratexts: Thresholds of Interpretation* (Cambridge, 1997), 218 (originally published in French as *Seuils* (Paris, 1987).

42. Madeline Harrison Caviness, "Reception of Images by Medieval Viewers," in *A Companion to Medieval Art: Romanesque and Gothic in Northern Europe*, ed. C. Rudolph (Malden, 2006), 65–85, esp. 71–72.

43. I thank Ephraim Shoham-Steiner for this idea. On the possible Jewish patron of a Romanesque ivory series of the Samson stories, see: Vivian Mann, "The Samson and Hercules Tablemen: A Case for Jewish Patronage in Twelfth-Century Cologne," in *Art & Ceremony in Jewish Life: Essays in the History of Jewish Art* (London, 2005), 153–173.

44. Einbinder, *Beautiful Death*, 106.

45. Ibid., 108–109.

46. For more on Isaac, blood, and martyrdom, see Israel Jacob Yuval, "God Will See the Blood: Sin, Punishment, and Atonement in the Jewish-Christian Discourse," in *Jewish Blood: Reality and Metaphor in History, Religion, and Culture*, ed. M. B. Hart (London, New York, 2009), 83–98. On Samson as a messianic figure see Shimon Fogel, "Shimson ke-mashiaḥ—mabbat nosaf," *JSIJ* 11 (2012), 1–25 (electronic journal: http://www.biu.ac.il/JS/JSIJ/11-2012/Fogel.pdf).

47. Davidson, *Thesaurus of Mediaeval Hebrew Poetry*, I, 4273; Goldschmidt, *Maḥzor*, 2: 568–73; Einbinder, *Beautiful Death*, 167; Marc Hirshman, " 'Al kiddush ha-shem ba-'et ha-'attikah ve-hishtakkefuto ba-piyyut *Eleh Ezkera*," in: *Neti'ot le-david: Jubilee Volume for David Weiss Halivni*, ed. Y. Elman, E. B. Halivni, and Z. A. Steinfeld (Jerusalem, 2005), 71–81. In our manuscript the lament is written on fols. 455b–456b. For a selective bibliography on the Ten Martyrs see Ra'anan S. Boustan and Annette Yoshiko Reed, "Blood and Atonement in the Pseudo-Clementines and the 'Story of the Ten Martyrs': The Problem of Selectivity in the Study of 'Judaism' and 'Christianity,'" *Henoch* 30 (2008), 333–364; Ra'anan S. Boustan, *From Martyr to Mystic: Rabbinic Martyrology and the Making of Merkavah Mysticism* (Tübingen, 2005); Joseph Dan, *Toldot torat ha-sod ha-'ivrit: yemé benayim*, 7 vols. (Jerusalem, 2008–2012), II, chapter 22; Shmuel Shepkaru, *Jewish Martyrs in the Pagan and Christian Worlds* (Cambridge, UK, 2006), chapters 3 and 5.

48. On memory and visual culture in the Middle Ages see Mary J. Carruthers, *The Book of Memory* (Cambridge, 1990); Idem., *The Craft of Thought: Meditation, Rhetoric, and the Making of Images, 400–1200* (Cambridge, 1998).

49. In another series of images in the manuscript, done at a later stage of production, there are two scenes related to one's willingness to sacrifice oneself as a martyr; on the opening on fols. 259b–260a we find four scenes from the Book of Daniel showing the Three Hebrew Youths in the Fiery Furnace and Daniel in the Lions' Den. The Hebrew youths are a known subject in martyrological writings, and see Einbinder, *Beautiful Death*, 111. On these scenes, see: Sed-Rajna, *Hebraic Bible*, 135; Zirlin, "Decoration of the *Miscellany*," 91–93.

CHAPTER 14

THE LAMENT ON THE MARTYRS OF TROYES AS A MONUMENT OF JUDEO-FRENCH ON THE VERGE OF THE EXPULSIONS

Cyril Aslanov

In April 1288, 13 Jews were burnt at the stake in Troyes as a result of a blood libel that was launched against the community that Passover.[1] A *seliḥah* in Old French was composed in memory of the martyrs. It was published twice by Arsène Darmsteter.[2] In the first of the two articles, Darmsteter also inserted two *seliḥot* in Hebrew that refer to the same event, one by Jacob b. Judah of Lotra (Lotharingia), who also seems to be the author of the Old French text,[3] and another by Meir b. Eli'av. In her article on those *seliḥot*, Susan Einbinder inserted the facsimile of the relevant pages of MS. Vatican Ebr. 322, fol. 188b–189b. She also proposed a transcription and translation of the Old French text.[4] Four years later, Mark Kiwitt put forward an alternative edition of the text where he contested some of Einbinder's readings.[5] Most recently, Kirsten Fudeman wrote an article on the Old French *seliḥah* with her own transcription, translation and commentary.[6] The present study addresses the questions raised by this text from a more literary and poetic perspective.

At the outset, I note that the model on which the author of the Old French *seliḥah* relied could not be that of the Hebrew liturgical poems, as those pieces were primarily composed with the cento (*shibbuts*) technique[7] and, thus, heavily reliant on Biblical quotations. Due to the difference of language between the Hebrew Bible and the language of the Old French text, the latter was far more emancipated from the intertextual indebtedness toward the Bible. However, the text was largely influenced by the *seliḥah Elleh ezkerah*,[8] which is recited during the additional prayer of the

Day of Atonment in the Ashkenazic communities and on the 9 of Av in the
Sephardic world. This influence is perceptible both in the narrative technique and in more formal aspects like rhyme or number of syllables in the
verse. Einbinder acknowledged the existence of the link with *Elleh ezkerah*
in both *seliḥot*—the Hebrew one and its Old French counterpart but she did
not illustrate her point.[9] In this chapter, I would like to bring this intertex-
tuality to the foreground.

Another important point that has not been stressed in previous research
on the Old French *seliḥah* is its status as one of the few examples of Judeo-
French—a swan song of medieval French Jewry before the successive
expulsions put an end to its existence during the fourteenth century.
Although there is much doubt as to the existence of Judeo-French in the
Middle Ages,[10] I argue that, toward the end of its history, medieval French
Jewry managed to develop an Old-French-based Jewish language. This is
all the more probable because, in the beginning of the thirteenth century,
the French Jews lived in a state of growing isolation from their Christian
neighbors.[11]

I would like to connect the two issues: the influence of the poetics of
the classical *piyyut* on the writing in Old French and the question of Judeo-
French. Of course, these two aspects correspond to very different levels.
The influence of Hebrew poetics on writing in Old French is the result of a
premeditated transfer from one cultural horizon to the other. Conversely, the
crystallization of a Jewish language is beyond the awareness of its speakers.
In other words, the question is whether the Jewishness of the *seliḥah* derives
from the adoption and adaptation of Hebrew poetics to the Old French or
also from the inherent character of a putative Judeo-French.

Taking into consideration the poetic and linguistic dimensions of the
seliḥah will help elucidate the question of Judeo-French from several vantage
points, both the aforementioned diachronic perspective (Judeo-French as a
late expression of French Jewish identity toward the end of the history of
Medieval French Jewry), and from a sociolinguistic perspective. It is possible
that the response to the question of whether a specific Judeo-French language
existed is dependent on the sociolinguistic function. Medieval French Jews
certainly spoke in the same language as their Christian neighbors. However,
once they embarked on Old French writing, the language was probably more
characteristic of literary models in their specific Hebrew culture rather than
those of the common medieval French horizon. In order to appreciate the
impact of the Hebrew *Dachsprache* on their writing in Old French, one need
only think of the huge influence exerted by Latin in the frame of medieval
Christian diglossia.

It is important to stress that the *seliḥah* was not translated from another
language. Rather, its language was informed by the poetics of Hebrew classical *piyyut* in an attempt to sanctify the otherwise vulgar language.

For the sake of comparison, we will also briefly discuss *s'Mamserbelwel* "the blood libel"—a nineteenth-century Judeo-Alsatian elegy that relies upon materials far more ancient than the nineteenth century.[12] In spite of the gaps between Medieval French Jewry and modern Jewish Alsace, *s'Mamserbelwel* can be considered part of the tradition also represented by the Old French *seliḥah*. In both cases, one can perceive the influences of the liturgical poem *Elleh ezkerah* on the Old French and Judeo-Alsatian in which they are written, and the consequent upgrading of these vulgar languages to an almost sacred status.

Narrative Technique and Poetics

Old French intertextuality

In order to fully appreciate the indebtedness of the *seliḥah* to the poetics of classical Hebrew *piyyut* as exemplified by *Elleh ezkerah* and the Hebrew *seliḥah* of Jacob b. Judah, it is important to evaluate the extent to which the Jewish French text esthetically differs from contemporaneous Old French narrative poetry. Einbinder who focused on the martyrological motifs included in the Old French *seliḥah*, stressed the "courtly" character of this text,[13] as well as its indebtedness to the conventions of hagiographic literature.[14] However, the use of the term "courtly" in this context is only partly justified. The courtly tonality is certainly heard in the Old French *seliḥah*. The only intertextual link given by Einbinder in order to corroborate her view is connected with the *Song of Roland*, 2364 (*Seliḥah* 16, 3).[15] Actually, the epic genre, in general, and the *Song of Roland*, in particular, do not belong to the category of courtly literature. The echoing of the *Song of Roland*, a pre-courtly epic, in the Old French *seliḥah* is just one more testimony to the importance of this *chanson de geste* in the cultural horizon of medieval France (to the extent that it crossed the boundary between Christian and Jewish culture). However, this does not constitute evidence in favor of the courtly character of the *seliḥah*.

Let us be more rigorous in the identification of the courtly components of the *seliḥah*. From a lexical point of view, the words *joie* "joy" and *desduit* "pleasure" (2, 1) are typical in the phrase, referring to the erotic gratification the troubadour receives from his beloved. Likewise, the phrase *d'ofrir son cors por Ge i n'avet pas ruse* (10, 3) "he did not hesitate to offer his body to God" can be considered an echoing of a courtly lyrical song by Conon de Béthune. We will deal with this issue later.

From the perspective of phraseology, it is worth noting that the *seliḥah* contains three occurrences of a formulation that is typical of Old French literary discourse, but not necessarily of the courtly genres. This phrase consists of anticipating the adverb *molt* (*mult; mout; mot;* or *mont* [1,1; 5,2; 11, 1]) at the beginning of the sentence (sometimes after the coordination *mes* "but" or after the relative pronoun *qui* "who"). Here are the occurrences of this idiosyncratic construction within the poem:

> *Mont sont a mechief Israel, l'egaree gent.* (1,1)
> "Israel, the abandoned people, is suffering great hardship."
>   (trans. K. Fudeman)
> *Mont li fit mal la departie; de ce jeta mot grant cri.* (5,2)
> "The separation was very hard for her, so she uttered a loud cry."
>   (trans. K.F.)
> *Mot etet envenime lo felon, le madit.* (11, 1)
> "The evildoer, the cursed one, he was filled with poisonous desire."
>   (trans. K.F.)

In the romance *Erec and Enide* by Chrétien de Troyes, this formulation that consists of anticipating the adverb *molt* in order to transform it into the main topic of the sentence occurs at least in 50 of the 6,950 verses contained in the book. However, this stylistic twist is not especially courtly. It is rather a general device that characterizes the literary style. However, the mere fact that the *selihah* begins with the anticipated adverb *molt* can be considered the echoing of Conon de Béthune's poem: *Mout me semont Amors ke je m'envoise* "Greatly Love spreads to me so that I may sing."[16]

The relationship of the Selihah to the poetics of the classical Hebrew piyyut

In spite of its relationship to the poetic conventions of contemporaneous Old French literature, the *selihah* offers first and foremost an example of the adaptation of the Old French vulgar to Hebrew poetics in general and to the art of classical *piyyut* in particular. The indebtedness to Hebrew poetics comes to the fore through the rhyme as every strophe is in monorhyme except for the appendix. This is strongly reminiscent of *Elleh ezkerah*. This pattern also appears in Jacob b. Judah's Hebrew *selihah*. As in *Elleh ezkerah*, his transition to the next strophe, which is marked by a change of rhyme, is also associated with a shift of focus to another martyr. In spite of Darmsteter's attempts to reconstruct alexandrine verses in the *selihah*, it is more likely that the number of syllables was variable (as in *Elleh ezkerah*).[17] It should be noted that, in Old French poetry, the use of the alexandrine verse was quite unique. In the frame of Old French narrative poetry, the octosyllable verse would be the more expected.

The rhyme exemplified by the Old French *selihah* functions in a different way than we see in Old French poetry where this prosodic device can consist of the repetition of the same vowel or of the same sequel vowel plus consonant, whereas the repetition of the consonant that precedes the vowel is only facultative. However, we see the difference in the *selihah* as the consonant preceding the rhyming vowel is also supposed to rhyme throughout the strophe according to the following schema: CV(C) instead of the V(C) schema of Old French poetry. The content of the *selihah* is also very similar to that of *Elleh ezkerah*. Both cases contain a horrifying description of death at the stake. To be sure, in *Elleh ezkerah* each of the ten martyrs receives a different death, whereas in the *selihah* all the thirteen martyrs are burnt alive. However, another kind of death is alluded to, namely the torture of flaying alive, which is the way Ishma'el was executed according to *Midrash Elleh ezkerah* and to the liturgical poem *Elleh ezkerah*. In 7, 4 of the Old French *selihah*, Isaac Chatelain's daughter-in-law expresses her willingness to be flayed alive instead of committing apostasy:

Je ne lerrai le Gé vif; por tant me porrez escorchier.
"I will not give up the living God, therefore you could flay me alive."
(trans. K.F.)

Likewise, other intertextual echoes of *Elleh ezkerah* are perceptible throughout the Old French *selihah*. In 8, 4, we read the following statement as to the martyrs' eagerness to face their destiny:

Oncques gens an ne vit si hetement aler.
"Never did a group of people come so joyfully out into the open air."
(trans. K.F.)

This formulation is reminiscent of the description of Ishmael's eagerness to die in *Elleh ezkerah*, 12, 1:

Lishpokh damo miher ke-shor par.
"To pour his blood he hurried up like a bullock."

This verse implicitly compares Ishmael who was nicknamed "the High Priest" to the bullock that was brought as a sacrifice by the priests. Through this metaphor, we understand that the one bringing the sacrifice and the sacrifice itself are the same person.

The very same paradox is recycled in the Old French *selihah*, where it is expressed even more explicitly in the utterance ascribed to Isaac Chatelain who was apparently a *kohen*:

Je sui Cohen: ofrande de mon cors voil ofrir. (14, 4)
"I am a Cohen: I want offer my body as a sacrifice." (my translation)

In the Hebrew *selihah* by Meir b. Eli'av, the metaphor that compares the martyr with the sacrifice becomes a full-fledged leitmotiv developed throughout the poem (strophes 1; 2; 4; 5; 7; and 9).[18]

The motive of self-sacrifice is further brought in 10, 3, although in a more attenuated way:

> *D'ofrir son cors por Ge i n'avet pas ruse.*
> "He did not hold back from offering his body to God." (trans. K. F.)

In spite of the strong indebtedness of the Old French *seliḥah* to *Elleh ezkerah*, the motive of the sacrifice of the body can also be considered an intertextual link to courtly lyric poetry. In the poem of Conon de Béthune mentioned above, the poet recycles the courtly opposition between the body (*cors*) and the heart (*cuers*) to the context of the Crusades:

> *Se li cors va servir Nostre Signor,*
> *Mes cuers remaint del tot en sa baillie.*[19]
> "If the body goes out to serve our Lord,
> My heart remains completely in her power."

Finally, in the aforementioned Judeo-Alsatian *seliḥah*, the metaphor that compares martyrdom with sacrifice appears in 7, 2:

> *Henn for ihr emüne g'opfert ihr Lewe.*[20]
> "For their faith they have sacrificed their lives."

Further, possible evidence of the indebtedness of the *seliḥah* to *Elleh ezkerah* lies in the mention of the profession of scribe (*sofer*) associated with the ninth martyr (*Simeon Sofer*) in 12, 4. It reminds one of the mention of Yeshev'av the scribe in *Elleh ezkerah*, 22, 4. On its own, the mention of this profession does not add much to the assumption that the Old French *seliḥah* heavily relied on *Elleh ezkerah*; however, in this case, the word *sofer* creater internal rhyme as the Old French pronunciation of the -*er* ending of the infinitive was still pronounced -er:

> *Ce fu R. Shim'on Sofer / qui si bien saveit orer.*
> "It was R. Simeon Sofer who knew how to pray so well."
>   (my translation)

Since the occurrence of *sofer* is not prosody-bound and only constitutes a facultative internal rhyme with the last word of the verse *orer* "to pray," it makes sense to view the use of a Hebrew title within the Old French text as an expression of deliberate intent of paradigmatic comparison between R. Simeon Sofer with R. Yeshev'av ha-Sofer.

Broadly speaking, the combination of descriptions of the cruel torments of the martyrs leading to their deaths, accompanied by the mention of their qualities during their lifetimes, is very typical of the poetic technique exhibited in *Elleh ezkerah*.

Curiously, the Old French *seliḥah* differs from *Elleh ezkerah* inasmuch as it does not contain an alphabetic acrostic. This essential difference is because writing in Old French with Hebrew letters does not allow use of all 22 letters of the Hebrew alphabet. In the Old French glosses, only 18 of the 22 Hebrew letters are used. This demonstrates a limit in the adaptation of Hebrew poetics to the Old French.

The Language of the Old French *Seliḥah* as a Specimen of Judeo-French

Despite Menahem Banitt's skepticism as to the existence of a medieval Judeo-French, the text of the Old French *seliḥah* displays some linguistic characteristics that can help us reconsider the position that Judeo-French was no more than a "ghost language."

Syntax

In the opening sentence that we have already analyzed above,

> *Mont sont a mechief Israel, l'egaree gent.* (1,1)
> "Israel, the stray nation, are greatly misfortuned/unfortunate."
> (my translation)

there is a striking syntactic feature that consists of imitating in French the agreement *kata synesin* whereby the plural form *sont* is used with the subject *Israel, l'egaree gent*—a singular with a plural meaning. This construction reminds us of a specific habit of Mishnaic Hebrew whereby Israel in the meaning of "the people of Israel" agrees *kata synesin* with a verb in plural. This is not only a matter of word-by-word translation cleaving to the syntactic structure of the Hebrew original because the copula *sont* has no parallel in Hebrew. Therefore, the use of the plural can be considered a creative adaptation of the *kata synesin* agreement characterizing Mishnaic Hebrew to the linguistic system of Old French.

Another syntactic matter is the imitation of the redundant expression of possession (*semikhut kefulah*) that characterizes Mishnaic Hebrew:

> *sa fin <de> d'Anvirey dam Bendit.* (11, 4)
> "his end, that of sir Bendit from Anvirey." (my translation)

I disagree with Kirsten Fudeman's interpretation of the toponym *Anvirey*, as an alternative or corrupted form for Avirey as *enivré* "intoxicated."[21] Darmsteter interpreted with reason the word דאנבאדיט as representing *danbadit*.[22] However, in another place in the same article, Darmsteter reconstructed the sequel as representing *de Bendit* "of Bendit,"[23] as did Einbinder[24] and Kiwitt.[25] Blondheim[26] correctly identified the element דאנ- with the honorific title *dan/ dam* "sir," a reflection of Latin *dominu(m)*, the parallel of *don* in Italian and Spanish, *dom* in Portuguese and *domnu* in Romanian. In the sequel שאפין דאנוירי דאנבאנדיט = *sa fin <de> d'Anvirey dam Bendit* "from Anvirey dam Bendit, his end," the preposition *de* that was supposed to connect *sa fin* with *dam Bendit d'Anvirey* was probably dropped as a result of a haplology. Indeed, the complete formula should have contained two occurrences of the preposition *de,* one immediately after the other: *sa fin <de> d'Anvirey dam Bendit,* the first one connecting *sa fin* and *D'Anviray dan Bendit* and the second one connecting *dam Bendit* with the toponym *Anvirey.*

However, the most important point here is the redundant use of *sa* in order to underline the possessive relationship between *fin* and *dam Bendit.* We see a similar application of the redundant mark of possession characteristic of Mishnaic Hebrew at work in Ladino, the written register of Judeo-Spanish. There, the Aramaic blessing בריך שמה דמרא עלמא *berikh shemeh de-mareh 'alma* "blessed be His name of the master of universe" was translated as

בנדטיג'ו סיאה סו נומברי דיל פאדרון דיל מונדו – *bendicho sea su nombre del padrón del mundo*

with a redundant expression of the possessive relation that unites *nombre* and *padrón del mundo.*

In French, however, the two components of the name of the possessor *dam Bendit d'Anvirey* underwent an inversion as a result of which the toponym appears first, before the name *Dam Bendit*: *D'Anvirey dam Bendit.* This inversion is a well-known device of French poetry that can be considered a Latinism transplanted into the vulgar.

We see here the mingling of three different linguistic systems: (1) the regular syntax of French represented by the latent structure *la fin de dam Bendit d'Anvirey*; (2) the Latinism consisting of the inversion of the two components of the latter phrase: *d'Anvirey dam Bendit*; (3) a syntactic calque of Mishnaic Hebrew with the repetition of the mark of possession: *sa fin de dam Bendit d'Anvirey.*

Whereas in the aforementioned Ladino example, the adoption of the redundancy characterizes the style of literal translation (from Aramaic in that specific case), the adoption of a similar syntactic structure in Old French does not continue any original Hebrew or Aramaic. It is rather the spontaneous imitation of a syntactic feature common in Judeo-Aramaic and Mishnaic Hebrew. In other words, the Aramaic or Hebrew syntax informs the Old French linguistic material.

Lexicon

Besides the application of Hebrew poetics to the writing in Old French and the occasional calque of syntactic structures imitated from Mishnaic

Hebrew or Judeo-Aramaic, the language of the *selihah* displays a tendency to reshape the semantic fields of some words according to the semantics of Hebrew. On its own, such a reshaping can be considered clear evidence in favor of the existence of a specific Jewish dialect in France toward the end of the thirteenth century. Needless to say, we see the presence of Hebrew *Kulturwörter*—a very banal phenomenon in Jewish interlinguistics. Such words are, of course, extant in the *selihah* but there is no need to indulge further in their description.[27] Let us just briefly mention תורה "Torah" in 2, 2; תוספות "Tosafot" in 4, 4; חתן *hatan*, bridegroom, in 9,1; קדושה, *kedusha*, "sanctification" in 9, 2; קדוש *kadosh*, "martyr" in 11,2 and 16, 1; the already mentioned סופר, *sofer*, in 12,4; כהן *kohen*, "priest" in 14, 1.

The only interesting Hebrew word is the title *kadmenet/ kadmenes* in 9,4. According to Darmsteter,[28] this form is the feminine of *kadmon* "old-timer." The derivation of a feminine form קדמנת, *kadmenet*, on the base of the masculine קדמון, *kadmon*, constitutes an interesting innovation in its own right; however, this has more to do with the traditions of Hebrew in northern France than with the issue of the existence of Judeo-French. Fudeman proposed an alternative meaning, "the Eastern one,"[29] but we do not see this paralleled enough in Hebrew.

In 2, 3 we also find a Hebrew term that was totally embedded in the structure of Old French. According to Blondheim's reading,[30] the verbal form *asqer*, that is, *asquer* or rather *aschier* with the allophone *-ier* of *-er*[31] after the [tʃ] (already reduced in [ʃ] in the thirteenth century),[32] is the adaptation of *'asak* "to deal with" and more specifically "to study (the Torah)," as in the formula *la-'asok be-divré torah* "to deal with the words of the Law," which appears in the *Birkat ha-torah*. Darmsteter deciphered this word in a different way and identified it with the verb *tascher* "to fulfill a task; to try hard."[33] If the reading *aschier* should be preferred, Kiwitt's statement regarding the absence of Hebrew-Old French hybridization in the *selihah*[34] does not hold true since *aschier* possibly displays a combination of the Hebrew verbal stem *'āsaq* (as its allomorph *'āsq-*) with the ending *-er/ -ier*.

The form *medeet*, that is, *medeient* "they studied" (2, 2) is perhaps more univocal. Although it is not a Hebrew component, it is nevertheless a specifically Jewish term. This verb *meder*, also attested in the form *miauder*, is the Romance avatar of the Latin *meletare*, is itself an adaptation of Greek μελετᾶν and is paralleled by Judeo-Spanish *meldar* "to read; to pray."[35]

In order to fully evaluate the nature of Judeo-French, it is also important to take into account the impact of Hebrew and of the Jewish way of life on the semantics of the specific blend of Old French that was in use in Jewish milieus. This impact is felt especially with regard to the semantic shifts that affected some Old French terms. In other words, the signifier of those words is the same in Old French and in the Jewish variety of Old French whereas their signified underwent a deep transformation (as in the case of the German term *Jahreszeit* "season," the Yiddish equivalent of which *yortseyt* is used in the meaning of "anniversary of the death of someone").

The *seliḥah* contains two semantic shifts of this kind: in 4, 4 the adjective *plain* meaning "simple" is used as a substantive in the meaning of "plain commentary."[36] Interestingly enough, the Old French word *plain* that was preserved in English and lost in modern French was recycled by English-speaking Jews as a canonic translation of Hebrew *peshat*. Needless to say, this encounter between medieval Judeo-French and modern Jewish English is not intentional. It does show how often modern English preserved the Old French lexicon better than did modern French.

In 17, 1 the noun *emprinere*, also attested as *empreneeur, emprenere, emprenire*, offers a good example of the aforementioned semantic shifts that are peculiar to the Jewish blend of Old French.[37] From the general meaning of "undertaker," the term was specialized for the translation of the term *kanna* (Exodus 34:14) and used as a determiner of *Gé* "God" (see below).

In addition to these expressions of Jewish identity in Old French, the language exemplified by the *seliḥah* contains an occurrence of *paradis* (6, 4), a Christian term recycled for Jewish use. This word is the superficial vulgarization of Latin *paradisus* that is used by Jerome in his translation of the Bible (cf. its vulgar counterpart *pareïs* found in the *Song of Roland* 2241). The Christian impregnation of this term did not prevent the French Jewish *paytan* from resorting to this word in order to refer to *Gan Eden*.

Moreover, it seems that beyond this terminological congruence between the Christian and Jewish cultures there is also an intertextual link between a certain formula found in the *seliḥah* and a verse of the Gospel—a text that was very remote from the Jewish cultural horizon. In the exhortation by one of the martyrs of Troyes to his younger brother, we see a formula close to that found in Luke 23:43. In 6, 3–4, the Judeo-French text reads as follows:

> *E dit: "Haro! J'ar toz!" E li granz li aprent*
> *E dit: "A Paradis seras tot, je t'acrant.*
> "And he said: 'Help! I am burning up!' And his older brother
>   instructed him
> And said to him: 'You will be soon in the Paradise, I promise you."
> (translation K.F.)

Darmsteter identified this word *tot* with the *toz/ tot* "all" and chose to connect this adverbial use of *tot* with the verb *je t'acrant* "I promise you."[38] However Blondheim, Einbinder, and Kiwitt[39] preferred to interpret *tot* as a reflection of *tost* "soon." The latter reading fits an intertextual link with Luke 23:43: "And Jesus said unto him: Verily I say unto thee, today shalt thou be with me in paradise" (King James version). In the cultural horizon of medieval France, this text was mostly known in Latin, according to the Vulgate: *Et dixit illi Jesus : Amen dico tibi : hodie mecum eris in paradiso.*

Likewise, the use of the verb *orer* "to pray" (12, 4) that Einbinder translated as "to sing"[40] constitutes a point of convergence between the Jewish and Christian discourses. Indeed, *orer/ourer* is the most widespread Old French verb for expressing the action of praying. This fact did not prevent the French Jewish *paytan* from using it in order to refer to Jewish prayer. The use of *orer/ourer* has been continued in a Germanized form as *oren*, the Western Yiddish counterpart of Eastern Yiddish *davenen*,[41] that could also continue an Old French etymon.[42]

On the other hand, the specifically Jewish theonym *Gé* "God" is recurrent throughout the *seliḥah*. It appears either alone (2,4; 3, 3; 4, 2; 7, 4; 10, 3; 13, 3; 14, 3; and 17, 4) or with an adjective: *Gé vif* "Living God" (4, 3 and 15, 3); *Gé vivant*, same meaning (16, 4); *Gé venchère* "avenging God" (17, 1), a reminiscence of Psalms 94:1. The form ײִג, G'Y, of the manuscript represents [dʒe] or rather [ʒe], the result of the palatalization of the initial [d-] in *Dié/ Dé* "God." Whereas in Christian pronunciation, the various Old French reflections of Latin *Deus* preserved [d-] (*Dieu; Deu; Dié; Di; Dé*), probably because of the pressure of Latin on Old French, the specific Jewish blend of Old French that was less exposed to Latin performed the palatalization of the initial [d-] that was usual before the semi-consonant [j] or before the front vowels [i] and [e] (cf. Latin *diurnum* "day" > Old French *jorn/ jurn*). In other words, the Old French word for God that was preserved from the palatalization in Christian milieus underwent this phonetic change only in Judeo-French.[43] This striking divergence between the general use and the Jewish one may also have been motivated by a deliberate intent to avoid the Christian theonym. The Jews of medieval France probably took advantage of the variations of the Latin etymon *Deus* on the various levels of Old French diglossia, in order to allow the expression of difference.

Onomastic Issues Reflected in the *Seliḥah*

The names of the martyrs reflect an interesting process of reshuffling the semantics of Old French in contact with Hebrew. Before we start to deal with onomastics, it is worth noting that, in the manuscript, all the names are preceded by the title *rabbi* according to a tradition well attested throughout the Ashkenazic world. However, one of the martyrs deserves the aforementioned title of *dan/ dan* "sir" that is more characteristic of Gentile onomastic.

As for the names themselves, it is important to stress that some of them display a complete adaptation to the Christian onomasticon. The most obvious example is provided by the name of R. *Itzhak Chatelain* (1, 4). The etymological meaning of *chastelain* (already leveled to *chatelain* by the thirteenth century) is "commander of a castle"—a function to which the Jews of medieval France did not have access. Nowadays, the second name *Châtelain* is widespread in the Aube department where Troyes is located.[44]

Toponymy is one of the origins of French patronyms and of patronyms in general, especially as far as the names of the cities are concerned. The recycling of toponyms as patronyms was probably at work with the determiner דאנווירי *d'Anvirey* before the mention of *Dam Bendit* (11, 4). Likewise, the toponym *Brinon* preceded by the proposition *de* (15, 4) is added to the name of Hayyim.

As for the first names, they often seem to be adapted to the linguistic horizon of medieval France. Thus, the name *Yonah* (13, 1) does not appear in its Hebrew form but as a translation into Old French: *Colon* (dove). It is worth noting that the Yiddish equivalent of *Colon*, which is *Toybe*, is a feminine name and not a masculine name like *Colon* used as an equivalent of *Yonah*. This difference between the medieval Judeo-French habit and its Yiddish counterpart may be due to the specific nature of Old French, a language where the noun *colon/coulon/colomb* "dove" is masculine to be distinguished from *colombe* that was the only one to survive in Modern French. The existence of a masculine term for the dove in Old French made it possible to translate the masculine name *Yonah* into the vernacular. This option was not available in Middle High German—a language where the name of the dove was exclusively feminine: *tûbe* continued in Yiddish as *toyb*, the base for the feminine name *Toybe*.

A common feature between the onomasticon of medieval French Jewry and German-speaking Jewries is the anthroponym *Bendit*, which is represented by the form באדיט that should be read [bãⁿdit] with a graphic representation of the nasal vowel [ã] by *aleph*. The interesting point from the onomastic perspective is the fact that the anthroponym *Barukh* was literally translated by *Bendit* "blessed." In its turn, this anthroponym, *Bendit* became a patronym among German Jews, probably as a result of the emigration of French Jews after the expulsions of the fourteenth century.

A Comparative Approach

From *Elleh ezkerah* to the French *selihot* and to the later Judeo-Alsatian *selihah s'Mamserbelwel* mentioned above, we are able perceive how the poetic devices and the martyrological motives of the classical *piyyut* were acclimated to the vulgar languages—either Old French or Judeo-Alsatian. It is difficult to understand the rationale for such a crossing of the boundary between the sacred language and the vulgar.

Is it possible that the *selihot* in vulgar were written for a female audience that did not have access to Hebrew?[45] This explanation might be relevant with regard to the Judeo-Alsatian *selihah* that ends with extracts taken from the ritual of prayers. However, in the Old French *selihah*, there is no tangible evidence in favor of Einbinder's assumption as to the performance of the poem in the frame of the synagogue, parallel to the recitation of the Hebrew version.[46] It is likely that, on the verge of the expulsions of the Jews from France or in its aftermath, this poem enjoyed a special resonance among the French Jewish refugees who found an abode in the neighboring countries. Indeed, before the expelled French Jews assimilated with other Jewries outside France—mainly Germany and northern Italy—they probably preserved their language for several generations, especially in such countries as Dauphiné or Savoy.[47] Although remaining outside the Kingdom of France (for Dauphiné until 1349), those lands were part of the French cultural space (despite the differences between French, and Franco-Provençal the vernacular language of both Dauphiné and Savoy). Once the descendants of the French Jews assimilated linguistically into the Jewish communities that received their forefathers, the Old French *seliḥah* was unable to continue to function as an equivalent of *Elleh ezkerah* in the local Jewish traditions. However, many generations later, when the Alsatian Jews who used to be part of German Jewry were swallowed into the Kingdom of France as a result of the Peace of Westphalia (1648), the tradition that consisted of singing a *seliḥah* in vulgar on the model of *Elleh ezkerah* was reinstated with the aforementioned *s'Mamserbelwel*. Can we conclude from the parallelism between the Old French *seliḥah* and *s'Mamserbelwel* that there was a real continuity from medieval French Jewry to early modern Alsatian Jews?

If this is at all the case, the continuity was primarily synchronic inasmuch that the tragic events undergone by French Jews had repercussions in Ashkenaz. This continuity is mainly due to the intensity of the contact between the Jews of northern France and their coreligionists of the Holy Roman German Empire throughout the Middle Ages.[48] A good example of such continuity is provided by the fact that the names of the martyrs of Troyes were preserved in the *Memorbuch* of Mayence.

However, the French *seliḥah* and *s'Mamserbelwel* differ from each other in terms of the Hebrew component. Although the Old French *seliḥah* contains some Hebrew words with which we dealt above, the presence of the sacred tongue is far more evident in the Judeo-Alsatian *piyyut*. This is mainly because Western Yiddish in general and Judeo-Alsatian in particular contained a special register called *ləshon əkaudish*, consisting of a secret language with many Hebrew components.[49] To be sure, the language of *s'Mamserbelwel* is not deliberately encoded. However, the language of the composition can be viewed as a literary expression of the cryptolalic language that was in use among German-speaking Jews.

Conclusions

Turning back to the Old French *seliḥah,* it can be said that it is written in a language that should be considered a specimen of Judeo-French used on the verge of the expulsion of French Jews from France. However, the Hebrew components embedded therein consist only of a few *Kulturwörter*, even fewer lexical items like *asquier/aschier* (<*'asak* "to deal with; to study") or *meder/miauder* "to study," a specifically Jewish verb, although of non-Hebrew origin. Thus, the Jewish character of the language exemplified by the Old French *seliḥah* is primarily due to the presence of full-fledged French words having received a specifically Jewish meaning. Likewise, the imprint of Hebrew can be seen not only at the lexical level but also on the syntax—a more essential dimension to understanding language structure than mere vocabulary. Since the Old French *seliḥah* is not really a translation, the presence of occasional Hebraisms in its syntax can be considered clear evidence of the structural influence of Hebrew on the blend of Old French that was in use among the Jews of medieval France rather than the result of pressure of the source language on the target language.

Thus, it appears that toward the first expulsion of the Jews from the Kingdom of France in 1306 an Old French-based Jewish language was already crystallized north of the Loire. However, unlike other Jewish languages that continued to be in use even after their speakers left their birthplaces, medieval Judeo-French did not succeed in striking roots in the Jewries that received the French Jewish refugees.

In my opinion, what distinguishes Judeo-French from Yiddish and Judeo-Spanish is precisely the fact that the latter languages did not crystallize in Germany or Spain but in Eastern Europe, in the first case, and in the Ottoman Empire, in the second. Conversely, the Judeo-French that crystallized in France in the wake of the expulsions, and whereof the *seliḥah* is a reliable testimony, came into existence in the place where French Jews spent so many centuries throughout the Middle Ages and not in the places of emigration where they just settled, as happened with the German Jews in Eastern Europe and the Spanish Jews in the Ottoman Empire. In other words, what made Yiddish and Judeo-Spanish so competitive with respect to other languages spoken by the Jews in their places of emigration was precisely the fact that both languages were already *koinés*, that is, composite dialects resulting from the synthesis originally spoken in various geographical areas. As already noted by Fudeman, the language represented in the *seliḥah* already underwent a process of dialectal mixture (a Lotharingian base colored by some interference from the dialects of Champagne and Burgundy).[50] It seems, therefore, that in order to be able to continue its existence outside the place where it was first spoken, a Jewish language needs to rely on more than one dialectal variety so that it may generate a new synthesis instead of being just a transplantation of a unique dialectal blend. Paradoxically enough, the fact that Judeo-French was not able to continue its existence outside France and can therefore be considered a kind of linguistic dead end, constitutes evidence in favor of the assumption that Yiddish and Judeo-Spanish crystallized outside Germany and Spain. Otherwise, as in the case of Judeo-French, a local koiné would not have survived once transplanted to other countries. Only a new creation in those countries was able to last for generations.

Notes

A Hebrew version of the present study has been published in a different form in *Massorot*, xvi–xvii (2014): 69–86.

1. On the historical circumstances of this tragic event, see Robert Chazan, *Medieval Jewry in Northern France: A Political and Social History* (Baltimore and London, 1973), 180–181; Emily Taitz, *The Jews of Medieval France: The Community of Champagne* (Westport, CT and London, 1994), 217–219; Simon Schwarzfuchs, *Yehude tsarfat bi-yemé ha-benayim* (Tel Aviv, 1991), 246–248.

2. Arsène Darmsteter, "Deux élégies du Vatican," *Romania* 3 (1874): 443–486; "L'autodafé de Troyes (24 avril 1288)," *Revue des Études Juives* 2 (1881): 199–247.

3. Ibid., 218.

4. Susan L. Einbinder, "The Troyes Laments: Jewish Martyrology in Hebrew and Old French," *Viator* 30 (1999), 203–205; 218–230.

5. Mark Kiwitt, "L'élégie de Troyes: une nouvelle lecture," *Études médiévales*, 5 (2003): 262–265.

6. Kirsten A. Fudeman, "Restoring a Vernacular Jewish Voice: The Old French Elegy of Troyes," *Jewish Studies Quarterly* 15 (2008): 197–204.

7. The *cento* technique, called *shibbuts*, consists of writing a text mainly composed of quotes of another text (the biblical text in a Jewish context).

8. This parallel was suggested by Kirsten A. Fudeman, "These Things I Will Remember: The Troyes Martyrdom and Collective Memory," *Prooftexts* 29 (2009): 1–30.

9. Einbinder, "The Troyes Laments," 202, 206.

10. Menahem Banitt, "Une langue-fantôme – le judéo-français," *Revue de Linguistique Romane* 27 (1963): 245–294.

11. Kirsten A. Fudeman, *Vernacular Voices: Language and Identity in Medieval French Jewish Communities* (Philadelphia, 2010), 36–39.

12. Freddy Raphaël, *Juifs en Alsace: Culture, société, histoire* (Toulouse, 1977), 320–322.

13. Einbinder, "The Troyes Laments," 208–209; 215, 217. See also by the same author, *Beautiful Death: Jewish Poetry and Martyrdom in Medieval France* (Princeton and Oxford, 2002), 134.

14. Einbinder, "The Troyes Laments," 209–210.

15. Ibid., 215; Einbinder, *No Place of Rest: Jewish Literature, Expulsion, and the Memory of Medieval France* (Philadelphia, 2009), 139.

16. Axel Wallensköld, *Les chansons de Conon de Béthune* (Paris, 1921), 5.

17. Darmsteter, "L'autodafé de Troyes," 211–213.

18. Ibid., 227–233.

19. Wallensköld, *Les chansons de Conon de Béthune*, 6. See also Cyril Aslanov, *Shiré ahavah ve-shiré milḥamah be-shirat ha-trubadurim: ben niggud le-hashlamah hadadit* (Jerusalem, 2010), 148.

20. Raphaël, *Juifs en Alsace: Culture, société, histoire*, 324.

21. Fudeman, "Restoring a Vernacular," 203.

22. Darmsteter, "L'autodafé de Troyes," 209, 240.

23. Ibid., 216.

24. Einbinder, "The Troyes Laments," 227.

25. Kiwitt, "L'élégie de Troyes," 264.

26. David S. Blondheim, "Contribution à l'étude de la poésie judéo-française," *Revue des Études Juives* 83 (1927): 160.

27. Einbinder, "The Troyes Laments," 209, 212–213.

28. Darmsteter, "L'autodafé de Troyes," 239.

29. Fudeman, "Restoring a Vernacular," 203.

30. Blondheim, "Contribution à l'étude de la poésie judéo-française," 83 (1927): 160.

31. Gérard Moignet, *Grammaire de l'ancien français* (Paris, 1973), 56.

32. On the equivalence *koph* = [tʃ]/ [ʃ] in the practice of writing Old French with Hebrew letters, see Menahem Banitt, introduction to *Le glossaire de Leipzig* (Jerusalem, 2005), 168.

33. Darmsteter, "L'autodafé de Troyes," 207, 215.

34. Kiwitt, "L'élégie de Troyes," 267.

35. Raphael Lévy, *Contribution à la lexicographie française selon d'anciens textes d'origine juive* (Syracuse, 1960), 429–430; *Trésor de la langue des Juifs français au Moyen Âge* (Austin, 1964), 155.

36. Kiwitt, "L'elégie de Troyes," 270; Fudeman, "Restoring a Vernacular," 206.

37. Kiwitt, "Lélégie de Troyes," 268–269. For a radically different interpretation see Fudeman, "Restoring a Vernacular," 211. Fudeman recognizes here the phrase *en prinra* "he will take (vengeance)."

38. Darmsteter, "L'autodafé de Troyes," 208; 214–215.

39. Blondheim, "Contribution à l'étude de la poésie judéo-française," 83 (1927): 160; Einbinder, "The Troyes Laments," 226; Kiwitt, "L'elégie de Troyes," 263.

40. Einbinder, "The Troyes Laments," 211.

41. On the complementary distribution of *oren* and *davenen* in Yiddish, see Marvin I. Herzog ed., *The Language and Culture Atlas of Ashkenazic Jewry*, (Tübingen, 1992–2000), III, 216–217.

42. Cyril Aslanov, "A Tentative Romance Etymology for Yiddish *Dav(e)nen*", in *Sha'arei Lashon: Studies in Hebrew, Aramaic, and Jewish Languages Presented to Moshe Bar-Asher*, ed. Aharon Maman, Steve Fassberg, and Yochanan Breuer, III (Jerusalem, 2007), 244–258.

43. As already stated by Kiwitt, "L'élégie de Troyes," 269–270.

44. http://www. nom-famille.com/nom-chatelain.html, © 2006–2014.

45. Einbinder, "The Troyes Laments," 216–217; Kiwitt, "L'élégie de Troyes," 271–272.

46. Einbinder, "The Troyes Laments," 217.

47. On the survival of the legacy of French Jewry in Savoy and Piedmont, see Einbinder, *No Place of Rest*, 137–157.

48. On the linguistic and cultural ties between French and German Jews in the Middle Ages see Cyril Aslanov, "The Juxtaposition Ashkenaz/ Tsarfat vs. Sepharad/ Provence Reassessed—A Linguistic Approach," *Simon-Dubnow-Institute Jahrbuch/ Yearbook*, VIII (2009), 51–55.

49. Florence Guggenheim-Grünberg, "The Horse Dealers' Language of the Swiss Jews in Endingen and Lengnau," in *The Field of Yiddish: Studies in Language, Folklore, and Literature*, ed. Uriel Weinreich (New York, 1954), 48–62.

50. Fudeman, "Restoring a Vernacular," 195.

CHAPTER 15

EXEGESIS AND ROMANCE: REVISITING THE
OLD FRENCH TRANSLATION OF *KALLIR*[1]

Susan L. Einbinder

Until recently, scholars rarely asked what language resounded in medieval places of Jewish prayer. The great liturgical and customary
compendium known as the *Maḥzor Vitry* emphasized the Hebrew prayer
practices of a literate (and male) community of users.[2] The chance survival
of liturgical hymns, or fragments of hymns, composed in the vernacular,
did little to unsettle the assumption that the formal worship experience
of medieval European Jews was dominated by Hebrew. A Judeo-French
lament for thirteen victims of an auto da fé in Troyes in 1288, a snippet of a
drinking song scrawled in a Passover *haggadah*, or even a bilingual wedding
song preserved in the *Maḥzor Vitry* could be associated with paraliturgical
activity.[3] Thus, they seemed to confirm the belief that the vernacular made
few, if any, inroads into the Jewish house of prayer. Neither the growing trend toward affective devotion in the larger culture, nor the rise of
Romance prose was seen as a factor that might have created an opening for
vernacular prayer.[4]

Nonetheless, there is evidence that at least some French Jews did choose
to pray in the language of daily life. Between 1933 and 1956, Hiram Peri
(Pflaum) published two articles detailing the contents of several stray
folios recovered from the binding of a late fifteenth-century biblical codex
in Heidelberg.[5] Among them, three parchment bifolia contained hymns
(*piyyutim*) by a revered poet of Late Antiquity, Eleazar beribbi Kallir. The
hymns were not, however, in their original Hebrew, but translated into Old
French inscribed in Hebrew characters. Pflaum's dating (ca. 1300) put these
fragments among the earliest of the known French vernacular compositions
preserved in Hebrew letters.[6] Largely ignored since their publication, these
texts are overdue for new attention.

The hymns preserved in the Heidelberg fragment are Kallir's *Ansikha malki/lefanav behithallekhi* and *Zekher tehillat kol maʿas*, with their connecting prose ligatures. They belong, respectively, to the *malkhuyot* and *zikhronot* sections of the *Musaf* liturgy for Rosh Hashanah. According to Pflaum, they may have been intended for a cantor or congregants not at ease with learned Hebrew, perhaps Jewish women.[7] Certainly, Jewish men as well as women might have found the vernacular a relief on long festival days, but that is not the only option. I would like to suggest that, rather than a default to a less learned style, the vernacular translations illustrate new ways of relating to sacred Hebrew texts, some anticipated in exegetical genres. They may also represent a concession to a yearning for a prayer experience that was close to the language of daily living and thought—much in keeping with the affective piety of the times.

This essay treats Kallir's *Ansikha Malki*, the first of the *piyyutim* preserved in MS Heidelberg Or. 490. What do these texts tell us about the intellectual world of the translator and the men and women for whom he translated this poem? As Ephraim Kanarfogel has demonstrated, northern French rabbis long associated with the talmudic dialectics of the Tosafist school also showed interest in biblical exegesis and piyyut composition.[8] Their eclectic approaches are reflected in this translator's work, as he demonstrates familiarity both with the tools of *peshat* reading that characterized twelfth-century French exegesis and the aggadic traditions that had long been enlisted to reconcile textual difficulties in the biblical text. *Peshat* readings typically turned to narrative as a way of smoothing snags or filling gaps between biblical verses, and our translator has also applied this technique to Kallir's hymn, replacing a difficult, non-narrative structure with one his audience would find easy to grasp and enjoy. This deliberate reworking challenges the view that the vernacular translation represents a "dumbing down" of the original for a late thirteenth-century audience. On the contrary, both the translator and his audience demonstrate awareness of recent literary, philological, exegetical, and cultural trends.

The translator's efforts are especially striking because classical liturgical poetry, especially from the Late Antique period represented by Kallir, did not lend itself to narrative. Early composers of *piyyutim* conflated past, present, and future. In place of "plot" or narrative, their phrases triggered a cascade of textual associations that emphasized the simultaneity of sacred and mundane history. Not only does this stylistic density make it difficult to disentangle past from present from messianic future, but the resulting "verticality" of the verses resists the forward progression that is the essence of narrative writing. The Old French translator's achievement is all the more remarkable when we realize that he has not only translated the language of the Hebrew original, but its way of thinking, too.

Appended to the essay is a full translation of the Hebrew and Old French versions of the hymn into English (see table 15A.1); the translations are the work of Professor Samuel N. Rosenberg, Professor Emeritus of Medieval French Literature at Indiana University, and myself.

Many aspects of the Judeo-French text merit close attention, but let me highlight three: (1) the translator's adaptation of exegetical traditions to explain Kallir's Hebrew and to make it sequentially coherent; (2) the translator's use of medieval realia; and (3) the selective elision in the vernacular of details or motifs present in the Hebrew original. The following observations rely upon a handful of roughly contemporary *piyyut* commentaries—glosses on the poetic text—two associated with French-rite liturgies and two with Ashkenaz. Biblical prooftexts have been filtered through the exegetical traditions associated with the French school, especially Rashi and Joseph Kara. In other words, I have sought to reconstitute the Hebrew text of *Ansikha Malki* as it would have been read by a learned thirteenth-century French Jew.[9]

The Old French translator has taken care to produce a text that is intelligible as well as artful. To do so, he has had to remove encumbrances that make Kallir's Hebrew a challenge, to simplify the difficult, clarify the obscure, and connect the disconnected. That is, like all good translators, he has been forced to interpret; consequently, the Old French composition constitutes a commentary as much as a translation. Indeed, many of the techniques engaged by the translator, whom we have named Monsieur OF, are familiar to scholars who study the method of contextual, or *peshat*, reading. Here they are applied to a liturgical, poetic genre with its own distinctive conventions, including a love of rabbinic allusions and a messianic theology not generally associated with the French Tosafists or exegetes. Monsieur OF must also have been familiar with the practice of writing commentaries to liturgical poetry, a type of gloss unique to Ashkenaz and northern French communities.[10] The application of *peshat* reading to Kallirian texts had a precedent in this commentary literature; the Old French translation extends this practice to verse, reflecting what Elisabeth Hollender has described as the commentary's growing assumption of responsibility for providing narrative and aesthetic value to inaccessible *piyyut* texts.[11]

The importation to verse of techniques associated with narrative prose marks this text's connection to a living, social world in which narrative was ascendant. It may also say something about the Hebrew source text's failure to convey meaning of the sort its users desired. Those users found themselves facing serious challenges; Pflaum's dating of the Old French text places it in the decade preceding the great expulsion of French Jews in 1306, a decade marked by intensifying instability, stress, and fear. In that context, the vernacular poem offered more than intelligibility: in familiar images, it promised a usable future as much as a usable past.

The vernacular translation of *Ansikha Malki* has two striking features. First, the translator has stripped the text of its midrashic density, bypassing the Kallir's puzzles and epithets. He has also filled in the gaps that characterize Kallir's Hebrew, crafting a narrative of messianic redemption whose sketchy outlines are suggested by the ritual drama of the shofar service to which the poem belongs. Curiously, the vernacular poem suppresses martyrological allusions in the source, raising questions to which I return below.

Composed in sixth- or seventh-century Palestine and transmitted via southern Italy, Kallir's hymns belonged to a semi-mythical past. Their language and style were foreign to the high medieval aesthetic, certainly in Sephardic circles, as we know from Abraham Ibn Ezra's famed critique of them, but also in Ashkenaz, more sympathetically disposed to Kallir's neologisms, fragmentary syntax, and rabbinic allusions.[12] Certainly, what for Ibn Ezra was evidence of willful obscurity and bad style struck the rabbis of France and Ashkenaz with considerable awe. In fact, Kallir's hymns were not only revered by the latter, but they generated an extensive commentary literature—produced by the same rabbis associated with Rashi and his circle, particularly Joseph Kara, who are most associated with biblical exegesis.[13] Kara, who studied with Rashi's old teachers in Worms, and then with Rashi, wrote much of his *piyyut* commentary in Rashi's Troyes—a center of the Jewish exegetical renaissance. So, too, Shema'yah, Rashi's student and copyist, was fascinated by Kallir.[14] Even Kallir's biography was adorned with legends of prophetic, supernatural powers: Joseph Kara knew the legend attributing Kallir's death to the jealousy of his teacher, Yannai (who put a scorpion in his shoe), and Rashi's grandson, Rabbenu Tam, transmitted the story of Kallir composing in a forest surrounded by divine flames.[15] Thus, the Kallirian legacy assumed mythic proportions in precisely the context of Monsieur OF.

Scholars of biblical exegesis have emphasized the outstanding innovations of the *peshat* school. Chief among them is the emphasis on *peshat*, or contextual reading, which I define as the drive to interpret the text in its immediate semantic and narrative setting, relying on related usages in other parts of Scripture.[16] This method freed both reader and sacred text from the accretions of post-biblical *midrash*. In exchange, it offered narrative: by emphasizing narrative contiguities, contextual reading shaped the meaning of a specific word or phrase and its place in a larger story. Narrative was, thus, a tool that permitted claims for biographical, historical, or theological sequence and causality.[17]

As Elisabeth Hollender notes, a deference to narrative increasingly characterized *piyyut* commentary also, a trend she identifies with a "shifting aesthetic" that responded to the diminished abilities of readers.[18] In contrast to *peshat* commentary on the biblical text, however, *piyyut* commentary—by the same exegetes—freely tapped *midrashic* sources, sometimes embellishing them in miniature narratives. Here, too, narrative was a tool, rephrasing enigmatic texts to harmonize with medieval theology and needs [19]. Both of the French-rite commentaries I examined, MSS Vat. 306

and Parma 3006, as well as the Ashkenazic Mahzor Nuremberg and *'Arugat ha-bosem*, illustrate this narrative trend. The same impulse characterizes the Old French translation, linking this work to the exegetical writings. Kallir's *Ansikha Malki* is composed of 22 couplets in an alphabetical acrostic, one couplet per letter. Each verse line consists of four subunits, the first and third beginning with the acrostic letter. The first three sub-units, which each contain two to four words, share an internal rhyme; the fourth unit concludes all 44 verses with the word ימלוך [*yimlokh*—He shall reign] —that is, **a** a **a** B/ **a** a **a** B; **c** c **c** B / **c** c **c** B etc., where bold font indicates the recurring acrostic. The drone *yimlokh*, like the thematic matter of the poem, links the composition to the *Malkhuyot* liturgy for Rosh Hashanah *Musaf* and its theme of divine sovereignty. The Old French poem is also 22 double-verses, each containing four units and conserving the Hebrew rhyme scheme (not otherwise attested in vernacular poetry). There are approximately eight syllables per verse. Pflaum tentatively placed the translator in Lorraine—a region identified as a center of Judeo-French writing.[20]

The content of Kallir's Hebrew text consists of fractured images and allu-sions (see table 15A.1). With deliberate ambiguity, Kallir conflates pronouns and royal imagery that refer sometimes to God, sometimes to the Messiah, and even sometimes to Elijah, the Messiah's herald. The Jews, suffering under gentile rule, await Elijah, who will herald the Messiah who will inaugurate God's rule on earth. In the first half of the *piyyut*, Kallir evokes the mis-rule of the nations and their ultimate doom, contrasting Israel's subjugation to illegitimate rulers with anticipation of Messianic redemption and God's vengeance. Allusions to the Day of Judgment are interlaced with allusions to the worshippers at prayer, shifting between an apocalyptic future and the present reality of the congregation. At the conclusion of double-verse 10, the congregation walks before God "like angels" and proclaims Him King; they joyously cry: יי ימלוך! [*adonai yimlokh*] "The Lord shall reign!"

In the second half of the Hebrew poem, God levels the gentile nations and raises up Israel to its rightful position at their head. Heavens and earth fall and are remade; "the nations totter, the prideful crash, the boastful col-lapse" [מעדו מתגאים / המו גאים / מטו גויים (*matu goyim / hamu ge'im / ma'adu mitga'im*)—v. 13a]. The gentile princes acknowledge Israel and return them to Jerusalem, and God metes out justice, showing mercy to His people and crushing Esau's descendants. When the Messiah arrives, God's throne will be made whole, and His rule established; song and rejoicing will fill heaven and earth. These verses, too, avoid linear progression. The apocalyptic images of the subject nations and God's trumpeting vengeance are simultaneously the songs of the worshippers and the blasts of the shofar. Double-verse 18 again ends with the congregation's shouting: הן לצדק ימלוך! (*hen le-tsedek yimlokh*) — "Behold in justice He shall reign!" Double-verses 19–21, which envision the people's return to Zion, add the roar of God's angelic and earthly creatures. The poem concludes with God's heavenly throne, fixed like the sun, the Messiah as radiant as that sun, God's kingdom stretching from sunrise to sunset, and God's exaltation of His people—a chiastic echo of the poem's opening description of the people exalting God. The Old French translation is sensitive to this link, which it emphasizes by using the same verb for both verses: "Esaterai mon roi"(v.1a) and "esacera adont/ sa gent" (v. 22b).

Monsieur OF's reading of the Hebrew poem is deeply informed by the concerns, approaches, and often conclusions of the commentary literature, some of which he must have known. MS Vat. Heb 306 preserves a commentary he seems to follow particularly closely. According to Avraham Kupfer, MS Vat. Heb 306's early thirteenth-century author was in the orbit of the French school.[21] The commentary's eclectic blend of peshat and aggadic interests is characteristic of a trend identified recently by Ephraim Kanarfogel among students of R. Tam.[22] The Old French translator's sympathy for MS Vat. 306's readings may place him in the same, somewhat later, orbit as the anonymous commentator. Comparison of the vernacular with the Hebrew reveals how much he shared the goals and methods of the exegetes, producing a new version of Kallir's text that is at once pleasing and intelligible. Consider the following examples:

The Old French translation elegantly substitutes for Hebrew epithets. Kallir's verse 1b reads:

אליל בהשליכי / לפני בא יום מלכי / איש מלאכי / ישלח ואז ימלוך.

Elil be-hashlikhi / lifné bo yom malki / ish mal'akhi / yishlaḥ ve-az yimlokh.

Literally: "When I cast out the idol before my King arrives, He (God) will send the messenger, so that He shall reign." Conventionally, the expression *ish mal'akhi* ("my messenger") from Mal.3:1, 23, signifies the prophet Elijah. In other words, "When I cast out the idol before my Messiah arrives, God will send Elijah, so that He (God) may reign." Monsieur OF has saved his readers the substitution:

Li volz getez sera / quant Messie venra.

Elie tremet[ra] /devant; lors regnera.

(His Messiah will come,with Elijah sent before; Vain idols will vanish, God alone then shall reign.)[23]

Similarly, Hebrew references to "the flatterer" (2a), an epithet for Esau, appear as "Rome" in Old French, a term that also does service for Hebrew references to "the nations," the Kittim and Chaldeans. So, too, allusions to biblical foreign gods, like Molokh or Bel, are subsumed under the vernacular "li volz" (the idol). Sometimes this simplifying agenda has the added benefit of resolving contradictory images. So, for example, verse 3 refers in Hebrew to the גברת ממלכות (*geveret mamlakhot*), "Lady of the kingdoms," the personi-fication of the gentile nations who seek Israel's ruin. The OF accordingly invokes the "Dame qui a fierté," who will be crushed by God ("quant Dé l'avra maté"). But in the following verse, Kallir abruptly jumps from this feminine image of gentile rule to remind us how that rule began. With his allusion to (masculine) "weepy pleading," the "Lady" is replaced by Esau, progenitor of the gentile nations and whose tears before his father Isaac led Isaac to pity him. The allusion to Esau originates in *midrashic* sources cited by the medieval commentaries. With their help, the gaps in the Hebrew can be filled. The Hebrew reads

דורכת נסיכות / בחינון קול בכות / דיברה אני במלכות / ומי יוכל למלוך

Dorekhet nesikhut / be-ḥinnun kol bakhut / dibbera ani be-malkhut / u-mi yukhal limlokh

I translate: "She (Lady Edom = the gentile nations) has justified her claim to fiefdoms by virtue of (Esau's) tearful pleading." Again, the Hebrew does not refer explicitly to either "Edom" or "Esau," whom I have inserted in paren-theses. Yet, just as I have been forced to do, Monsieur OF must translate by inserting a proper name:

Dé fit ja coroner / Esav par son plorer

(God granted Esau a crown in response to his tears)

A similar process is evident in verse 11a, where the Hebrew alludes to two seemingly disjunctive events:

כיתים בכתתו / איים בהכותו / כס ממלכתו / יכון ואז ימלוך

Kittim be-khatteto / iyyim be-hakkoto / kes mamlakhto / yikkon ve-az yimlokh.

Literally: "When he crushes the Kittim and strikes the islands, He will estab-lish his throne and then he shall reign." The islands of the Kittim are men-tioned several times in Scriptures and now identified with Cyprus. The Old French translator found them an unnecessary obfuscation and substituted the all-purpose "Rome"—an identification reinforced by the piyyut commen-taries. The commentaries also understand the reference to establishing the throne to refer to the repair or completion of God's throne; the expression becomes a shorthand way of saying that when the time is ripe for messianic redemption, God's throne will be firmly established and "whole." The com-mentary preserved in MS Vat. Heb 306 connects the two verse-halves by linking them both to Israel's eternal foe, Amalek. (He may be riffing on the appearance of the Kittim in Num. 24:24, joining the forces of Amalek.) The commentator writes: "God has vowed that His throne would not be whole until He took vengeance on Amalek; only then would He establish it and reign..." The Old French picks up on this tradition, rendering the verse as follows:

> Romains defoissera / e realtez otera
> Son siege donc sera / entiers; si regnera.
> (The heathen will fall, their kingdom torn apart; God's throne will be whole, and He alone shall reign.)

The image of the restored throne might also have been familiar to Monsieur OF from a *piyyut* composed by R. Natanel of Chinon, a thirteenth-century French rabbi. R. Natanel's hymn, "Seder Tamid," also found a home in the French Jewish liturgy for *Seliḥot*. The messianic motif of the throne that must be made whole has *midrashic* precedents; it signals the defeat of the gentile nations and the re-establishment of God's reign.[24] This is precisely the meaning intended by Kallir and evoked by Monsieur OF, confirming evidence for the circulation of a tightly controlled set of motifs among a later thirteenth-century French audience.

Midway through the poem, the throne stands against the defeated enemies of God and Israel; in the poem's final Hebrew verse, the throne reappears, permanent and presumably radiant like the sun, תוכן כס כשמש (*tukkan kes ka-shemesh*), citing Ps. 89: 37–38. The commentaries acknowledge the messianic context, glossing *tukkan* (established) as מתוקן (*metukkan*, repaired). This time, however, Monsieur OF ignores the throne, preferring to invoke the biblical king David:

> David qui a été / de grant atorité
> En joie e en clarté / avec Dé regnera.

Michael Signer and Robert A. Harris have both framed Rashi's approach to the so-called "Messianic Psalms"—among them Ps. 89—as part of a larger anti-Christian polemic. Where Christian exegesis understood these psalms as explicit allusions to Jesus, Rashi explained them as biographical incidents in the life of King David.[25] However, Rashi was not always consistent in this approach, glossing several verses in Ps. 89 to refer to a future messiah.[26] I am not sure what Monsieur OF wished to accomplish here, but first, he has *removed* messianic speculation by adopting Rashi's general practice of referring such references to King David. At the same time, he has also *permitted* messianic speculation by conflating the anticipated return of the Davidic dynasty with future restoration of the cult. Fittingly, the verse emphasizes authority and rule—the liturgical themes of the *malkhuyot* prayers. These associations link the biblical past and its promise of redemption for the worshippers nearing the conclusion of the New Year's liturgy. But in the process of doing so, Monsieur OF has had to rebalance the ring-structure of Kallir's poetic architecture to suggest a linear progression from past to present to future: he needed narrative.

It is worth noting how hard it is to translate a writer like Kallir and not try to "make sense" of his verses by supplying them with narrative. Kallir's intertextual referents permit him to tap the surface of a textual tradition and leap on paratactically. Whether Kallir "felt" his poem as a narrative, we cannot know; the question may be whether *we* are capable of reading it any other way. The fact that we speak of the enlistment of narrative by Rashi and his disciples as such an extraordinary development suggests that they may have been more aware than we that there were other options. Certainly, the Old French translator has gone to some pains to smooth out the Hebrew text. His temporal markers offset the messianic time of the Hebrew and anchor it in the liturgical present of the worship service—thus, "those who seek acquittal on the Day of Judgment" becomes those "who seek mercy *today*" (4b); "when He restores legitimate sovereignty [to Israel]" becomes "the throne will *now* be restored to its rightful holder" (8a).[27] The vernacular insistence on present-ness shifts in the second half of the poem to God's *anticipated* actions. The Hebrew text skips from the songs of homage offered the Jews by the defeated gentiles (14), to the song of God's people praising His Name (15), God's thunderous shofar blasts (17), the song of earth and heaven (18), and then the fused trumpeting of the angels and earthly creatures (21). The Old French clarifies and sequences these images, offering a moral progression from a world where injustice and insecurity challenge God's majestic promise, to a redemptive (and noisy) climax in which that promise triumphs.

Medieval realia and romance convention also translate a seventh-century composition into another world. The Hebrew גברת ממלכות (*geveret mamlakhot*, Lady of the Kingdoms) becomes the "Dame qui a fierté" (proud ruling Lady) of v. 3. The oppressiveness of gentile rule also assumes a feudal cast when the Hebrew דכאי רוח נמיכות (*dakke'é ruaḥ nemikhut*) those of humbled spirit) becomes "nos qui soms si soujiez' (we who are his subjects). As Pflaum noted, the OF translator also eliminated the Hebrew's multicultural references to the gentiles and their gods in favor of Esau, Rome, and their idols. Pointedly, the beginning of verse 15, סיכות אלילים / כיון גילולים (*sikkut elilim / kiyyun gillulim*—the idols of false gods, the icons, and statues) becomes "ces volz, cez crucefiz / ces images dépiz" (the idols, *the crosses*, the odious images).

Monsieur OF could also censor, as when he suppppresses martyrological allusions in the Hebrew. Verse 9b reads:

טוהר זכיות / ושאג בקול בכיות / טבע צול דוכיות / יפן ובם ימלוך

Tohar zekhiyyot / ve-sha'ag be-kol bikhyot / teva' tsul dokhyot / yifen u-vam yimlokh.

I translate the verse as follows:

> The purity of the worthy ones [Israel], the roar of their weeping [in prayer]!
> He will turn to those who were drowning in the sea and through them he
> shall reign.

Both the Vatican and Parma commentaries remarked on the allusion to the rabbinic martyrs who, as captives at sea, threw themselves overboard rather than be sodomized by their captors.[28] The Old French elides this clause altogether:

> Cete émérée gent / qui ont lo cor plorant
>
> De peine e de torment / en eus Dé regnera.
>
> (The pure, who in torment have wept until then, will find God in their midst, and He shall reign.)

Likewise, verse 14's "princes of peoples" is drawn from Ps. 47:10, where Rashi reads it to refer to those "princes" among the Jews who volunteered to murder other Jews as martyrs. Monsieur OF avoids this reading, translating "li contes e li rois" (the counts and kings). Cumulatively, these deviations imply a deliberate refusal to valorize martyrdom. Since even the minimal information we have about the translator places him in the circles of Tosafist scholars whose endorsement of the martyrological ideal is otherwise ubiquitous, why the change here?

Unfortunately, we cannot know. Monsieur OF, whoever he was, lived through a period marked by intensifying anti-Jewish measures, culminating in the Great Expulsion of 1306. In 1288, in nearby Troyes, thirteen French Jews—eleven men and two women—were burned in an auto da fé.[29] Perhaps Monsieur OF was not consoled by the idea of resistance unto death, and if so, his lack of enthusiasm is striking. Anti-martyrological positions among his contemporaries were rare, although Monsieur OF might have taken comfort in passages like the one Judah Galinsky, one of this volume's editors, called to my attention. In a Tosafist commentary to Gen. 9:5 preserved in the compilation *Da'at Zekenim*, the writer scathingly describes the suicidal and homicidal acts of contemporary fellow Jews that fall under the category of martyrdom ("sanctification of God's Name"). He concludes with the following anecdote:

> Once there was a certain rabbi who slaughtered many infants during a pogrom, because he feared that they would be converted. There was another rabbi with him who grew very angry with him and called him a murderer, but he didn't fear. That (second) rabbi said, if I am right let that rabbi die an unnatural death! And so it was. The idolaters captured him, flayed his skin, and put sand between the skin and the flesh. Afterward the pogrom was halted and if he hadn't slaughtered those infants they would have been saved...[30]

More research on this question, and on any number of points I have made in this chapter, awaits. Nonetheless, even this preliminary analysis suggests several intriguing possibilities. As Pflaum observed, the Heidelberg binding fragments suggest that use of the vernacular was more widespread among medieval French Jews than is customarily considered. Fudeman's more recent work has also persuasively demonstrated a vernacular *mentalité* in French Jewish life, especially evident in the Lorraine region.[31] The Heidelberg bifolia confirm that investment in the vernacular reached to the highest circles of medieval Jewish society. In the hands of scholars and exegetes, it became a medium for the same ideological concerns that characterized biblical and *piyyut* commentary literature. It was also amenable to the same methodological approaches: simplification, rationalization, and narrative. Using these tools, medieval French rabbis also managed to enhance the polemical value of otherwise obscure if revered texts, and package them in aesthetically appealing narratives.

Today, it is easy to confront Kallir's gaps and vertical echoes, his intrinsic resistance to sequential reading, and conclude that the task of reader or translator is to supply ligature and linearity. Nonetheless, to the extent we become persuaded that ligature and linearity constitute a natural or necessary "explanation" of what Kallir wrote, the more we become unable to distinguish between the text and a socially determined form of reading. Kallir's Old French translator may have been savvier in this regard than we are. So, too, his embrace of the vernacular was neither naïve nor a concession to degraded public literacy and tastes. On the contrary, it was a decision to engage a powerful and expressive instrument for conveying a vision of political, social, and human history that underscored both causality and divine justice to its listeners. Like many a translator of technical, scientific, or medical works, Monsieur OF turned to the vernacular because he could do things with it that he couldn't do in Hebrew. He knew the difference. And we owe him at least a similar degree of awareness about the power and privilege of narrative thinking, not to mention its implications and its consequences, in the world it tries to read.

Notes

1. This essay originated in a paper, "Exegesis and Romance: Revisiting an Old French Translation of Kallir," delivered at Rühr University in Bochum, Germany, in September 2011. My thanks to this volume's editors for the invitation to include a revised version, and to them and their anonymous reader for their helpful suggestions.

2. *Maḥzor Vitry*, ed. Shim'on Hurwitz and A. Berliner (Nürnberg, 1923).

3. Kirsten Fudeman, *Vernacular Voices: Language and Identity in Medieval French Jewish Communities* (Philadelphia, 2010).

4. The affective piety of the thirteenth century has been widely treated; see André Vauchez, *Sainthood in the Later Middle Ages* (Cambridge, 1997). For Romance (French) hagiography, see, for example, Brigette Cazelles, *The Lady as Saint* (Berkeley, 1991). On Jewish familiarity with Romance texts, see Ivan Marcus, "Why is this Knight Different: A Jewish Self-Representation in

Medieval Europe," in *Tov Elem: Memory, Community and Gender in Medieval and Early Modern Jewish Societies: Essays in honor of Robert Bonfil* (Jerusalem, 2011), 139–152.

5. Hiram Peri (Pflaum), "Deux Hymnes Judéo-Français du Moyen Âge," *Romania* 59 (1933): 389–422; Idem., "Piyyutim me-ha-maḥzor be-tsarfattit 'attika,"*Tarbitz* 25 (1956): 154–186.

6. Pflaum, "Deux hymnes," 393. In Pflaum's account, the fragments were recycled as binding material in the sixteenth century; they were removed from the Heidelberg binding in 1923. Pflaum, "Deux hymnes," 390–391. Pflaum called the manuscript Heidelberg 362a N. 28 XII; it is now catalogued as MS Heidelberg Or. 490 (Institute of Microfilmed Hebrew Manuscripts [=IMHM] F 34411).

7. Pflaum, "Piyyutim," 155; Pflaum, "Deux hymnes," 393.

8. Ephraim Kanarfogel, *The Intellectual History and Rabbinic Culture of Medieval Ashkenaz* (Detroit, 2012).

9. The following analysis does not rely on the "best manuscript" of Daniel Goldschmidt's critical edition, but on an emendation of that text in accordance with the French-rite variants indicated in his notes. See appendix.

10. Kanarfogel, *Intellectual History,* chapter 5.

11. Elisabeth Hollender, "Narrative Exegesis in Ashkenas and Zarfat: The case of Piyyut-Commentary," in *Jewish Studies at the Turn of the Twentieth Century* (proceedings of the 6th EAJS Congress, Toledo 1998), ed. Judit Targarona Borrás and Angel Sáenz-Badillos (Brill, 1999): 429–435.

12. Yosef Yahalom, "Ats kotses": gishot ve-'emdot bi-she'elot signon ha-piyyut u-leshono," *Meḥkeré yerushalayim be-sifrut 'ivrit* 1 (1980): 167–182.

13. Abraham Grossman, *Ḥakhmé tsarfat ha-rishonim (Jerusalem, 1994),* 339, re Kara; Idem., "Shivḥé R. El'azar beribbi Kallir be-ferush ha-piyyutim shel R.Y. Kara," in *Keneset Ezra: Literature and Life in the Synagogue,* ed. Shulamit Elizur, M. D. Herr, Gershon Shaked and Avigdor Shinan (Jerusalem, 1994), 293–308.

14. Grossman, *Ḥakhmé tsarfat,* 391.

15. Ibid., citing *Maḥzor Vitry,* 364. The story is also cited in Ephraim Kanarfogel, *Peering through the Lattices: Mystical, Magical, and Pietistic Dimensions in the Tosafist Period* (Detroit, 2000), 168–169, and in E. Landshuth, *'Ammudé ha-'avodah* (Berlin, 1857), 103. Landshuth refers also to the "unnatural" legends surrounding the life of Kallir, E. Landshuth, 103. See also Ruth Langer, "Kalir was a Tanna," *Hebrew Union College Annual* 67 (1996): 95–106.

16. This is my definition. See Kanarfogel, *Intellectual History,* chapters 2–3. On *peshat,* see the following note.

17. The literature is huge. See, for example, Avraham Grossman, *Rashi* (Jerusalem, 2006); Robert A. Harris, "Structure and Composition in Isaiah 1–12: A Twelfth-Century Northern French Perspective," in *"As Those Who are Taught": The Interpretation of Isaiah from the LXX to the SBL,* ed. Claire Matthews McGinnis and Patricia K. Tull (Boston and Leiden, 2006), 171–187; Robert A. Harris, "Twelfth-Century Biblical Exegetes and the Invention of Literature," in *The Multiple Meanings of Scripture: The Role of Exegesis in Early Christian and Medieval Culture,* ed. Ineke van't Spijker (Boston and Leiden, 2009), 311–330; Sarah Japhet, "Major Trends in the Study of

Medieval Jewish Exegesis in Northern France," *Trumah* 9 (2000): 43–61; Sarah Japhet, "Rashi's Commentary on the Song of Songs: The Revolution of the *Peshat* and its Aftermath," in *Mein Haus wird ein Bethaus für alle Völker gennant warden (Jes 56, 7)*, ed. Julia Mannchen (Neukirchen-Vluyn, 2007), 199–219; Hanna Liss, *Creating Fictional Worlds: Peshat-exegesis and Narrativity in Rashbam's Commentary on the Torah* (Boston and Leiden, 2011); Michael A. Signer, "'Peshat,' 'Sensus litteralis' and Sequential Narrative: Jewish Exegesis and the School of St Victor in the Twelfth Century," in *The Frank Talmage Memorial Volume,* ed. Barry Walfish (Haifa and Lebanon, NH, 1993), 1:203–216; "Rashi as Narrator," *Rashi et la culture juive,* ed. Gilbert Dahan et al. (Paris, 1997), 103–110.

18. Hollender, "Narrative Exegesis," 430.
19. My thanks to the editors for reminding me that this also describes Rashi's approach.
20. Pflaum, "Deux hymnes," 395. Fudeman, *Vernacular Voices,* 10–11, 160.
21. A. Kupfer, "A commentary on Azharot" [in Hebrew], *Kovets 'al yad* 11, part 2 (n.s.) (1989): 109–207, see p. 110. Kupfer hypothesizes that he was a colleague of the sons of Haim b. Hananel ha-Cohen, a student of R. Tam's (d. 1171).
22. Kanarfogel, *Intellectual History,* especially chapter 4.
23. Unless otherwise indicated, the prose translations of the Old French are the work of Samuel N. Rosenberg.
24. Abraham Grossman, R. Netan'el mi-Kinon, mi-gedolé ba'alé ha-tosafot be-Tsarfat be-me'ah ha-yud-gimel," in *Meḥkeré talmud: kovets meḥkarim be-talmud u-vi-teḥumim govlim, mukdash le-zikhro shel Prof. Efrayim E. Urbach,* ed. Yaakov Zussman and David Rosenthal (Jerusalem, 1990), 1: 174–189, especially 187.
25. Michael A. Signer, "King/Messiah: Rashi's Exegesis of Psalm 2," *Prooftexts* 3 (1983): 273–78; Robert A. Harris, "Rashi and the Messianic Psalms," in *Birkat Shalom: Studies in the Bible, Ancient Near Eastern Literature and Postbiblical Judaism presented to Shalom M. Paul..."* ed. Chaim Cohen et al. (Winona Lake, 2008), 845–862.
26. Harris, "Rashi and the Messianic Psalms," 855.
27. The translation in the appendix does not reflect the literal translation here.
28. See Ps. 69:3, Ps. 93:3 and related midrash.
29. Susan L. Einbinder, *Beautiful Death: Jewish Poetry and Martyrdom in Medieval France* (Princeton, 2002), chapter 5.
30. *Da'at zekenim mi-ba'alé ha-tosafot* (Budapest, 1834), Gen. 9:5.
31. Fudeman, *Vernacular Voices.*

CHAPTER 15: APPENDIX

A HEBREW *PIYYUT* AND ITS OLD
FRENCH TRANSLATION

Susan L. Einbinder and Samuel N. Rosenberg

The following translations represent the fruits of a rewarding collaboration, over whose duration many of the concerns treated in the preceding essay emerged. As noted above, an Old French translation of two hymns by Kallir was discovered, in the 1930s, in the binding of a Latin codex by Hiram Peri (Pflaum), who published a transcription and discussion of the fragments in two articles.[1] Four of the folios belonged to the festival liturgy for Rosh Hashanah; Pflaum dated them to approximately 1300 and believed that they were the surviving remnants of what must have been a vernacular *maḥzor*.

The texts preserved are as interesting as the phenomenon they document. Kallir's compositions, from sixth- or seventh-century Palestine, stirred ambivalent reactions among medieval European Jews. In regions dominated by the biblical purity and elegant aesthetic of Sephardic Hebrew poetry, they were largely disdained.[2] However, in nearby Ashkenaz and northern France, these same compositions were treated with a reverence usually associated with sacred texts. Here, the *piyyutim* of Kallir, despite (or because of) their difficult style, even accumulated a rich commentary literature.

Medieval vernacular translation of the sort represented here is an extension of exegetical activity. The translator seeks to convey his understanding of the Hebrew text, and to align it with the tastes and attitudes of contemporary readers. Far from attesting to a diminished level of Hebrew learning, the use of the vernacular illustrates a finely honed appreciation for Kallir's difficult Hebrew style. The vernacular composition also skillfully incorporates the *peshat* style of contemporary exegesis. In so doing, the unknown translator demonstrates how much translation occupies one end of a spectrum of exegetical activity that includes the more familiar forms of biblical commentary and the less familiar genre of *piyyut* commentary.

What we offer in the following pages is a way to gauge how this process worked in the first of the two *piyyutim*, Kallir's *Ansikha Malki*.[3] First, we present a new English translation of Kallir's Hebrew text, and then an English translation of the Old French translation of the Hebrew. Through our own translations we hope to emphasize the interrelationship of the Hebrew and vernacular versions, and their dominant features. At the same time, we have opted for a set of poetic rather than literal translations, hoping to suggest something of the poetic appeal of the originals.

The Hebrew Text

The translator's efforts, embodied in the vernacular text introduced below by Samuel N. Rosenberg, provide us with valuable insight into the way Kallir's Hebrew was understood by late medieval French Jews. I have translated the Hebrew with certain caveats. First, as noted in the preceding essay, the Hebrew text is not that found in Daniel Goldschmidt's monumental work on the Hebrew liturgy.[4] Goldschmidt based his texts on what he felt was the "best manuscript" for the Ashkenazic rite. I have emended that text to reflect the French-rite variants indicated in his notes. The Old French translation confirms that these variants, and not the Ashkenazic readings, were before the Romance translator. I have also relied upon a handful of *piyyut* commentaries more or less contemporary to the Old French translation. Two are drawn from French-rite liturgies, and two come from Ashkenaz.[5] When possible, I have read biblical prooftexts through a French exegetical lens, particularly that of Rashi and Joseph Kara. The result is hopefully a translation that reflects as much as possible the Hebrew text as it would have been read by a learned French Jew around 1300. That year, significantly, places the Old French translator and the users of his *maḥzor* in the decade prior to the Great Expulsion of French Jewry in August 1306, testifying by a strange historical fluke to the depth of Jewish attachment to the land and language they would leave a few years later.

Kallir is not an easy poet to render into readable English idiom. His Hebrew is deliberately dense and layered; the verses unfold in fractured images and allusions that conflate past, present, and future as well as cosmic and human characters. Pronouns are ambiguous, so that, like the Old French translator, I have had to interpret references that seem sometimes to belong to God and sometimes to the Messiah or his prophetic herald, Elijah. Where the English translations from Hebrew and Old French diverge, it is possible to see where the Old French translator departed from received exegetical conventions. Formally, the Hebrew consists of twenty-two couplets in an alphabetical acrostic, one couplet per letter. Each verse contains four subunits of two to four words; the first three subunits share a rhyme and the fourth concludes all 44 verses with the drone word ימלוך (*yimlokh*, "He shall reign"). The reiterated drone emphasizes the theme of royalty linked to God's anticipated reign. This theme is fitting for the *Malkhuyot* liturgy, which emphasizes God's sovereignty. The following two liturgical segments emphasize remembrance (*Zikhronot*) and the shofar blasts that conclude this part of the liturgy (*Shofarot*). Together, these segments are known as "*teki'ot*" ("blasts"), as they all conclude with prescribed blasts on the *shofar*; our hymn is of the type known as a "*teki'ata.*"

The first half of the Hebrew poem describes the situation of the Jews under an oppressive gentile rule. In the second half, God destroys the gentile nations and exalts Israel to its rightful position at their head. The messianic trajectory is conflated with the dramatic progression of the Rosh Hashanah liturgy, culminating in the *shofar* blasts that simultaneously announce divine vengeance and represent the worshippers at song. The poem concludes with the people's return to Zion and the image of God's (or the Messiah's) throne, fixed firmly in place, and from which God reigns and praises His people—a symmetrical echo of the poem's opening, in which the people give praise to God.

I have followed the Old French translator in reading the Kallirian text as a narrative. Whether Kallir would have approved or not is not at issue so much as the evidence that this was the way a thirteenth-century French Jew would have resolved its difficulties and made "sense" of it. Rhyme and acrostic are also important to the Hebrew text. I have not attempted to reproduce them, relying instead on rhythm, alliteration, and assonance to create a cohesive verse line. I have, however, retained the Hebrew's use of a drone word to conclude each couplet; each English couplet concludes with the word "reign."

The translation follows.

Ansikha Malki

Sources:

Daniel Goldschmidt, *Mahzor la-yamim ha-nora'im* (Jerusalem, 1970), 1: 233–37.

Hiram Peri (Pflaum), "Piyyutim me-ha-mahzor be-tsarfattit 'attika," *Tarbitz* 25 (1956): 154–186.

Old French text, MS Cod. Heid. Or. 490 (IMHM microfilm no. F 34411).

Commentaries: Jerusalem MS PH Scholem 225 (IMHM F 45414) fols. 66ab (15th cent. Ashkenaz)

Parma 3006 (Da Rossi 654), (IMHM F 13730) (Tallard, dated 1304).

Vatican heb. 306 (IMHM F 357) (early fifteenth century, Byzantine script).

Nuremberg Mahzor (online, National Library of Israel; part II, images 152–153)

Mateh Levi, in *Mahzor 'im shelosha be'urim: matté levi, bet levi, ma'ase oreg; ve-shem ha-kolel me-ha-be'urim korban aharon* (Lemberg, 1863), part I: 35–36.

Abraham b. Azriel, *Arugat ha-bosem*, ed. Ephraim E. Urbach, 4 vols. (Jerusalem, 1963).

Table 15A.1 *Ansikha Malki*: Facing Translations from the Hebrew and Judeo-French

H1.	F1.
I shall exalt my King as I walk before the Ark. He will gird Himself in strength when I proclaim him King. Then He shall reign. When I cast out the idol before the Messiah arrives, God will send Elijah. Then the Messiah shall reign.	I shall glorify my God, whom I worship and adore, the King who gathers strength and forever shall reign. His Messiah will come, with Elijah sent before; vain idols will vanish; God alone then shall reign.
H2.	**F2.**
When Elijah comes to crush Esau's rule, He will destroy his haughty dynasty so they no longer reign. He will walk in my midst when he comes to reign. Israel shall rule in God's kingdom: then God alone shall reign.	Thus Elijah sets forth; idols will splinter and fall and hubris reach its end, for God shall reign. If He looks at me when He rules over all, in my eyes He will see what joy greets His reign.
H3.	**F3.**
When God overthrows peoples and kingdoms, He will rout the Lady of the Kingdoms. And then He shall reign. On this day, unfurl the scroll of events, the record of our deeds, to acquit those who hope for His reign.	Overthrown and confounded will she be who ruled with pride and might before His coming to reign. Judge our deeds, unscrolled now, Lord, not crude, but worthy of You, O God who shall reign!
H4.	**F4.**
Moved by Esau's tearful pleading, Lady Edom claims her fiefs. She says, "I am sovereign! Who else should reign?" The humbled and contrite, who seek acquittal on this Judgment Day, she crushes with her royal yoke – until the Rock shall reign.	God granted Esau a crown in response to his tears, and Esau scoffs at any threat to his reign. We are his subjects, crushed and humbled by fear, but certain of freedom once God comes to reign.
H5.	**F5.**
Resplendent, God traversed the heavens to have His sovereignty proclaimed, in might to reign. By what right was Bel crowned sovereign? Who granted him permission when he hastened to reign?	Our mighty God fights for us; He came down from on high and pulled us up from the sea; with strength shall He reign. The idol now in command—a command to defy! I will not kneel before sin, nor submit to its reign.

252

H6.

God lived before the reign of any king,
and when all kings are gone, He alone shall reign.
What power has Molokh before God's judgment?
When the storm passes, he will cease to reign.

H7.

When He arraigns us in judgment, the Pure One will show mercy.
In trampling the wicked, He seeks vengeance. Then He shall reign.
He retrieves the crown from the wicked to empower his Messiah.
Granting sovereignty to pure Israel, over all He shall reign

H8.

When He restores rightful sovereignty to Israel,
His royal offshoot in justice will reign.
He will heal the distress of long exile.
He will dress the wound when He shall reign.

H9.

Oh, those idolaters, the burden of the kingdoms!
They have polluted the beauty of the Temple, so in arrogance they might reign.
Oh, the purity of the worthy, and the cry of their weeping!
God will turn to the martyrs who drowned in the sea. Through them He shall reign.

H10.

Children of kings, Israel cast its fate with God.
On this day, they await: He will surely come to reign.
They will walk before Him like angels,
in unison proclaim Him king: "The Lord shall reign!"

F6.

There was no king till Israel knew our Lord;
when others have fallen, our King shall still reign.
How can the idol not fall before God's mighy sword?
Wind will blow him away, and no more will he reign.

F7.

With mercy, as ever, will God judge His people;
harsh justice will come to our foes when He reigns.
The Messiah will stamp out all doers of evil,
recall us to life, restore our rule; and God shall reign.

F8.

The throne will come back to its ruler by right,
the usurper cast out and crushed; just God shall reign.
The long darkness of exile will give way to light;
God will bind up our wounds, and He shall reign.

F9.

All grief that the wicked have brought us will end;
the Temple-profaner will perish, not reign.
The pure, who in torment have wept until then,
will find God in their midst, and He shall reign.

F10.

My people look toward God in trust and expectation;
the children of kings, they long for the day of his reign.
Like wingèd angels today in joy and celebration,
they know God as their King, God who shall reign

Continued

Table 15.1A *Continued*

H11.

When God crushes the Kittim, striking their islands,
He will make His royal throne whole, and then He shall reign.
This is His kingdom's glory, and the sanctification of his deeds.
When He completes His work, in the sight of all He shall reign.

H12.

He will level every height, topple mountain and hill.
He will cast the nations into darkness. Like breaking dawn, He shall reign.
He shall fold up the heavens and make them anew.
He has ordained this day, when from Zion He shall reign.

H13.

The nations totter, the prideful crumble, the boastful collapse.
God is triumphant when He comes to reign.
When the many shall rule and the mighty are removed,
the King of all nations shall come to reign.

H14.

The peoples' princes will assemble among the nations
to bear the least of peoples to their place to reign.
The nations will play beautiful melodies before them.
God has lifted them up among peoples, over all of them to reign.

H15.

The idols of false gods, the icons and statues,
will be dragged and discarded like corpses, never to reign.
You children of the mighty! Speak God's secret Name!
Lift up song and praises to the Lord, for He shall reign.

F11.

The heathen will fall, their kingdoms torn apart;
God's throne will be whole, and He alone shall reign.
The defeat of the heathen will be a clear mark
of dominion and honor, and God's splendor shall reign.

F12.

He will level all hills and make rough places smooth;
He will humble kings and resplendently reign.
He will split the heavens apart and create them anew;
Zion today will hail Him as Lord, and He shall reign.

F13.

The arrogant will fall and kingdoms will crumble,
for their power cannot hold once the Lord reigns.
My people will rise, as kings falter and tumble;
our King will now rule; everywhere shall He reign.

F14.

Counts and kings of every nation and faith
shall follow our God to the place where He reigns.
Crowds from all corners will come for His grace,
to sing in jubilation and celebrate God's reign.

F15.

The idols, the crosses, the hateful images will be flung down
like dogs, unable to reign.
Exalt the Lord's name! Sing praise and give thanks!
Glorify and celebrate the One who shall reign!

H16.
When the Almighty raises His hand to lift up His Messiah,
and raise those weighed down, He'll show His power to reign.
High in Heaven, He raised His hand to swear
by the splendor of His throne, where He shall sit to reign.

H17.
The earth will be rent asunder in utter destruction,
a snare for the children of Esau. He shall rattle the kingdoms and then He shall reign.
The mighty terror of the shofar blasts! He will blow three times, then destroy the wicked.
With the third glorious blast, the dead will rise from the ends of the earth. Then He shall reign.

H18.
Song will rise from the earth, and praise from the sea.
In song that rings from high heaven, they will rejoice in His reign.
The Almighty will send healing for the wounds of all His creatures.
From far and wide, they will raise wondrous song: "In righteousness, He shall reign!"

H19.
Those who ruled will cast off their royal robes.
They will shout aloud and proclaim the king, for he shall reign.
Those who were called Israel will rule. They will follow God.
They will go proudly upright, and at their head He shall reign.

F16.
God will lift up His people; His power will grow;
He will lead His nation to triumph, and He shall reign.
Did He not swear on His throne to undo His foes?
We will hail Him as King, and as King shall He reign.

F17.
The world will be confounded and earth undone;
the wicked will be trapped, and Lord God shall reign.
Three times the horn will sound, and Rome will succumb,
cut down like hay. Come, let us praise God's reign!

F18.
Hymns will rise from the land and flow from the sea;
watery depths, like the skies above, will praise His reign.
The hungry will be fed; the infirm will be healed;
all rejoicing will sing "On this day, God shall reign."

F19.
Kings on their thrones will cast off their royal cloaks;
they will cede their rule to the One who shall reign.
Your people, Lord, from bondage freed and unyoked,
will proclaim Your law and exult: You shall reign!

Continued

Table 15.1A *Continued*

H20.	**F20.**
The secret of redemption has been hidden, recorded for its proper time. On this day, the Avenging God shall reign. Coming from the south, the Faithful Shepherd will blast the winds through Yemen. Then in Gilead He shall reign.	Unveil Your secret, God! Say when Messiah will come! Today let us see who on Your throne shall reign. The loyal king, our Messiah, bright as the sun, will vanquish the heathen and in Zion shall reign.
H21.	**F21.**
Angelic creatures on high – a company of angels! – will burst into song from heaven's hills: "He shall reign!" The din of the lower world joins the heavenly bodies, the vast roar of creatures blaring: "He shall reign!"	The angels on high, like us in valleys below, will declare that God rules, our God who shall reign. In portent-bearing heavens, as in the depths of woe, for every creature and creation, God shall reign.
H22.	**F22.**
The Messiah's throne will be fixed firmly as the sun. He is radiant like the rising sun. When he reigns, God shall reign. God upholds heaven and earth from sunrise to sunset. He will exalt Israel, pure as the sun, and then He shall reign.	Our ruler by right, shoot and branch of David the king, will come back in joy, and with God shall reign. From summit to summit, the whole world will sing. Echo and resound, praise of God! For He shall reign!

Notes

1. Pflaum, "Deux hymnes," 389–422; updated and revised in "Piyyutim," 154–186.
2. See Yahalom, "Ats kotses," 167–182.
3. The second hymn is a translation of Kallir's "*Zekher tehillat kol ma'as*" [זכר תחילת כל מעש], which belongs to the *Zikhronot* section of the shofar service. It would have followed the hymn treated here, which belongs to the *Malkhuyot* liturgy.
4. Daniel Goldschmidt, ed., *Mahzor la-yamim ha-nora'im – le-fi minhagé bené Ashkenaz le-khol 'anfehem*, 2 vols. (Jerusalem: 1970). Our piyyut, "Ansikha Malki," is found in the "additional" (musaf) service for the first day Rosh Hashanah, 233–237.
5. MS Vatican Heb. 306; Parma MS 3006. On MS Vat. 306 and its French intellectual lineage, see A. Kupfer, "A commentary on Azharot" [in Hebrew], *Kovets 'al yad* 11, part 2 (n.s.) 1989: 109–207, esp. p. 110.

CHAPTER 16

ABSTINENCE IN MEDIEVAL NORTHERN
FRANCE: A COMPARISON OF "A SLAVE FOR
SEVEN YEARS" IN *SEFER HA-MA'ASIM* TO
"THE LIFE OF ST. ALEXIS"

Rella Kushelevsky

$\int$*efer ha-ma'asim* (A Book of Tales) is a large compilation of stories from northern France preserved in a single manuscript from the thirteenth century.[1] The compilation, with its 69 stories covering 78 pages (39 leaves) includes a varied selection of sources and literary genres. Each story begins with the graphically accentuated phrase "ma'aseh be-"—"A tale of," or if you wish, "Once there was"—that adorns the manuscript's beautiful and clear Ashkenazic script. Some stories that entered the collection were known to the medieval exegetes and can be found among the commentaries of Rashi and the Tosafists. Many were recopied over the years, and they were apparently recounted and read aloud on various occasions before listeners, as was the accepted practice with the poetry and narratives of the period. The stories—some of which were exempla and others novellas or brief narratives containing romantic elements—are deeply rooted in the cultural expanse in which they were created or adapted. Their study in the cultural context of Ashkenaz, and especially of northern France, can contribute both to the research of this compilation as a literary creation as well as to the historical study of various types of discourse in which the stories participate.

One of the longest stories in the compilation, not known from earlier sources, is *'Eved le-sheva' shanim* (A Slave for Seven Years) (325a–325b). In this chapter, I will suggest that this story is part of the discourse on abstinence in Jewish and Christian sources in the twelfth and thirteenth centuries in northern France. The chapter will examine this story from a number of perspectives: a study of the story itself; a comparison with a talmudic story that shares the motif of temporary abstinence between husband and wife; a comparison to a well-known Christian legend, "The Life of St. Alexis," here discussed as a parallel to the Jewish story; and, finally, an examination of some sources of the Ashkenazic Pietists and the polemic literature, relevant to the story.

The story begins with a childless man whose prayers for a son are answered, who devotes himself to teaching the boy the Torah. After he dies, the boy's mother insists that her son must learn his father's trade and engage in commerce. Her son, however, is unable to accept the norms of deception and theft inherent in trade, and returns to his mother empty handed. A funeral happens to pass by and he joins the mourners in order to pay his respects to the dead. He then meets Elijah, who is plowing, a clean profession that captures his heart. Elijah allows him to make a wish and he wishes for a worthy, God-fearing wife. Elijah immediately takes him to the place of one of three women of valor in the world where he asks her if she would marry the young man, and she agrees.

On the seventh day after the wedding ceremony, Elijah returns to the young man and finds him "sporting with his wife," an expression of clearly erotic connotations.[2] Elijah rebukes him for abandoning the Torah because of his passion for his wife and informs him that he will be sold into slavery for seven years against the seven days of nuptial festivities. The young man bursts into tears, which his bride, who was not witness to his meeting with Elijah, takes as a sign for his yearning for his family. She decides to return with him to his mother's home, but their plan does not turn out as expected. While on their way, the young man goes to bathe in the river, Elijah appears, abducts, and sells him into slavery. When her husband does not return, the woman realizes that this must be from God. She accepts the decree and decides to settle there, in that place. In her wisdom, she foresees a famine in the land, and advances a plan that will return her husband to her. With the help of her slaves and maidservants, she builds a city and plants a field.

Her plan succeeds. When the famine comes and people from all over travel to the city to trade for food, she identifies her husband with his master. She reveals herself to him and learns about his life during the last five years of slavery. Despite their emotional encounter, the young man decides, in agreement with his wife, to leave her again in order to complete the two remaining years of his slavery. When his time is up, Elijah brings the young back to his wife and together they travel to see his mother. The epilogue concludes with praise for the wife, as it says of her "A woman of valor who can find" (Prov. 30).

This story is unknown from previous sources in the Talmud or compilations of stories from the east. As far as we know, the first written version of the story is this one in *Sefer ha-ma'asim*. Versions of this story in Ashkenaz, in the Middle Ages follow the *Midrash 'aseret ha-dibberot* (Midrash of the Ten Commandments) in the context of the commandment of "Thou shalt not commit adultery,[3] up until but not included in the *Mayseh bukh*, which was printed in the early seventeenth century.[4] It may be concluded to a large degree of likelihood that the story originated in Ashkenaz and, as we will see, probably in France.

The story describes the initiation process of a cultural hero who, already from birth, is designated for God's work. Beginning with his wondrous birth to a childless father and his training for his vocation: "And he taught him Torah greatly." Two events complicate this initiation: One is the death of his father, in the wake of which he is sent to engage in trade in order to preserve the family inheritance. His resistance to the plan is intuitive. Although disgusted by the norms of commerce, by the deceit and dishonesty that it involves, he still lacks the tools to offer an appropriate alternative as he sees it. His charitable act of joining in the funeral procession is more satisfying to him. The other complication involves his becoming addicted to his passion for his bride. His love games with her, that the stranger in the image of Elijah happens to witness on the seventh day after the wedding, distract the groom from his duty to the Torah for which he was destined.[5] The position taken by the narrator is that surrendering to one's urges (sex and money) leaves no room for a spiritual experience, undermines morality, and disrupts the proper order of the world. This is especially so when it involves a cultural hero who was trained and destined from the time of his birth to devote himself to God through the study of the Torah.

The complications in the story are resolved through the mediation of Elijah who offers the protagonist alternative models involving a life of asceticism and abstinence: farming instead of commerce that leaves room for reflection and study (Elijah plows and, while he is doing so, studies a book that is placed atop the plow), and the period of slavery and separation from his wife for seven years, which are intended to cause him to submit to the authority above him. His process of initiation is emphasized in light of his wife as an ideal symbol of a "God-fearing" "woman of valor." Only at the internalization that love of God as a value is more sublime than love for a woman will he be permitted to return to his wife. Toward the end of the story, it indeed becomes evident that the message has been learned. When he is reunited with his wife after five years of bondage, he leaves her again of his own volition for two more years of slavery in order to complete the seven years.

The model of abstinence in the story deviates conspicuously from the accepted norms in earlier Jewish sources. It implies reservation from marital relations (albeit not their complete repudiation) as a factor that competes with one's love of God and His Torah. The abduction of the groom from his bride seven days after the wedding ceremony makes this even more extreme—an

approach that has no parallel, not even in the sage Ben 'Azzai, who preferred
not to marry because his soul was drawn to the Torah, while criticizing
himself for this at the same time.[6] A series of stories in tractate BT *Ketubbot*
61b–63a about sages who absented themselves for long periods from home in
order to study the Torah in Babylon offers a conflict that resembles the one
we see in our story between marital life and the duty to learn Torah, based
on the injunction "And you shall meditate therein day and night" (Josh.
1:8). On the one hand, these stories offer examples of the practice among
sages to leave their wives and go away for a long period following their
marriage to centers of Torah study,[7] whereas on the other, they warn of the
husband's duty to fulfill his marital obligations toward his wife that, along
with food and clothing, include a sexual obligation. The preferred norm in
the Babylonian Talmud to marry before embarking on the intense study of
the Torah represents the view that satisfying one's sexual urges in the context
of marriage enables one to study the Torah in purity even during the periods
of abstinence required for initiation into that world.

The stories, however, also illustrate the problematic nature of this practice and its implications for family life, and the scholars are urged to maintain constant contact with their home during periods of absence. They also
represent the added value of the period of initiation, when it is the result
of agreement between the man and his wife.[8] The story of R. Akiva, who
started out as an ignorant shepherd and who, at his wife's behest and with her
encouragement, became a great Torah scholar, is the climax in this series of
stories (BT *Ketubbot* 62b). At first, he leaves her for a period of twelve years,
and then receives her permission to go away again, and returns to her at the
head of thousands of students following a second period of twelve years.
Like the "woman of valor" in our story, the figure of the wife of R. Akiva
is extolled.

Despite the similarities between the two stories, they represent different views in regard to abstinence. In the Talmud, the purpose of the life of
abstinence is ultimately to attain a proper balance between conjugal relations
and the study of the Torah. Our story in *Sefer ha-ma'asim* is an example of
someone who became a slave to his passion for his wife, thus, neglecting the
study of the Torah—a value that competes with the value of marriage, without canceling it out. Accordingly, the demand not to neglect Torah study
even during the celebratory seven days following the marriage ceremony
is more extreme than any previous one, especially in light of the romantic
description in tractate BT *Nedarim* (50a) of Akiva after his marriage picking
the straw out of his wife's hair in the barn where they lived. Compared to the
demand in the Talmud to maintain constant contact with home during the
period of initiation abroad as a Torah scholar, in "A Slave for Seven Years,"
the wife only hears for the first time about her husband's fate five years after
his abduction. It would appear then that the series of stories in BT *Ketubbot*

does not really contribute to our understanding of "A Slave for Seven Years," and it is, therefore, necessary to take a closer look at the discourse of abstinence held in the story in light of the popular literature in its surroundings in northern France at the time.

De Vita S. Alexi

The hagiographic legend of "The Life of St. Alexis," which has sources in Syriac and Greek in the second half of the fifth century, was very widespread in the High Middle Ages in western Europe in Latin and in various local vernaculars. Outstanding among them are its versions in old French, the earliest of which is from the eleventh century, and which were adapted throughout the twelfth, thirteenth, and fourteenth centuries.[9]

Historical processes led to changes in the versions of the story; throughout its development, the story was accepted as a paradigmatic tale, and in the thirteenth century, as a model of religious devotion among the laity, especially for men.[10] The story was accompanied by a widespread cult throughout the Middle Ages that was expressed in the establishment of churches, chapels, and altars named for St. Alexis in various locations, a feast day in his honor in the Christian calendar (July 17), and his emulation based on values of suffering, humility, self-denial, prayer, and fasting, and the commemoration of episodes from his life in the visual arts. Alexis also became the patron saint of travelers, pilgrims, beggars, and lepers, as well as a role model for the giving of charity.[11]

In the next two sections, I will analyze the Latin legend and its versions in old French as a parallel to "A Slave for Seven Years," and as a point of departure for the medieval discourse of abstinence. According to the Latin version in *Acta Sanctorum*, Alexis was born to wealthy, previously childless, parents in response to their prayers for an heir, and as a reward for their piety and charity to the poor and needy. When he was born, his parents decided to take on a life of purity and abstinence in the context of their marriage and hired teachers to instruct their son in the sacraments of the church and other subjects of learning, especially spiritual studies. When he reached the right age, they chose him a worthy wife from the family of the emperor and they were married in a magnificent church ceremony. When evening fell, the father urged his son to approach the festive bridal bed and draw his wife close. When the couple was alone, Alexis lectured his bride on the principles of the faith, gave her the buckle of his belt, and left her in order to set out on a life of abstinence.[12] He then traveled to the port, boarded a ship, and arrived in Leodikya, and from there went to Edessa in Syria to the Church of the Virgin Mary. The belongings he took with him he distributed among the poor, while he himself wore rags and lived among the destitute beggars in the church courtyard.

When it became known in Rome that Alexis had left, his father sent out his servants to search for him, but when they arrived in Edessa, they did not recognize him. His young bride remained with his mother throughout all the years, both grieving his absence. For 17 years, Alexis lived among the beggars and poor in the courtyard of the Church of the Virgin Mary, until she revealed that he was a saint and ordered him to enter the church. But Alexis could not bear the adulation of his admirers and boarded a ship to take him to a different destination. However, a storm took the ship to Rome, where his parents lived. Assuming that he would remain unrecognized and to avoid becoming a burden to strangers, he came to his parents' home, where he lived for another 17 years under a staircase, never revealing his true name. His identity was ultimately revealed by a heavenly voice after his death and in the story of his life that he wrote on parchment. His parents were inconsolable, and Alexis was declared a saint and buried in the Church of Boniface.

Although containing similarities, the stories are, of course, far from identical. Well-known topoi from Jewish folklore are evident, such as the childless father who begets a son in his old age; the biblical story of Joseph, who reveals his identity to his brothers during the famine in Canaan; and the story of the Crescentia type included in *Sefer ha-ma'asim* (310b–311a), motifs from which have also been integrated into the story under discussion here.[13] Nevertheless, through the heterogeneous texture of the story, the influence of the legend of "The Life of St. Alexis" is especially evident.

The most outstanding aspect that "The Life of St. Alexis" and "A Slave for Seven Years" share is the groom's decision to retire to a life of abstinence and asceticism following the wedding ceremony, for what appear to be completely opposed reasons. The ceremony itself becomes a crossroads leading to a life of abstinence under compulsion or by choice. In the Jewish story, the decision to take up a life of abstinence belongs to Elijah, who becomes the young man's guardian and abducts him from his wife. In the Christian story, it is Alexis himself who makes this decision. In both stories, the wife accepts her husband's departure, albeit after the fact—whether as an expression of acceptance of God's justice in the Jewish story, which is further confirmed in their reunion five years later,[14] or as a recognition of Alexis's resolve and lack of any choice in the Christian one.

A series of additional shared motifs allow us to draw conclusions regarding the affinity of "A Slave for Seven Years" to the legend of Alexis: the character of the childless father who is given a son thanks to his piety; the father's devotion to his son's spiritual education; the initiation process that involves self-negation and experiences of abasement (either as a slave or an anonymous beggar); the temporary return home that increases the difficulty in the period of abstinence; and, finally, the return to the mother's or parents' home. On this shared background, the difference in the shaping of the conflict between the love of God and love of woman that underlies the story becomes evident.

The Latin version of the Alexis legend was translated and adapted with considerable changes into old French, both orally as well as in writing in the documented versions, starting from the eleventh century, and especially in the two centuries that followed. I will argue that the Hebrew story resembles the versions in French more than it does the Latin one presented above, in respect to the voice given in them to the woman and the extent of emphasis on the emotional dimensions of the story. I conclude from this that the version in the *Sefer ha-ma'asim* is typically French, and was influenced by the vernacular versions of the story, both orally and in writing, as opposed to the Latin version.

The vernacular versions of the story in French have been studied extensively, and for our discussion, it is of particular interest to note a finding that relates to the parting scene between Alexis and his bride on their wedding night.[15] Three scholars, Carl Odenkirche, Charles Stebbins, and Emma Campbell, who studied different versions in Latin and French, noted a consistent trend in the French versions to describe the emotional aspects, erotic implications, and intensification of the conflict in Alexis between sexual passion and love of God. Odenkirche compares the emotional description in the Hildesheim version from the eleventh century of Alexis's struggle with his sexual urges to the matter-of-fact description in the earlier versions in Syriac and Greek, and in the assumed Latin version from the eleventh century.[16] Stebbins points to the further intensification of this trend in the thirteenth century, in MS Paris (P), as is implied by the detailed description of the bedroom, the woman's beauty, the intensity of the temptation, her response to Alexis's decision, his struggle with leaving, and the emotions that accompany their parting. The narrator identifies with the wife-bride's great pain and shares with the reader his difficulty in describing it due to its immensity.[17] Emma Campbell also draws conclusions, hers with a gender orientation, regarding the emphasized emotional expression of the feelings of the bride in the two French versions, from the twelfth and thirteenth centuries.[18]

These studies evince a clear later development that is dependent on their historical and cultural context.[19] A further investigation of the French versions of the legend not discussed by the above scholars bolsters their claims: In MS 2471 Fr. from the twelfth century, Alexis gazes at his wife as the candles burn bright all around, and she is noble, desirable, and lovely, and he turns his eyes away to God, whom he loves more than anything else, and confesses his torment in fighting the sin and his fear of losing Him if he does not leave immediately.[20] In response to the anticipated parting, she grieves over her future loneliness[21] and declares: "*S'encor ne t' voi, de duel m'estuet morir,*"[22] /.../*S'a ten consel le peusse trouver,* / *Qu'ensamble toi me laissaisses aler,* / *Je me veroies gentement conreer,* / *Tondre mes crins, un capel a fubler,* / *Et prendre escerpe et un bourdon ferré;/ Servirai toi de tes dras relaver,/ Ne ja luxure ne m' verras demener,/ Ne adultére, ne autre putteé.*[23] The tendency to intensify the conflict in the character of Alexis along with the erotic tension, and to provide a detailed description of his feelings for his bride, can also be found in another version from the thirteenth century.[24]

In light of the French versions of the legend of Alexis, we can now return to the Hebrew narrative. Two scenes in the story are emotional—contrary to the practice in folktales, which tend mostly to focus on the actions rather than introspections of the protagonist: the response of the young man to the news that he will be separated from his wife for seven years of slavery (weeping and lamentation); and the response of the woman to their reunion after five years of separation ("she stood and embraced and kissed him").[25] Except that, this time, it is different: This time, in contrast to his behavior after the wedding ceremony, the young man gives precedence to duty over emotion. In consultation with his wife, he leaves her for another two years of bondage, until he has completed his seven-year quota of abstinence and asceticism. The emotional expression in both of these scenes intensifies the conflict between the love of a woman and love of God and His Torah.

The story approaches the legend of the life of St. Alexis as it was adapted in France in the vernacular in two ways: One is through the radicalization of the story of abstinence compared to the talmudic story of R. Akiva and his wife as discussed above; and the other by giving of expression to the characters' feelings in accordance with the trend in the French versions of the legend of Alexis. Can we point to a social-cultural substrate in Ashkenaz that enabled the creation and acceptance of "A Slave for Seven Years" despite its unusual message?

The Discourse of Abstinence in Ashkenaz

The discourse on abstinence in Ashkenaz as a whole, and particularly in the context of the conflict between the love of God and His Torah and the love of a woman and pleasures, was held in a number of sources. Abstinence was considered worthy behavior for a pietist in Ashkenaz. On the basis of the external Mishnah quoted in the name of R. Pinḥas ben Ya'ir in tractate BT 'Avodah zarah 20b that discusses the levels of worship of God,[26] R. Eleazar of Worms instructs his followers in the norms of purity, abstinence, and caution, explaining that they must be very strict with themselves regarding what is permitted and what is forbidden where women are concerned and to refrain from looking at them, or "even at clothing laid out to dry on the wall," should they belong to a women he does not know.[27]

In *Sefer ḥasidim*—sexual temptation is presented as an obstacle to attaining absolute adherence to God through the study of the Torah.[28] In the tract "Matters of the study of Torah" in *Sefer ḥasidim*, the author recommends that

young men that come to their teacher to study the Torah sit in a vessel of
cold water whenever they feel their urges overcoming them (paragraph 798,
p. 201); in paragraph 400 in the same tract, he recommends that the teacher
should have a separate entrance to his home and a separate one for the study
hall so as not to cause the young students to fall into temptation by looking
at the females of his household. Even normative married life can constitute
an obstacle: "When a man speaks long with a woman or with his wife, he is
wasting time that should be devoted to the study of Torah (paragraph 770).
This idea is further expanded:

> When a person ponders day and night a woman or money, and is willing
> to give his life for them...playing with children and women and laughing
> with friends and excursions and idle chatter cause a person to waste time that
> should be devoted to the study of Torah, consequently you must with all your
> heart and all your soul abandon your love and work to worship and love the
> Almighty...And that same love [of God] prevents a person from wasting time
> that should be devoted to Torah study because of illusions and to amuse his
> children and the love of seeing woman and talking, he must also abandon
> excursions and this will cause him to sing pleasantly to fill his heart with love
> of God, and work and toil on the path that is the will of the Almighty...[29]

These ideas receive even greater emphasis in the Margaliyot edition
(paragraph 14) of *Sefer ḥasidim*, based on the Bologna Press, where the connection between these matters is explicitly expounded on in a discussion of
the essence of the love of God: "The root of the love of God is 'And you shall
love the Lord your God with all your heart and with all your soul and with
all your might...' (Deuteronomy 6:4)."[30]

These sources and others represent the dilemma in "A Slave for Seven
Years" and the repercussions, according to *Sefer ḥasidim*, of excessive preoccupation with love for a woman at the expense of Torah study. Nevertheless,
these excerpts from *Sefer ḥasidim* do not preach extreme abstinence or the
complete negation of sexuality per se among the followers of the Pietist
movement.[31] The very same sources themselves, as Grossman claims, make
it possible to distinguish between the Jewish discourse on abstinence and
the Christian one.[32] *Sefer ḥasidim* describes passion for God in terms of the
passion of a man for a woman so as to highlight the conflict that they create
without supporting sexual abstinence: "And that intense joy that overcomes
the heart that even a young man who has not come to his wife for many days
and has great passion when his seed shoots like an arrow and takes pleasure,
which cannot be compared to the intense strength of his joy at his love of
God" (paragraph 815). This image, the purpose of which is to illustrate the
intensity of love for God, at the same time, gives full legitimacy to sexual
pleasure in the context of marriage. Considerable freedom is given to a husband and wife in their sexual relations in order to prevent sinful thoughts,

which are worse than the sin itself.[33] This is closer to the position noted above in the Babylonian Talmud that sexual satisfaction in marital life makes it possible for the scholar to learn the Torah in purity, even while abroad, in sharp contrast to the fundamentally negative approach taken by the Christian church toward sexuality. In Christianity, marriage, even after it has been consecrated by the church, is perceived as a life that is essentially inferior to one of abstinence and asceticism.

Another expression of this that is relevant to the legend of Alexis is abstinence between a married couple, such as the decision made by Alexis's parents to live a life of abstinence after their prayers were answered and they were given a son, and, of course, the example of Alexis himself who left his wife on their wedding night before his marriage was consummated.[34] These fundamental differences in approach in regard to sexuality are also expressed in the polemical literature. In his edition of *Nitsahon Vetus*, David Berger points to the aggressive attacks on the Christian ideal of celibacy in contrast to the value of marriage in Jewish society, in which it was believed to serve as a protection against adultery and licentiousness.[35]

Sefer hasidim contains a discourse on abstinence in the context of the laws of penitence as well. The penitence of the fence is a lifestyle that the sinner adopts in order not to stumble back into sin, and is expressed in a system of "fences" or restrictions that forbid that which is permitted, in addition to the previously existing restrictions in Jewish law.[36] The typical example that appears in *Sefer hasidim* and *Sefer ha-rokeah* is a response to the sin of adultery. The sinner must refrain "from any pleasures from a woman except his wife," not even to look into the face of another woman in order not to engage even in sinful thought.[37] In *Sefer ha-rokeah,* in the context of the laws of Rosh Hashanah, it is a condition of repentance "that he not see the face of a woman or her clothes, except of his wife,"[38] and in the paragraph on the laws of repentance, greater detail is provided.[39]

The sanctification of God's name, as a supreme value among the Hasidé Ashkenaz, is yet another expression of the value of qualified abstinence among them. As Joseph Dan noted, "The war on the wicked desires and the evil inclination, abstinence from the pleasures of the world, self-mortification for penance, withstanding the temptations of the world...[were a preparation] for the great, total test of sanctification of God's name, which is the absolute negation of this world and its pleasures, of Christianity and its symbols, and that means total abstinence and supreme mortification."[40] We can see that various types of discourses of abstinence, which are not necessarily the practice of abstinence, were held in Germany and France in different Jewish sources, without denying the fundamental difference between the Jewish sources' generally positive view of sexuality in the context of marriage and the reservations and negative view taken by the Christian approach.

Notes

1. Oxford, Bodleian Library, Or. 135 (Neubauer, 1466), ff.300a—339b. This article is the fruit of research under the sponsorship of the Israeli Academy of Sciences (no. 6470, 2008–2012) on *Sefer ha-ma'asim* in preparation of a critical edition. For a number of studies on the compilation as a whole and on the manuscript copied in it, see Eli Yassif, "Sefer ha-ma'asim," *Tarbiz*, 53 (1984): 409–429 and his "'Penai' ve-'ruaḥ reḥavah': halakhah u-ma'aseh be-hithavvut ha-sippur ha-'ivri be-shalhé yemé ha-benayim," *Kiryat Sefer* 62 (1988–1989); 887–892. See as well Malachi Beit-Arie, "Ketav yad Oxford Bodl. Or. 135: be-shulé ma'amaro shel E. Yassif," *Tarbiz* 54 (1984): 631–634. I would like to express my heartfelt thanks to Elisheva Baumgarten, my colleague and partner for the research of *Sefer Ha-ma'asim*, for her helpful comments all along our mutual work. Special thanks to Tovi Bibring for her help with locating and translating a selection of vernacular versions of "The Life of Alexis,"which are a major contribution to this chapter.

2. See Gen. 26:8: "And it came to pass...that Abimelekh king of the Philistines looked out at a window, and saw, and, behold, Isaac was sporting with Rebecca his wife." Rashi notes: "He saw him engaging in marital relations." In the current story, the expression refers to love games and courting, rather than to sexual relations that are forbidden by Jewish law immediately after the wedding night, due to the virginal blood.

3. *Midrash of the Ten Commandments* is a compilation of stories and homilies that illustrate the commandments. The story appears in manuscripts from Ashkenaz: Wolfenbüttel 36.25, fol. 19–20 (fourteenth century); Parma 2269 (de Rossi 473), fol. 76a–77a (fourteenth century); Oxford, Bodleian Library 268 (Opp. 27), fol. 242a-–242b (sixteenth-seventeenth centuries) and in manuscripts in Spanish script: Vatican 107, fol. 175a-176a (Provence 1438); Moscow-Guenzburg 111, fol. 123a–124a (1462).

4. *Mayseh Bukh*, Basel 1602, fol. 161–163, paragraph 197. The story does not appear in the manuscripts of the *Mayseh Bukh*.

5. The groom's weeping at what Elijah tells him, his bride's attempt to discover the reason and her numerous hypotheses, and ultimately, her response to her groom's disappearance in my opinion express her sorrow at being parted from him and her acceptance of the judgment, rather than feelings of guilt and repentance at having engaged in forbidden sexual relations.

6. Theodore Albeck ed., [Midrash] *Bereshit rabbah* (Jerusalem, 1995), 34:6, 326–327; BT *Yevamot* 63b. Also notable in this context is the exemption from having to go out to war given in the Bible to a groom in the first year of marriage (Deut. 20:7).

7. Daniel Boyarin calls this phenomenon "the married monk," see *Carnal Israel: Reading Sex in Talmudic Culture* (Berkeley, Los Angeles, 1993), 154–155.

8. The wife's permission for the period of absence is a factor that the Mishna and Talmud discuss, as well as the negative repercussions if that permission is forced, compared to the benefits when it is given freely.

9. There are many versions of the legend. The partial selection here represents versions of one story and not literary adaptations that digress considerably from the core of the story. For a survey of the history of the legend and

its versions in Syriac, Greek and Latin, as well as in old French from the eleventh century, based on MS Hildesheim, see Carl J. Odenkirchen, *The Life of St. Alexis*, Classical Folia Editions (Brookline, 1978), 92–141; Gaston Paris and Léopold Pannier, eds. *La vie de Saint Alexis, Poème du XI͏ᵉ siècle et renouvellements des XII͏ᵉ, XIII͏ᵉ et XIV͏ᵉ siècles* (Paris, 1887) [1872]. Additional versions that I will refer to later are: *Acta Sanctorum*, Julii, Vol. IV, 251–253, which appears along with a translation into English in Odenkirchen, 34–51; "The Golden Legend" by Jacobus de Voragine, which is very similar to the *Acta Sanctorum* version. In translation into English: Jacobus de Voragine, *The Golden Legend, Readings on the Saints*, #94, trans. William Granger Ryan (Princeton, 1995), 1: 371–374. These two later sources, *Acta Sanctorum* and *The Golden Legend*, make it possible to reconstruct the ancient Latin version that we do not have. Additional versions relevant to the discussion are: (1) a version from the thirteenth century in old French (MS Paris 2162 marked as MS P), published in Charles E. Stebbins, *A Critical Edition of the 13th and 14th Centuries Old French Poem Versions of the 'Vie de Saint Alexis'* (Tübingen, 1974), 21–63. A comparison of this version to the original Latin source in *Acta Sanctorum* can be found on pages 73–81; (2) a version from the twelfth century in MS S (Fr. 12471), 222–260, can be found in the above edition of Paris and Pannier, *La vie de Saint Alexis*, 222–60; (3) a version from the thirteenth century based on MS B (M) Imp.fr 1553, which is different from the version in MS Paris, as in Paris and Pannier, 279–317.

10. Dyan Elliott, *Spiritual Marriage, Sexual Abstinence in Medieval Wedlock* (Princeton, 1993), 7, 105–106.

11. For a full survey of the development of the legend and how it became accepted, including a comprehensive bibliographical appendix of the existing scholarship on it, see Louk J. Engels, "The West European Alexis Legend," in *The Invention of Saintliness*, ed. Anneke B. Mulder-Bakker (London and New York, 2002), 93–144.

12. Odenkirchen, *The Life of St. Alexis* 37.

13. Crescentia, falsely accused of adultery and driven out of her home, becomes a well-known healer, and many of the ill and diseased seek her remedies, including her husband, who is reunited with her. See Hans-Jörg, Uther, *The Types of International Folktales*. A classification and Bibliography based on the system of Antti Aarne and Stith Thompson. Part I, Helsinki: Suomalainen tiedeakatemia academia scientiarum (Fennica, 2004), 522, 712, Tubach, 1898.

14. "And she neither screamed nor shouted, but rather gave thanks to the Almighty."

15. Compare a similar conflict between the ideal of chivalrous *virtu* and love for a woman in the well-known romance by Chrétien de Troyes, *Erec and Enide*. See: Chrétien de Troyes, *Erec and Enide*, translated with an introduction by Dorothy Gilbert (Berkeley Los Angeles and Oxford, 1992), vv. 2432–2459, 115–116. I thank Anne Lester for pointing this out.

16. Odenkirchen, *The Life of St. Alexis*, 31, 68, 96, columns 56–60, and his translation on p. 97. This in no way rules out emotional rhetoric in other scenes in the Hildesheim version from the eleventh century, for example, in monologues by the mother and wife about their yearning for Alexis.

17. Stebbins, *A Critical Edition of the 13th and 14th Centuries*, 72–80, verses VII, IX, X, in MS Paris, compared to the Latin version in *Acta Sanctorum*, Stebbins, 37.

18. Emma Campbell, "Clerks and Laity," *The Cambridge Companion to Medieval French Literature*, ed. Simon Gaunt and Sarah Kay (Cambridge, 2008), 215–219.

19. On emotions as an object of historical rather than biological or universal research, see Barbara H. Rosenwein, "Problems and Methods in the History of Emotions," retrieved from http://www.passionsincontext.de/index. php?id=557.

20. A paraphrase based on Tovi Bibring's translation here and later in the text, and in notes 20–24. In the source: Sains Alessins esgarda la *pucele*./ *Assés i ardent candoiles et lanternes*/ *Mout la vit gente et couvoiteuse et bele;*/ Ses oels en torne vers le signour celestre/ Qu'il amoit plus que nule riens terrestre:/ "Elas", dit-il, "com fors pechiés m'apresse!/ S'or nen m'en vois, jou crien que ne te perde;/ (italics here and below are in the source). XII, columns 124–130, in the anthology by Paris and Pannier, *La vie de Saint Alexis*, 225–226.

21. *Jou remanrai en estrange pais,*/ *Et esgarée entre tous mes amis*, ibid., XXIII-XXIV, columns 293–294, [I will stay on a foreign land,/ cast away from all my friends]. P. 230.

22. Ibid., column 296, [If I do not see you again, I must die from sorrow]. P. 230.

23. Columns 307–314 in the edition. [If you can find a way/ To let me go together with you/ I could attire myself quite richly/Crop my hair, put on a cap/ And wear a scarf and take up a pilgrim's staff/I will be servant to you and wash your clothing/And you will never see me act out of lust/ Or adultery or debauchery.] P. 230.

24. Kant Alexis ot se femme veue,/ Ki tant par est cortoise et bien creue/Et covoitose et blance en se car nue,/ Et voit le cambre ki si est portendue,/ [...] Dont me cuida bien mes pére aloer/ Kant il me fist cheste dame esposer? / S'or ne m'en fui tot me veut afoler/ Et en infier el plus parfont jeter." XII-XIII, columns 101–120, and in translation, p. 282–283: When Alexis had seen his wife/ Who is so elegant and so well groomed/ And desirable and so white in her naked skin/ And he sees that the room is so adorned/ . . ./ What good did my father want to arrange for me/ When he made me marry this lady?/ If I don't escape now, this will drive me to distraction/ And throw me into the deepest part of hell.

25. In later versions, there is a further development of the characters' emotions, for example in MS Vatican 107 from Provence: "She immediately stood and embraced and kissed him, took out food and fed him and kissed him, at first she cried and gave praise and thanks to the Almighty for His miracles"; and in another manuscript from the sixteenth and seventeenth centuries, the emotional response of the young man is mentioned, and not only that of his wife, "She immediately embraced and kissed him and they began to weep" (Oxford. Bodl. Op. 27).

26. R. Pinḥas ben Ya'ir said: Study leads to caution, caution leads to zeal, zeal leads to cleanliness, cleanliness leads to abstinence, abstinence leads to purity, purity leads to holiness, holiness leads to meekness, meekness, leads to fear

of sin, fear of sin leads to saintliness, saintliness leads to the possession of the holy spirit, the holy spirit leads to life eternal and saintliness is greater than any of these.

27. Rabbi Eleazar of Worms, *Sefer ha-rokeaḥ ha-gadol*, ed. Barukh Shimon Schneerson (Jerusalem, 1967), 14.

28. The citations will be from the edition of *Sefer ḥasidim* edited by Judah Wistinetzki (Berlin, 1891, repr. Jerusalem, 1998) unless otherwise stated.

29. Paragraph 415, p. 206. The paragraph is cited in the context of the tract "Matters of the study of Torah."

30. *Sefer ḥasidim*, ed. Reuven Margaliot (Jerusalem, 1957), 64.

31. See Haggai Ben Artzi, "Ha-perishut be-sefer ḥasidim," *Da'at* 11 (1983): 39–45.

32. Avraham Grossman, *Ve-hu yimshol bakh? Ha-isha be-mishnatam shel ḥakhmé yisra'el bie-yemé ha-benayim* (Jerusalem, 1990), 174–211.

33. Ibid., 183–188, in response to J. Baskin, "Mabbat ḥadash 'al ha-ishah ha-yehudiyyah be-ashkenaz," in *Harimi ba-koaḥ kolekh* [Lift Up Your Voice], ed. Renée Levine Melammed (Tel Aviv, 2001), 72–84.

34. On periods of abstinence in the context of marriage, albeit not related to the Pietists of Ashkenaz, but rather to Ḥasidism of the modern age, see Ada Rapoport-Albert, "'Al ha-nashim ba-ḥasidut u-mesoret ha-betulah mi-Ludmir," in *Tsaddik ve-'edah*, ed. David Assaf (Jerusalem, 2001), 499–503.

35. David Berger, *The Jewish-Christian Debate in the High Middle Ages, A Critical Edition of the Niẓẓahon Vetus with an Introduction, Translation and Commentary* (Philadelphia, 1979), 27. And see his reference in n. 71 to the relevant sources in his edition. In the note, Berger qualifies this determination as a hypothesis that is difficult to prove unequivocally. I would like to thank Judah Galinsky for referring me to this source.

36. See Ivan G. Marcus, *Piety and Society, The Jewish Pietists of Medieval Germany*, (Leiden, 1981).

37. *Sefer ḥasidim*, ed. Judah Wistinetzki, # 35, p. 39

38. Eleazar b. Judah, *Sefer ha-rokeaḥ*, #207, p. 98.

39. Ibid., Laws of Repentance, # 9, p. 26.

40. Joseph Dan, "Hishtakkefut kiddush ha-shem ba-sifrut ha-'iyyunit shel ḥasidut ashkenaz," in *Milḥemet kodesh u-martirologiya be-toldot yisra'el u-ve-toldot ha-'amim*" (Jerusalem,1967), 122.

INDEX

CPI Antony Rowe
Eastbourne, UK
August 15, 2019